Richard Morris, Geoffrey Chaucer

Chaucer's Translation of Boethius's

Richard Morris, Geoffrey Chaucer

Chaucer's Translation of Boethius's

ISBN/EAN: 9783337068516

Printed in Europe, USA, Canada, Australia, Japan

Cover: Foto ©ninafisch / pixelio.de

More available books at **www.hansebooks.com**

Chaucer's Translation

of

Boethius's "De Consolatione Philosophiæ."

EDITED FROM

THE ADDITIONAL MS. 10,340 IN THE BRITISH MUSEUM.
COLLATED WITH THE CAMBRIDGE UNIV. LIBR. MS. Ii. 3. 21.

BY

RICHARD MORRIS,

EDITOR OF CHAUCER'S POETICAL WORKS, SPENSER'S WORKS, DAN MICHEL'S AYENBITE
OF INWYT, ETC.; MEMBER OF COUNCIL OF THE PHILOLOGICAL AND
EARLY ENGLISH TEXT SOCIETIES.

LONDON:
PUBLISHED FOR THE EARLY ENGLISH TEXT SOCIETY
BY N. TRÜBNER & CO., 57 & 59, LUDGATE HILL.

MDCCCLXVIII.

[*Reprinted from Stereotype Plates, 1889.*]

INTRODUCTION.

WHEN master hands like those of Gibbon and Hallam have sketched the life of *Boethius*, it is well that no meaner man should attempt to mar their pictures. They drew, perhaps, the most touching scene in Middle-age literary history,—the just man in prison, awaiting death, consoled by the Philosophy that had been his light in life, and handing down to posterity for their comfort and strength the presence of her whose silver rays had been his guide as well under the stars of Fortune as the mirk of Fate. With Milton in his dark days, Boece in prison could say,—

> 'I argue not
> Against Heaven's hand or will, nor bate a jot
> Of heart or hope; but still bear up and steer
> Right onward. What supports me, dost thou ask?
> The conscience, friend, to have lost them overplied
> In liberty's defence, my noble task,
> Of which all Europe rings from side to side.'

For, indeed, the echoes of Boethius, Boethius, rang out loud from every corner of European Literature. An Alfred awoke them in England, a Chaucer, a Caxton would not let them die; an Elizabeth revived them among the glorious music of her reign.[1] To us, though far off, they come with a sweet sound. 'The angelic' Thomas Aquinas commented on him, and many others followed the saint's steps. Dante read him, though, strange to say, he speaks of the

---

[1] Other translations are by John Walton of Osney, in verse, in 1410 (Reg. MS. 18, A 13), first printed at Tavistock in 1525, and to be edited some time or other for the E. E. T. S. An anonymous prose version in the Bodleian. George Colvile, alias Coldewel, 1556; J. T. 1609; H. Conningesbye, 1664; Lord Preston, 1695, 1712; W. Causton, 1730; Redpath, 1785; R. Duncan, 1789; anon. 1792 (Lowndes).

Consolation as 'a book not known by many.'[1] Belgium had her translations—both Flemish[2] and French[3]; Germany hers,[4] France hers,[5] Italy hers.[6] The Latin editors are too numerous to be catalogued here, and manuscripts abound in all our great libraries.

No philosopher was so bone of the bone and flesh of the flesh of Middle-age writers as Boethius. Take up what writer you will, and you find not only the sentiments, but the very words of the distinguished old Roman. And surely we who read him in Chaucer's tongue, will not refuse to say that his full-circling meed of glory was other than deserved. Nor can we marvel that at the end of our great poet's life, he was glad that he had swelled the chorus of Boethius' praise; and 'of the translacioun of Boece de Consolacioun,' thanked 'oure Lord Ihesu Crist and his moder, and alle the seintes in heuen.'

The impression made by Boethius on Chaucer was evidently very deep. Not only did he translate him directly, as in the present work, but he read his beloved original over and over again, as witness the following list, incomplete of course, of passages from Chaucer's poems translated more or less literally from the *De Consolatione*:

I. LOVE.

Wost thou nat wel the olde clerkes sawe,
That who schal yeve a lover eny lawe,
Love is a grettere lawe, by my pan,
Then may be yeve to (of) eny erthly man?

(*Knightes Tale, Aldine Series*, vol. ii. p. 36, 37.)

But what is he þat may ȝeue a lawe to loueres. loue is a gretter lawe and a strengere to hym self þan any lawe þat men may ȝeuen.

(*Chaucer's Prose Translation*, p. 108.)

Quis legem det amantibus?
Major lex amor est sibi.—(Boeth., lib. iii. met. 12.)

---

[1] Dante, in his *Convito*, says, "Misimi a legger quello *non conosciuto da molti* libro di Boezio, nel quale captivo e discacciato consolato s'avea."
[2] Printed at Ghent, 1485.
[3] By Reynier de Seinct Trudon, printed at Bruges, 1477.
[4] An old version of the 11th cent., printed by Graff, and a modern one printed at Nuremberg, 1473.
[5] By Jean de Méung, printed at Paris, 1494.
[6] By Varchi, printed at Florence, 1551; Parma, 1798.

II. A DRUNKEN MAN.

A dronke man wot wel he hath an hous,
But he not[1] which the righte wey is thider.
(*Knightes Tale*, vol. ii. p. 39.)

Ryȝt as a dronke man not nat[2] *by whiche paþe he may retourne home to hys house.*—(Chaucer's Trans., p. 67.)

Sed velut ebrius, domum quo tramite revertatur, ignorat.
(Boeth., lib. iii. pr. 2.)

III. THE CHAIN OF LOVE.

The firste moevere of the cause above,
Whan he first made the fayre cheyne of love,
Gret was theffect, and heigh was his ententc ;
Wel wist he why, and what therof he mente ;
For with that faire cheyne of love he bond
The fyr, the watir, the eyr, and eek the lond
In certeyn boundes, that they may not flee.
(*Knightes Tale*, p. 92.)

That þe world with stable feith / varieth acordable chaungynges // þat the contraryos qualite of elementȝ holden amonge hem self aliaunce perdurable / þat phebus the sonne with his goldene chariet / bryngeth forth the rosene day / þat the mone hath commaundement ouer the nyhtes // whiche nyhtes hesperus the eue sterre hat[h] browt // þat þe se gredy to flowen constreyneth with a certeyn ende hise floodes / so þat it is nat l[e]ucful to strechche hise brode termes or bowndes vp-on the erthes // þat is to seyn to couere alle the erthe // Al this a-cordaunce of thinges is bownden with looue / þat gouerneth erthe and see / and [he] hath also commaundementȝ to the heuenes / and yif this looue slakede the brydelis / alle thinges þat now louen hem to-gederes / wolden maken a batayle contynuely and stryuen to fordoon the fasoun of this worlde / the which they now leden in acordable feith by fayre moeuynges // this looue halt to-gideres poeples / ioygned with an hooly bond / and knytteth sacrement of maryages of chaste looues // And loue enditeth lawes to trewe felawes // O weleful weere mankynde / yif thilke loue þat gouerneth heuene gouerned yowre corages /.—(*Chaucer's Boethius*, bk. ii. met. 8.)

   Quod mundus stabili fide
   Concordes variat vices,
   Quod pugnantia semina
   Fœdus perpetuum tenent,
   Quod Phœbus roseum diem
   Curru provehit aureo,
   Ut quas duxerit Hesperus

---

[1] The Harl. MS. reads *not nat*, to the confusion of the metre.
[2] = ne wot nat = knows not.

Phœbe noctibus imperet,
Ut fluctus avidum mare
Certo fine coerceat,
Ne terris liceat vagis
Latos tundere terminos;
Hanc rerum seriem ligat,
Terras ac pelagus regens,
Et cælo imperitans amor.
Hic si fræna remiserit,
Quicquid nunc amat invicem,
Bellum continuo geret:
Et quam nunc socia fide
Pulcris motibus incitant,
Certent solvere machinam.
Hic sancto populos quoque
Junctos fœdere continet,
Hic et conjugii sacrum
Castis nectit amoribus,
Hic fidis etiam sua
Dictat jura sodalibus.
O felix hominum genus,
Si vestros animos amor,
Quo cælum regitur, regat.—(*Boeth.*, lib. ii. met. 8.)

Love, that of erth and se hath governaunce!
Love, that his hestes hath in hevene hye!
Love, that with an holsom alliaunce
Halt peples joyned, as hym liste hem gye!
Love, that knetteth law and compaignye,
And couples doth in vertu for to dwelle!
   (*Troylus & Cryseyde*, st. 243, vol. iv. p. 296.)

That, that the world with faith, which that is stable
Dyverseth so, his stoundes concordynge;—
That elementz, that ben so discordable,
Holden a bond, perpetualy durynge;—
That Phebus mot his rosy carte forth brynge,
And that the mone hath lordschip overe the nyghte;—
Al this doth Love, ay heryed be his myght!

That, that the se, that gredy is to flowen,
Constreyneth to a certeyn ende so
Hise flodes, that so fiersly they ne growen
To drenchen erth and alle for everemo;
And if that Love aught lete his brydel go,
Al that now loveth asonder sholde lepe,
And lost were al that Love halt now to kepe.
   (*Ibid.* st. 244, 245.)

IV. MUTABILITY DIRECTED AND LIMITED BY AN IMMUTABLE AND DIVINE INTELLIGENCE.

> That same prynce and moevere eek, quod he,
> Hath stabled, in this wrecched world adoun,
> Certeyn dayes and duracioun
> To alle·that er engendrid in this place,
> Over the whiche day they may nat pace,
> Al mowe they yit wel here dayes abregge;
> . . . .
> Than may men wel by this ordre discerne
> That thilke moevere stabul is and eterne.
> . . . .
> And therfore of his wyse purveaunce
> He hath so wel biset his ordenaunce,
> That spices of thinges and progressiouns
> Schullen endure by successiouns
> And nat eterne be, withoute any lye.
>   (*Knightes Tale*, vol. ii. p. 92, 93.)

> Þe engendrynge of alle þinges quod she and alle þe progressiouns of muuable nature. and alle þat moeueþ in any manere takiþ hys causes. hys ordre, and hys formes, of þe stablenesse of þe deuyne þou3t [and thilke deuyne thowht] þat is yset and put in þe toure. þat is to seyne in þe hey3t of þe simplicite of god. stablisiþ many manere gyses to þinges þat ben to don.—(*Chaucer's Boethius*, bk. iv. pr. 6, p. 134.)

V. THE PART IS DERIVED FROM THE WHOLE, THE IMPERFECT FROM THE PERFECT.

> Wel may men knowe, but it be a fool,
> That every partye dyryveth from his hool.
> For nature hath nat take his bygynnyng
> Of no partye ne cantel of a thing,
> But of a thing that parfyt is and stable,
> Descendyng so, til it be corumpable.
>   (*Knightes Tale*, vol. ii. p. 92.)

> For al þing þat is cleped inperfit . is proued inperfit by þe amenusynge of perfeccioun . or of þing þat is perfit . and her-of comeþ it . þat in euery þing general . yif þat . þat men seen any þing þat is inperfit . certys in þilke general þer mot ben somme þing þat is perfit. For yif so be þat perfeccioun is don awey . men may nat þinke nor seye fro whennes þilke þing is þat is cleped inperfit . For þe nature of þinges ne token nat her bygynnyng of þinges amenused and inperfit . but it procediþ of þingus þat ben al hool . and absolut . and descendeþ so doune iu-to outerest þinges and in-to þingus empty and wiþ-oute fruyt .

but as I haue shewed a litel her byforne. þat yif þer be a blisfulnesse
þat be frele and vein and inperfit. þer may no man doute. þat þer nys
som blisfulnesse þat is sad stedfast and perfit.'—(bk. iii. pr. 10, p. 89.)

Omne enim quod imperfectum esse dicitur, id deminutione perfecti
imperfectum esse perhibetur. Quo fit ut si in quolibet genere imperfectum quid esse videatur, in eo perfectum 'quoque aliquod esse necesse
sit. Etenim perfectionè sublata, unde illud, quod imperfectum perhibetur, extiterit, ne fingi quidem potest. *Neque enim ab diminutis incon-
summatisque natura rerum cepit exordium, sed ab integris absolutisque
procedens in hæc extrema atque effœta dilabitur.* Quod si, uti paulo ante
monstravimus, est quædam boni fragilis imperfecta felicitas, esse aliquam
solidam perfectamque non potest dubitari.—(*Boeth.*, lib. iii. pr. 10.)

VI. GENTILITY.

  For gentilnesse nys but renomé
  Of thin auncestres, for her heigh bounté
  Which is a straunge thing to thy persone.
    (*The Wyf of Bathes Tale*, vol. ii. p. 241.)

For if þe name of gentilesse be referred to renoun and clernesse of
linage. þan is gentil name but a foreine þing.
    (*Chaucer's Boethius*, p. 78.)

Quæ [nobilitas], *si ad claritudinem refertur, aliena est.*
    (*Boethius*, lib. iii. pr. 6.)

VII. NERO'S CRUELTY.

  No teer out of his eyen for that sighte
  Ne cam ; but sayde, a fair womman was sche.
  Gret wonder is how that he couthe or mighte
  Be domesman on hir dede beauté.
    (*The Monkes Tale*, vol. iii. p. 217.)

Ne no tere ne wette his face, but he was so hard-herted þat he
myȝte ben domesman or iuge of hire dede beauté.
    (*Chaucer's Boethius*, p. 55.)

  Ora non tinxit lacrymis, sed esse
  Censor extincti potuit decoris.
    (*Boethius*, lib. ii. met. 6.)

VIII. PREDESTINATION AND FREE-WILL.

In 'Troylus and Cryseyde' we find the following long passage
taken from Boethius, book v. prose 2, 3.

    Book iv. st. 134, vol. iv. p. 339.

(1) Syn God seth every thynge, out of doutaunce,
  And hem disponeth, thorugh his ordinannce,

In hire merites sothely for to be,
As they shul comen by predesteyné

136

(2) For som men seyn if God seth al byforne,
Ne God may not deseyved ben pardé!
Than moot it fallen, theigh men hadde it sworne,
That purveyaunce hath seyn befor to be,
Wherfor I seye, that, from eterne, if he
Hathe wiste byforn our thought ek as oure dede,
We have no fre choys, as thise clerkes rede.

137

(3) For other thoughte, nor other dede also,
Myghte nevere ben, but swich as purveyaunce,
Which may nat ben deceyved nevere moo,
Hath feled byforne, withouten ignoraunce;
For if ther myghte ben a variaunce,
To wrythen out fro Goddes purveyinge,
Ther nere no prescience of thynge comynge;

138

(4) But it were rather an opinyon
Uncertein, and no stedfast forseynge;
And certes that were an abusyon
That God shold han no parfit clere wetynge,
More than we men, that han douteous wenynge,
But swich an erroure upon God to gesse
Were fals, and foule, and wikked corsednesse.

139

(5) They seyn right thus, that thynge is nat to come,
For that the prescience hath seyne byfore
That it shal come; but they seyn that therfore
That it shal come, therfor the purveyaunce
Woot it bifore, withouten ignorance.

140

(6) And in this manere this necessité
Retourneth in his part contrarye agayn;
For nedfully byhoveth it not to be,
That thilke thynges fallen in certeyn
That ben purveyed; but nedly, as they seyne,
Bihoveth it that thynges, which that falle,
That thei in certein ben purveied alle.

141

(7) I mene as though I labourede me in this,
To enqueren which thynge cause of whiche thynge be;.

(8) As, whether that the prescience of God is
The certein cause of the necessité
Of thynges that to comen ben, pardé!
Or, if necessité of thynge comynge
Be cause certein of the purveyinge.

142

(9) But now nenforce I me nat in shewynge
How the ordre of causes stant; but wel woot I
That it bihoveth that the bifallynge
Of thynges, wiste bifor certeinly,
Be necessarie, al seme it nat therby
That prescience put fallynge necessaire
To thynge to come, al falle it foule or faire.

143

(10) For, if ther sit a man yonde on a see, [seat]
Than by necessité bihoveth it,
That certes thyn opinioun soth be,
That wenest or conjectest that he sit;
And, further over, now ayeinwarde yit,
Lo right so is it on the part contrarie,
As thus,—nowe herkene, for I wol nat tarie :—

144

(11) I sey, that if the opinion of the
Be soth for that he sit, than seye I this,
That he moot sitten by necessité;
And thus necessité in either is,
For in hym nede of sittynge is, ywis,
And in the, nede of soth; and thus forsoth
Ther mot necessité ben in yow bothe.

145

(12) But thow maist seyne, the man sit nat therfore,
That thyn opinioun of his sittynge sothe is;
But rather, for the man sat there byfore,
Therfor is thyn opinioun soth, ywys;
And I seye, though the cause of soth of this
Cometh of his sittynge, yet necessité
Is interchaunged both in hym and the.

146

(13) Thus in the same wyse, out of doutaunce,
I may wel maken, as it semeth me,
My resonynge of Goddes purveiaunce,
And of the thynges that to comen be; ...

147

(14) For although that for thynge shal come, ywys,
Therfor it is purveyed certeynly,
Nat that it cometh for it purveied is;
Yet, natheles, bihoveth it nedfully,
That thyngo to come be purveied trewly; .
Or elles thynges that purveied be,
That they bitiden by nocessité.

148

(15) And this sufficeth right ynough, certeyn,
For to distruye oure fre choys everydele.

(1) Quæ tamen ille ab æterno cuncta prospiciens providentiæ cernit intuitus, et suis quæque meritis prædestinata disponit. . . . . (*Boethius*, lib. v. pr. 2.) . . . .

(2) Nam si cuncta prospicit Deus neque falli ullo modo potest, evenire necesse est, quod providentia futurum esse præviderit. Quare si ab æterno non facta hominum modo, sed etiam consilia voluntatesque prænoscit, nulla erit arbitrii libertas;

(3) Neque enim vel factum aliud ullum vel quælibet existere poterit voluntas, nisi quam nescia falli providentia divina præsenserit. Nam si res aliorsum, quam provisæ sunt detorqueri valent, non jam erit futuri firma præscientia;

(4) Sed opinio potius incerta; quod de Deo nefas credere judico.

(5) Aiunt enim non ideo quid esse eventurum quoniam id providentia futurum esse prospexerit; sed e contrario potius, quoniam quid futurum est, id divinam providentiam latere non possit.

(6) Eoque modo necessarium est hoc in contrariam relabi partem; neque enim necesse est contingere quæ providentur, sed necesse est quæ futura sunt provideri.

(7) Quasi vero quæ cujusque rei causa sit,

(8) Præscientiane futurorûm necessitatis an futurorum necessitas providentiæ, laboretur.

(9) At nos illud demonstrare nitamur, quoquo modo sese habeat ordo causarum, necessarium esse eventum præscitarum rerum, etiam si præscientia futuris rebus eveniendi necessitatem non videatur inferre.

(10) Etenim si quispiam sedeat, opinionem quæ eum sedere conjectat veram esse necesse est: at e converso rursus,

(11) Si de quopiam vera sit opinio quoniam sedet eum sedere necesse est. In utroque igitur necessitas inest : in hoc quidem sedendi, at vero in altero veritatis.

(12) Sed non idcirco quisque sedet, quoniam vera est opinio : sed hæc potius vera est, quoniam quempiam sedere præcessit. Ita cum causa veritatis ex altera parte procedat, inest tamen communis in utraque necessitas.

(13) Similia de providentia futurisque rebus ratiocinari patet.

(14) Nam etiam si idcirco, quoniam futura sunt, providentur: non vero ideo, quoniam providentur, eveniunt: nihilo minus tamen a Deo vel ventura provideri, vel provisa evenire necesse est :

(15) Quod ad perimendam arbitrii libertatem solum satis est.

(lib. v. pr. 3.)

See *Chaucer's Boethius*, pp. 154-6.

IX. THE GRIEF OF REMEMBERING BYGONE HAPPINESS.

For, of fortunes scharp adversité,
The worste kynde of infortune is this,
A man to han ben in prosperité,
And it remembren, when it passed is.
(*Troylus and Cryseyde*, bk. iii. st. 226, vol. iv. p. 291.)

Sed hoc est, quod recolentem me vehementius coquit. Nam in omni adversitate fortunæ infelicissimum genus est infortunii, fuisse felicem.[1]— (*Boethius*, lib. ii. pr. 4.)

X. VULTURES TEAR THE STOMACH OF TITYUS IN HELL.

————Syciphus in Helle,
Whos stomak fowles tyren everemo,
That hyghten volturis.
(*Troylus and Cryseyde*, book i. st. 113, p. 140.)

þe fowel þat hyȝt voltor þat etiþ þe stomak or þe giser of ticius.
(*Chaucer's Boethius*, p. 107.)

XI. THE MUTABILITY OF FORTUNE.

For if hire (Fortune's) whiel stynte any thinge to torne
Thanne cessed she Fortune anon to be.
(*Troylus and Cryseyde*, bk. i. st. 122, p. 142.)

If fortune bygan to dwelle stable. she cesed[e] þan to ben fortune.
(*Chaucer's Boethius*, p. 32.)

[1] Cf. Dante, *Inferno*, V. 121.
Nessun maggior dolore
Che ricordarsi del tempo felice
Nella miseria; e ciò sa 'l tuo Dottore.

(Compare stanzas 120, 121, p. 142, and stanza 136, p. 146, of
'Troylus and Cryseyde' with pp. 31, 33, 35, and p. 34 of Chaucer's
Boethius.)

At omnium mortalium stolidissime, si manere incipit, fors esse
desistit.—(*Boethius*, lib. ii. prose 1.)

XII. WORLDLY SELYNESSE

. . . .
Imedled is with many a bitternesse.
Ful angwyshous than is, God woote, quod she,
Condicion of veyn prosperité!
For oyther joies comen nought yfeere,
Or elles no wight hath hem alwey here.
(*Troylus and Cryseyde*, bk. iii. st. 110, p. 258.)

þe swetnesse of mannes welefulnesse is yspranid wiþ many[e] bitter-
nesses.—(*Chaucer's Boethius*, p. 42.)

—ful anguissous þing is þe condicioun of mans goodes. For
eyþer it comeþ al to-gidre to a wyȝt. or ellys it lasteþ not perpetuely.
(*Ib.* p. 41.)

Quam multis amaritudinibus humanæ felicitatis dulcedo respersa
est!—(*Boethius*, lib. ii. prose 4.)

Anxia enim res est humanorum conditio bonorum, et quæ vel nunquam tota proveniat, vel nunquam perpetua subsistat.—(*Ib.*)

O, brotel wele of mannes joie unstable!
With what wight so thow be, or how thow pleye,
Oither he woot that thow joie art muable,
Or woot it nought, it mot ben on of tweyen:
Now if he woot it not, how may he seyen
That he hath veray joie and selynesse,
That is of ignoraunce ay in distresse?

Now if he woote that joie is transitorie,
As every joie of worldly thynge mot fle,
Thanne every tyme he that hath in memorie,
The drede of lesyng maketh hym that he
May in no parfyte selynesse be:
And if to lese his joie, he sette not a myte,
Than semeth it, that joie is worth ful lite.
(*Troylus and Cryseyde*, bk. iii. st. 111, 112, vol. iv. p. 258.)

(1) What man þat þis toumblyng welefulnesse leediþ, eiþer he woot
þat [it] is chaungeable. or ellis he woot it nat. And yif he woot it
not. what blisful fortune may þer be in þe blyndenesse of ignoraunce.

(2) And yif he woot þat it is chaungeable. he mot alwey ben adrad
þat he ne lese þat þing. þat he ne douteþ nat but þat he may leesen it.

. . . . . For whiche þe continuel drede þat he haþ ne suffriþ hym nat to ben weleful. Or ellys yif he leese it he wene[þ] to be dispised and forleten hit. Certis eke þat is a ful lytel goode þat is born wiþ euene hert[e] whan it is loost.—(*Chaucer's Boethius*, pp. 43, 44.)

(1) Quem caduca ista felicitas vehit, vel scit eam, vel nescit esse mutabilem. Si nescit, quænam beata sors esse potest ignorantiæ in cæcitate?

(2) Si scit, metuat necesse est, ne amittat, quod amitti posse non dubitat ; quare continuus timor non sinit esse felicem. An vel si amiserit, negligendum putat? Sic quoque perexile bonum est, quod æquo animo feratur amissum.—(*Boethius*, lib. ii. prose 4.)

XIII. FORTUNE.

————Fortune
That semeth trewest when she wol bigyle,
. . . .
And, when a wight is from hire whiel ithrowe,
Than laugheth she, and maketh hym the mowe.
· (*Troylus and Cryseyde*, bk. iii. st. 254, vol. iv. p. 299.)

She (Fortune) vseþ ful flatryng familarité wiþ hem þat she enforceþ to bygyle.—(*Chaucer's Boethius*, p. 30.)

. . . . She lauȝeþ and scorneþ þe wepyng of hem þe whiche she haþ maked wepe wiþ hir free wille . . . . Yif þat a wyȝt is seyn weleful and ouerþrowe in an houre.—(*Ib.* p. 33.)

In book v., stanza 260, vol. v. p. 75, Chaucer describes how the soul of Hector, after his death, ascended 'up to the holughnesse of the seventhe spere.' In so doing he seems to have had before him met. 1, book 4, of Boethius, where the 'soul' is described as passing into the heaven's utmost sphere, and looking down on the world below. See *Chaucer's Boethius*, p. 110, 111.

Ætas Prima is of course a metrical version of lib. ii. met. 5.

Hampole speaks of the wonderful sight of the Lynx ; perhaps he was indebted to Boethius for the hint.—(See *Boethius*, book 3, pr. 8, p. 81.)

I have seen the following elsewhere :

(1) Value not beauty, for it may be destroyed by a three days' fever.
(See *Chaucer's Boethius*, p. 81.)

(2) There is no greater plague than the enmity of thy familiar friend.
(See *Chaucer's* translation, p. 77.)

Chaucer did not English Boethius second-hand, through any early French version, as some have supposed, but made his translation with the Latin original before him.

Jean de Méung's version, the only early French translation, perhaps, accessible to Chaucer, is not always literal, while the present translation is seldom free or periphrastic, but conforms closely to the Latin, and is at times awkwardly literal. A few passages, taken haphazard, will make this sufficiently clear.

Et dolor ætatem jussit inesse suam. And sorou haþ comaunded his age to be in me (p. 4).
   Et ma douleur *commanda* a vieillesse
   Entrer en moy / ains quen fust hors ieunesse.

Mors hominum felix, quæ se nec dulcibus annis
Inserit, et mæstis sæpe vocata venit.
þilke deeþ of men is welful þat ne comeþ not in ȝeres þat ben swete (i. *mirie*). but comeþ to wrecches often yclepid. (p. 4.)
   On dit la mort des homes estre cureuse
   Qui ne vient pas en saison planturense
   Mais des tristes moult souuent appellee
   Elle y affuit nue / seche et pelee.

Querimoniam lacrymabilem. Wepli compleynte (p. 5). Fr. ma complainte moy esmouuant a pleurs.

Styli officio. Wiþ office of poyntel (p. 5). Fr. (que ie reduisse) par escript.

Inexhaustus. Swiche ... þat it ne myȝt[e] not be emptid (p. 5). Fr. inconsumptible.

Scenicas meretriculas. Comune strumpetis of siche a place þat men clepen þe theatre (p. 6). Fr. ces ribaudelles fardees.

Præcipiti profundo. In ouer-þrowyng depnesse (p. 7).
   [L]As que la pensee de lomme
   Est troublee et plongie comme
   En *abisme precipitee*
   Sa propre lumiere gastee.

Nec pervetusta nec incelebris. Neyþer ouer-oolde ne vnsolempne (p. 11). Fr. desquelz la memoire nest pas trop ancienne ou non recitee.

Inter secreta otia. Among my secre restyng whiles (p. 14). Fr. entre mes secrettes *et* oyseuses estudes.

Palatini canes. þe houndys of þe palays (p. 15). Fr. les chiens du palais.

Masculæ prolis. Of þi masculyn children (p. 37). Fr. de ta lignie masculine.

Ad singularem felicitatis tuæ cumulum venire delectat. It deliteþ me to comen now to þe singuler vphepyng of þi welefulnesse (p. 37). Fr. Il me plait venir au singulier monceau de ta felicite.

Consulare imperium. Emperie of consulers (p. 51). Fr. lempire consulaire.

Hoc ipsum brevis habitaculi. Of þilke litel habitacle (p. 57). Fr. de cest trespetit habitacle.

Late patentes plagas. þe brode shewyng contreys (p. 60).
        QViconques tend a gloire vaine
        Et le croit estre souueraine
        Voye *les regions patentes*
        Du ciel . . . . .

Ludens hominum cura. þe pleiyng besines of men (p. 68).
        Si quil tollist par doulz estude
        Des hommes la solicitude . .

Hausi cælum. I took heuene (p. 10). Fr. ie ... regarday le ciel.

Certamen adversum præfectum prætorii communis commodi ratione suscepi. I took strif aȝeins þe prouost of þe pretorie for comune profit (p. 15). Fr. ie entrepris lestrif a lencontre du prefect du parlement royal a cause de la commune vtilite.

At cujus criminis arguimur summam quæris? But axest þou in somme of what gilt I am accused? (p. 17). Fr. Mais demandes tu la somme du pechie duquel pechie nous sommes arguez?

Fortuita temeritate. By fortunouse fortune (p. 26). Fr. par fortuite folie.

Quos premunt septem gelidi triones. Alle þe peoples þat ben vndir þe colde sterres þat hyȝten þe seuene triones (p. 55). Fr. coulx de septentrion.

Ita ego quoque tibi veluti corollarium dabo. Ryȝt so wil I ȝeue þe here as a corolarie or a mede of coroune (p. 91). Fr. semblablement ie te donneray ainsi que vng correlaire.

In stadio. In þe stadie or in þe forlonge (p. 119). Fr. ou (for au) champ.

Conjecto. I coniecte (p. 154). Fr. ie coniecture.

Nimium ... adversari ac repugnare videtur. It semeþ ... to repugnen and to contrarien gretly. Fr. Ce semble chose trop contraire et repugnante.

Universitatis ambitum. Envirounynge of þe vniuersite (p. 165). Fr. lauirouncment de luniuersalite.

Rationis universum. Vniuersite of resoun (p. 165). Fr. luniuersalite de Raison.

Scientiam nunquam deficientis instantiæ rectius æstimabis. þou shalt demen [it] more ry3tfully þat it is science of presence or of instaunce þat neuer ne fayleþ (p. 174). Fr. mais tu la diras plus droittement et mieulx science de instante presentialite non iamais defaillant mais eternelle.

Many of the above examples are very bald renderings of the original, and are only quoted here to show that Chaucer did not make his translation from the French.

Chaucer is not always felicitous in his translations:—thus he translates *clavus atque gubernaculum* by *keye* and a stiere (p. 103), and *compendium* (gain, acquisition) by *abreggynge* (abridging, curtailment), p. 151. Many terms make their appearance in English for the first time,—and most of them have become naturalized, and are such as we could ill spare. Some few are rather uncommon, as *gouernaile* (gubernaculum), p. 27; *arbitre* (arbitrium), p. 154. As Chaucer takes the trouble to explain *inestimable* (inæstimabilis), p. 158, it could not have been a very familiar term.

Our translator evidently took note of various readings, for on p. 31 he notes a variation of the original. On p. 51 he uses *armurers* (= armures) to render *arma*, though most copies agree in reading *arva*.

There are numerous glosses and explanations of particular passages, which seem to be interpolated by Chaucer himself. Thus he explains what is meant by the *heritage of Socrates* (p. 10, 11); he gives the meaning of *coemption* (p. 15); of *Euripus* (p. 33); of the *porch* (p. 166).[1] Some of his definitions are very quaint; as, for instance, that of Tragedy—'*a dité of a prosperité for a tyme þat endiþ in wrechednesse*' (p. 35). One would think that the following definition of Tragedian would be rather superfluous after this,—'*a maker of dites þat hy3ten* (are called) *tregedies*' (p. 77).

Melliflui . . . oris Homerus

is thus quaintly Englished: *Homer wiþ þe hony mouþe, þat is to seyn. homer wiþ þe swete dites* (p. 153).

[1] See pages 39, 50, 61, 94, 111, 133, 149, 153, 159.

The present translation of the *De Consolatione* is taken from Additional MS. 10,340, which is supposed to be the *oldest* manuscript that exists in our public libraries. After it was all copied out and ready for press, Mr Bradshaw was kind enough to procure me, for the purpose of collation, the loan of the Camb. University MS. Ii. 3. 21, from which the various readings at the foot of the pages are taken.

Had I had an opportunity of examining the Cambridge MS. carefully throughout before the work was so far advanced, I should certainly have selected it in preference to the text now given to the reader. Though not so ancient as the British Museum MS., it is far more correct in its grammatical inflexions, and is no doubt a copy of an older and very accurate text.

The Additional MS. is written by a scribe who was unacquainted with the force of the final *-e*. Thus he adds it to the preterites of strong verbs, which do not require it; he omits it in the preterites of weak verbs where it is wanted, and attaches it to passive participles (of weak verbs), where it is superfluous. The scribe of the Cambridge MS. is careful to preserve the final *-e* where it is a sign (1) of the definite declension of the adjective; (2) of the plural adjective; (3) of the infinitive mood; (4) of the preterite of weak verbs; (5) of present participles;[1] (6) of the 2nd pers. pret. indic. of strong verbs; (7) of adverbs; (8) of an older vowel ending.

The Addit. MS. has frequently *thilk* (singular and plural), and *-nes* (in *wrechednes*, &c.), when the Camb. MS. has *thilke*[2] and *-nesse*.

For further differences the reader may consult the numerous collations at the foot of the page.

If the Chaucer Society obtains that amount of patronage from the literary public which it deserves, but unfortunately has yet not succeeded in getting, so that it may be enabled to go on with the great work which has been so successfully commenced, then the time may come when I shall have the opportunity of editing the Camb. MS. of Chaucer's Boethius for that Society, and lovers of Early English Literature will have two texts instead of one.

[1] In the Canterbury Tales we find participles in *-yngë*.
[2] It is nearly always *thilkë* in the Canterbury Tales.

APPENDIX TO INTRODUCTION.

THE last of the ancients, and one who forms a link between the classical period of literature and that of the middle ages, in which he was a favourite author, is Boethius, a man of fine genius, and interesting both from his character and his death. It is well known that after filling the dignities of Consul and Senator in the court of Theodoric, he fell a victim to the jealousy of a sovereign, from whose memory, in many respects glorious, the stain of that blood has never been effaced. The *Consolation of Philosophy*, the chief work of Boethius, was written in his prison. Few books are more striking from the circumstances of their production. Last of the classic writers, in style not impure, though displaying too lavishly that poetic exuberance which had distinguished the two or three preceding centuries, in elevation of sentiment equal to any of the philosophers, and mingling a Christian sanctity with their lessons, he speaks from his prison in the swan-like tones of dying eloquence. The philosophy that consoled him in bonds, was soon required in the sufferings of a cruel death. Quenched in his blood, the lamp he had trimmed with a skilful hand gave no more light ; the language of Tully and Virgil soon ceased to be spoken ; and many ages were to pass away, before learned diligence restored its purity, and the union of genius with imitation taught a few modern writers to surpass in eloquence the Latinity of Boethius.—(Hallam's *Literature of Europe*, i. 2, 4th ed. 1854.)

The Senator Boethius is the last of the Romans whom Cato or Tully could have acknowledged for their countryman. As a wealthy orphan, he inherited the patrimony and honours of the Anician family, a name ambitiously assumed by the kings and emperors of the age ; and the appellation of Manlius asserted his genuine or fabulous descent from a race of consuls and dictators, who had repulsed the Gauls from the Capitol, and sacrificed their sons to the discipline of the Republic. In the youth of Boethius the studies of Rome were not totally abandoned ; a Virgil is now extant, corrected by the hand of a consul ; and the professors of grammar, rhetoric, and jurisprudence, were maintained in their privileges and pensions by the liberality of the Goths. But the erudition of the Latin language was insufficient to satiate his ardent curiosity ; and

Boethius is said to have employed eighteen laborious years in the schools of Athens, which were supported by the zeal, the learning, and the diligence of Proclus and his disciples. The reason and piety of their Roman pupil were fortunately saved from the contagion of mystery and magic, which polluted the groves of the Academy, but he imbibed the spirit, and imitated the method, of his dead and living masters, who attempted to reconcile the strong and subtle sense of Aristotle with the devout contemplation and sublime fancy of Plato. After his return to Rome, and his marriage with the daughter of his friend, the patrician Symmachus, Boethius still continued, in a palace of ivory and [glass] to prosecute the same studies. The Church was edified by his profound defence of the orthodox creed against the Arian, the Eutychian, and the Nestorian heresies; and the Catholic unity was explained or exposed in a formal treatise by the *indifference* of three distinct though consubstantial persons. For the benefit of his Latin readers, his genius submitted to teach the first elements of the arts and sciences of Greece. The geometry of Euclid, the music of Pythagoras, the arithmetic of Nicomachus, the mechanics of Archimedes, the astronomy of Ptolemy, the theology of Plato, and the logic of Aristotle, with the commentary of Porphyry, were translated and illustrated by the indefatigable pen of the Roman senator. And he alone was esteemed capable of describing the wonders of art, a sun-dial, a water-clock, or a sphere which represented the motions of the planets. From these abstruse speculations, Boethius stooped, or, to speak more truly, he rose to the social duties of public and private life: the indigent were relieved by his liberality; and his eloquence, which flattery might compare to the voice of Demosthenes or Cicero, was uniformly exerted in the cause of innocence and humanity. Such conspicuous merit was felt and rewarded by a discerning prince: the dignity of Boethius was adorned with the titles of consul and patrician, and his talents were usefully employed in the important station of master of the offices. Notwithstanding the equal claims of the East and West, his two sons were created, in their tender youth, the consuls of the same year. On the memorable day of their inauguration, they proceeded in solemn pomp from their palace to the forum amidst the applause of the senate and people; and their joyful father, the true Consul of Rome, after pronouncing an oration in the praise of his royal benefactor, distributed a triumphal largess in the games of the circus. Prosperous in his fame and fortunes, in his public honours and private alliances, in the cultivation of science and the consciousness of virtue, Boethius might have been styled happy, if that precarious epithet could be safely applied before the last term of the life of man.

A philosopher, liberal of his wealth and parsimonious of his time, might be insensible to the common allurements of ambition, the thirst of gold and employment. And some credit may be due to the asseveration of Boethius, that he had reluctantly obeyed the divine Plato, who enjoins every virtuous citizen to rescue the state from the usurpation of vice and ignorance. For the integrity of his public conduct he appeals to the memory of his country. His authority had restrained the pride and oppression of the royal officers, and his eloquence had delivered Paulianus from the dogs of the palace. He had always pitied, and often relieved, the distress of the provincials, whose fortunes were exhausted by public and private rapine; and Boethius alone had courage to oppose the tyranny of the Barbarians, elated by conquest, excited by avarice, and, as he complains, encouraged by impunity. In these honourable contests his spirit soared above the consideration of danger, and perhaps of prudence; and we may learn from the example of Cato, that a character of pure and inflexible virtue is the most apt to be misled by prejudice, to be heated by enthusiasm, and to confound private enmities with public justice. The disciple of Plato might exaggerate the infirmities of nature, and the imperfections of society; and the mildest form of a Gothic kingdom, even the weight of allegiance and gratitude, must be insupportable to the free spirit of a Roman patriot. But the favour and fidelity of Boethius declined in just proportion with the public happiness; and an unworthy colleague was imposed to divide and control the power of the master of the offices. In the last gloomy season of Theodoric, he indignantly felt that he was a slave; but as his master had only power over his life, he stood without arms and without fear against the face of an angry Barbarian, who had been provoked to believe that the safety of the senate was incompatible with his own. The Senator Albinus was accused and already convicted on the presumption of *hoping*, as it was said, the liberty of Rome.

"If Albinus be criminal," exclaimed the orator, "the senate and myself are all guilty of the same crime. If we are innocent, Albinus is equally entitled to the protection of the laws." These laws might not have punished the simple and barren wish of an unattainable blessing; but they would have shown less indulgence to the rash confession of Boethius, that, had he known of a conspiracy, the tyrant never should. The advocate of Albinus was soon involved in the danger and perhaps the guilt of his client; their signature (which they denied as a forgery) was affixed to the original address, inviting the emperor to deliver Italy from the Goths; and three witnesses of honourable rank, perhaps of infamous reputation, attested the treasonable designs of the Roman patrician. Yet his innocence must be presumed, since he was deprived by Theodoric of the means of justification, and rigorously confined in the tower of Pavia, while the senate, at the distance of five hundred miles, pronounced a sentence of confiscation and death against the most illustrious of its members. At the command of the Barbarians, the occult science of a philosopher was stigmatized with the names of sacrilege and magic. A devout and dutiful attachment to the senate was condemned as criminal by the trembling voices of the senators themselves; and their ingratitude deserved the wish or prediction of Boethius, that, after him, none should be found guilty of the same offence.

While Boethius, oppressed with fetters, expected each moment the sentence or the stroke of death, he composed in the tower of Pavia the

Consolation of Philosophy; a golden volume not unworthy of the leisure of Plato or Tully, but which claims incomparable merit from the barbarism of the times and the situation of the author. The celestial guide, whom he had so long invoked at Rome and Athens, now condescended to illumine his dungeon, to revive his courage, and to pour into his wounds her salutary balm. She taught him to compare his long prosperity and his recent distress, and to conceive new hopes from the inconstancy of fortune. Reason had informed him of the precarious condition of her gifts; experience had satisfied him of their real value; he had enjoyed them without guilt; he might resign them without a sigh, and calmly disdain the impotent malice of his enemies, who had left him happiness, since they had left him virtue. From the earth, Boethius ascended to heaven in search of the SUPREME GOOD; explored the metaphysical labyrinth of chance and destiny, of prescience and free-will, of time and eternity; and generously attempted to reconcile the perfect attributes of the Deity with the apparent disorders of his moral and physical government. Such topics of consolation, so obvious, so vague, or so abstruse, are ineffectual to subdue the feelings of human nature. Yet the sense of misfortune may be diverted by the labour of thought ; and the sage who could artfully combine in the same work the various riches of philosophy, poetry, and eloquence, must already have possessed the intrepid calmness which he affected to seek. Suspense, the worst of evils, was at length determined by the ministers of death, who executed, and perhaps exceeded, the inhuman mandate of Theodoric. A strong cord was fastened round the head of Boethius, and forcibly tightened till his eyes almost started from their sockets ; and some mercy may be discovered in the milder torture of beating him with clubs till he expired. But his genius survived to diffuse a ray of knowledge over the darkest ages of the Latin world ; the writings of the philosopher were translated by the most glorious of the English kings, and the third emperor of the name of Otho removed to a more honourable tomb the bones of a Catholic saint, who, from his Arian persecutors, had acquired the honours of martyrdom and the fame of miracles. In the last hours of Boethius, he derived some comfort from the safety of his two sons, of his wife, and of his father-in-law, the venerable Symmachus. But the grief of Symmachus was indiscreet, and perhaps disrespectful ; he had presumed to lament, he might dare to revenge, the death of an injured friend. He was dragged in chains from Rome to the palace of Ravenna; and the suspicions of Theodoric could only be appeased by the blood of an innocent and aged senator.—Gibbon's *Decline and Fall,* 1838, vol. vii. p. 45—52 (without the notes).

INDEX

(*Giving the first line of each Metre, the first words of each Prose, and the corresponding page of the translation*).

Book	Metre	Prose		Page
I	1	—	Carmina qui quondam studio florente peregi ...	4
,,	—	1	Hæc dum mecum tacitus ipse reputarem ...	5
,,	2	—	Heu, quam præcipiti mersa profundo	7
,,	—	2	Sed medicinæ, inquit, potius tempus est ...	8
,,	3	—	Tunc me discussa liquerunt nocte tenebræ ...	9
,,	—	3	Haud aliter tristitiæ nebulis dissolutis, hausi cœlum	10
,,	4	—	Quisquis composito serenus ævo	12
,,	—	4	Sentisne, inquit, hæc, atque animo illabuntur tuo ?	13
,,	5	—	O stelliferi conditor orbis	21
,,	—	5	Hæc ubi continuato dolore delatravi	23
,,	6	—	Cum Phœbi radiis grave	25
,,	—	6	Primum igitur paterisne me pauculis rogationibus	26
,,	7	—	Nubibus atris	29
II	—	1	Posthæc paulisper obticuit	29
,,	1	—	Hæc cum superba verterit vices dextra ...	33
,,	—	2	Vellem autem pauca tecum fortunæ ipsius ...	33
,,	2	—	Si quantas rapidis flatibus incitus	35
,,	—	3	His igitur si pro se tecum fortuna loqueretur ...	36
,,	3	—	Cum polo Phœbus roseis quadrigis	39
,,	—	4	Tum ego, Vera, inquam, commemoras ...	39
,,	4	—	Quisquis volet perennem	44

Book	Metre	Prose		Page
II	—	5	Sed quoniam rationum jam in te mearum fomenta	45
,,	5	—	Felix nimium prior ætas	50
,,	—	6	Quid autem de dignitatibus, potentiaque disseram	51
,,	6	—	Novimus quantas dederit ruinas	55
,,	—	7	Tum ego, Scis, inquam, ipsa	56
,,	7	—	Quicumque solam mente præcipiti petit ...	60
,,	—	8	Sed ne me inexorabile contra fortunam ...	61
,,	8	—	Quod mundus stabili fide	62
III	—	1	Jam cantum illa finierat	63
,,	1	—	Qui serere ingenuum volet agrum	64
,,	—	2	Tum defixo paululum visu	64
,,	2	—	Quantas rerum flectat habenas	68
,,	—	3	Vos quoque, o terrena animalia	69
,,	3	—	Quamvis fluente dives auri gurgite	71
,,	—	4	Sed dignitates honorabilem reverendumque ...	72
,,	4	—	Quamvis se Tyrio superbus ostro	74
,,	—	5	An vero regna regumque familiaritas efficere potentem valent?	75
,,	5	—	Qui se volet esse potentem	77
,,	—	6	Gloria vero quam fallax sæpe, quam turpis est!	77
,,	6	—	Omne hominum genus in terris	78
,,	—	7	Quid autem de corporis voluptatibus loquar?	79
,,	7	—	Habet omnis hoc voluptas	80
,,	—	8	Nihil igitur dubium est, quin	80
,,	8	—	Eheu, quam miseros tramite devio	81
,,	-	9	Hactenus mendacis formam felicitatis ostendisse	82
,,	9	—	O qui perpetua mundum ratione gubernas ...	87
,,	—	10	Quoniam igitur quæ sit imperfecti	88
,,	10	—	Huc omnes pariter venite capti	94
,,	—	11	Assentior, inquam.	95
,,	11	—	Quisquis profunda mente vestigat verum ...	100
,,	—	12	Tum ego, Platoni, inquam, vehementer assentior	101
,,	12	—	Felix qui potuit boni	106
IV	—	1	Hæc cum Philosophia, dignitate	108

Book	Metre	Prose		Page
IV	1	—	Sunt etenim pennæ volucres mihi	110
,,	—	2	Tum ego, Papæ, inquam, ut magna promittis!	112
,,	2	—	Quos vides sedere celso	118
,,	—	3	Videsne igitur quanto in cœno probra volvantur	119
,,	3	—	Vela Neritii ducis	122
,,	—	4	Tum ego, Fateor, inquam, nec injuria dici video	123
,,	4	—	Quid tantos juvat excitare motus	130
,,	—	5	Hic ego, Video, inquam, quæ sit vel felicitas ...	131
,,	5	—	Si quis Arcturi sidera nescit	132
,,	—	6	Ita est, inquam.	133
,,	6	—	Si vis celsi jura tonantis	143
,,	—	7	Jamne igitur vides, quid hæc omnia quæ diximus, consequatur?	144
,,	7	—	Bella bis quinis operatus annis	147
V	—	1	Dixerat, orationisque cursum ad alia quædam	149
,,	1	—	Rupis Achæmeniæ scopulis, ubi versa sequentum	151
,,	—	2	Animadverto, inquam, idque uti tu dicis, ita esse consentio.	152
,,	2	—	Puro clarum lumine Phœbum	153
,,	—	3	Tum ego, En, inquam, difficiliori rursus ambiguitate confundor.	154
,,	3	—	Quænam discors fœdera rerum	159
,,	—	4	Tum illa, Vetus, inquit, hæc est de Providentia querela	161
,,	4	—	Quondam porticus attulit	166
,,	—	5	Quod si in corporibus sentiendis, quamvis ...	168
,,	5	—	Quam variis terras animalia permeant figuris!	170
,,	—	6	Quoniam igitur, uti paulo ante monstratum est	171

Appendix.—Ætas Prima 180
    ,,   Balades de Vilage sanz Peinture 182

TABLE OF CONTENTS.

[I]NCIPIT TABULA LIBRI BOICII DE CON-
SOLAC*IO*N E PHILOSOPHIE.

[*Additional MS.* 10,340, *fol.* 3.]

LIBER PRIMUS. [fol. 3.]

1 Carmina qui quondam studio flore*nte* p*er*egi.
2 Hic dum mecum tacitus.
3 Heu qu*a*m precipiti.
4 Set medicine inquit tempus.
5 Tunc me discussa.
6 Haut¹ aliter tristicie.   ¹ MS. hanc.
7 Quisquis composito.
8 Sentis ne inquit.
9 O stelliferi conditor orbis.
10 Hic ubi continuato dolore.
11 Cum phebi radijs.
12 Prim*um* igit*ur* pateris rogacio*n*ibu*s*.
13 Nubib*us* atris condita.

EXPLICIT LIBER PRIMUS.

LIBER SECUNDUS.

1 Postea paulisper² conticuit.   ² MS. lllper.
2 Hec cum superba.
3 Uellem autem pauea.
4 Si quantas rapidis.
5 His igitur si *et* pro se.

1

TABLE OF CONTENTS.

6 Cum primo polo.
7 Tunc ego uera inqvam.
8 Contraque.
9 Quisquis ualet perhennem cantus.
10 Set cum racionum iam in te.
11 Felix in mirum iam prior etas.
12 Quid autem de dignitatibus.
13 Nouimus quantos dederat.
14 Tum ego scis inquam.
15 Quicunque solam mente.
16 Set ne me inexorabile.
17 Quod mundus stabile fide.

EXPLICIT LIBER SECUNDUS.

LIBER TERCIUS.

1 Iam tantum illa.
2 Qui serere ingenium.
3 Tunc defixo paululum.
4 Quantas rerum flectat.
5 Uos quoque terrena animalia.
6 Quamuis fluenter diues.
7 Set dignitatibus.
8 Quamuis se tirio.
9 An uero regna.
10 Qui se ualet esse potentem.
11 Gloria uero quam fallax.
12 Omne hominum genus in terris.
13 Quid autem de corporibus.
14 Habet hoc uoluptas.
15 Nichil igitur dubium est.
16 Heu que miseros tramite.
17 Hactenus mendacio formam.
18 O qui perpetua.
19 Quoniam igitur qui scit.
20 Nunc omnes pariter.
21 Assencior inquam cuncta.

22 Quisq*ue* profunda.
23 Tunc ego platoni inq*ua*m.
24 Felix qui poterit.

  EXPLICIT LIBER TERCIUS.

LIBER QUARTUS.

1 Hec cum philosophia.
2 Sunt etenim penne.
3 Tunc ego pape inq*ua*m.
4 Quos uides sedere celsos.
5 Uides ne igitur quanto.
6 U[e]la naricij ducis.
7 Tunc ego fateor inq*ua*m.
8 Quid tantos iuuat.
9 Huic ego uideo inq*ua*m.
10 Si quis arcturi [1] sydera.   [1] MS. aritu:a.
11 Ita est inq*ua*m.
12 Si uis celsi iura.
13 Iam ne igit*ur* uides.
14 Bella bis quinis.

  EXPLICIT LIBER QUARTUS.

INCIPIT LIBER QUINTUS.

1 Dixerat orac*i*onis q*ue* cursu*m*.
2 Rupis achemenie.
3 Animaduerto inq*ua*m.
4 Puro claru*m* lumine.
5 Tamen ego en inq*ua*m.
6 Que nam discors.
7 Tamen illa uetus.
8 Quonda*m* porticus attulit.
9 Quod si i*n* corporib*us*.
10 Qua*m* uarijs figuris.
11 Quonia*m* igit*ur* uti paulo ante.

  EXPLICIT LIBER QUINTUS ET ULTIMUS.

BOETHIUS DEPLORES HIS MISFORTUNES. [BOOK I. MET. 1.

[* fol. 3 b.]

*LIBER PRIMUS.

[The fyrste Metur.]

INCIPIT LIBER BOICII DE CONSOLACIONE PHILOSOPHIE.
Carmina qui quondam studio florente peregi.

Boethius deplores his misfortunes in the following pathetic elegy.

Allas I wepyng am constreined to bygynne vers of sorouful matere. ¶ þat whilom in florysching studie made delitable ditees. For loo rendyng muses of poetes enditen to me þinges to be writen. and drery vers of wrecchednes weten my face wiþ verray teers. ¶ At þe leest no drede ne my3t[e] ouer-come þo muses.

ypalage antithesis

þat þei ne weren felawes and folweden my wey. þat is to seyne when I was exiled. þei þat weren glorie of my you3th whilom weleful and grene conforten now þo

Laments his immature old age.

sorouful werdes of me olde man. for elde is comen vnwarly vpon me hasted by þe harmes þat I haue. and sorou haþ comaunded his age to be in me. ¶ Heeres hore ben schad ouertymelyche vpon myne heued. and þe slak[e] skyn trembleþ vpon myn emty body. þilk[e]

Death turns a deaf ear to the wretched.

deeþ of men is welful þat ne comeþ not in 3eres þat ben swete (.i. mirie.) but comeþ to wrecches often yclepid.

¶ Allas allas wiþ how deef an cere deeþ cruel tourneþ awey fro wrecches and naieþ to closen wepyng eyen. ¶ While fortune vnfeiþful fauored[e] me wiþ ly3te goodes (.s. temporels.) þe sorouful houre þat is to seyne þe deeþ had[de] almost dreynt myne heued.

When Fortune was favourable Death came near Boethius,

but in his adversity life is unpleasantly protracted.

¶ But now for fortune clowdy haþ chaunged hir disceyuable chere to me warde. myn vnpitouse lijf draweþ a long vnagreable dwellynges in me. ¶ O 3e my

1 of—MS. of of.
2 florysching—floryssynge
3 rendyng—rendynge
4 be—ben
5 wrecchednes — wrecchednesse
teers—teeres
6 leest—leeste
my3t[e] ouer-come—myhte ouercomen
8 seyne when—seyn whan
9 you3th—MS. þo3t, O. yowthe
10 sorouful werdes — sorful wierdes [l. fata]
12 sorou—sorwe

12 haþ—MS. haþe
be—ben
13 hore—hoore
ben—arn
myne—myn
14 slak[e]—slake
{ vpon—of
emty —emptyd
þilk[e]—thilke
15 welful—weleful
comeþ not—comth nat
16 .i. mirie—omitted
19 tourneþ—torneth
naieþ—nayteth
wepyng—wepynge

20 While—Whil
fauored[e]—fauorede
21 ly3te—lyhte
.s. temporels—omitted
sorouful houre — sorwful howre
22 seyne—seyn
had[de]—hadde
myne—myn
23 haþ—MS. haþe
chaunged hir disceyuable—chaungyd hyre deceyuable
24 vnpitouse lijf—vnpietous lyf

PHILOSOPHY APPEARS TO BOETHIUS.

frendes what or wherto auaunted[e] ʒe me to be wele- *Why did his*
ful : for he þat haþ fallen stood not in stedfast degree. *friends call him happy? He stood not firm that hath thus fallen.*

HIC DUM MECUM TACITUS.

IN þe mene while þat I stille recorded[e] þise þinges [The firste prose.]
wiþ my self. and markede my wepli compleynte wiþ. 29
office of poyntel. I saw stondyng aboue þe heyʒt of my *Philosophy appears to Boethius,*
heued a woman of ful greet reuerence by semblaunt
hir eyen brennyng and clere seing ouer þe comune *like a beautiful woman,*
myʒt of men. wiþ a lijfly colour and wiþ swiche vigoure 33
and strenkeþ þat it ne myʒt[e] not be emptid. ¶ Al
were it so þat sche was ful of so greet age. þat men ne *and of great age.*
wolde not trowe in no manere þat sche were of oure 36
elde. þe stature of hir was of a doutous iugement. for *Her height could not be determined,*
sumtyme sche constreyned[e] and schronk hir seluen
lyche to þe comune mesure of men. and sumtyme it
semed[e] þat sche touched[e] þe heuene wiþ þe heyʒte 40
of hir heued. and when sche hef hir heued heyer sche *for there were times when she raised her head higher than the heavens.*
perced[e] þe seluc heuene. so þat þe syʒt of men lokyng
was in ydel. ¶ Hir cloþes weren maked of ryʒt delye
þredes and subtil crafte of perdurable matere. þe wyche 44
cloþes sche hadde wouen wiþ hir owen hondes : as I *Her clothes were finely wrought and indissoluble,*
knew wel aftir by hir selfe. declaryng and schewyng
to me þe beaute. þe wiche cloþes a derkenes of a for- 47
leten and dispised elde had[de] duskid and dirkid as *but dark and dusky, like old besmoked images.*
it is wont to dirken by-smoked ymages. ¶ In þe ne-

26 *auaunted[e]*—auauntede
    be—ben
27 *haþ*—MS. haþo
    not—nat
    stedfast—stidefast
28 *In þe mene*—omitted
    recorded[e]—recordede
30 *saw*—MS. sawe, C. sawh
    stondyng aboue—MS. studiyng aboue, C. stondinge abouen
    heyʒt—heyhte
    my—myn
31 *greet*—gret
32 *brennyng*—brennynge
    clere seing—cleer seynge
33 *swiche*—swych
34 *strenkeþ*—strengthe
    it — emptid — it myhte

34 *Al*—alle
36 *wolde——trowe*—wolden nat trowen
37 *iugement*—Iuggement
38 *sumtyme*—somtyme
    constreyned[e] — constreynede
    schronk—MS. schronke, C. shronk
39 *lyche*—lyk
40 *semed[e]*—semede
    touched[e]—towchede
41 *when*—whan
    hef—MS. heued, C. hef
    heyer—hyere
42 *perced[e]*—percede
    syʒt—syhte
    lokyng—lookynge

44 *crafte*—craft
45 *wouen*—MS. wonnen, C. wouen
    owen hondes — owne handes
46 *knew* — MS. knewe, C. knewh
    selfe declaryng — self declarynge
    schewyng—shewynge
47 *derkenes*—dirknesse
    forleten—forletyn
48 *dispised*—despised
    had[de] duskid — hadde dusked
    dirkid—derked
49 *by-smoked*—the smokede
    neþeres[e]—netherest

A DESCRIPTION OF PHILOSOPHY. [BOOK I. PROSE I.]

On the lower hem of her garment was the letter Π and on the upper Θ.

þerest[e] hem or bordure of þese cloþes men redden ywouen in swiche a gregkysche .P. þat signifieþ þe lijf actif. And abouen þat lettre in þe hey3est[e] bordure a grekysche T. þat signifieþ þe lijf contemplatif.

Between the letters were steps like a ladder.

¶ And by-twene þese two lettres þere weren seien degrees nobly wrou3t in manere of laddres. By wyche degrees men my3t[en] clymbe fro þe neþemast[e] lettre

Philosophy's garments were tattered and torn, and pieces had been carried violently off.

to þe ouermast[e]. ¶ Naþeles hondes of sum men hadde korue þat cloþe by vyolence and by strenkeþ. ¶ And eueryche man of hem hadde born away syche peces as he my3te geet[e]. ¶ And forsoþe þis forsaide

In her right hand she bore her books, and in her left a sceptre.

woman ber bookes in hir ry3t honde. and in hir lefte honde sche ber a ceptre. ¶ And when sche sau3 þese poetical muses aprochen aboute my bedde. and endytyng wordes to my wepynges. sche was a lytel ameued

Philosophy bids the Muses leave Boethius,

and glowed[e] wiþ cruel eyen. ¶ Who quod sche haþ suffred aprochen to þis seek[e] man þise comune strumpetis of siche a place þat *men clepen þe theatre.

[* fol. 4.]

¶ þe wyche only ne asswagen not his sorowes. wiþ no

as they only increase his sorrow with their sweet venom.

remedies. but þei wolde fede and norysche hem wiþ swete venym. ¶ Forsoþe þise ben þo þat wiþ þornes and prykkynges of talent3 or affeciouns wiche þat ben no þing fruteliyng nor profitable destroyen þe

They may accustom the mind to bear grief, but cannot free it from its malady.

cornes plenteuouse of frutes of reson. ¶ For þei holden þe hertes of men in usage. but þei ne delyuere not folk fro maladye. but if 3e muses hadde wiþdrawen

---

50 þese—thise
51 swiche—omitted
  gregkysche—grekysshe
  signifieþ—syngnifieth
52 hey3est[e]—heyeste
54 by-twene þese—bytwixen thise
  þere—ther
  seien—seyn
55 nobly wrou3t—nobely y-wroght
  wyche—whiche
56 my3t[en] clymbe—myhten clymbyn
  neþemast[e]—nethereste
57 ouermast[e]—vppereste
  sum—some
59 hadde korue—hadden korueu

58 cloþe—cloth
  strenkeþ—strengthe
59 born—MS. borne, C. born
  away syche—awey swiche
60 geet[e]—geten
  forsaide—forseide
61 ber—MS. bere, C. bar
  bookes—smale bookes
  honde—hand
  lefte honde—left hand
62 ber—MS. bere, C. baar
  sau3 þese—say thise
63 bedde—bed
  endytyng—enditynge
64 ameued—amoued
65 glowed[e]—glowede
  haþ—MS. haþe, C. hath
66 seek[e]—sike
  þise—the

66 strumpetis—strompetes
67 siche—swich
  clepen—clepyn
68 only ne—nat oonly ne
  not his—nat hise
  no—none
69 wolde fede—wolden feeden
  norysche hem — noryssyn
  hym
72 ben—ne ben
  fruteflyng—fruteflynge
73 cornes plenteuouse—corn plentyuos
74 þe and ne—both omitted
75 not—nat
  if 3e—MS. if þe, C. yif ye
  hadde—hadden

fro me wiþ ȝoure flateries. any vnkonnyng *and* vnprofit-   Philosophy is deeply grieved,
able man as men ben wont to fynde comunely amonges   because they have not seduced one
þe peple. I wolde wene suffre þe lasse greuously.   of the profane,
¶ For-why in syche an vnprofitable man myne ententes
weren no þing endamaged. ¶ But ȝe wiþdrawen me   80
þis man þat haþ ben norysched in studies or scoles of   but one who has been brought up
Eleaticis *and* of achademicis in grece. ¶ But goþ now   in Eleatic and Academic studies.
raþer awey ȝe meremaydenes wyche ben swete til it
be at þe laste. *and* suffreþ þis man to be cured *and*   84
heled by myne muses. þat is to say by notful sciences.   She bids the syrens begone.
¶ And þus þis compaygnie of muses I-blamed casten
wroþely þe chere adounward to þe erþe *and* schewyng   87
by redenesse hir schame þei passeden sorowfuly þe   Blushing for shame they pass
preschefolde. ¶ And I of whom þe syȝt plonged in   the threshold.
teres was derked so þat I ne myȝt[e] not knowe what
þat woman was of so *i*mperial auctorite. ¶ I wex al   91
a-besid *and* astoned. *and* caste my syȝt adoune in to þe   Boethius is astonished at the
erþe. *and* bygan stille forto abide what sche wolde don   presence of the august dame.
afterwarde. ¶ Þo come sche nere *and* sette hir doun
vpon þe vterrest[e] corner of my bedde. *and* sche by-   95
holdyng my chere þat was cast to þe erþe heuy *and*   Philosophy expresses her
greuous of wepyng. compleinede wiþ þise wordes þat I   concern for Boethius.
schal sey þe *pe*rtur*ba*cioun of my þouȝt.   98

HEU QU*AM* PRECIPITI MERSA PROFUNDO.

Allas how þe þouȝt of man dreint in ouer þrowyng   [The 2de Metur.]
depnesse dulleþ *and* forletiþ hys propre clere-   Drowned in the depth of cares
nesse. myntynge to gone in to foreyne derknesses as   the mind loses its proper
ofte as hys anoious bisines wexiþ wiþ-outen mesure.   clearness.

76 *vnkonnyng*—vnkunnynge
78 *peple*—poeple
79 *syche*—swhiche
    myne—myn
80 *weren*—ne weeren
    ȝe—ye
81 *haþ*—MS. haþe, C. hath
    ben—be
    scoles—schooles
82 *goþ*—MS. goþe, C. goth
83 *wyche*—whiche þat
85 *say*—seyn
85 *notful*—notcful
86 *I-blamed*—Iblamyd
87 *wroþely*—wrothly
    adounward—downward
88 *redenesse*—rednesse
    sorowfuly—sorwfully
89 *preschefolde*—thresshfold
    syȝt—syhte
90 *derked*—dyrked
    myȝt[e]——*knowe*—myhte nat knowen
91 *wex*—wax
92 *a-besid*—abaysshed
    caste—cast
92 *adoune in to*—down to
93 *don*—MS. done
95 *vterrest[e] corner*—vtereste cornere
    bedde—bed
97 *compleinede*—compley[n]de
98 *sey*—seyen
101 *gone*—goon
102 *bisines*—bysynesse
    outen—owte

PHILOSOPHY ADDRESSES BOETHIUS. [BOOK I. PROSE 2.

Man in his freedom knew each region of the sky,

þat is dryuen to *and* fro wiþ worldly wyndes. ¶ þis man þat sumtyme was fre to whom þe heuene was open
105 and knowen *and* was wont to gone in heuenelyche paþes. *and* sauȝ þe lyȝtnesse of þe rede sunne. *and* sauȝ þe sterres of þe colde moone. *and* wyche sterre *in*

the motions of the planets, and was wont to investigate the causes of storms,

heuene vseþ wandryng risorses yflit by dyuerse speres. ¶ þis man ouer comere hadde comprehendid al þis by noumbre. of accountyng in astronomye. ¶ And ouer þis he was wont to seche þe causes whennes þe soun-
112 yng wyndes moeuen *and* bisien þe smoþe water of þe see. *and* what spirit turneþ þe stable heuene. *and* whi þe sterre ryseþ oute of þe reede eest. to falle

the nature and properties of the seasons,

in þe westren wawes. *and* what attempriþ þe lusty houres of þe fyrste somer sesou*n* þat hiȝteþ *and* ap-
117 paraileþ þe erþe wiþ rosene floures. ¶ And who makeþ þat plenteuouse autumpne in fulle ȝeres fletiþ wiþ heuy grapes. ¶ And eke þis ma*n* was wont to

and the hidden causes of nature.

telle þe dyuerses causes of nature þat weren yhid.
121 ¶ Allas now lieþ he emptid of lyȝt of hys þouȝt. *and*

But now, alas, he is constrained to keep his face to the ground.

hys nekke is pressid wiþ heuy cheynes *and* bereþ his chere enclined adoune for þe greet[e] weyȝt. and is
124 constreyned to loke on foule erþe.

SET MEDICINE INQUIT TEMPUS.

[The IJde prose.]

More need of medicine than of complaint.

Bvt tyme is now q*uo*d sche of medicine more þen of compleynte. ¶ Forsoþe þen sche entendyng to me warde wiþ al þe lokyng of hir eyen saide. ¶ Art
128 not þou he q*uo*d sche þat sumtyme I-norschid wiþ my

Philosophy addresses Boethius.

mylke *and* fostre[d] wiþ my meetes were ascaped *and* comen to corage of a perfit man. ¶ Certys I ȝaf þe

---

103 *worldly*—wordely	114 *ryseþ oute*—aryseth owt	124 *loke*——*foule*—looken on the fool
104 *sumtyme*—whilom	*falle*—fallen	125, 126 *þen*—than
105 *gone*—goon	115 *westren*—westrene	127 *al*—alle
106 *paþes*—paathes	116 *fyrste*—fyrst	*saide*—seyde
sauȝ—sawh	119 *eke*—ek	128 *sumtyme*—whilom
lyȝtnesse—lythnesse	120 *dyuerses*—diuerse	*I-norschid* — MS. I-norschide, C. noryssed
sunne—sonne	*yhid*—MS. yhidde	129 *fostre[d]*—fostered
sauȝ—MS. sue, C. sawgh	121 *lieþ*—lith	*my*—myne
107 *wyche*—which	*emptid*—emted	130 *Certys*—Certes
108 *risorses*—recourses	123 *adoune*—adown	ȝaf, yaf
111 *seche*—seken	*greet[e] weyȝt* — grete weyhte	
sounyng—sownynge		

syche armures þat ȝif þou þi self ne haddest first caste
hem away. þei schulden haue defendid þe in sykernesse 132
þat may not be ouer-comen. ¶ Knowest þou me not.
* Why art þou stille. is it for schame or for astonynge.   [* fol. 4 b.]
It were me leuer þat it were for schame. but it semeþ   She fears his silence proceeds from shame
me þat astonynge haþ oppressed þe. ¶ And whan   rather than from stupidity.
sche say me not oonly stille. but wiþ-outen office of 137
tonge and al doumbe. sche leide hir honde softely vpon   She finds him, however, in a
my brest and seide. ¶ Here nis no peril quod sche.   lethargy, the distemper of a disordered mind.
¶ He is fallen in to a litargie. whiche þat is a comune
sekenes to hertes þat ben desceiued. ¶ He haþ a litel 141
forȝeten hym self. but certis he schal lyȝtly remembren   To make his recovery an easy
hym self. ¶ Ȝif so be þat he haþ knowen me or now.   matter, she wipes his eyes, which
and þat he may so done I wil wipe a litel hys eyen.   were darkened by the clouds of
þat ben derked by þe cloude of mortel þinges ¶ þise   mortal things,
wordes seide sche. and wiþ þe lappe of hir garment 146
yplitid in a frounce sche dried[e] myn eyen þat were   and dries up his tears.
ful of þe wawes of my wepynges.

         TUNC ME DISCUSSA.   *i.e. dispelled*

Þus when þat nyȝt was discussed and chased awey.   [The 3de Metur.]
    derknesses forleften me. and to myn eyen repeyre   Her touch dispels the darkness of his soul,
aȝeyne her firste strenkeþ. and ryȝt by ensample as 151
þe sonne is hid when þe sterres ben clustred. þat is to   just as the heavy vapours, that
sey when sterres ben couered wiþ cloudes by a swifte   darken the skies and obscure the
wynde þat hyȝt chorus. and þat þe firmament stont   sunlight, are chased away by
derked by wete ploungy cloudes. and þat þe sterres not   the north wind,
apperen vpon heuene. ¶ So þat þe nyȝt semeþ sprad 156
vpon erþe. ¶ Yif þan þe wynde þat hyȝt borias

---

131 syche—swiche
   ȝif—yif
   caste—C. cast
132 away—awey
   schulden haue — sholden han
133 not be—nat ben
   Knowest þou—knowestow
134 art þou—artow
136 haþ—MS. haþe
138 tonge—tunge
   doumbe—dowmb
   honde—hand

139 Here—her
140 litargie whiche—litarge which
141 sekenes—sykenesse
141, 143 haþ—MS. haþe
144 done—doon
   wil wipe—wol wypen
146 garment—garnemeut
147 dried[e]—dryedo
   were—weeren
148 ful—fulle
149 when—whan
150 myn—myno

150 repeyre—repeyrede
151 aȝeyne—omitted
   her firste—hir fyrst
152 hid—MS. hidde, C. hid
   when—whan
153 sey—seyn
   when—whan
154 hyȝt—heyhte
   chorus—MS. thorus
   stont—MS. stonde, C. stant
157 þan—thanne
   wynde—wynd
   hyȝt—hyhte

158 sent out of þe kaues of þe contre of Trace betiþ þis

causing the return of the hidden day, when the sun smites our wondering sight with his sudden light.

nyȝt. þat is to seyn chasiþ it away *and* descoureþ þe closed day. ¶ þan schineþ phebus yshaken wiþ sodeyne lyȝt *and* smyteþ wiþ hys bemes in meruelyng

162 cyen.

¹ MS. hanc.　　　HAUT ¹ ALITER TRISTICIE.

[The 3ᵈᵉ prose.]
The cloudes of sorrow being dispelled, Boethius recollects the features of his Physician,

Ryȝt so *and* none oþer wyse þe cloudes of sorowe dissolued *and* don awey. ¶ I took heuene. *and* receyuede mynde to knowe þe face of my fyciscien. ¶ So þat I sette myne cyen on hir *and* festned[e] my

whom he discovers to be Philosophy.

lokyng. I byholde my norice philosophie. in whos houses I hadde conuersed *and* haunted fro my ȝouþe.

169 *and* I seide þus. ¶ O þou maistresse of alle uertues

He addresses her.

descendid fro þe souereyne sete. Whi art þou comen in to þis solitarie place of myn exil. ¶ Art þou comen

172 for þou art mad coupable wiþ me of fals[e] blames.

She expresses her concern for him,

¶ O q*uod* sche my norry scholde I forsake þe now. and scholde I not parte wiþ þe by comune trauaille þe charge þat þou hast suffred for envie of my name. ¶ Certis

176 it nar[e] not leueful ne sittyng to philosophie to leten

and tells him that she is willing to share his misfortunes.

wiþ-outen compaignie þe wey of hym þat is innocent. ¶ Scholde I þan redoute my blame *and* agrisen as þouȝ

179 þer were byfallen a newe þing. q. d. non. ¶ For

She fears not any accusation, as if it were a new thing.

trowest þou þat philosophi be now alþerfirst assailed in perils by folk of wicked[e] maneres. ¶ Haue I not

For before the age of Plato she contended against folly,

stryuen wiþ ful greet strife in olde tyme byfore þe age of my plato aȝeins þe foolhardines of foly *and*

184 eke þe same plato lyuyng. hys maistre socrates

and by her help Socrates triumphed over an unjust death.

deserued[e] victorie of vnryȝtful deeþ in my presence. ¶ þe heritage of wyche socrates. þe heritage is to seyne

158 *sent*—lsent
160 *þan*—thanne
161 *sodeyne*—sodeyn
163 *none oþer*—non oother
　sorowe—sorwe
165 *knowe*—knowen
166 *myne*—myn
　festned[e]—fastnede
170 *fro*—from
170, 171 *art þou*—artow

172 *mad*—MS. made, C. mak-
　fals[e]—false　　　[ed
174 *parte*—parten
176 *nar[e]*—nere
　sittyng—sittinge
178 *þan*—thanne
179 *þing*—thing
　q. d. *non*—omitted
180 *trowest þou*—trowestow
　alþerfirst—alderfirst

181 *wicked[e]*—wikkede
182 *strife*—strif
183 *aȝeins*—aȝenis
　foolhardines — foolhardi-
　　nesse
foly—folie
184 *eke*—ek
185 *deserued[e]*—desseruede
186 *wyche*—the which
　seyne—seyn

þe doctrine of þe whiche socrates in hys oppiniouʒ of felicite þat I clepe welfulnesse ¶ Whan þat þe people of epicuriens *and* stoyciens *and* many oþer enforceden hem to go rauische eueryche man for his part þat is 190 to seyne. þat to eueryche of hem wolde drawen to þe defence of his oppiniouʒ þe wordes of socrates. ¶ Þei as in *p*artic of hir preye todrowen me criynge *and* debatyng þer aʒeins. *and* tornen *and* torenten my cloþes 194 þat I hadde wouen wiþ myn handes. *and* wiþ þe cloutes þat þei hadden arased oute of my cloþes. þei wenten awey wenyng þat I hadde gon wiþ hem euery dele. In whiche epicuryens *and* stoyciens. for as 198 myche as þer semed[e] somme traces *and* steppes of myne habit. þe folye of men wenyng þo epicuryens *and* stoyciens my *familers *p*eruertede (.s. *p*ersequend*a*) somme þoruʒ þe errour of þe wikked[e] or vnkunn- 202 yng[e] multitude of hem. ¶ Þis is to seyne for þei semeden philosophres: þei weren *p*ursued to þe deeþ and slayn. ¶ So yif þou hast not knowen þe exilynge of anaxogore. ne þe empoysenyng of socrates. ne þe 206 tour*m*entʒ of ʒeno for þei [weren] straungers. ¶ ʒit myʒtest þou haue knowen þe senectiens *and* þe Canyos *and* þe sorancis of wyche folk þe renouʒ is neyþer ouer oolde ne vnsolempne. ¶ Þe whiche men no þing ellys 210 ne brouʒt[e] hem to þe deeþ but oonly for þei weren enfourmed of my maneres. *and* semeden moste vnlyke to þe studies of wicked folk. ¶ And forþi þou auʒtest not to wondre þouʒ þat I in þe bitter see of þis lijf be 214

Of the inheritance of Socrates the rout of Epicureans and Stoics wanted to get a part.

Philosophy withstood them, whereupon they tore her robe, and, departing with the shreds,

Imagined that they had got possession of her.

Thus, clothed with her spoils, they deceived many.

[* fol. 5.]

Philosophy adduces examples of wise men, who had laboured under difficulties on account of being her disciples.

188 *welfulnesse* — weleful-
189 *oþer*—oothre [nesse
190 *go*—gon
  eueryche—euerich
191 *seyne*—seyn
  to—omitted
  eueryche—euerich
194 *tornen*—read coruen, C.
  korueu
195 *wouen*—MS. wonnen, C.
  wouen
196 *arased*—arraced
197 *gon*—MS. gone, C. gon
198 *dele*—del
199 *myche*—moche

199 *semed*[e]—semede
  and—or
200 *myne*—myn
  wenyng—MS. wevyng, C.
  weninge
202 *þoruʒ*—thorw
  wikked[e]—wikkede
  vnkunnyng[e] — vnkuun-
203 *seyne*—seyn þat   [ynge
204 *semeden*—semede
  pursued — MS. pursuede,
  C. pursued
205 *slayn* — MS. slayne, C.
  slayn
207 [*weren*]—weeren

208 *myʒtest* þou *haue* —
  myhtestow han
209 *sorancis*—sorans
  wyche—which
  is—nis
210 *oolde*—MS. colde, C. old
211 *brouʒt*[e]—browhte
212 *enfourmed* — MS. vn-
  fourmed, C. enformyd
  my—myne
  vnlyke—vnlyk
213 *wicked folk* — wikkede
  auʒtest—owhtest [foolke
214 *wondre*—wondren
  bitter —bittre

THE AIM OF PHILOSOPHY. [BOOK I. MET. I.

It is the aim of Philosophy to displease the wicked,

fordryuen wiþ tempestes blowyng aboute. in þe whiche tempeste þis is my most purpos þat is to seyn to dis-
217 plese to wikked[e] men. ¶ Of whiche schrews al be

who are more to be despised than dreaded, for they have no leader.

þe oost neuer so grete it is to dispyse. for it nis gouerned wiþ no leder of resoune. but it is rauysched only by
220 flityng errour folyly *and* ly3tly. ¶ And if þei somtyme makyng an ost a3eynest vs assaile vs as strengere. oure

If Philosophy is attacked by the wicked, she retires within her fortress,

leder draweþ to gedir hys rycchesse *in* to hys toure. *and* þei ben ententif aboute sarpulers or sachels vn-profitable forto taken. but we þat ben hey3 abouen syker
225 fro al tumulte *and* wode noise. ben stored *and* enclosed

leaving the enemy busy among the useless baggage, and laughing to scorn such hunters of trifles.

in syche a palays. whider as þat chateryng or anoying folye ne may not attayne. ¶ We scorne swiche rauiners *and* honters of foulest[e] þinges.

QUISQUIS COMPOSITO.

*The fertile Metur.]
He who hath triumphed over fate, and remained insensible to the*

Who so it be þat is clere of vertue sad *and* wel ordinat of lyuyng. þat haþ put vnderfote þe prowed[e] wierdes *and* lokiþ vpry3t vpon eyþer fortune. he may
232 holde hys chiere vndiscomfited. ¶ þe rage ne þe manace

changes of Fortune, shall not be moved by storms, nor by the fires of Vesuvius, nor by the fiercest thunderbolts.

of þe commoeuyng or chasyng vpwarde hete fro þe botme. ne schal not moeue þat man. ne þe vnstable mountaigne þat hy3t veseuus. þat wircheþ oute þoru3
236 hys broken[e] chemineys smokyng fires. ¶ Ne þe wey of þonder ly3t þat is wont to smyte hey3e toures ne

Fear not the tyrant's rage.

schal not mouene þat man. ¶ Wherto þen wrecches drede 3e tyrauntes þat ben wode *and* felownes wiþ-outen

He who neither fears nor hopes

ony strenkeþ. ¶ Hope after no þing ne drede nat. *and*

---

216 *displese*—displesen
217 *wikked*[*e*]—wikkede
   schrews—shrewen
218 *oost*—glossed *acies* in C.
   grete—gret
219, 222 *leder*—ledere
220 *flityng*—flectynge
   ly3tly—lythly
   v̄—yif
221 *a3eynest*—ayenis
222 *to*——*rycchesse*, to gydere hise rychesses
   toure—towr
224 *hey3*—heye

225 *al*—alle
   ben—omitted
   stored—warnestored
226 *syche*—swich
   þat—omitted
227 *scorne*—schorne
228 *rauiners* —— *þinges*—rauyneres & henteres of fowleste thinges
229 *clere*—cleer
230 *lyuyng*—leuynge
   haþ—MS. hape
   vnderfote—vndir-foot
   pr)*wed*[*e*]—prowde

231 *may*——*chiere*—may his cheere holde
232 *manace*—manesses
233 *þe*—þe see
235 *hy3t*—hihte
   veseuus—MS. veseuus
   wircheþ—writith
236 *brokn*[*e*]—brokene
   smokyng—smokynge
237 *smyte*—smyten
238 *Wherto þen*—wharto thanne
239 *felownes* —— *ony*—felonos withowte any

so schalt þou desarmen þe ire of þilke vnmyȝty tyraunt. *for anything disarms the tyrant.*
¶ But who so þat quakyng dredeþ or desireþ þing þat *He whose heart fails him, yields*
nis not stable of his ryȝt. þat man þat so doþ haþ cast *his arms, and forges his*
awey hys schelde *and* is remoeued fro hys place. *and* *own fetters.*
enlaceþ hym *in* þe cheyne wiþ whiche he may be 245
drawen.

SENTIS NE INQUIT.

FElest þou q*uod* sche þise þinges *and* entren þei ouȝt [*The verthe prose.*]
in þi corage. ¶ Art þou like an asse to þe harpe. *Philosophy seeks to know the*
Whi wepest þou whi spillest þou teres. ¶ Yif þou *malady of Boethius.*
abidest after helpe of þi leche. þe byhoueþ discouere þi 250
wounde. ¶ þo .I. þat hadde gadered strenkeþ in my *Boethius complains of For-*
corage answered[e] *and* seide. *and* nedeþ it ȝitte q*uod* *tune's unrelenting rage.*
.I. of rehersyng or of amonic*i*ou*n*. *and* scheweþ it not 253
ynouȝ by hym self þe scharpnes of fortune þat wexeþ *Is not she moved, he asks, with the*
woode aȝeynes me. ¶ Ne moeueþ it nat þe to seen þe *aspect of his prison?*
face or þe man*er*e of þis place (.i. priso*un*.). ¶ Is þis
þe librarie wyche þat þou haddest chosen for a ryȝt 257
certeyne sege to þe *in* myne house. ¶ Þere as þou *His library, his habit, and his*
desputest of[te] wiþ me of þe sciences of þinges touch- *countenance are all changed.*
ing diuinitee *and* touchyng mankynde. ¶ Was þan
myn habit swiche as it is now. was þan my face or 261
my chere swiche as now. ¶ Whan I souȝt[e] wiþ þe
quasi dicerct non.
secretys of nature. whan þou enfou*r*medest my maners
and þe resou*n* of al my lijf. to þe ensaumple of þe ordre 264
Ironice
of heuene. ¶ Is nat þis þe gerdou*n* þat I refere to þe *Is this, he asks,*
to whom I haue be obeisaunt. ¶ Certis þou enfou*r*- *the reward of his fidelity?*
medist by þe mouþe of plato þis sentence. þat is to *Plato (de Rep. v.) says that those*
seyne þat commune þinges or comunabletes weren *Commonwealths*

241 *schalt þou desarmen*—shaltow deseruien
243 *doþ*—MS. doþe, C. doth haþ—MS. haþe, C. hath
cast—MS. caste, C. cast
244 *schelde*—sheld
remoeued fro — remwed from
245 *which*—the which
be—ben
247 *Frlest þou*—Felistow
ouȝt—awht

248 *art þou*—artow
249 *wepest þou*—wepistow
spillest þou—spillestow
252 *answered[e]* — answerede
255 *woode*—wood
257 *wyche*—which
258 *myne house þere*—myn hows ther
259 *desputest of[te]* — desputedest ofte
260 *þan*—thanne

261 *it* and *þan*—both omitted
261, 262 *swiche*—swich
262 *souȝt[e]*—sowhte
263 *secretys*—secretȝ
my—MS. me, C. my
264 *al*—alle
265 *gerdoun*—gerdouns
266 *enfourmedist*—conformedest
267 *mouþe*—mowht
268 *comunabletes*—comunalitees

blysful yif þei þat haden studied al fully to wisdom
gouerneden þilke þinges. or ellys yif it so by-felle þat
þe gouernours *of communalites studieden in grete wis-
domes. ¶ þou saidest eke by þe mouþe of þe same
plato þat it was a necessarie cause wyse men to taken
and desire þe gouernaunce of comune þinges. for þat þe
gouernementes of comune citees y-left in þe hondes of
felonous tourmentours Citi3enis ne scholde not brynge
inne pestilence and destruccioun to goode folk. ¶ And
þerfore I folowynge þilk auctoritee (.s. platonis). desiryng
to put[te] furþe in execusioun and in acte of comune
administracioun þo þinges þat .I. hadde lerned of þe
among my secre restyng whiles. ¶ þou and god þat
put[te] þee in þe þou3tis of wise folk ben knowen wiþ
me þat no þing brou3t[e] me to maistrie or dignite : but
þe comune studie of al goodenes. ¶ And þer-of comeþ
it þat by-twixen wikked folk and me han ben greuouse
discordes. þat ne my3ten not be relesed by prayeres.
¶ For þis libertee haþ fredom of conscience þat þe wraþþe
of more my3ty folk haþ alwey ben despised of me for
saluacioun of ry3t. ¶ How ofte haue .I. resisted and
wiþstonde þilk man þat hy3t[e] conigaste þat made
alwey assautes a3eins þe propre fortunes of poure feble
folke. ¶ How ofte haue .I. 3itte put of. or cast out
hym trigwille prouost of þe kynges hous boþe of þe
wronges þat he hadde bygon[ne] to done and eke fully
performed. ¶ How ofte haue I couered and defended
by þe auctorite of me put a3eins perils. þat is to seine put
myne auctorite in peril for þe wreched pore folke. þat

þe couetise of straungeres vnpunysched to*ur*mentid alwey | thority in peril for the defence of poor folk.
wiþ myseses *and* greuaunces oute of noumbre. ¶ Neuer
man drow me ȝitte fro ryȝt to wrong. When I say þe | I never deviated, he says, from the path of justice.
fortunes *and* þe rychesse of þe people of þe prouinces
ben harmed eyþer by priue rauynes or by comune 302
tributis or cariages. as sory was I as þei þat suffred[e] | I felt for those that were wrongfully oppressed.
þe harme. *Glosa.* ¶ Whan þat theodoric þe kyng of
gothes in a dere ȝere hadde hys gerners ful of corne
and comaundede þat no man ne schold[e] bie no corne 306
til his corne were solde *and* þat at a dere greuous pris.
¶ But I wi*th*stod þat ordinaunce *and* ouer-com it
knowy*n*g al þis þe kyng hym self. ¶ Coempcioun þat
is to seyn comune achat or bying to-gidere þat were 310
establissed vpon poeple by swiche a manere imposicio*n*
as who so bouȝt[e] a busshel corn he most[e] ȝeue þe
ky*n*g þe fifte part. *Textus.* ¶ Whan it was in þe 313
soure hungry tyme þere was establissed or cried greuous | I opposed successfully Coemption in Campaula.
and inplitable coempcio*n* þat men seyn wel it schulde
greetly tou*r*mentyn *and* endamagen al þe prouince of 316
compaigne I took strif aȝeins þe prouost of þe pretorie
for comune profit. ¶ And þe kyng knowyng of it I | I saved Paulinus out of the hands of the hounds of the palace *(Palatini canes).*
ouercom it so þat þe coempciou*n* ne was not axed ne
took effect. ¶ Paulyn a counseiller of Rome þe rychesse
of þe whyche paulyn þe houndys of þe palays. þat is to 321
seyn þe officeres wolde han deuoured by hope *and*
couetise.. ¶ Ȝit drow I hym out of þe Iowes .s. faucib*us*
of hem þat gapede*n*. ¶ And for as myche as þe peyne 324
of þe accusacio*u*n ainged byforn ne scholde not sodeynly | I defended Albinus against Cyprian.
henten ne punischen wrongfuly Albyn a counseiller of

---

298 *vnpunysched*—vnpunyssed
299 *myseses*—myseyses
300 *drow*—MS. drowe, C. weth drowh
  ȝitte—yit
  wrong—wronge
301 *rychesse*—richesses
  þe (2)—omitted
302 *harmed eyþer*—harmyd or amenused owther
303 *tributis*—trihutȝ
  suffred[e]—suffreden

304 *harme*—harm
305 ȝere—yer
305 *hys*—hise
305, 306, 307 *corne*—corn
306 *schold[e] bie* — sholde byen
308 *But I withstod* — Boece withstood (MS. withstode)
  com—MS. come, C. com
311 *swiche*—swich
312 *bouȝt[e]*—bowhte
  busshel—bossel

312 *most[e] ȝeue*—moste yeue
315 *inplitable*—vnplitable
  seyn—sayen
319 *ouercom* — MS. ouercome, C. ouer com
320 *counseiller*—consoler
  rychesse—rychesses
321 *whyche*—which
322 *wolde*—wolden
323 *drow*—MS. drowe, C. drowh
324 *myche*—moche
326 *punischen*—punisse

Rome. I put[te] me aȝenis þe hates *and* indiguaciouns of þe accusou*r* Ciprian. ¶ Is it not þan ynought yseyn þat I haue p*ur*chased greet[e] discordes aȝeins my self. but I aughte be more assured aȝenis alle oþer folk þat for þe loue of ryȝtwisnesse .I. ne rescrued[e] neuer no þing to my self to hem ward of þe kynges halle .s. officers. by þe whiche I were þe more syker. ¶ But þoruȝ þe same accusou*r*s accusyng I am co*n*dempned. ¶ Of þe noumbre of whiche accusou*r*s one basilius þat somtyme was chased out of þe kynges seruice. is now co*m*pelled i*n* accusyng of my name for nede of foreine moneye. ¶ Also opilion *and* Gaudencius han accused me. al be it so þat þe Iustice regal hadde su*m*tyme demed hem boþe to go in to exil. for her treccheries *and* fraudes wiþ-outen noumbre. ¶ To whiche iugement þei wolde not obeye. but defended[e] hem by sykernesse of holy houses. *þat is to seyne fledden in to seyntuaries. a*nd* whan þis was ap*er*ceiued to þe kyng. he comaunded[e] but þat þei voided[e] þe citee of Rauenne by certeyne day assigned þat men scholde merken hem on þe forheued wiþ an hoke of iren *and* chasen hem out of toune. ¶ Now what þing semeþ þe myȝt[e] be lykned to þis cruelte. For certys þilk same day was receyued þe accusyng of my name by þilk[e] same accusou*r*s. ¶ What may be seid herto. haþ my studie *and* my konnyng deserued þus. or ellys þe forseide dampnaciou*n* of me. made þat hem ryȝtful accusours or no (q.d. non). ¶ Was not fortune asshamed of þis. [Certes alle hadde nat fortune ben asshamyd] þat i*n*nocence was accused. ȝit auȝt[e] sche haue had schame of þe filþe of myn ac-

---

327 *put[te]*—putte
328 *yseyn*—MS. yseyne
329 *greet[e]*—grete
330 *aughte be*—owhte be the
  oþer—oothre
333 *by þe whiche*—by which
  þoruȝ þe—thorw tho
335 *whiche*—the whiche
  one—oon
  somtyme—whilom
339 *sumtyme*—whilom
340 *go*—gon
  her—hir

341 *wiþ-outen*—withowte
  wolde not—nolden nat
342 *defended[e]*—defendedyn
  by—by the
343 *seyne*—seyn
  seyntuaries—sentuarye
344 *was*—omitted
  comaunded[e] — comaundede
345 *voided[e]*—voidede
  certeyne—certeyn
346 *men*—me
  merken—marke

347 *hoke of iren*—hoot yren
348 *þe*—omitted
  myȝt[e] be—myhte ben
349 *þilk*—thilke
350 *þilk[e]*—thilke
351 *be*—ben
  seid—MS. seide, C. seyd
  haþ—MS. haþe
354, 355 [*Certes — asshamyd*]—from C.
356 *auȝt[e]*—owte
  haue had—han had, MS. hadde

cusours. ¶ But axest þou in somme of what gilt .I. 357
am accused. men seyne þat I wolde sauen þe compaignie of þe senatours. ¶ And desirest þou to here
in what manere .I. am accused þat I scholde han distourbed þe accusour to beren lettres. by whiche he
scholde han maked þe senatours gilty aȝeins þe kynges 362
Real maieste. ¶ O meistresse what demest þou of
þis. schal .I. forsake þis blame þat I ne be no schame to
þe (q. d. non). ¶ Certis .I. haue wold it. þat is to 365
seyne þe sauuacioun of þe senat. ne I schal neuer leten
to wilne it. *and* þat I confesse *and* am a-knowe. but
þe entent of þe accusour to be destourbed schal cese.
¶ For schal I clepe it a felonie þan or a synne þat I 369
haue desired þe sauuacioun of þe ordre of þe senat.
and certys ȝit hadde þilk same senat don by me þoruȝ
her decretȝ *and* hire iugementys as þouȝ it were a synne
or a felonie þat is to seyne to wilne þe sauuacioun of 373
hem (.s senat*us*). ¶ But folye þat lieth alwey to hym
self may not chaunge þe merit of þinges. ¶ Ne .I.
trowe not by þe iugement of socrates þat it were leue- 376
ful to me to hide þe soþe. ne assent[e] to lesynges.
¶ But certys how so euer it be of þis I put[te] it to gessen
or preisen to þe iugeme*n*t of þe *and* of wise folk. ¶ Of
whiche þing al þe ordinaunce *and* þe soþe for as moche 380
as folk þat ben to comen aftir oure dayes schollen
knowen it. ¶ I haue put it in scripture *and* remem-
braunce. for touching þe le*tt*res falsly maked. by
whiche le*tt*res I am accused to han hooped þe fredom of
Rome. What apperteneþ me to speken þer-of. Of 385
whiche le*tt*res þe fraude hadde ben schewed apertly if

[BOOK 1, PROSE 4] Boethius says he is accused of trying to save the Senate, and of having embarrassed an informer against the Senate.

It is true that he tried to save the Senate, for he has and will have its best interests always at heart.

(Folly cannot change the merit of things.

According to Socrates' judgment it is not lawful to hide the truth nor assent to a falsehood.)

Boethius determines to transmit an account of his prosecution to posterity.

---

357 *axest þou*—axestow
358 *seyne*—seyn
sauen—saue
359 *desirest þou*—desires thow
here—hereen
362 *maked*—MS. maken, C. makyd
363 *demest þou*—demestow
365 *wold*—MS. wolde, C.

wold
366 *seyne*—seyn
367 *þat*—omitted
am—I am
368 *be*—ben
369 *it*—it thanne
þan—omitted
371 *þilk*—thilke
372 *her*—hir
hire—hir

372 *þouȝ*—thogh
373 *or*—and
seyne—seyn
374 *lieth*—MS. lieþe, C. lieth
377 *assent[e]*—assente
381 *schollen*—shellen
382 *and*—and in
385 *speken*—speke
of——lettres—C. omits
386 *if*—yif

18 BOETHIUS COMPLAINS TO PHILOSOPHY. [BOOK 1. PROSE 4.

Boethius says that he could have defeated his accusers had he been allowed the use of their confessions.

I hadde had libertee forto han vsed *and* ben at þe confessiou*n* of myn accusou*rs*. ¶ þe whiche þing in alle nedys haþ grete strenkeþ. ¶ For what oþer fredo*m* may men hopen. Certys I wolde þat some oþer fredom

391 myȝt[e] be hoped. ¶ I wolde þan haue answered by þe wordes of a man þat hyȝt[e] Canius. for whan he was

But there is now no remains of liberty to be hoped for.

accused by Gayus Cesar Germeins son þat he (caniu*s*) was knowyng *and* consentyng of a coniuracio*un* maked aȝeins hym (.s. Gaiu*s*). ¶ þis Canius answered[e]

396 þus. ¶ Yif I had[de] wist it þou haddest not wist

It is not strange that the wicked should conspire against virtue.

it. In whiche þing sorwe haþ not so dulled my witte þat I pleyne oonly þat schrewed[e] folk apparailen folies aȝeins vertues. ¶ But I wondre gretly how þat

400 þei may p*er*forme þinges þat þei had[de] hoped forto done. For why. to wylne schrewednesse þat comeþ

The will to do ill proceeds from the defects of human nature.

parauenture of oure defaute. ¶ But it is lyke to a monstre *and* a meruaille. ¶ How þat in þe p*r*esent

404 syȝt of god may ben acheued *and* p*er*formed swiche þinges. as euery felonous man haþ conceyued in hys

It is a marvel how such evil acts can be done under the eye of an Omniscient God.

þouȝt aȝeins innocent. ¶ For whiche þing oon of þi familers not vnskilfully axed þus. ¶ ȝif god is. whennes comen wikked[e] þinges. *and* yif god ne is whennes

409 comen goode þinges. but al hadde it ben leueful þat

If there be a God, whence proceeds evil? If there is none, whence arises good?

felonous folk þat now desiren þe bloode *and* þe deeþ of alle goode men. *and* eke of al þe senat han wilned to gone destroien me. whom þei han seyn alwey batailen

413 *and* defenden goode men *and* eke al þe senat. ȝit hadde I not desserued of þe fadres. þat is to seyne of þe senatours þat þei scholde wilne my destruccio*un*.

---

387 *had*—MS. hade, C. had
388 *myn*—myne
389 *haþ*—MS. haþe, C. hath
grete—gret
what—omitted
390 *some*—som
391 *myȝt[e] be*—myhte ben
þan haue—thanne han
392 *hyȝt[e]*—hyhte
394 *maked*—ymaked
395 *answered[e]*—answerode
396 *had[de]*—hadde

397 *whiche*—which
sorwe—sorw
haþ—MS. haþe
witte—wit
398 *schrewed[e]*—shrewede
399 *folies*—felonies
vertues—vertu
400 *had[de]*—han
401 *done*—don
comeþ—comth
402 *lyke to a*—lyk a
404 *syȝt*—syhte

405 *haþ*—MS. haþe
406 *innocent*—innocentȝ
whiche—which
408 *wikked[e]*—wykkede
410 *bloode*—blod
411 *eke*—ek
412 *gone*—gon *and*
seyn—seyen
413 *eke*—ek
414 *seyne*—seyn
415 *scholde*—sholden

OF HIS FALSE ACCUSERS.

¶ þou remembrest wele as I gesse þat whan I wolde *Boethius defends the integrity of his life.* [* fol. 6 b.]
don or *seyn any þing. þou þi self alwey present re-
weledest me. ¶ At þe citee of verone whan þat þe *He defended the Senate at Verona.*
kyng gredy of comune slau3ter. caste hym to trans-
porten vpon al þe ordre of þe senat. þe gilt of his real 420
maieste of þe whiche gilt þat albyn was accused. wiþ
how grete sykernesse of peril to me defended[e] I al 422
þe senat. ¶ þou wost wel þat I seide soþe. ne I *He spake only the truth, and did not boast.*
auaunted[e] me neuer in preysyng of my self. ¶ For
alwey when any wy3t resceiueþ preciouse renoun in *(Boasting lessens the pleasure of a self approving conscience.)*
auauntyng hym self of hys werkes: he amenusiþ þe
secre of hys conscience. ¶ But now þou mayst wel 427
seen to what ende I am comen for myne innocence.
I receiue peyne of fals felonie in gerdoun of verray *But as the reward of his innocence he is made to suffer the punishment due to the blackest crime.*
vertue. ¶ And what open confessioun of felonie
had[de] euer iugis so accordaunt in cruelte. þat is to
seyne as myne accusyng haþ. ¶ þat oþer errour of 432
mans witte or ellys condicioun of fortune þat is vncerteyne
to al mortal folk ne submytted[e] summe of hem. þat is
to scyne þat it ne cheyned[e] summe iuge to han pitee 435
or compassioun. ¶ For al þou3 I had[de] ben accused *Had he been accused of a design to burn temples, massacre priests, he would have been allowed to confront his accusers.*
þat I wolde brenne holy houses. and strangle prestys
wiþ wicked swerde. ¶ or þat .I. had[de] grayþed deeþ
to alle goode men algatis þe sentence scholde han
punysched me present confessed or conuict. ¶ But 440
now I am remewed fro þe Citee of rome almost fyue- *But now this is denied him, and he is proscribed and condemned to death.*
hundreþ þousand pas. I am wiþ outen defence dampned
to proscripcioun and to þo deeþ. for þe studie and
bountees þat I haue done to þe senat. ¶ But o wel ben 444
þei worþi of mercye (as who seiþ nay.) þer my3t[e] neuer

---

416 *wele*—wel
417 *don*—MS. done, C. doon
   seyn—seyen
418 *þe* (1)—omitted
419 *slau3ter*—slawhtre
420 *transporten vpon*—transpor vp
422 *grete*—gret
   defended[e]—deffendede
423 *seide soþe*—seye soth
424 *auaunted[e]*—auauntede
425 *when*—whan
   preciouse—presious
429 *in*—for
430 *vertue*—vertu
431 *had[de]*—hadde
432 *seyne*—seyn
   myne—myn
   haþ—MS. haþe
433 *witte*—wit
   vncerteyne—vncertcyn
434 *al*—alle
434 *submytted[e]*—submittede
435 *seyne*—seyn [tede
   cheyned[e]—enclinede
436 *had[de]*—hadde
438 *wicked*—wykkede
   had[de]—hadde
441 *almost*—almest
442 *þousand*—MS. þousns
   wiþ outen—withowte
444 *done*—doon
445 *my3t[e]*—myhte

446 ȝit non of hem ben conuicte. Of swiche a blame as
myn is of swiche trespas myn accusours seyen ful wel
þe dignitee. þe wiche dignite for þei wolde derken it
wiþ medelyng of some felonye. þei beren me on honde
450 *and* lieden. þat I hadde polute *and* defouled my conscience wiþ sacrelege. for couetise of dignite. ¶ And
certys þou þi self þat art plaunted in me chacedest oute
þe sege of my corage al couetise of mortal þinges. ne
454 sacrilege ne had[de] no leue to han a place in me byforne
þine eyen. ¶ For þou drouppedest euery day in myn
eeres *and* in my þouȝt þilk comaundement of pictogoras.
þat is to seyne men schal serueu to god. *and* not to
458 goddes. ¶ Ne it was no couenaunt ne no nede to
taken helpe of þe foulest spirites. ¶ I þat þou hast
ordeyned or set in syche excellence þat [þou] makedest
461 me lyke to god. and ouer þis þe ryȝt clene secre
chaumbre of myn house. þat is to seye my wijf *and* þe
compaignie of myn honeste frendis. *and* my wyues
fadir as wel holy as worþi to ben reuerenced þoruȝ
465 hys owen dedis. defenden me of al suspeccioun of syche
blame. ¶ But o malice. ¶ For þei þat accusen me
taken of þe philosophie feiþe of so grete blame. ¶ For
þei trowen þat .I. haue had affinite to malyfice or en-
chauntementȝ by cause þat I am replenissed *and* ful-
470 filled wiþ þi techynges. *and* enformed of þi maners.
¶ And þus it sufficeþ not only þat þi reuerence ne auayle
me not. but ȝif þat þou of þi fre wille raþer be blemissed
wiþ myne offensioun. ¶ But certys to þe harmes þat I
474 haue þere bytydeþ ȝit þis encrece of harme. þat þe

Boethius says that his enemies accused him of sorcery.

He affirms that he has always followed the golden maxim of Pythagoras,—ἕπου Θεῷ.

His family and friends could clear him from all suspicion of the crime of sorcery.

Because he has given himself up to Philosophy, his enemies accuse him of using unlawful arts.

446 *ben*—be
swiche—swich
447 *myn (both)*—myne
swiche—whiche
seyen—sayen
449 *wolde*—wolden
449 *some*—som
beren—baren
on honde—an hand
450 *polute*—polut
451 *sacrelege*—C. has sorcerie *as a gloss to* sacrilege
453 *al*—alle

454 *had[de]*—hadde
byforne—byforn
455 *drouppedest*—droppedest
myn—myne
456 *þilk*—thilke
457 *seyne*—seyn
seruen—serue
god—godde
459 *helpe*—help
spirites—spirite
460 *set*—MS. sette, C. set
syche—swiche
[*þou*]—thow

461 *lyke*—lyk
462 *house*—hows
seye—seyn
463 *myn*—my
465 *owen*—owne
of al—from alle
syche—swich
467 *philosophie*—philosophre
feiþe—feyth
grete—gret
468 *had*—MS. hadde, C. had
473 *myne*—myn
474 *þere*—ther
harme—harm

gessinge *and* þe iugement of myche folk ne loken no 475
þing to þe[de]sertys of þinges but only to þe aue*ntu*re *Most people imagine that that only should be judged to be undertaken with prudent foresight which is crowned with success.*
of fortune. ¶ And iugen þat only swiche þinges ben
p*u*rueied of god. whiche þat temporel welefulnesse
commendiþ. *Glosa.* ¶ As þus þat yif a wy3t haue
prosperite. he is a good man *and* worþi. to haue þat 480
prosperite. and who so haþ aduersite he is a wikked
man. *and* god haþ forsake hym. *and* he is worþi to *The unfortunate lose the good opinion of the world.*
haue þat aduersite. ¶ þis is þe opinio*un* of so*m*me
folke. *and þer of comeþ þat good gessyng. ¶ Fyrste of [* Text begins again.]
al þing forsakeþ wrecches certys it greueþ me to þink[e] 485
ry3t now þe dyuerse sentences þat þe poeple seiþ of
me. ¶ And þus moche I seye þat þe laste charge of 487
contrarious fortune is þis. † þat whan þat ony blame is [† fol. 7.]
laid vpon a caytif. men wenen þat he haþ deserued þat *Boethius laments the loss of his dignities and reputation.*
he suffreþ. ¶ And I þat am put awey from goode men
and despoiled from dignitees *and* defoulid of my name
by gessyng haue suffred torment for my goode dedis. 492
¶ Certys me semeþ þat I se þe felonus couines of
wikked men abounden in ioie *and* in gladnes. ¶ And *The wicked, he says, sin with impunity,*
I se þat euery lorel shapiþ hy*m* to fynde oute newe
fraudes forto accusen goode folke. and I se þat goode 496
men ben ouerþrowen for drede of my pe*r*il. ¶ and
euery luxurious tou*r*mentour dar don alle felonie vnpunissed *and* ben excited þerto by 3iftes. and i*n*nocent3 499
ne ben not oonly despoiled of sykernesse but of de- *while the innocent are deprived of security, protection, and defence.*
fence *and* þerfore me list to crien to god in þis manere. *and*

O STELLIFERI CONDITOR ORBIS.

O þou maker of þe whele þat bereþ þe sterres. whiche [The fifthe met*ur*.]
þat art fastned to þi pe*r*durable chayere. *and* *Author of the starry sky, Thou,*

---

475 *myche*—moche
476 þe[*de*]*sertys*—the desert3
479 *Glosa*—glose
480 *good*—MS. goode, C. good
haue—han
481 *so*—omitted in C.
491, 492 *haþ*—MS. haþe
483 *haue*—han .

484 *Fyrste*—fyrst
485 *al*—alle
þink[*e*]—thinke
488 *ony*—any
489 *laid*—MS. laide, C. leyd
haþ—MS. haþe
490 *put*—MS. putte, C. put
491 *from*—of
494 *abounden*—habownden

494 *gladnes*—gladnesse
495 *oute*—owt
496 *accusen*—accuse
497 *ben*—beth
501 *manere*—wise
502 *whele*—whel
whiche—which
503 *fastned*—yfastned
chayere—chayer

seated on high, turnest the spheres, and imposest laws upon the stars and planets.

turnest þe heuene wiþ a rauyssyng sweighe *and* con-streinest þe sterres to suffren þi lawe. ¶ So þat þe mone somtyme schynyng wiþ hir ful hornes metyng

507 wiþ alle þe bemes of þe sonne. ¶ Hir broþer hideþ þe

The sun obscures the lesser lights, and quenches even the moon's light.

sterres þat ben lasse. *and* somtyme whan þe mone pale wiþ hir derke hornes approcheþ þe sonne. leesith hir ly3tes. ¶ And þat þe cuesterre esperus whiche

511 þat in þe first[e] tyme of þe ny3t bryngeþ furþe hir

Thou raisest Hesperus to usher in the shades of night, and again causest him to be the harbinger of day, whence his name Lucifer.

colde arysynges comeþ eft a3eynes hir vsed cours. *and* is pale by þe morwe at þe rysynge of þe sonne. and is þan cleped lucifer. ¶ þou restreinest þe day by schorter dwellyng in þe tyme of colde wynter þat makeþ þe

516 leues to falle. ¶ þou diuidest þe swifte tides of þe ny3t when þe hote somer is comen. ¶ þi my3t at-

Thou controllest the changing seasons of the year.

tempre[þ] þo variaunt3 sesons of þe 3ere. so þat 3epherus þe deboneire wynde bringeþ a3ein in þe first[e]

520 somer sesou*n* þe leues þat þe wynde þat hy3t[e] boreas haþ reft awey in autu*m*pne. þat is to seyne in þe laste eende of somer. and þe sedes þat þe sterre þat hy3t arc-

523 tur*us* saw ben waxen hey[e] cornes whan þe sterre

All nature is bound by thy eternal law.

sirius eschaufeþ hym. ¶ þere nis no þing vnbounde from hys olde lawe ne forleteþ hym of hys *p*ropre estat.

526 ¶ O þou gouerno*ur* gouernyng alle þinges by certeyne

Why, then, leavest thou man's actions uncontrolled?

ende. why refusest þou oonly to gouerne þe werkes of men by dewe manere. ¶ Whi suffrest þou þat slid-

Why should fickle fortune be allowed to work such mighty changes in the world?

yng fortune turneþ to grete vtter chaungynges of þinges. so þat anoious peyne þat scholde duelly punisshe fel-ouns punissit3 innocent3. ¶ And folk of wikked[e]

532 maneres sitten in hei3e chaiers. *and* anoienge folk

504 *sweighe*—sweyh
  constreinest, MS. con-treinest, C. constreynest
506 *hir*—here
508 *lasse*—lesse
510 *esperus whiche* — hes-perus which
511 *first[e]*—fyrste
  furþe—forth
512 *eft*—est
514 *restreinest* — MS. re-strenlest
516 *to*—omitted
518 *attempre[þ] þo*—atemp-reth the
518 *sesons*—sesoun
  3*ere*—yer
519 *wynde bringeþ*—wynd brengeth
520 *wynde*—wynd
  hy3t[e]—hihte
521 *reft*—MS. refte, C. reft
  seyne—seyn
522 *hy3t*—hihte
  arcturus—MS. ariturus
523 *saw* — MS. saweþ, C. sawgh
  hey[e]—hyye
524 *hym*—hem
  þere—ther
  þing—thinge
525 *from*—fram
  forleteþ hym of—forleet-heth þe werke of
527 *refusest þou* — refows-estow
529 *to* — *þinges*—so grete entrechaunginges of thynges
531 *punissit3*—punysshe
  wikked[e]—wykkede
532 *hei3e*—heere

treden *and* þat vnryʒtfully in þe nekkes of holy men. 533
¶ And vertue clere *and* schynyng naturely is hid in The wicked are prosperous, while the righteous are in adversity.
dirke dirkenesses. *and* þe ryʒtful man beriþ þe blame
and þe peyne of þe felowne. ¶ Ne þe forsweryng ne 536
þe fraude couered *and* kembd wiþ a fals colour ne
a-noyeþ not to schrewes. ¶ þe whiche schrewes whan
hem lyst to vsen her strengþe þei reioisen hem to
putten vndir hem þe souerayne kynges. whiche þat 540
poeple wiþ[outen] noumbre dreden. ¶ O þou what so O thou that bindest the disagreeing elements, look upon this wretched earth,
euer þou be þat knyttes[t] alle bondes of þinges loke
on þise wrecched[e] erþes. we men þat ben nat a
foule party but a faire party of so grete a werke we 544
ben turmentid in þe see of fortune. ¶ þou gouernour
wiþdraw *and* restreyne þe rauyssinge flodes *and* fastne and, as thou dost govern the spacious heavens, so let the earth be firmly bound.
and forme þise erþes stable wiþ þilke [bonde] wiþ
whiche þou gouernest þe heuene þat is so large.

HIC UBI CONTINUATO DOLORE.

Whan I hadde wiþ a continuel sorwe sobbed or [The fyfthe prose.] Philosophy consoles Boethius.
broken out þise þinges sche wiþ hir chere peisible
and no þing amoeued. wiþ my compleyntes seide þus. 551
whan I say þe q*uod* sche sorweful *and* wepyng I wist[e]
on-one þat þou were a wrecche *and* exiled. but I
wist[e] neuer how fer þine exile was : ʒif þi tale ne
hadde schewed it to me. but certys al be þou fer fro þi 555
contre. þou nart * nat put out of it. but þou hast [* fol. 7 b.]
fayled of þi weye *and* gon amys. ¶ and yif þou hast
leuer forto wene þan þou be put out of þi contre. þan She speaks to his of his country.
hast þou put oute þi self raþer þen ony oþer wyʒt haþ.
¶ For no wyʒt but þi self ne myʒt[e] neuer haue don 560

---

533 *in*—oon
534 *and*—omitted
536 *Ne þe forsweryng*—Ne forswerynge
537 *kembd*—MS. kembde, C. kembd
541 *wiþ[outen]*—withhowtyn
542 *knyttes[t]*—knyttest
543 *wrecched[e]*—wrecchede
544 *a* (2)—omitted

545 *þe*—this
546 *wiþdraw* — MS. wiþdrawe, C. withdrawh
þe—thei
547 *forme*—ferme
(*bonde*)—from C.
wiþ—to
550 *broken*—borken
552 *wist[e]*—wyste
553 *on-one*—anon
554 *wist[e]*—wyste

554 *fer*—ferre
555 *ne hadde*—nadde
557 *gon*—MS. gone, C. gon
558 *leuer*—leuere
558, 559 *put*—MS. putte, C. put
559 *haþ*—MS. haþe
560 *myʒt[e]*—myhte
haue—han
don—MS. done, C. don

561 þat to þe. ¶ For ȝif þou remembre of what contre þou
art born. it nis not gouerned by emperoures. ne by
gouernement of multitude. as weren þe contres of hem
of athenes. ¶ But o lorde *and* o kyng *and* þat is god
þat is lorde of þi contree. whiche þat reioiseþ hym of
566 þe dwellyng of hys Citeȝenis. *and* not forto putte hem
in exile. Of þe whiche lorde it is a souerayne fredom
to be gouerned by þe bridel of hym and obeie to his
iustice. ¶ Hast þou forȝeten þilke ryȝt olde lawe of þi
570 Citee. in þe whiche Citee it is ordeyned *and* establissed
þat what wyȝt þat haþ leuer founden þer i*n*ne hys sete
or hys house. þen ellys where : he may not be exiled
573 by no ryȝt fro þat place. ¶ For who so þat is co*n*tened
in-wiþ þe paleis [*and* the clos] of þilke Citee. þer nis
no drede þat he may deserue to ben exiled. ¶ But
who þat letteþ þe wille forto enhabit[e] þere. he for-
577 leteþ also to deserue to ben Citeȝein of þilke Citee.
¶ So þat I seye þat þe face of þis place ne amoeueþ me
nat so myche as þine owen face. Ne .I. ne axe not
raþer þe walles of þi librarie apparailled *and* wrouȝt
wiþ yvory *and* wiþ glas þan after þe sete of þi þouȝt.
582 In whiche I putte nat somtyme bookes. but .I. putte
þat þat makeþ bookes worþi of pr*is* or precious þat is
to sein þe sentence of my books. ¶ *And* certeinly of
585 þi decertes by-stowed in commune good. þou hast seid
soþe but after þe multitude of þi goode dedys. þou hast
seid fewe. *and* of þe vnhonestee or falsnesse of þinges
588 þat ben opposed aȝeins þe. þou hast remembred þinges
þat be*n* knowe to alle folk. and of þe felonies *and*
fraudes of þine accusours. it semeþ þe haue I-touched
it forsoþe ryȝtfully *and* schortly. ¶ Al myȝten þo

She reminds him that he is a citizen of a country not governed by a giddy multitude, but εἰς χοίρανος ἔστιν, εἰς βασιλεύς.

The Commonwealth of Boethius.

Philosophy says she is moved more by the looks of Boethius than by his gloomy prison.

Books are to be valued on account of the thoughts they contain.

Boethius has rightfully and briefly recounted the frauds of his accusers.

562 *born*—MS. borne, C. born
566 *hys*—hise
putte—put
568 *be*—ben
571 *haþ*—MS. haþe
572 *house*—howss
574 [*and——clos*]—from C.
576 *wille*—wyl
enh,bit[e]—enhabyte
578 *seye*—sey
amoeueþ—moueth
579 *myche*—mochel
owen—owne
ne (2)—omitted
582 *putte (both)*—put
582 *somtyme*—whilom
585 *decertes*—desertes
seid—MS. seide, C. seyde
586 *soþe*—soth
587 *seid*—MS. seide, C. seyd
588 *opposed*—aposyd
589 *knowe*—knowyn

AND PROPOSES TO ADMINISTER REMEDIES. 25

same þinges beltere *and* more plentiuousely be couth 592
in þe mouþe of þe poeple þat knoweþ al þis. ¶ þou
hast eke blamed gretly *and* compleyned of þe wrongful
dede of þe senat. ¶ And þou hast sorwed for my *Thou hast, said Philosophy, be-*
blame. *and* þou hast wepen for þe damage of þi re- *wailed the loss of thy good name.*
noune þat is appaired. *and* þi laste sorwe eschaufed 597
aȝeins fortune *and* compleinest þat gerdouns ne ben not *thou hast complained against*
euenliche ȝolde to þe desertes of folk. *and* in þe la*tt*re *Fortune, and against the*
ende of þi woode muse þou priedest þat þilke pees þat *unequal distribution of rewards*
gouerneþ þe heuene scholde goue*rn*e þe erþe ¶ But *and punishments.*
for þat many tribulac*ioun*s of affecc*ioun*s han assailed 602
þe. *and* sorwe *and* Ire *and* wepyng todrawen þee
dyuersely ¶ As þou art now feble of þouȝt. myȝtyer *Strong medicines are not proper for*
remedies ne schullen not ȝit touchen þe for whiche *thee now, distracted by grief,*
we wil[e] vsen somedel lyȝter medicines. So þat þilk[e] *anger, and sadness.*
passiou*n*s þat ben woxen harde in swellyng by per- 607
turbac*ioun* folowyng in to þi þouȝt mowen woxe esy *Light medicines must prepare*
and softe to receyue*n* þe strenkeþ of a more myȝty *and* *thee for sharper remedies.*
more egre medicine by an esier touchyng. 610

CUM PHEBI RADIIS GR*A*UE CA*N*CR*I* SID*U*S ENESTUAT.

Whan þat þe heuy sterre of þe cancre eschaufeþ by [The sixte met*ur*.]
 þe beme of pheb*us*. þat is to seyne whan þat pheb*us* *He who sows his seed when the*
þe sonne is in þe signe of þe Cancre. Who so ȝeueþ *sun is in the Sign of Cancer,*
þan largely hys sedes to þe feldes þat refuse to re- *must look for no produce.*
ceiuen hem. lete hym gon bygyled of trust þat he 615
hadde to hys corn. to acorns or okes. yif þou wilt *Think not to ingather violets in*
gadre violettȝ. ne go þou not to þe purp*er* wode whan *the wintry and stormy season.*
þe felde chirkynge agriseþ of colde by þe felnesse of
þe wynde þat hyȝt aquilon ¶ Yif þou desirest or 619

592 *be couth*—MS. be couthe, 606 *wil[e]*—wol 614 *refuse*—refuseu
  O. ben cowth *lyȝter*—lyhtere 615 after *hem* C. adds [s.
596 *wepen*—wopen *þilk[e]*—thilke corn]
597 *laste*—lnst 607 *harde*—hard *lete hym gon* (MS. *gone*)—
  eschaufed—eschaufede 608 *folowyng*—Flowyng lat hym gon
598 *not*—omitted *woxe*—wexen 616 *or*—of
599 *ȝolde*—yolden 610 *esier*—esyere *wilt gadre*—wolt gadery
602 *many*—manye 612 *beme*—beemes 618 *felde*—feeld
604 *myȝtyer*—myhtyere *seyne*—seyn *felnesse*—felnessee
605 *whiche*—which 614 *hys*—hise 619 *hyȝt*—hyhte

If you wish for wine in autumn let the tendrils of the vine be free in the spring.	wolt vsen grapes ne seke þou nat wiþ a glotonus hande to streine and presse þe stalkes of þe vine in þe first somer sesoun. for bachus þe god of wyne haþ raþer
623	ȝeuen his ȝiftes to autumpne þe latter ende of somer.
[* fol. 8.] To every work God assigns a proper time, nor suffers anything to pass its bounds. Success does not await him who departs from the appointed order of things.	¶ God tokeniþ and assigneþ *þe tymes. ablyng hem to her propre offices. ¶ Ne he ne suffreþ not stoundes whiche þat hym self haþ deuided and constreined to be medeled to gidre ¶ And forþi he þat forleteþ certeyne ordinaunce of doynge by ouerþrowyng wey. he ne haþ no glade issue or ende of hys werkes.

PRIMUM IGITUR PATERIS ROGACIONIBUS.

[The syxte prose.] Philosophy proposes to question Boethius.	First wolt þou suffre me to touche and assaie þe stat of þi þouȝt by a fewe demaundes. so þat I may vnderstonde what be þe manere of þi curacioun. ¶ Axe
633	me quod .I. atte þi wille what þou wilt. and I schal
P. Is the world governed by Chance?	answere. ¶ Þo saide sche þus. wheþer wenest þou quod sche þat þis worlde be gouerned by foolisshe happes
636	and fortunes. or elles wenest þou þat þer be in it any
B. By no means. The Creator presides over his own works.	gouernement of resoun. Certes quod .I. ne trowe not in no manere þat so certeyne þinges scholde be moeued by fortunouse fortune. but I wot wel þat god maker
640	and mayster is gouernour of þis werk. Ne neuer nas
I shall never swerve from this opinion.	ȝit day þat myȝt[e] putte me oute of þe soþenesse of þat sentence. ¶ So is it quod sche. for þe same þing
643	songe þou a lytel here byforne and byweyledest and
P. Yes! Thou didst say as much when thou didst declare man alone to be destitute of divine care. Still thou seemest to labour under some defect even in this conviction.	byweptest. þat only men weren put oute of þe cure of god. ¶ For of alle oþer þinges þou ne doutest nat þat þei nere gouerned by reson. but how (.i. pape.). I wondre gretly certes whi þat þou art seek. siþen þou art put in to so holesom a sentence. but lat vs seken

620 hande—hond
622 haþ—MS. haþe
625 her propre—heere propres
    not—nat the
626 haþ—MS. haþe
627 be medeled—ben I-medled
629 certeyne—certeyn

629 haþ—MS. haþe
630 wolt þou—woltow
    stat—estnt
633 atte—at
    wilt—wolt
635 worlde—world
    foolisshe—foolyssh
636 fortunes—fortunows

638 scholde—sholden
639 wot—MS. wote, C. woot
641 myȝt[e] putte—myhte put
644 put—MS. putte
645 doutest—dowtedest
646 how—owh
647 seek siþen—syke syn
648 put—MS. putte, C. put

… DISCOVERS THE CAUSE OF HIS DISTEMPER.

depper. I coniecte þat þere lakkeþ I not what. but 649
sey me þis. siþen þat þou ne doutest nat þat þis worlde
be gouerned by god ¶ wiþ swycche gouernailes takest
þou hede þat it is gouerned. ¶ vnneþ quod .I. knowe 652
.I. þe sentence of þi questioun. so þat I ne may nat
ȝit answeren to þi demaundes. ¶ I nas nat decciued
quod sche þat þere ne faileþ sumwhat. by whiche þe
maladie of perturbacioun is crept in to þi þouȝt. so
as þe strengþe of þe paleys schynyng is open. ¶ But
seye me þis remembrest þou ouȝt what is þe ende of
þi þinges. whider þat þe entencioun of al kynde tendeþ.
¶ I haue herd told it somtyme quod .I. but drery- 660
nesse haþ dulled my memorie. ¶ Certys quod sche
þou wost wel whennes þat alle þinges ben comen and 662
proceded. I wot wel quod .I. and ansewered[e] þat
god is þe bygynnyng of al. ¶ And how may þis be
quod sche þat siþen þou knowest þe bygynnyng of
þinges. þat þou ne knowest not what is þe endyng of
þinges. but swiche ben þe customes of perturbaciouns. 667
and þis power þei han. þat þei may moeue a man fro
hys place. þat is to seyne from þe stablenes and perfeccioun of hys knowyng. but certys þei may not al
arace hym ne alyene hym in al. ¶ But I wolde þat 671
þou woldest answere to þis. ¶ Remembrest þou þat
þou art a man ¶ Boice. ¶ Whi scholde I nat remembre þat quod .I. Philosophie. ¶ Maiste þou not telle
me þan quod sche what þing is a man. ¶ Axest not
me quod I. wheþir þat be a resonable best mortel. I
wot wel and I confesse wel þat I am it. ¶ Wistest
þou neuer ȝit þat þou were ony oþer þing quod she.

Tell me how the world is governed.

B. I do not thoroughly comprehend your question.
P. I was not deceived, then, when I said there was some defect in thy sentiment.
Tell me what is the chief end of all things; and whither all things tend.

B. God is the beginning of all things.
P. How, then, art thou ignorant of their end?

But it is the nature of these perturbations (which thou endurest) to unsettle men's minds.

Dost thou remember that thou art a man?
B. Certainly I do.
P. What is man?
B. If you ask me whether I am a rational and mortal creature, I know and confess I am.
P. But dost thou not know that thou art more than this?

---

649 depper—deppere
  not what—not nere what
650 siþen—syn
  worlde—world
651 takest þou—takestow
658 seye—sey
  remembrest þou — re-
    menbres thow
  ouȝt—omitted
659 al—alle

660 herd told — MS. herde tolde
  herd told it—herd yt toold
661 haþ—MS. haþe
663 proceded—procedeth
  ansewered[e]—answerede
664 þe—omitted
  al—alle
665 siþen—syn
669 fro—owt of

669 seyne from—seyn fro
672 Remembrest þou— Re-
    menbresthow
674 Maiste þou—Maysthow
675 þan—þanne
  þing—thinge
  Axest—Axestow
677 Wistest þou — wystest-
    how
679 þing—thinge

B. No. No q*uod* .I. now wot I q*uod* she oþer cause of þi
680 maladie *and* þat ryȝt grete ¶ þou hast left forto
P. Now I know the principal cause of thy distemper. knowe þi self what þou art. þoruȝ whiche I haue pleynelyche knowen þe cause of þi maladie. or ellis þe
683 entre of recoueryng of þin hele. ¶ Forwhy for þou·
Thou hast lost the knowledge of thyself, art confounded wiþ forȝetyng of þi self. forþi sorwest
þou þat þou art exiled of þi propre goodes. ¶ And
thou knowest not the end of things, and hast forgotten how the world is governed. for þou ne wost what is þe ende of þinges. for[þi] demest
[þou] þat felono*us and* wikked men ben myȝty *and* weleful
for þou hast forȝeten by whiche gouernementȝ þe worlde
689 is gouerned. ¶ Forþi wenest þou þat þise mut*a*ciouns
These are not only great occasions of disease, but also causes of death itself. I thank God that Reason hath not wholly deserted thee. of fortune fleten wiþ outen gouernour. þise ben grete
causes not oonly to maladie. but certes grete causes to
deeþ ¶ But I þanke þe auctour *and* þe makere of
heele þat nature haþ not al forleten þe. *and* I haue
694 g[r]ete norissinges of þi hele. *and* þat is þe soþe sen-
I have some hope of thy recovery since thou believest that the world is [fol. 8 b.] under Divine Providence, for this small spark shall produce vital heat.* tence of gouer*n*aunce of þe worlde. þat þou byleuest
þat þe gouer*n*ynge of it nis nat subgit ne vnderput
to þe folie *of þise happes auenterouses. but to þe
resou*n* of god ¶ And þer fore doute þe noþing. For
of þis litel spark þine heet of lijf schal shine. ¶ But
700 for as muche as it is not tyme ȝitte of fastere remedies
But as this is not the time for stronger remedies, and because it is natural to embrace false opinions so soon as we have laid aside the true, from whence arises a mist that darkens the understanding, I shall endeavour therefore to dissipate these vapours so that you may perceive the true light. ¶ And þe nature of þouȝtes disseiued is þis þat as ofte
as þei casten aweye soþe opyniou*n*s: þei cloþen hem in
fals[e] opiniou*n*s. [of which*e* false opyniou*n*s] þe derknesse
of p*er*turbaciou*n* wexeþ vp. þat comfoundeþ þe verray
insyȝt. *and* þat derkenes schal .I. say somwhat to
maken þinne *and* wayk by lyȝt *and* meenclyche remedies. so þat after þat þe derknes of desseyuynge
desyrynges is don awey: þou mow[e] knowe þe schynyng of verray lyȝt.

680 *hast left*—MS. haste lefte, C. hast left	wykkyd	698 *noþing*—nothinge
681 *knowe*—knowen *pleynelyche knowen*—pleynly fwonde [= founde]	688 *worlde*—world	699 *spark þine heet*—sparke
	689 *wenest þou*—wenestow	700 *muche*—meche [thin hete
	690 *outen*—owte	702 *aweye*—away
	693 *haþ*—MS. haþe *al*—alle	703 [*of——opyniouns*]—from
684 *sorwest þou*—sorwistow	694 *þi*—thin	705 *insyȝt*—insyhte [C. *say*—assaye
686 *for[þi] demest* [þou]— For thy demesthow	696 *vnderput*—vndyrputte	706 *lyȝt*—lyhte
687 *wikked*—MS. wilked, C.	697 *to* (2)—omitted	708 *don*—MS. done *mow[e]*—mowe
	698 *fore*—for	

NUBIB*US* ATRIS CONDITA.

Þ E sterres cou*ered* wiþ blak[e] cloudes ne mowen [The seuende Metyr.]
geten a dou*n* no lyʒt. ʒif þe trouble wy*n*de þat Black clouds obscure the light
hyʒt auster stormynge *and* walwy*n*g þe see medleþ þe of the stars.
heete þat is to seyne þe boylyng vp from þe botme 713
¶ þe wawes þ*at* somtyme weren clere as glas *and* If the south wind renders the sea
lyke to þe fair[e] bryʒt[e] dayes wiþstant anon þe tempestuous, the waves, fouled
syʒtes of men. by þe filþe *and* ordure þat is resolued. with mud, will lose their glassy
and þe fletyng streme þat royleþ dou*n* dyuersely fro clearness.
heyʒe mou*n*taignes is arestid *and* resisted ofte tyme
by þe encou*n*trynge of a stoon þat is depa*r*tid *and* 719
fallen from some roche. ¶ And forþi yif þou wilt If thou wouldst see truth by the
loken *and* demen soþe wiþ clere lyʒt. *and* holde þe clearest light, pursue the path
weye wiþ a ryʒt paþe. ¶ Weyue þou ioie. drif fro þe of right. Away with joy,
drede. fleme þou hope. ne lat no sorwe apr*o*che. þat is fear, hope, and sorrow.
to sein lat noon of þise four passiou*n*s ouer come þe. Let none of these passions cloud
or blynde þe. for cloudy *and* dirke is þilk þouʒt *and* thy mind. Where these
bounde w*ith* bridles. where as þise þinges regnen. 726 things control, the soul is bound by strong fetters.

EXPLICIT LIBER PRIMUS.

INCIPIT LIBER SECUNDUS.

POSTEA [PAU]LISPER CONTICUIT.

A ftcr þis she stynte a litel. and after þat she hadde [The fyrst prose.]
gadred by atempre stillenesse myn attenciou*n* she 728
seide þus. ¶ As who so myʒt[e] seye þus. After þise Philosophy exhorts Boethius
þinges she stynt[e] a lytel. *and* whanne she aper- not to torment himself on
cciued[e] by atempre stillenesse þat I was ententif to account of his losses.
herkene hire. she bygan to speke in þis wyse. ¶ Yif 732

---

710 *blak[e]*—blake
712 *stormynge*—turnyng
713 *from*—fro
714 *somtyme*—whilom
715 *lyke*—lyk
   fair[e] —— *wiþstant* (MS. *wiþstante*)—fayre cleere
   dayes *and* brihte withstand

716 *syʒtes*—syhtes
717 *streme*—strem
718 *heyʒe*—hy
720 *from some*—fram som
   wilt—wolt
721 *soþe*—soth
   clere—cleer
   holde—holden
722 *weye*—wey

722 *paþe*—paath
724 *come*—comen
725 *blynde*—blende
   þilk—thilke
727 *she* (2)—I
729 *myʒt[e] seye*—myhte seyn
730 *stynt[e]*—stynte
732 *hire*—here

733 I *quod* she haue vnderstonden *and* knowe vtterly þe
causes *and* þo habit of þi maladie. þou languissed *and*
art deffeted for talent *and* desijr of þi raþer fortune.
736 ¶ She þat ilke fortune only þat is chaunged as þou
feinest to þe ward. haþ peruerted þe clerenesse *and* þe
astat of þi corage. ¶ I vnderstonde þe felefolde
colour *and* deceites of þilke merueillous monstre fortune. and how she vseþ ful flatryng familarite wiþ hem
741 þat she enforceþ to bygyle. so longe til þat she confounde wiþ vnsuffreable sorwe hem þat she haþ left
743 in despeir vnpurueyed. ¶ and if þou remembrest wel
þe kynde þe maners *and* þe desert of þilke fortune. þow
shalt wel knowe as in hir þou neuer ne haddest no
hast ylost any fair þing. But as I trowe I shal not
747 gretly trauaile to don þe remembren of þise þinges.
¶ For þou were wont to hurtlen [*and* despysen] hir
wiþ manly wordes whan she was blaundissinge *and*
presente *and* pursewedest hir wiþ sentences þat were
751 drawen oute of myne entre. þat is to seyne out of
myn informacioun ¶ But no sudeyne mutacioun ne
bytideþ nat wiþ outen a maner chauŋgyng of curages.
and so is it byfallen þat þou art departed a litel fro
þe pees of þi þouȝt. but now is tyme þat þou drynke
and atast[e] some softe *and* delitable þinges. so þat whan
þei ben entred wiþ inne þe. it mow make weye to
strenger drynkes of medycynes. ¶ Com nowe furþe
þerfore þe suasioun of swetnesse Rethoryen. whiche
þat goþ oonly þe ryȝt wey whil she forsakeþ not myne
estatutȝ. ¶ And wiþ Rethorice com forþe musice a
762 damoisel of oure house þat syngeþ now lyȝter moedes

Thou art, she says, affected by the loss of thy former fortune.

It hath perverted thy faculties.
I am well acquainted with all the wiles of that Prodigy (i. e. Fortune).

Though she has left thee, thou hast not lost anything of beauty or of worth.

Thou wert once proof against her allurements.

But sudden change works a great alteration in the minds of men, hence it is that thou art departed from thy usual peace of mind.
But with some gentle emollients I shall prepare thee for stronger medicines.
Approach then, Rhetoric, with thy persuasive charms, and therewith let Music also draw near.

---

733 *knowe vtterly*—knowen owtrely
734 *languissed*—languyssest
737 *haþ*—MS. haþe
738 *astat*—estat
   felefolde—feelefold
739 *colour*—colours
   deceites (MS. decrites) — deceytes
   merueillous—meruayles
742 *haþ*—MS. haþe
743 *if*—yif

746 *any* (MS. my)—any
   þing—thinge
747 *trauaile*—travaylen
   don—do
   remembren of—remenbre on
748 [*and despysen*]—from C.
749 *was*—omitted
750 *were*—weren
751 *myne*—myn
   seyne—sayn
752 *sudeyne*—sodeyn

753 *outen*—owte
757 *inne*—in
   mow — weye — mowe maken wey
759 *strenger*—strengere
   Com nowe furþe — MS. Come; C. Com now forth
760 *goþ*—MS. goþe
761 *com*—MS. come, C. com
762 *house*—hows
   lyȝter—lyhtere

or prolaciouns now heuyer. *what ayleþ þe man. what [* fol. 9.]
is it þat haþ cast þe in to murnyng *and* in to wepyng. 764
I trow[e] þat þou hast sen some newe þing *and* un- Thou thinkest that Fortune is
couþe. ¶ þou wenest þat fortune be chaunged aʒeins changed towards thee.
þe ¶ But þou wenest wrong. yif þou [þat] wene. But thou art deceived.
Alwey þo ben hire maners. she haþ raþer [kept] as to 768
þe ward hire propre stablenes in þe chaungyng of hyre In this misadventure of thine
self. ¶ Ryʒt swyche was she whan she flatered[e] she hath preserved her constancy in
þe. *and* desseiued[e] þe wiþ vnleueful lykynges of changing.
false welefulnesse. þou hast now known *and* ataynt 772
þe doutous or double visage of þilke blynde goddesse You have seen the double face
fortune. ¶ She þat ʒit couereþ hir *and* wympleþ hir of this blind divinity.
to oþer folk. haþ shewed hir euerydel to þe. ¶ ʒif
þou approuest hir *and* þenkest þat she is good. vse 776
hir maners *and* pleyne þe nat. ¶ And if þou agrisest If thou dost abhor her perfidy
hir fals[e] trecherie. dispise *and* cast aweye hir þat cast her off, for her sports are
pleyeþ so harmefully. for she þat is now cause of so dangerous.
myche sorwe to þe. sholde be to þe cause of pees *and* 780
[of] ioie. ¶ she haþ forsaken þe forsoþe. þe whiche
þat neuer man may be syker þat she ne shal forsake
hym. *Glose.* ¶ But naþeles some bookes han þe text
þus. For soþe she haþ forsaken þe ne þer nis no man 784
syker þat she ne haþ not forsaken. ¶ Holdest þou Is that happiness which is so
þan þilke welefulnesse preciouse to þe þat shal passen. transient?
and is present fortune derworþi to þe. whiche þat nis Is the attendance of Fortune so dear
not feiþful forto dwelle. *and* whan she goþ aweye þat to thee, whose stay is so uncertain, and whose
she bryngeþ a wyʒt in sorwe ¶ For syn she may nat removal causes such grief?
be wiþholden at a mans wille. she makeþ hym a wrecche
when she departeþ fro hym. ¶ What oþer þing is 791

763 *prolaciouns* — probasyons
heuyer—heuyere
ayleþ—eyleth
765 *trow[e]*—trowe
sen—MS. sene, C. seyn
some—som
þing—thinge
uncouþe—vnkowth
766 *aʒeins*—ayein
767 *wenest*—weenes
[*þat*]—C. that
768 *haþ*—MS. haþe
[*kept*]—from C.

769 *stablenes in þe*—stabylnesse standeth in the
770 *swyche*—swich
771 *vnleueful*—vnleffull
775 *haþ*—MS. had, C. hat
776 *good*—MS. goode, C. god
777 *agrisest*—MS. agrised, C. agrysyst
778 *fals[e]*—false
780 *myche*—mochel
781 [*of*]—from C.
haþ—MS. haþe
783 *text*—texte
784 *haþ*—MS. haþe

785 *forsaken*—forsake
Holdest þou—holdestow
786 *þan*—thanne
preciouse—presyes
787 *derworþi*—dereworthe
whiche—which
788 *feiþful*—feythfulle
goþ—MS. goþe
aweye—awey
790 *mans*—mannys
791 *when*—wan
þing—thinge

What is she (Fortune) but the presage of future calamity?	flitting fortune but a manere shewyng of wrycchednesse þat is to comen. ne it ne suffriþ nat oo[n]ly to loken
	794 of þing þat is present byforne þe eyen of man. but wisdom lokeþ and mesureþ þe ende of þinges. and þe
	796 same chaungyng from one to an oþer. þat is to seyne
Her mutability should make men neither fear her threats nor desire her favours.	fro aduersite to prosperite makeþ þat þe manaces of fortune ne ben not forto dreden. ne þe flatrynges of hir to ben desired. ¶ þus atte þe last it byhoueþ þe to suffren wiþ euene wille in pacience al þat is don
	801 inwiþ þe floor of fortune. þat is to seyne in þis worlde.
If you submit to her yoke you must patiently endure her inflictions.	¶ Syþen þou hast oones put þi nekke vnder þe ȝokke of hir. for if þou wilt write a lawe of wendyng and of dwellyng to fortune whiche þat þou hast chosen frely
	805 to be þi lady ¶ Art þou nat wrongful in þat and
Impatience will only embitter your loss.	makest fortune wroþe and aspere by þin inpacience. and ȝit þou mayst not chaungen hir. ¶ Yif þou com-
You cannot choose your port if you leave your vessel to the mercy of the winds.	mittest [and] bitakest þi sayles to þe wynde. þou shalt be shouen not þider þat þou woldest(:) but whider þat þe wynde shoueþ þe ¶ Yif þou castest þi scedes in þe
	811 feldes þou sholdest haue in mynde þat þe ȝeres ben
You have given yourself up to Fortune; it becomes you therefore to obey her commands.	oþer while plenteuous and oþer while bareyne. ¶ þou hast bytaken þiself to þe gouernaunce of fortune. and forþi it byhoueþ þe to ben obeisaunt to þe manere
Would you stop the rolling of her wheel?	of þi lady. and enforcest þou þe to aresten or wiþ- stonden þe swyftnesse and þe sweyes of hir tournyng
Fool! If Fortune once became stable she would cease to exist.	whele. ¶ O þou fool of alle mortel fooles if fortune bygan to dwelle stable. she cesed[e] þan to ben fortune.

793 *suffriþ*—suffiseth
794 *of þing*—on thynge
 byforne—MS. byforne byforne
 man—a man
795 *mesureþ*—amesureth
796 *from one*—fram oon
 seyne—seyn
797 *fro*—from
 to—into
799 *atte þe last*—at the laste

801 *seyne*—seyn
 worlde—world
802 *Syþen*—Syn
 ȝokke—yoke
803 *if*—yif
 write—wryten
804 *whiche*—which
805 *lady*—ladye
 Art þou—Artow
806 *wroþe*—wroth
 þin—thine

807 *chaungen*—chaunge
808 [*and*]—from C.
809 *þider*—thedyr
 whider—whedyr
811 *haue*—han
814 *manere*—maneres
815 *and*—omitted
 wiþstonden—withholden
816 *sweyes*—sweyȝ
818 *cesed[e]*—cesede

THE INCONSTANCY OF FORTUNE.

HEC CUM SUPERBA.

Whan fortune wiþ a proude ryȝt hande haþ turnid hir chaungyng stoundes she fareþ lyke þe maners of þe boillyng eurippe. *Glose.* Eurippe is an arme of þe see þat ebbith *and* flowiþ. *and* somtyme þe streme 822 is on one syde *and* somtyme on þat oþer. *Texte* ¶ She cruel fortune kasteþ adoune kynges þat somtyme weren ydred. *and* she deceiuable enhaunseth vp þe humble chere of hym þat is discomfited. *and* she neyþer hereþ 826 ne reccheþ of wrecched[e] wepynges. *and* she is so harde þat she lauȝeþ *and* scorneþ þe wepyng of hem þe whiche she haþ maked wepe wiþ hir free wille. ¶ þus she pleyeþ *and* þus she preueþ hir strengþe *and* sheweþ a grete wondre to alle hir seruauntȝ. ¶ Yif þat a wyȝt is seyn weleful *and* ouerþrowe in an houre. 832

[The fyrst metur. Fortune is as inconstant as the ebb and flow of Euripus.

She hurls kings from their thrones, and exalts the captive.

She turns a deaf ear to the tears and cries of the wretched.

Thus she sports and boasts her power and presents a marvel to her servants

if, in the space of an hour, a man is hurled from happiness into adversity.]

VELLEM AUTEM PAUCA.

CErtis I wolde plete wiþ þee a fewe þinges vsynge þe wordes of fortune tak heede now þi self. yif þat she axeþ ryȝt. *¶ O þou man wher fore makest þou me gilty by þine euerydayes pleynynges. what wronges haue I don þe. what goodes haue I byreft þe þat weren þine. stryf or plete wiþ me by fore what iuge þat þou wilt of þe possessioun of ryechesse or of dignites ¶ And yif þou maist shewe me þat euer any mortal man haþ 840 receyued any of þese þinges to ben his in propre. þan wol I graunt[e] frely þat [alle] þilke þinges weren þine whiche þat þou axest. ¶ Whan þat nature brouȝt[e] þe forþe out of þi moder wombe. I receyued[e] þe naked

[The secunde prose.] Philosophy expostulates with [* fol. 9 b.] Boethius in the name of Fortune. Why do you accuse me (Fortune) as guilty? What goods or advantages have I deprived you of?

Can you prove that ever any man had a fixed property in his riches?

You came naked into the world,

---

819 *proude*—prowd
hande—hand
haþ—MS. haþe
820 *lyke*—lik
821 *arme*—arm
822 *streme*—strem
823 *one*—o
824 *adoune*—adown
somtyme—whilom
825 *ydred* (MS. ydredde)—
humble—vmble [ydrad
827 *reccheþ*—rekkeþ

827 *wrecched*[e]—wrecchede
harde—hard
829 *lauȝeþ*—lyssheth
wepyng—wepynges
830 *strengþe*—strengthes
833 *plete*—pleten
834 *tak*—MS. take, C. tak
835 *makest* þou—makes thow
836 *wronges*—wronge
837 *don*—MS. done, C. don
byreft—MS. byrefte, C. byreft

838 *stryf*—MS. stryue, C. stryf
plete—pleten
by fore—by forn
839 *wilt*—wolt
ryechesse—rychesses
840 *shewe*—shewyn
euer—euere
haþ—MS. haþe
841 *þese*—tho
his—hise
842 *graunt*[e]—graunte
[*alle*]—from C.

3

PROSPERITY DOES NOT CONSTITUTE FELICITY. [BOOK 2. PROSE 2.

and I cherished you

and nedy of al þing. *and* I norysshed[e] þe wiþ my rychesse. *and* was redy *and* ententif þoru3 my fauo*ur* to

847 sustene þe. ¶ And þat makeþ þe now i*n*pacient a3eins

and encompassed you with affluence. Now that I have a mind to withdraw my bounty, be thankful and complain not.

me. *and* I envirounde þe wiþ al þe habundaunce *and* shinyng of al goodes þat ben in my ry3t. ¶ Now it lykeþ me to wiþ drawe myne hande. þou hast had grace as he þat haþ vsed of foreyne goodes. þou hast no ry3t to pleyne þe. as þou3 þou haddest vtterly lorn alle þi

853 þinges. whi pleynest þou þan. I haue don þe no wrong.

Riches and honours are s..bject to me. They are my servants, and come and go with me.

Ricches hono*ur*es *and* swyche oþer þinges ben of my ry3t. ¶ My seruauntes knowen me for hir lady. þei comen wiþ me *and* departen whan I wende. I dar wel affermen hardyly. þat yif þo þinges of whiche þou

858 pleynest þat þou hast forlorn hadde ben þinc. þou ne

Shall I alone be forbidden to use my own right? Doth not heaven give us sunny days and obscure the same with dark nights? Is not the earth covered with frost as well as with flowers?

haddest not lorn hem. ¶ shal I þan only be defended to vse my ry3t. ¶ Certis it is leueful to þe heuene to make clere dayes. *and* after þat to keuere þe same dayes wiþ derke ny3tes. ¶ þe erþe haþ eke leue to apparaile þe visage of þe erþe now w*ith* floures *and* now wiþ fruyt. *and* to confo*u*nde hem somtyme wiþ raynes *and*

865 wiþ coldes. ¶ þe see haþ eke hys ry3t to be som-

The sea sometimes appears calm, and at other times terrifies us with its tempestuous waves. Shall I be bound to constancy by the covetousness of men?

tyme calme *and* blaundyshing wiþ smoþe water. *and* somtyme to be horrible wiþ wawes *and* wiþ tempestes. ¶ But þe couetyse of men þat may not be staunched shal it bynde me to be stedfast. syn þat stedfastnesse is vnkouþ to my maneres. ¶ Swyche is my strengþe.

871 *and* þis pley. I pley[e] co*n*tinuely. I tourne þe whirlyng

I turn my rolling wheel and amuse myself with exalting what

whele wiþ þe tournyng cercle ¶ I am glade to chaunge þe lowest to þe heyeste. *and* þe heyest to þe loweste.

---

845 *al þing*—alle thinges
 norysshed[*e*]—noryssede
846 *rychesse*—rychesses
848, 849 *al*—alle
848 *habundaunce*—aboundaunce
850 *wiþ* —— *hande* — withdrawen myn hand
 had—MS. hadde, C. had
851 *haþ*—MS. haþe
852 *vtterly*—outrely
 lorn — MS. lorne, C. for lorn

853 *don*—MS. done, C. don
854 *Ricches*—Rychesses
858 *forlorn*—MS. forlorne, C. forlorn
859 *lorn*—MS. lorne, C. lorn
860 *vse*—vsen
861 *keuere* þe—coeueryn tho
862 *derke*—dirk
 erþe—yer
 haþ—MS. haþe
864 *confounde*—confownden
865 *haþ*—MS. haþe
866 *calme*—kalm

867 (2nd) *wiþ*—omitted
869 *stedfast*—stidefast
 stedfastnesse — stidefastnesse
870 *vnkouþ*—MS. vnkouþe, C. vnkowth
 Swyche—Swych
871 *pley*[*e*]—pleye
872 *whele*—wheel
 glade—glad
 chaunge—chaungyn

worþe vp yif þou wilt. so it be by þis lawe. þat þou <small>was low, and bringing down</small>
ne holde not þat I do þe wronge þou3 þou descende <small>what was high. Ascend if you</small>
dou*n* whanne resou*n* of my pleye axeþ it. Wost þou <small>will, but come down when my sport requires it.</small>
not how Cresus kyng of lyndens of whiche kyng Cir*us*
was ful sore agast a litel byforne þat þis rewlyche 878
Cresus was cau3t of Cirus *and* lad to þe fijr to be <small>Know you not the history of Crœsus and of</small>
brent. but þat a reyne descended[e] dou*n* from heuene <small>Paulus Æmilius?</small>
þat rescowed[e] hym ¶ And is it out of þi mynde how
þat Paulus consul of Rome whan he hadde take þe
kyng of perciens weep pitou[s]ly for þe captiuitee of þe 883
self[e] kyng. What oþer þinges bywaylen þe criinges of <small>What else does the weeping</small>
Tragedies. but only þe dedes of fortune. þat wiþ an <small>muse of Tragedy deplore but the</small>
vnwar stroke ouertu*r*neþ þe realmes of grete nobley <small>overthrow of kingdoms by</small>
¶ *Glose*. Tragedie is to seyne a dite of a *prosperite* for <small>the Iudiscriminate strokes of Fortune?</small>
a tyme þat endiþ in wrechednesse. Lernedest nat þou <small>Did you not learn whilst a youth,</small>
in grek whan þou were 3onge þat in þe entre or in þe <small>that at the gates of Jove's palace</small>
seler of Iuppiter þer ben couched two tunnes. þat on <small>stand two vessels, one full of bless-</small>
is ful of good þat oþer is ful of harme. ¶ What ry3t <small>ings, the other of woes?</small>
hast þou to pleyne. yif þou hast taken more plenteuously <small>What if you have drunk too deep of</small>
of þe goode syde þat is to seyne of my rycchesse a*nd* <small>the first vessel?</small>
prosperites. *and* what eke. yif I be nat departed fro þe. 894
What eke. yif my mutabilitee 3iueþ þe ry3tful cause of <small>My mutability gives thee hope</small>
hope to han 3it better þinges. ¶ Naþeles desmaie þe <small>of happier days.</small>
nat in þi þou3t. and þou þat art put in comune realme <small>Desire not to be exempted from</small>
of alle : ne desijr[e] nat to lyue by þine oonly propre ry3t. <small>the vicissitudes of humanity.</small>

SI QU*A*NTAS RAPIDIS.

Þ Ou3 plentee þat is goddesse of rycches hielde adoun <small>[the secu*n*de metur.]</small>
wiþ ful horn. *and* wiþdraweþ nat hir hand. ¶ As <small>Though Plenty, from her teeming horn, poured</small>
many recches as þe see turneþ vpwardes sandes whan it <small>down as many</small>

---

874 *worþe*—worth
  wilt—wolt
876 *doun*—adou*n*
  whanne—wan
  pleye—pley
  Wost þou—wistesthow
877 *kyng* (1)—the kyng
  lyndens—lydyens
878 *byforne*—byforn
880 *reyne descended[e]* —

rayn dessendede
880 *from*—fro
881 *rescowed[e]*—rescowede
882 *take*—takyn
885 *an*—a
886 *þe*—omitted
887 *seyne*—seyn
890 *tunnes*—tonnes
891 *harme*—harm
892 *hast þou*—hasthow

803 *seyne*—seyn
  rycchesse—rychesses
894 *I be nat*—I ne be nat al
896 *better*—beters
898 *lyue*—lyuen
  þine—thin
899 *rycches*—rychesses
901 *recches*—rychesses
  vpwardes—vpward

THE COVETOUS ARE EVER DISCONTENTED. [BOOK 2. PROSE 3

riches on the world as there are sands on the sea-shore, or stars in heaven, mankind would not cease to complain.
[* fol. 10.; plain.]

is moeued wiþ rauysshing blastes. or ellys as many rycches as þer shynen bry3t[e] sterres on heuene on þe sterry ny3t. 3it for al þat mankynde nolde not cesce to wope wrecched[e] pleyntes. ¶ And al be it so *þat

906 god receyueþ gladly her prayers *and* 3eueþ hem as ful

Though Heaven may grant every desire, they will still cry for more.

large muche golde *and* apparaileþ coueytous folk wiþ noble or clere hono*urs*. 3it semeþ hem haue I-gete no-þing. but alwey her cruel ravyne deuourynge al þat þei

910 han geten shewiþ oþer gapinges. þat is to seye gapen

What rein can restrain unbounded avarice?

and desiren 3it after moo rycchesse. ¶ What brideles my3ten wiþholde to any certeyne ende þe desordene

He who thinks himself poor, though he be rich, doth truly labour under poverty.

coueitise of men ¶ Whan euere þe raþer þat it fletiþ in large 3iftis : þe more ay brenneþ in hem þe prest of hauyng. ¶ Certis he þat quakyng *and* dredeful weneþ

916 hym seluen nedy. he ne lyueþ neuere mo ryche.

HIIS IGITUR SI PRO SE.

[The thrydde prose.]
If Fortune spake thus to you, you could not defend your complaint.

Þerfore yif þat fortune spake wiþ þe for hir self in þis manere. For soþe þou ne haddest [nat] what þou my3test answere. and if þou hast any þing wher-wiþ. þou mayist ry3tfully tellen þi compleynt. ¶ It

921 byhoueþ þe to shewen it. *and* .I. wol 3eue þe space to

B. What you have said is very specious, but such discourses are only sweet while they strike our ears. They cannot efface the deep impressions that misery has made in the heart.

tellen it. ¶ Certeynely q*uod* I þan þise ben faire þinges *and* enoyntid wiþ hony swetnesse of rethorike *and* musike. *and* only while þei ben herd þei ben de-liciouse. ¶ But to wrecches is a deppere felyng of harme. þis is to seyn þat wrecches felen þe harmes þat þei suffren more greuously þan þe remedies or þe delites

928 of þise wordes mowe gladen or comforten hem. so þat

---

902 *rauysshing*—rauyssynge
903 *rycches*—rychesses
    bry3t[e]—bryhte
    on (1)—in
904 *ny3t*—nyhtes
905 *wope wrecched[e]*—wope wrecchede
906 *her*—hir
    ful—fool
907 *muche*—mcche
    folk—men

908 *haue*—hauen
    I-geto—I-getyn
909 *her*—hir
910 *seye*—seyn
911 *rycchesse*—rychesses
912 *wiþholde*—wytholden
    certeyne—certeyn
914 *prest*—thurst
915 *dredeful*—dredful
916 *lyueþ*—leueth
918 [*nat*]—from C.

919 *if*—yif
920 *mayist*—mayst
    tellen—defendyn
921 *3eue*—yeuyn
922 *þan*—thanne
    ben—bet (= beth)
923 *swetnesse*—swetenesse
924 *while*—whil
    herd—MS. herde
926 *harme*—harm
928 *mowe*—mowen

whan þise þinges stynten forto soun[e] in eres. þe sorwe 929
þat is inset greueþ þe þouȝt. Ryȝt so is it *quod* she.
¶ For þise ne ben ȝit none remedies of þi maladie. but
þei ben a manere norissinges of þi sorwe ȝit rebel
aȝeyne þi cura*cioun*. ¶ For whan þat tyme is. I shal
moue swiche þinges þat *percen* hem self depe. ¶ But
naþeles þ*at* þou shalt not wilne to leten þi self a
wrecche. ¶ Hast þou forȝeten þe nou*m*bre *and* þe
manere of þi welefulnesse. I holde me stille how þat
þe souerayn men of þe Citee toke*n* þe in cure *and*
kepynge whan þou were orphelyn of fadir *and* modir.
and were chosen i*n* affinite of princes of þe Citee.
¶ And þou bygu*n*ne raþer to ben leef *and* deere þan 941
forto ben a neyȝbour. þe whiche þing is þe most ' preciouse kynde of any pr*o*pinquitee or aliau*n*ce þat may
ben. ¶ Who is it þat ne seide þou nere ryȝt weleful 944
wiþ so grete a nobley of þi fadres in lawe. ¶ *And* wiþ
þe chastite of þi wijf. *and* wiþ þe oportunite *and*
noblesse of þi masculyn children. þat is to seyne þi
sones *and* ouer al þis me lyst to passe of comune þinges. 948
¶ How þou haddest in þi þouȝt dignitees þat weren
warned to olde men. but it deliteþ me to comen now to
þe singuler vphepyng of þi welefulnesse. ¶ Yif any
fruyt of mortal þinges may han any weyȝte or price of 952
welefulnesse. ¶ Myȝtest þou euere forȝeten for any
charge of harme þat myȝt[e] byfallen. þe remembrau*n*ce
of þilke day þat þou sey[e] þi two sones maked conseillers. *and* ylad to gidre from þin house vndir so gret
assemble of senatours. *and* vndir þe blyþenesse of poeple. 957
and whan þou say[e] hem sette in þe court in her

P. So it is indeed; for my arguments are not designed as remedies, but as lenitives only. When time serves, I will administer those things that shall reach the seat of your disease. But you are not among the number of the wretched. I shall not speak of your happiness in being provided for (in your orphanage) by the chief men of the city;

nor of your noble alliance with Festus and Symmachus;

nor of your virtuous wife, and manly sons.

Can you ever forget the memorable day that saw your two sons invested with the dignity of Consuls?

---

929 *soun[e]*—sowne
930 *inset*—MS. insette, C. inset
932 *sorwe*—sorwes
933 *aȝeyne*—ayein
934 *moue swiche*—moeue swych
939 *souerayn*—souerane
943 *neyȝbour*—neyssheboúr
944 *nere*—were

945 *nobley*—nobleye
  fadres—fadyr-is
947 *seyne*—seyn
948 *lyst*—lyste
  passe of—passen the
949 *þouȝt*—yowthe
950 *warned*—werned
952 *fruyt*—frute
  price—pris
953 *Myȝtest þou* — myhtes.

thow
954 *harme*—harm
  myȝt[e] byfallen — myhte befalle
955 *sey[e]*—saye
956 *from*—fro
  gret—MS. grete, C. gret
958 *say[e]*—saye
  sette—set
  her—heere

When in the circus you satisfied the expectant multitude with a triumphal largess?

chaieres of dignites. ¶ þou rethorien or pronouncere of kynges preysinges. deseruedest glorie of wit and of eloquence. whan þou sittyng bytwix þi two sones conseillers in þe place þat hyȝt Circo. and fulfildest þe

963 abydyng of multitude of poeple þat was sprad about þe wiþ large praysynge and laude as men syngen in victories. þo ȝaue þou wordes of fortune as I trowe. þat

By your expressions you flattered Fortune, and obtained from her a gift which never before fell to any private person.

is to seyne. þo feffedest þou fortune wiþ glosynge wordes and desseiuedest hir. whan she accoied[e] þe and norsshed[e] þe as hir owen delices. ¶ þou hast

969 had of fortune a ȝifte þat is to seyn swiche gerdoun þat she neu[er]e ȝaf to preue man ¶ Wilt þou þerfore

Will you therefore call Fortune to account? She now begins, I own, to look unkindly on you; but if you consider the number of your blessings, [* fol. 10 b.] you must confess that you are still happy.

leye a rekenyng wiþ fortune. she haþ now twynkeled first vpon þe wiþ a wykked eye. ¶ Yif þou considere þe noumbre and þe manere of þi blysses. and of þi sorwes. *þou maist nat forsake þat þou nart ȝit blysful. For if þou þerfore wenest þi self nat weleful for þinges

976 þat þo semeden ioyful ben passed. ¶ þer nis nat whi

These evils that you suffer are but transitory.

þou sholdest wene þi self a wrecche. for þinges þat now semen soory passen also. ¶ Art þou now comen firste

979 a sodeyne gest in to þe shadowe or tabernacle of þis

Can there be any stability in human affairs, when the life of man is exposed to dissolution every hour?

lijf. or trowest þou þat any stedfastnesse be in mannis þinges. ¶ Whan ofte a swifte houre dissolueþ þe same man. þat is to seyne whan þe soule departiþ fro þe body. For al þouȝ þat yelde is þer any feiþ þat fortunous þinges willen dwelle. ȝit naþeles þe last[e] day

The last day of life puts an end to Prosperity.

of a mannis lijf is a manere deeþ to fortune. and also

What matters it then, whether you by death leave it, or it (Fortune) by flight doth leave you?

to þilke þat haþ dwelt. and þerfore what wenist þou þar recche yif þou forlete hir in deynge or ellys þat she fortune forlete þe in fleenge awey.

961 *bytwix*—bytwyen
962 *hyȝt*—hihte
963 *of* (1)—of the
    about—abowten
964 *wiþ—with* so
965 *ȝaue*—MS. þau, C. yaue
    of—to
966 *seyne*—seyn
967 *accoied*[*e*]—acoyede
968 *norsshed*[*e*]—noryssede
    owen—owne
    þou —— *of* — thew bar
    away of

969 *had*—MS. hadde
    swiche—swich
970 *preue*—pryue
971 *leye*—lye
    haþ—MS. haþe
972 *wykked*—wyckede
973 *blysses*—blysse
974 *forsake*—forsakyn
    nart—nrt
    blysful—blysseful
978 *soory*—sorye
    firste—fyrst
979 *sodeyne*—sodeyn

979 *shadowe*—shadwe
980 *stedfastnesse*—stedefast-
981 *swifte*—swyft   [nesse
    dissolueþ—dyssoluede
983 *al þouȝ þat* — al þat
    \ thowgh
    fortunous—fortune
984 *willen dwelle* — wolen
    last[*e*]—laste   [dwellyn
986 *haþ*—MS. haþe
    wenist þou—weenostow
987 *þar recche*—dar recke
988 *awey*—away

[BOOK 2. MET. 3. PROSE 4.] MANY BLESSINGS STILL REMAIN.

CUM PRIMO POLO.

Whan phebus þe sonne bygynneþ to spreden his clere- *[The .iij. Metur.]*
nesse wíth rosene chariettes. þan þe sterre ydimmyd *The stars pale before the light of*
paleþ hir white cheres. by þe flamus of þe sonne þat *the rising sun.*
ouer comeþ þe sterre ly3t. ¶ þis is to seyn whan þe
sonne is risen þe day sterre wexiþ pale *and* lesiþ hir 993
ly3t for þe grete bry3tnesse of þe sonne. ¶ Whan þe *Westerly winds*
wode wexeþ redy of rosene floures in þe first somer *deck the wood with roses, but easterly winds*
sesoun þoru3 þe breþe of þe wynde Zephirus þat wexeþ *cause their beauty to fade.*
warme. ¶ Yif þe cloudy wynde auster blowe folliche. 997
þan goþ awey þe fayrnesse of þornes. Ofte þe see is *Now the sea is calm, and again*
clere *and* calme wiþoute moeuyng floodes. And ofte *it is tempestuous.*
þe horrible wynde aquilon moeueþ boylyng tempestes 1000
and ouer whelweþ þe see. ¶ Yif þe forme of þis worlde *If all things thus vary, will you*
is so [3eelde] stable. *and* yif it tourniþ by so many *trust in transitory riches?*
entrechaungynges. wilt þou þan trusten in þe trublynge
fortunes of men. wilt þou trowen in flittyng goodes. 1004
It is certeyne *and* establissed by lawe perdurable þat' no *All here below is unstedfast and*
þing þat is engendred nys stedfast no stable. *unstable.*

TUNC EGO UERA INQUAM.

þAnne seide I þus. O norice of alle uertues þou *[The ferthe prose.]*
seist ful soþe. ¶ Ne I may nat forsake þe ry3t[e] *B. I cannot deny my sudden and*
swifte cours of my prosperitee. þat is to seine. þat *early prosperity.*
prosperitee ne be comen to me wondir swiftly *and* 1010
soone. but þis is a þing þat gretly smertiþ me whan it *It is the remembrance of former*
remembreþ me. ¶ For in alle aduersitees of fortune þe *happiness that adds most to*
most vnsely kynde of contrariouse fortune is to han *man's infelicity.*
ben woleful. ¶ But þat þou *quod* she abaist þus þe *P. Recollect that*
tourment of þi fals[e] opinioun þat maist þou not ry3t- *you have yet much affluence.*

---

989 *his*—hyr
990 *þan*—thanne
991 *flamus*—flambes
995 *redy*—rody
  rosene—rosyn
997 *warme*—warm
998 *goþ*—MS. *goþe*, C. goth
  fayrnesse—fayrenesse
999 *clere*—cleer
  calme—kalm

1000 *wynde*—wynd
1001 *whelweþ*—welueeth
1002 [3eelde]—from C.
1003, 1004 *wilt þou*—wolthow
1003 *þan*—thanne
  trublynge—towmblynge
1004 *in flittyng* — on flet-
1005 *It is*—is it [tynge
1006 *no*—ne
  stable—establc

1008 *soþe*—soth
  Ne I may—Ne I ne may
1009 *seine*—seyn
1011 *a*—omitted
  gretly—gretely
1012 *aduersitees*—aduersytc
1013 *most*—mooste
1014 *abaist*—abyest
1015 *tourment*—torment;
  fals[e]—false

fully blamen ne aretten to þinges. as who seiþ for þou hast ȝitte many habundaunces of þinges. ¶ Textus.

1018. For al be it so þat þe ydel name of auenterouse welefulnesse moeueþ þe now. it is leueful þat þou rekene with me of how many[e] þinges þou hast ȝit plentee. ¶ And þerfore yif þat þilke þing þat þou haddest for most precious in alle þi rycchesse of fortune be kept 1023 to þe by þe grace of god vnwemmed und vndefouled. Mayst þou þan pleyne ryȝtfully vpon þe myschief of fortune. syn þou hast ȝit þi best[e] þinges. ¶ Certys ȝit 1026 lyueþ in goode poynt þilke precious honour of mankynde. ¶ Symacus þi wyues fadir whiche þat is a man maked al of sapience and of vertue. þe whiche 1029 man þou woldest b[i]en redely wiþ þe pris of þin owen lijf. he byweyleþ þe wronges þat men don to þee. and not for hym self. for he liueþ in sykernesse of any sentence put aȝeins hym. ¶ And ȝit lyueþ þi wif þat is attempre of witte and passyng oþer women in clennes 1034 of chastitee. and for I wol closen shortly her bountes she is lyke to hir fadir. I telle þe welle þat she lyueþ looþ of hir life. and kepiþ to þee oonly hir goost. and is al maat and ouer-comen by wepyng and sorwe for 1038 desire of þe ¶ In þe whiche þing only I mot graunten þat þi welefulnesse is amenused. ¶ What shal I seyn eke of þi two sones conseillours of whiche as of children of hir age þer shineþ *þe lyknesse of þe witte of hir fadir and of hir eldefadir. and siþen þe souereyn cure of alle mortel folke is to sauen hir owen lyues. ¶ O how weleful art þou þouȝ þou knowe þi goodes.

What you esteemed most precious in your happy days, you still retain,

and ought therefore not to complain.

Symmachus, dear to you as life,

is safe and in health.

Your wife Rusticiana is also alive,

and bewaileth her separation from you.

Why need I mention your two sons, in whom so much of the wit [* fol. 11.] and spirit of their sire and grandsire doth shine?

And since it is the chief care of man to preserve life; you are still

---

1016 seiþ—MS. selþe, C. seyh
1017 ȝitte—yit
1019 leueful—leefful
1020 many[e] þinges—manye grete thinges
1022 alle—al
1023 þe by—the yit by
1024 myschief—meschef
1025 best[e]—beste
1026 lyueþ—leueth goode—good.
1027 whiche—which
1028 al—alle

1028 of (2)—omitted
1029 b[i]en—byen owen—owne
1030 byweyleþ—bewayleth don—MS. done, C. don
1031 lineþ—leueth
1033 witte—wyt women—wymmen
1034 shortly—shortely
1035 lyke—lik welle—wel
1036 hir life—this lyf
1037 maat—maud

1038 whiche—weche
1039 amenused—amenyssed seyn—(MS. seyne) seyn
1041 lyknesse—lykenesse witte—wyt
1042 and (1)—or eldefadir—eldyr fadyr siþen—syn
1043 folke—folk
1044 art þou þouȝ—arthow yif

¶ But ȝitte ben þer þinges dwellyng to þe wardes þat no most happy in the possession of
man douteþ þat þei ne ben more derworþe to þe þen blessings which all men value more than life.
þine owen lijf. ¶ And forþi drie þi teres for ȝitte nys Dry up thy
nat eueriche fortune al hateful to þe warde. ne ouer tears, thou hast still present com-
greet tempest haþ nat ȝit fallen vpon þe. whan þat þin fort and hope of future felicity.
ancres cliue fast[e] þat neiþer wole suffre þe comfort of þis 1050
tyme present. ne þe hope of tyme comynge to passen
ne to fallen. ¶ And I preie quod, I þat fast[e] mot[en] B. I hope these will never fail me.
þei holden. ¶ For whiles þat þei halden. how so euere
þat þinges ben. I shal wel fleten furþe and eschapen. 1054
¶ But þou mayst wel seen how greet[e] apparailes and But do you not see how low I am fallen?
aray þat me lakkeþ þat ben passed awey fro me. ¶ I P. I should think
haue sumwhat auaunced and forþered þe quod she. if that I had made progress if you did not repine so
þat þou anoie nat or forþenke nat of al þi fortune. As at your fate.
who seiþ. ¶ I haue somwhat comforted þe so þat þou It grieves me to hear you com-
tempest nat þe þus wiþ al þi fortune. syn þou hast plain while you possess so many comforts.
ȝit þi best[e] þinges. ¶ But I may nat suffre þin
delices. þat pleinst so wepyng. and anguissous for þat 1062
oþer lakkeþ somwhat to þi welefulnesse. ¶ For what Every one, how-ever happy, has
man is so sad or of so perfit welefulnesse. þat he ne something to complain of.
stryueþ or pleyneþ on some half aȝeine þe qualitee of 1065
his estat. ¶ For whi ful anguissous þing is þe con- The condition of human enjoy-
diciou*n* of mans goodes. ¶ For eyþer it comeþ al to ment is anxious; for either it
gidre to a wyȝt. or ellys it lasteþ not perpetuely. comes not all at once, or makes no long stay when
¶ For som man haþ grete rycchesse. but he is as- it does come. One man is very
shamed of hys vngentil lynage. and som man is re- wealthy, but his birth is obscure.
nomed of noblesse of kynrede. but he is enclosed in so Another is con-spicuous for
grete angre for nede of þinges. þat hym were leuer þat nobility of de-scent, but is
he were vnknowe. and som man habundeþ boþe in surrounded by indigence.
rychesse and noblesse. but ȝit he bywaileþ hys chast[e] A third is blest with both ad-

---

1045 *But ȝitte*—for yit
  dwellyng—dwellyd
  wardes—ward
1046 *þat*—than
  derworþe—dereworthe
  þen þine—than thin
1047 ȝitte—yit
1049 *haþ*—MS. haþe
  þin—thyne
1050 *cliue fast[e]*—cleuen
  faste
  wole suffre—wolen suffren

1052 *fallen*—faylen
1053 *fast[e] mot[en]*—faste
  moten
1053 *holden*—halden
1054 *furþe*—forth
1055 *mayst*—mayste
  greet[e]—grete
1058 *forþenke*—forthinke
1061 *best[e]*—beste
  suffre þin—suffren thi
1063 *oþer*—ther
1064 *perfit*—parfyt

1065 *or*—and
  some half aȝeine — som
  halue ayen
1067 *mans*—mannes
  comeþ al—comth nat al
1068 *lasteþ*—last
  perpetuely—perpetue*i*
1069 *rycchesse*—Rychesses
1070 *renomed*—renowned
1072 *angre for*—Angwyssh*e*
  leuer—leuere [of
1074 *chast[e]*—caste

vantages, but is unmarried.	lijf. for he haþ no wijf. ¶ and som man is wel *and*
This man is happy in a wife, but is childless, while that other man has the joy of children, but is mortified by their evil ways.	solily maried but he haþ no children. *and* norissheþ his ricchesse to þe heires of straunge folk. ¶ And som man is gladded wiþ children. but he wepiþ ful sory for þe trespas of his son or of his douȝtir. ¶ and for þis
Thus we see that no man can agree easily with the state of his fortune.	þer accordeþ no wyȝt lyȝtly to þe condicio*un* of his fortune. for alwey to euery man þere is i*n* mest somwhat
1082	þat vnassaieþ he ne wot not or ellys he drediþ þat he
The senses of the happy are refined and delicate, and they are impatient if anything is untoward.	haþ assaied. ¶ *And* adde þis also þat euery weleful man haþ a wel delicat felyng. ¶ So þat but yif alle þinges fallen at hys owen wille for he inpacient or is nat vsed to han none aduersitee. an-oone he is þrowe
The happiness of the most fortunate depends on trifles.	adoūne for euery lytel þing. ¶ And ful lytel þinges ben þo þat wiþdrawen þe somme or þe *per*feccio*un* of
1089	blisfulnesse fro hem þat ben most fortunat. ¶ How
How many would think themselves in heaven if they had only a part of the remnant of thy fortune! Thy miseries proceed from the thought that thou art miserable. Every lot may be happy to the man who bears his condition with equanimity and courage.	many men trowest þou wolde demen hem self to ben almost in heuene yif þei myȝten atteyne to þe leest[e] *par*tie of þe remenaunt of þi fortune. ¶ þis same place þat þou clepist exil is contre to hem þat enhabiten here. *and* forþi. Noþing wrecched. but whan þou wenest it ¶ As who seiþ. þouȝ þi self ne no wyȝt ellys nys no wrecche but whan he weneþ hym self a
1097	wrecche by reputacio*un* of his corage.

CONTRAQUE.

1098 And aȝeinewarde al fortune is blisful to a man by þe agreablete or by þe egalite of hym þat suffreþ it.

When patience is lost then a change of state is desired.	¶ What man is þat. þat is so weleful þat nolde chau*n*gen his estat whan he haþ lorn pacience. þe swetnesse of
1102	mannes welefulnesse is yspranid wiþ many[e] bitternesses.

1075, 1076 *haþ*—MS. haþe	1083, 1084 *haþ*—MS. haþe	1095 *who*—ho
1076 *maried*—ymaryed	1084 *wel*—ful	1096 *no*—a
his—hise	1085 *fallen*—byfalle	1098 *aȝeinewarde al*—ayein-
1077 *ricchesse*—Rychesses	*wille*—wyl	ward alle
heires—eyres	1086 *none*—non	1099 *it*—hyt
folk—foolkys	*an-oone*—Anon	1101 *whan*—what
1080 *þer*—þer ne	*þrowe*—throwen	*haþ*—MS. haþe
1081 *mest*—omitted	1087 *adoūne*—adoun	*lorn*—MS. lorne, C. lost
1082 *vnassaieþ*—vnassaied	1090 *wolde*—wolden	1102 *yspranid*—spraynyd
wot—MS. wote, C. wot	1095 *it*—hyt	*bitternesses*—beternesses

þe whiche welefulnesse al þouȝ it seme swete *and* ioyeful to hym þat vseþ it. ȝit may it not be wiþ-holden þat it ne goþ away whan it woL ¶ þan is it wel sen how wrecched is þe blisfulnesse of mortel þinges. þat neiþer it dwelliþ perpetuel wiþ hem þat euery fortune receyuen agreablely or egaly. ¶ Ne it ne deliteþ not in al. to hem þat ben anguissous. ¶ O ye mortel folkes what seke *ȝe þan blisfulnesse oute of ȝoure self. whiche þat is put in ȝoure self. Errour *and* folie confoundeþ ȝow ¶ I shal shewe þe shortly. þe poynt of souereyne blisfulnesse. Is þer any þing to þe more preciouse þan þi self ¶ þou wilt answere nay. ¶ þan if it so be þat þou art myȝty ouer þi self þat is to seyn by tranquillitee of þi soule. þan hast þou þing *in* þi power þat þou noldest neuer lesen. ne fortune may nat by-nyme it þe. *and* þat þou mayst knowe þat blisfulnesse [ne] may nat standen in þinges þat ben fortunous *and* temperel. ¶ Now vndirstonde *and* gadir it to gidir þus yif blisfulnesse be þe souereyne goode of nature þat lieuþ by resou*n* ¶ Ne þilke þing nis nat souereyne goode þat may be taken awey in any wyse. for more worþi þing *and* more digne is þilke þing þat may nat be taken awey. ¶ þan shewiþ it wele þat þe vnstablenesse of fortune may nat attayne to receyue verray blisfulnes. ¶ And ȝit more ouer. ¶ What man þat þis toumblyng welefulnesse leediþ. eiþer he woot þat [it] is chaungeable. or ellis he woot it nat. ¶ And yif he woot it not. what blisful fortune may þer be in þe blyndenesse of ignoraunce. and yif he woot þat·it is chaungeable. he mot alwey ben adrad þat he ne lese þat þing. þat he ne douteþ nat but þat he may leesen

Marginalia:
How much is human felicity embittered! 1104
It will not stay with those that endure their lot with equanimity, nor bring comfort to anxious minds. 1109
Why then, O mortals, do ye seek abroad for that felicity which is to be found within yourselves? [* fol. 11 b.] Nothing is more precious than thyself. If thou hast command over thyself, Fortune cannot deprive thee of it. 1117
Happiness does not consist in things transitory. 1121
If happiness be the supreme good of nature, then that thing cannot be it which can be withdrawn from us. Instability of fortune is not susceptive of true happiness. He who is led by fading felicity, either knows that it is changeable or does not know it. If he knows it not, what happiness has he in the blindness of his ignorance? If he knows it is fleeting he must be afraid of losing

---

1104 *hym*—hem
it—hyt
be—ben
1105 *goþ*—MS. geþe
wol—woole
sen—MS. sene
1107 *dwelliþ*—dureth
1109 *folkes*—folke
1110 *oute*—owt
1112 *shortly*—shortely
1114 *wilt*—MS. wilte. C. wolt
if—yif
1117 *by-nyme*—be-neme
1118 *blisfulnesse* [ne] — blyssefulnesse ne
1120 *to gidir*—to gidere
1121, 1122 *souereyne goode*— souereyn good
1125 *wele*—wel
1126 *receyue*—resseyuen
1129 [*if*]—from C.
it—hyt
1130 *be*—ben
1131 *blyndenesse* — blyndnesse

RICHES DO NOT CONSTITUTE HAPPINESS.

it, and this fear will not suffer him to be happy.

it. ¶ As whoo seiþ he mot ben alwey agast lest he leese þat he wot wel he may leese. ¶ For whiche þe 1136 continuel drede þat he haþ ne suffriþ hym nat to ben weleful. ¶ Or ellys yif he leese it he wene to be dispised *and* forleten hit. ¶ Certis eke þat is a ful lytel goode þat is born wiþ euene hert[e] whan it is 1140 loost. ¶ þat is to seyne þat men don no more force.

Since thou art convinced of the soul's immortality, thou canst not doubt that if death puts an end to human felicity, that all men when they die, are plunged into the depths of misery.

of þe lost þan of þe hauynge. ¶ And for as myche as þou þi self art he to whom it haþ ben shewid *and* proued by ful many[e] demonstraciouns. as I woot wel þat þe soules of men ne mowen nat dien in no wise. and eke syn it is clere. *and* certeyne þat fortunous welefulnesse endiþ by þe deeþ of þe body. ¶ It may nat ben douted 1147 þat yif þat deeþ may take awey blysfulnesse þat al þe

But we know that many have sought to obtain felicity, by undergoing not only death, but pains and torments. How then can this present life make men truly happy, since when it is ended they do not become miserable?

kynde of mortal þingus ne descendiþ in to wrecchednesse by þe ende of þe deeþ. ¶ And syn we knowen wel þat many a man haþ souȝt þe fruit of blisfulnesse nat only wiþ suffryng of deeþ. but eke wiþ suffryng of peynes *and* tourmentes. how myȝt[e] þan þis present lijf make men blisful. syn þat whanne þilke self[e] lijf is endid. it ne makeþ folk no wrecches.

* MS. ualet.

QUISQUIS UOLET* PERHENNEM CAUTUS.

[The ferthe metur.] He who would have a stable and lasting seat must not build upon lofty hills; nor upon the sands, if he would escape the violence of winds and waves.

What maner man stable *and* war þat wil founden hym a perdurable sete *and* ne wil not be cast doune wiþ þe loude blastes of þe wynde Eurus. *and* wil dispise þe see manassynge wiþ floodes ¶ Lat hym eschewe to bilde on þe cop of þe mountayngne. or in þe moyste 1160 sandes. ¶ For þe fel[le] wynde auster tourmenteþ þe cop of þe mountayngne wiþ alle his strengþes. ¶ and þe

1134 *it*—hyt
  seiþ—MS. seiþe, C. seyth
1135 *woot*—MS. wote, C. wot
  leese (2)—leese it
  whiche—which
1136 *haþ*—MS. haþe
1137 *ellys*—omitted
  wene—weneth
1138 *hit*—omitted
1139 *goode*—good
  born—MS. borne, C. born
  hert[e]—herte

1140 *seyne*—seyn
  don—MS. done, C. do
  force—fors
1142 *haþ*—MS. haþe
1143 *many[e]*—manye
1144 *mowen*—mowe
  dien—deyen
1145 *clere*—cleer
  certeyne—certeyn
1147 *al*—alle
1150 *haþ*—MS. haþe
  fruit—frut

1152 *myȝt[e]*—myhte
1153 *make*—maken
  self[e]—selue
1155, 1156, 1157 *wil*—wole
1156 *be cast*—MS. be caste, C. ben cast
1157 *wynde*—wynd
1158 *eschewe*—eschewen
1160 *fel[le]*—felle
1161 *his*—hise

lowe see sandes refuse to beren þe heuy wey3te. *and* 1162
forþi yif þou wolt flee þe perilous auenture þat is to *If thou wilt flee perilous fortune,*
seine of þe worlde ¶ Haue mynde certeynly to ficchyn *lay thy foundation upon the firmer stone, so*
þi house of a myrie site in a lowe stoone. ¶ For al *that thou mayst grow old in thy*
þou3 þe wynde troublyng þo see þondre wiþ ouere- *stronghold.*
þrowynges ¶ þou þat art put i*n* quiete *and* welful by
strengþe of þi palys shalt leden a cleer age. scornyng
þe wodenesses and þe Ires of þe eir. 1169

SET CUM RACIONUM IAM IN TE.

But for as moche as þe noryssinges of my resou*n*s [The fythe prose.]
descenden now in to þe. I trowe it were tyme to *It is now time to use stronger medicines, since lighter remedies have taken effect. What is there in the gifts of Fortune that is not vile and despic-*
vsen a litel strenger medicynes. ¶ Now vndirstonde
here al were it so þat þe 3iftis of fortune nar[e] nat
brutel ne transitorie. what is þer in hem þat may be
þine *in any tyme. or ellis þat it nys foule if þat it be *[* fol. 12.] able ?*
considered *and* lokid perfitely. ¶ Richesse ben þei 1176
preciouse by þe nature of hem self. or ellys by þe *Are riches precious in themselves, or in men's*
nature of þe. What is most worþi of rycchesse. is it *estimation ? What is most*
nat golde or my3t of moneye assembled. ¶ Certis *precious in them, quantity or quality ?*
þilke golde *and* þilke moneye shineþ *and* 3eueþ better *Bounty is more*
renou*n* to hem þat dispenden it. þen to þilke folke þat *glorious than niggardliness.*
mokeren it. For auarice makeþ alwey mokeres to be *Avarice is always*
hated. *and* largesse makeþ folke clere of renou*n* *hateful, while liberality is praise-worthy.*
¶ For syn þat swiche þing as is transfered from o
man to an oþer ne may nat dwellen wiþ no man. 1185
Certis þan is þilke moneye precious. whan it is trans- *Money cannot be more precious*
lated in to oþer folk. *and* stynteþ to ben had by *than when it is dispensed liberally to others.*
vsage of large 3euy*n*g of hym þat haþ 3euen it. *and*
also yif al þe moneye þat is ouer-al in þe world were *If one man's coffers contained all*

1162 *lowe*—lavse
    see—omitted
    refuse—refusen
    wey3te—wyhte
1163 *flee*—fleen
1164 *seine*—seyn
1165 *þi*—thin
    lowe stoone—lowh stoon
1167 *welful*—weleful
1169 *wodenesses* — wood-

nesses
1172 *strenger*—strengere
    vndirstonde—vndyrstond
1173 *nar[e]*—ne weere
1174 *be þine*—ben thyn
1175 *foule*—fowl
1176 *Richesse*—Rychessis
1178 *rycchesse*—rychesses
1179, 1180 *golde*—gold
1180 *better*—betere

1181 *þen*—thanne
1182 *mokeres*—mokereres
1183 *folke clere*—folk cler
1184 *swiche*—swich
    from—fram
1187 *stynteþ*—stenteth
1188 *haþ*—MS. haþe
1189 *world*—worlde

<small>the money in the world, every one else would be in want of it.</small> gadered towar[d] o man. it sholde maken al oþer men to ben nedy as of þat. ¶ And certys a voys al hool
1192 þat is to seyn wiþ-oute amenusynge fulfilleþ to gyder
<small>Riches cannot be dispensed without diminution.</small> þe heryng of myche folke. but Certys ȝoure rycchesse ne mowen nat passen vnto myche folk wiþ-oute amen-
1195 ussyng ¶ And whan þei ben apassed. nedys þei maken
<small>O the poverty of riches, that cannot be enjoyed by many at the same time, nor can be possessed by one without impoverishing others!</small> hem pore þat forgon þe rycchesses. ¶ O streite and nedy clepe I þise rycchesses. syn þat many folke [ne] may nat han it al. ne al may it nat comen to on man wiþ-oute pouerte of al oþer folke. ¶ And þe shynynge
1200 of gemmes þat I clepe preciouse stones. draweþ it nat þe eyen of folk in to hem warde. þat is to seyne for þe
<small>The beauty of precious stones consists only in their brightness, wherefore I marvel that men admire that which is motionless, lifeless, and irrational.</small> beaute. ¶ For certys yif þer were beaute or bounte in shynyng of stones. þilke clerenesse is of þe stones hem self. and nat of men. ¶ For whiche I wondre gretly þat men merueilen on- swiche þinges. ¶ For whi what þing is it þat yif it wanteþ moeuyng and
1207 ioynture of soule and body þat by ryȝt myȝt[e] semen a faire creature to hym þat haþ a 'soule of resoun.
<small>Precious stones are indeed the workmanship of the Creator, but their beauty is infinitely below the excellency of man's nature.</small> ¶ For al be it so þat gemmes drawen to hem self a litel of þe laste beaute of þe worlde. þoruȝ þe entent of hir creatour and þoruȝ þe distinccioun of hem self. ȝit for as myche as þei ben put vndir ȝoure excellence.
1213 þei han not desserued by no weye þat ȝe shullen
<small>Doth the beauty of the field delight thee?
B. Why should it not? for it is a beautiful part of a beautiful whole.</small> merueylen on hem. ¶ And þe beaute of feeldes deliteþ it nat mychel vnto ȝow. Boyce. ¶ Whi sholde it nat deliten vs. syn þat it is a ryȝt fayr porcioun of þe ryȝt fair werk. þat is to seyn of þis worlde. ¶ And ryȝt
<small>Hence, we admire the face of the sea, the heavens,</small> so ben we gladed somtyme of þe face of þe see whan it is clere. And also merueylen we on þe heuene and

<small>
1190 al—alle
1191 al hool—omitted
1193 myche folke — moche folke
rycchesse—rychesses
1194 myche—moche
1196 forgon—MS. forgone
1197 þise—this
rycchesses—rychesse
[ne]—from C.
1198 on—o
1199 wiþ-oute—with-owten
</small>

<small>
1190 al—alle
folke—folke
1200 preciouse—presyous
1201 in—omitted
warde—ward
seyne—seyn
1202 beaute (1)—beautes
For—but
1203 in—in the
1204 whiche—which
1207 ioynture—Ioyngture
1208 faire—fayr
</small>

<small>
1208 haþ—MS. haþe
1210 laste—last
worlde—world
1212 myche—mochel
1213 desserued — MS. desseyued, C. desseruyd
weye—wey
shullen—sholden
1215 mychel—mochel
1217 fair werk—fayre werke
worlde—world
1219 clere—cler
</small>

on þe sterres. *and* on þe sonne. *and* on þe mone.
Philosophie. ¶ Apperteineþ qu*od* she any of þilke
þinges to þe. whi darst þou glorifie þe in þe shynynge
of any swiche þinges. Art þou distingwed *and* em- 1223
belised by þe spryngyng floures of þe first somer
sesou*n*. or swelliþ þi plente in fruytes of somer. whi
art þou rauyshed wiþ ydel ioies. why enbracest þou
straunge goodes as þei weren þine. Fortune shal neuer
maken þat swiche þinges ben þine þat nature of þinges
maked foreyne fro þe. ¶ Syche is þat wiþ-oute*n*
doute þe fruytes of þe erþe owen to ben on þe
norssinge of bestes. ¶ And if þou wilt fulfille þi
nede after þat it suffiseþ to nature þan is it no nede
þat þou soke after þe superfluite of fortune. ¶ For
wiþ ful fewe þinges *and* wit*h* ful lytel þing nature
halt hire appaied. *and* yif þou wilt achoken þe ful-
fillyng of nature wiþ superfluites ¶ Certys þilke 1236
þinges þat þou wilt presten or pouren in to nature
shullen ben vnioyeful to þe or ellis anoies. ¶ Wenest
þou eke þat it be a fair þinge to shine wiþ dyuerse
cloþing. of whiche cloþing yif þe beaute be agreable
to loken vpon. I wol merueylen on þe nature of þe
matere of þilke cloþes. or ellys on þe werkeman þat
wrou3t[e] hem. but al so a longe route of meyne. makiþ
þat a blisful *man. þe whiche seruauntes yif þei ben
vicioūs of condicio*u*ns it is a greet charge *and* a de-
strucciou*n* to þe house. *and* a greet enmye to þe lorde
hym self ¶ And yif þei ben goode men how shal
straung[e] or foreyne goodenes ben put in þe nou*m*bre
of þi rycchesse. so þat by alle þise forseide þinges. it is
clerly shewed þat neuer none of þilke þinges þat þou
accoumptedest for þin goodes nas nat þi goode. ¶ In
þe whiche þinges yif þer be no beaute to ben desired.

Does it add to a man's worth to shine in variety of costly clothing? The things really to be admired are the beauty of the stuff or the workmanship of it. Doth a great retinue make thee happy? If thy servants be vicious, they are [* fol. 12 *b*.] a great burden to the house, and pernicious enemies to the master of it. If they be good, why should the probity of others be put to thy account? Upon the whole, then, none of those enjoyments which thou didst consider as thy own did ever properly belong to thee.

as well as the sun, moon, and stars. *P*. Do these things concern thee? darest thou glory in them? Do the flowers adorn you with their variety? Why embracest thou things wherein thou hast no property? Fortune can never make that thine which the nature of things forbids to be so. The fruits of the earth are designed for the support of beasts. If you seek only the necessities of nature, the affluence of Fortune will be useless. Nature is content with a little, and superfluity will be both disagreeable and hurtful.

1222 *darst þou glorifie* — darsthow gloryfyen
1225 *in* — in the
1229 *Syche* — Soth
1230 *on* — to
1231, 1235, 1237 *wilt* — wolt

1238 *shullen* — shollen
1239 *fair* — fayre
1240 *whiche* — which
1242 *werkeman* — werkman
1246 *house* — hows
lorde — lord

1248 *goodenes* — goodnesse
1250 *shewed* — I-shewyd
none — oon
1251 *þin* — thine
goode — good

If they be not desirable, why shouldst thou grieve for the loss of them?	whi sholdest þou be sory yif þou leese hem. or whi sholdest þou reioysen þe to holden hem. ¶ For if þei
If they are fair by nature, what is that to thee?	ben fair of hire owen kynde. what apperteneþ þat to
They would be equally agreeable whether thine or not.	þe. for as wel sholde þei han ben faire by hem self. þou3 þei weren depa*r*tid from alle þin rycchesse. ¶ For-
They are not to be reckoned precious because they are counted amongst thy goods, but because they seemed so before thou didst desire to possess them.	why faire ne precioūs ne weren þei nat. for þat þei comen amonges þi rycchesse. but for þei semeden fair *and* precious. þerfore þou haddest leuer rekene hem amonges þi rycchesse. but what desirest þou of fortune wiþ so greet a noyse *and* wiþ so greet a fare ¶ I
What, then, is it we so clamorously demand of Fortune? Is it to drive away indigence by abundance? But the very reverse of this happens, for there is need of many helps to keep a variety of valuable goods. 1268	trowe þou seke to dryue awey nede wiþ habundaunce of þinges. ¶ But certys it turneþ to 3ow al in þe contrarie. for whi certys it nediþ of ful many[e] help- ynges to kepen þe dyuersite of preciouse ostelment3. and soþe it is þat of many[e] þinges han þei nede þat many[e] þinges han. *and* a3eyneward of litel nediþ
They want most things who have the most. They want the fewest who measure their abundance by the necessities of nature, and not by the superfluity of their desires.	hem þat mesuren hir fille after þe nede of kynde *and* nat after þe outrage of couetyse ¶ Is it þan so þat ye men ne han no propre goode. I-set in 3ow. For whiche 3e moten seken outwardes 3oure goodes in foreine *and* subgit þinges. ¶ So is þan þe condicio*u*n
Is there no good planted within ourselves, that we are obliged to go abroad to seek it? Are things so changed and in- verted, that god- like man should think that he has no other worth but what he de- rives from the possession of in- animate objects? Inferior things are satisfied with their own endow- ments, while man (the image of God) seeks to adorn his nature	of þinges turned vpso dou*n*. þat a man þat is a de- vyne beest by merit of hys resou*n*. þinkeþ þat hy*m* self nys neyþer fair ne noble. but if it be þoru3 possessiou*n* of ostelmentes. þat ne han no soules. ¶ And certys al oþer þinges ben appaied of hire owen beautes. but 3e men þat ben semblable to god by 3oure resonable þou3t desiren to apparaille 3oure excellent kynde of þe lowest[e] þinges. ne 3e ne vndirstonde nat how gret a wrong 3e don to 3oùre creatou*r*. for he wolde þat man kynde were moost worþi *and* noble of

1255 *fair*—fayre
  hire owen—hyr owne
1256 *sholde*—sholden
  self—seluc
1257 *þin rycchesse*—thyne
  rychesses
1259 *amonges*—amonge
1259, 1261 *rycchesse*—Rych-

cases
1259 *fair*—fayre
1260 *leuer rekene*—leuere
  rekne
1262 *greet* (2)—grete
1265, 1267 *many[e]*—manye
1267 *soþe*—soth
1272 *outwardes*—owtward

1276 *fair*—fayre
  if—yif
1278 *hire owen*—hir owne
1281 *ne* (2)—omitted
  vndirstonde—vndyrstond-
  yn
1282 *gret*—MS. grete, C. gret

any oþer erþely þinges. and ȝe þresten adoun ȝoure dignitees by-neþen þe lowest[e] þinges. ¶ For if þat al þe good of euery þing be more preciouse þan is þilk þing whos þat þe good. is. syn ȝe demen þat þe foulest[e] þinges ben ȝoure goodes. þanne summytten ȝe *and* putten ȝoure self vndir þo foulest[e] þinges by ȝoure estimacioun. ¶ And certis þis bitidiþ. nat wiþ out ȝoure desert. For certys swiche is þe condicioun of al man kynde þat oonly whan it haþ knowyng of it self. þan passeþ it in noblesse alle oþer þinges. and whan it forletiþ þe knowyng of it self. þan it is brouȝt byneþen alle beestes. ¶ For-why alle oþer [leuynge] beestes han of kynde to knowe not hem self. but whan þat men leten þe knowyng of hem self. it comeþ hem of vice. but how brode sheweþ þe errour *and* þe folie of ȝow men þat wenen þat ony þing may ben apparailled wiþ straunge apparaillementȝ ¶ but for-soþe þat may nat be don. for yif a wyȝt shyneþ wiþ þinges þat ben put to hym. as þus. yif þilke þinges shynen wiþ whiche a man is apparailled.. ¶ Certis þilke þinges ben commendid *and* preised wiþ whiche he is apparailled. ¶ But naþeles þe þing þat is couered *and* wrapped vndir þat dwelleþ in his filþe. and I denye þat þilke þing be good þat anoyeþ hym þat haþ it. ¶ Gabbe I of þis. þou wolt seye nay. ¶ Certys rycchesse han anoyed ful ofte hem þat han þo rycchesse. ¶ Syn þat euery wicked shrew *and* for hys wickednesse þe more gredy aftir oþer folkes rycchesse wher so euer it be in any place. be it golde. or

with things infinitely below him, not understanding how much he dishonours his Maker. God intended man to excel all earthly creatures, yet you debase your dignity and prerogative below the lowest beings. In placing your happiness in despicable trifles, you acknowledge yourselves of less value than these trifles, and well do you merit to be so esteemed. Man only excels other creatures when he knows himself. When he ceases to do so, he sinks below beasts. **1297** Ignorance is natural to beasts, but in men it is unnatural and criminal. How weak an error is it to believe that anything foreign to your nature can be an ornament to it. If a thing appear beautiful on account of its external embellishments, we admire and praise those embellishments alone. The thing covered still continues in its natural impurity. I deny that to be a good which is hurtful to its owner. Am I deceived in this? You will say no; for riches have often hurt their possessors. Every wicked man desires

---

1284 *oþer erþely* — oothre wordly
  þresten — threste
1285 *by-neþen* — by-nethe
  if — yif
1286 *good* — MS. goode, C. good
  þing — thinge
  preciouse — preyyos
  þilk þing — thilke thinge
1287 *þe (2)* — tho
1288 *summytten* — submitten
1289 *self* — seluen

1289 *foulest[e]* — fowleste
1290 *bitidiþ* — tydeth
1291 *out* — owte
  desert — desertes
1292 *al* — alle
1293 *self* — selue
1294 *it is* — is it
1296 [*leuynge*] — from C.
  hem — hym
1297 *þat* — omitted
1298 *comeþ* — comth
1299 *þing* — thinge
1302 *put* — MS. putte, C. put

1303 *whiche* — which
1306 *filþe* — felthe
1307 *þing* — thinge
  good — MS. goode, C. good
1308 *haþ* — MS. hnþe
1309 *rycchesse* — Rychesses
  þe — tho
1310 *rycchesse* — Rychesses
  shrew — shrewe
1311 *rycchesse* — rychesses
1312 *golde* — gold

[* fol. 13.]
another's wealth, and esteems him alone happy who is in possession of riches.
You, therefore, who now so much dread the instruments of assassination, if you had been born a poor wayfaring man, might, with an empty purse, have sung in the face of robbers. O the transcendant felicity of riches! No sooner have you obtained them, than you cease to be secure.

precious stones. *and* weniþ hym *only most worþi þat
haþ hem ¶ þou þan þat so besy dredest now þe swerde
and þe spere. yif þou haddest entred in þe paþe of þis
lijf a voide wayfaryng man. þan woldest þou syng[e]
by-fore þe þeef. ¶ As who seiþ a poure man þat bereþ
no rycchesse on hym by þe weye. may boldly syng[e]
byforne þeues. for he haþ nat wher-of to ben robbed.
¶ O preciouse *and* ryȝt clere is þe blysfulnesse of
mortal rycchesse: þat whan þou hast geten it. þan hast
þou lorn þi syke[r]nesse.

FELIX IN MIRUM PRIOR ETAS.

[The fyfthe metur.]
Happy was the first age of men. They were contented with what the faithful earth produced. With acorns they satisfied their hunger. They knew not Hypocras nor Hydromel.

They did not dye the Serian fleece in Tyrian purple.

1332

They slept upon the grass, and drank of the running stream, and reclined under the shadow of the tall pine. No man yet ploughed the deep, nor did the merchant traffick with foreign shores.

Blysful was þe first age of men. þei helden hem
apaied wiþ þe metes þat þe trewe erþes brouȝten
furþe. ¶ þei ne destroyed[e] ne desceyued[e] not hem
self wiþ outerage. ¶ þei weren wont lyȝtly to slaken
her hunger at euene wiþ acornes of okes ¶ þei ne
couþe nat medle þe ȝift of bacus to þe clere hony.
þat is to seyn. þei couþe make no piment of clarre.
ne þei couþe nat medle þe briȝt[e] flies of þe contre
of siriens wiþ þe venym of tirie. þis is to seyne. þei
couþe nat dien white flies of sirien contre wiþ þe
blode of a manar shelfysshe. þat men fynden in tyrie.
wiþ whiche blode men deien purper. ¶ þei slepen
holesom slepes vpon þe gras. and dronken of þe rynnyng
watres. *and* laien vndir þe shadowe of þe heyȝe
pyne trees. ¶ Ne no gest ne no straunger [ne] karf
ȝit þe heye see wiþ oores or wiþ shippes. ne þei ne

1314 *haþ*—MS. haþe, C. hat	1322 *lorn*—MS. lorne, C. lorn	1331 *seyne*—seyn
besy—bysy	1324 *erþes*—feeldes	1332 *couþe*—cowde
swerde—swerd	1325 *furþe*—forth	*dien*—deyen
1315 *paþe*—paath	*destroyed[e]*—dystroyede	*flies*—fleȝes
1316 *wayfaryng*—wayferynge	1327 *her*—hyr	1333 *blode*—blood
syng[e]—synge	*at*—MS. as, C. at	*shelfysshe*—shyllefyssh
1317 *by-fore*—by-forn	*euene*—euen	1334 *blode*—blood
seiþ—MS. selþe, C. seyth	1328 *couþe*—cowde	1335 *holesom*—holsom
poure—pore	*medle*—medly	*rynnyng watres*—rennynge wateres
bereþ—berth	*ȝift*—yifte	*shadowe*—shadwes
1318 *boldly syng[e]*—boldely synge	*clere*—cleer	*heyȝe*—heye
1319 *haþ*—MS. haþe	1329 *couþe*—cowde	1337 *pyne*—pyn
1320 *preciouse*—precyos	*of*—nor	*no (2)*—omitted
clere—cler	1330 *couþe*—cowde	*[ne]*—from C.
1321 *rycchesse*—rychesses	*briȝt[e] flies*—bryhte ficeȝes	*karf*—karue
	1331 *siriens*—Seryens	

hadden seyne ȝitte none newe stroudes to loden mer- 1339
chaundyse in to dyuerse contres. ¶ þo weren þe cruel *The warlike trumpet was*
clariouns ful whist and ful stille. ne blode yshed by *hushed and still. Bloodshed had*
egre hate ne hadde nat deied ȝit armurers. for wherto *not yet arisen through hateful*
or whiche woodenesse of enmys wolde first moeuen *quarrels. Nothing could stimulate their*
armes. whan þei seien cruel woundes ne none medes *rage to engage in war, when they*
ben of blood yshad ¶ I wolde þat oure tymes sholde *saw that wounds and scars were*
turne aȝeyne to þe oolde maneres. ¶ But þe anguissous *the only meeds. O that those days would come*
loue of hauyng brenneþ in folke moore cruely þan þe *again! The thirst of*
fijr of þe Mountaigne of Ethna þat euer brenneþ. *wealth torments all; it rages more*
¶ Allas what was he þat first dalf vp þe gobets or *fiercely than Ætna's fires.*
þe weyȝtys of gold couered vndir erþe. and þe precious *Cursed be the wretch who first*
stones þat wolden han ben hid. he dalf vp precious *brought gold to light.*
perils. þat is to seyne þat he þat hem first vp dalf. he 1352
dalf vp a precious peril. for-whi. for þe preciousnesse *It has since proved perilous*
of swyche haþ many man ben in peril. *to many a man.*

QUID AUTEM DE DIGNITATIBUS ET CETERA.

[The sixte prose.]

But what shal I seyne of dignitees and of powers. *But why should I discourse of dig-*
þe whiche [ye] men þat neiþer knowen verray dig- *nities and powers which (though*
nitee ne verray power areysen hem. as heye as þe *you are ignorant of true honour*
heuene. þe whiche dignitees and powers yif þei come *and real power) you extol to the*
to any wicked man þei don [as] greet[e] damages and *skies? When they fall to the lot of a*
distruccioun as doþ þe flamme of þe Mountaigne *wicked man, they produce greater*
Ethna whan þe flamme wit walwiþ. vp ne. no deluge *calamities than the flaming*
ne doþ so cruel harmes. ¶ Certys ye remembriþ wel *eruption of Ætna, or the most im-*
as I trowe þat þilke dignitee þat men clepiþ þe em- *petuous deluge. You remember*
perie of consulers þe whiche þat somtyme was by- *that your an- cestors desired to*
gynnyng of fredom. ¶ ȝoure eldres coueiteden to han *abolish the Con- sular government*
don a-wey þat dignitee for þe pride of þe conseilers. *(the commence- ment of the Roman liberty),*

1339 *hadden seyne ȝitte*—
hadde seyn yit
1341 *whist*—hust
blode yshed—blod I-shad
1343 *whiche woodenesse*—
whych wodnesse
1344 *seien*—say
1346 *turne aȝeyne*—torne
ayein
1347 *folke*—folk
1348 *þe*—omitted

1348 *euer*—ay
1351 *hid*—MS. hidde, C. hydd
1352 *seyne*—seyn
he (2)—omitted
1354 *swyche*—swych thinge
haþ—MS. haþe
1355 *seyne*—seye
1358 *come*—comen
1359 *don*—MS. done, C. don
[*as*] *greet[e]*—as grete

1360 *distruccioun*—destruc-
ciouns
doþ—MS. doþe, C. doth
flamme—flaumbe
1361 *flamme*—flawmbe
wit—omitted
1362 *doþ*—MS. doþe, C. doth
1363 *clepiþ*—clepyn
1364 *whiche*—whych
somtyme—whilom
1366 *for*—MS. of, C. for

¶ And ry3t for þe same pride 3oure eldres byforne þat tyme hadden don awey out of þe Citee of rome þe kynges name. þat is to seien. þei nolden haue no lenger no kyng ¶ But now yif so be þat dignitees and powers ben 3euen to goode men. þe whiche þing is ful 3elde. what agreable þinges is þer in þo dignitees. or powers. but only þe goodenes of folk þat vsen hem. ¶ And þerfore it is þus þat honour ne comeþ nat to vertue for cause of dignite. but a3einward. honour comeþ to dignite by cause of vertue. but whiche is 3oure derworþe power þat is so clere and so requerable ¶ O 3e erþelyche bestes considere 3e nat ouer whiche þing þat it semeþ þat 3e han power. ¶ Now yif þou say[e] a mouse amongus *oþer myse þat chalenged[e] to hymself ward ry3t and power ouer alle oþer myse. how gret scorne woldest þou han of hit. ¶ Glosa. ¶ So fareþ it by men. þe body haþ power ouer þe body. For yif þow loke wel vpon þe body of a wy3t what þing shalt þou fynde moore frele þan is mannes kynde. þe whiche ben ful ofte slayn wiþ bytynge of smale flies. or ellys wiþ þe entryng of crepyng wormes in to þe priuetees of mennes bodyes. ¶ But wher shal men fynden any man þat may exercen or haunten any ry3t vpon an oþer man but oonly vpon hys body. or ellys vpon þinges þat ben lower þen þe body. whiche I clepe fortunous possessiouns ¶ Mayst þou euer haue any comaundement ouer a fre corage ¶ Mayst þou remuen fro þe estat of hys propre reste. a þou3t þat is cleuyng to gider in hym self by stedfast resoun. ¶ As somtyme a tiraunt wende to confounde a freeman of

corage ¶ *And* wende to constreyne hym by tourment 1397
to maken hym dyscoueren *and* acusen folk þat wisten
of a coniuracio*un*. whiche I clepe a confedcracie þat
was cast aȝeins þis tyraunt ¶ But þis free man boot *Have you not read how Anaxarchus bit off his tongue and spat it in the face of Nicocreon?*
of hys owen tunge. *and* cast it in þe visage of þilke
woode tyraunte. ¶ So þat þe tourmentȝ þat þis
tyraunt wende to han maked matere of cruelte. þis 1403
wyse man maked[e it] matere of vertues. ¶ But what *What is it that one man can do to another that does not admit of retaliation?*
þing is it þat a man may don to an oþer man. þat he
ne may receyue þe same þing of oþer folke *in* hym
self. or þus. ¶ What may a man don to folk. þat folk 1407
ne may don hym þe same. ¶ I haue herd told of *Busiris used to kill his guests, but at last himself was killed by Hercules, his guest.*
busirides þat was wont to sleen hys gestes þat her-
burghden in hys hous. and he was slayn hym self of
ercules þat was hys gest ¶ Regulus had[de] taken in *Regulus put his Carthaginian prisoners in chains, but was afterwards obliged to submit to the fetters of his enemies.*
bataile many men of affrike. and cast hem in to fet-
teres. but sone after he most[e] ȝiue hys handes to
ben bounden w*ith* þe cheynes of hem þat he had[de]
somtyme ouercomen. ¶ Wenest þou þan þat he be *Is he mighty that dares not inflict what he would upon another for fear of a requital? If powers and honours were intrinsically good, they would never be attained by the wicked.*
myȝty. þat may nat don a þing. þat oþer ne may don
hym. þat he doþ to oþer. *and* ȝit more ouer yif it so
were þat þise dignites or poweres hadden any propre
or naturel goodnesse in hem self neuer nolden þei
comen to shrewes. ¶ For contrarious þinges ne ben *An union of things opposite is repugnant to nature.*
not wont to ben yfelawshiped togidres. ¶ Nature re-
fuseþ þat contra[r]ious þinges ben yioigned. ¶ And so 1422
as I am in certeyne þat ryȝt wikked folk han dignitees *But as wicked men do obtain the highest honours, it is clear that honours are not in themselves good, otherwise they would not fall to the share of the unworthy.*
ofte tymes. þan sheweþ it wel þat dignitees *and* powers
ne ben not goode of hir owen kynde. syn þat þei suffren hem self to cleue*n* or ioynen hem to shrewes.
¶ And certys þe same þing may most digueliche Iugen

1399 *whiche*—which
1401 *owen*—owne
1406 *receyue*—resseyuen
 oþer—oothre
1408 *herd told*—MS. herde tolde, C. herd told
1409 *hys*—hise
 herburghden — herberweden
1410 *slayn*—sleyn
1411 *had[de]*—hadde
1413 *most[e]*—moste
1414 *bounden*—bownde
 cheynes —MS. þenes, C. cheynes
 had[de]—hadde
1415 *somtyme*—whylom
1416 *þat*——*þing*—that hath
 no power to don a thinge
 oþer—oothre
1417 *hym*—in hym
 doþ—MS. doþe, C. doth
 to oþer—in oothre
1421 *togidres*—to-gidere
1423 *certeyne*—certein
1424 *tymes*—tyme
1425 *owen*—owne

The worst of men have often the largest share of Fortune's gifts.	*and* seyen of alle þe ȝiftis of fortune þat most plen- teuously comen to shrewes. ¶ Of þe whiche ȝiftys I
We judge him to be valiant who has given evidence of his fortitude.	trowe þat it auȝt[e] ben considered þat no man doutiþ þat he nis strong. in whom he seeþ strengþe. *and* in
1432	whom þat swiftnesse is ¶ Soþe it is þat he is swyfte.
So music maketh a musician, &c.	Also musyk makeþ musiciens. *and* fysik makeþ phi-
The nature of everything consists in doing what is peculiar to itself, and it repels what is contrary to it.	siciens. *and* rethorik rethoriens. ¶ For whi þe na- ture of euery þing makiþ his propretee. ne it is nat entermedled wiþ þe effectis of contrarious þinges. ¶ And as of wil it chaseþ oute þinges þat to it ben
Riches cannot restrain avarice. Power cannot make a man master of himself if he is the slave of his lusts.	contrarie ¶ But certys rycchesse may nat restreyne auarice vnstaunched ¶ Ne power [ne] makeþ nat a man myȝty ouer hym self. whiche þat vicious lustis holden destreined wiþ cheins þat ne mowen nat ben
Dignities conferred upon base men do not make them worthy, but rather expose their want of merit. Why is it so? 'Tis because you give false names to things. You dignify riches, power, and [* fol. 14.] honours, with names they have no title to.	vnbounden. *and* dignitees þat ben ȝeuen to shrewed[e] folk nat oonly ne makiþ hem nat digne. but it sheweþ raþer al openly þat þei ben vnworþi *and* vndigne. ¶ And whi is it þus. ¶ Certis for ȝe han ioye to clepen þinges wiþ fals[e] names. þat beren hem al in þe contrarie. þe whiche names ben ful ofte reproued by þe effect of þe same þinges. so þat *þise ilke rycch- esse ne auȝten nat by ryȝt to ben cleped rycchesse.
1450	ne whiche power ne auȝt[e] not ben cleped power. ne whiche dignitee ne auȝt[e] nat ben cleped dignitee.
In fine, the same may be said of all the gifts of Fortune, in which nothing is desirable, nothing of natural good in them, since they are not always allotted to good men, nor make them good to whom they are attached.	¶ And at þe laste I may conclude þe same þinge of al þe ȝiftes of fortune in whiche þer nis no þing to ben desired. ne þat haþ in hym self naturel bounte. ¶ as it is ful wel sene. for neyþer þei ne ioygnen hem nat alwey to goode men. ne maken hem alwey goode to whom þei ben y-ioigned.

1429 *whiche*—which	1441 *ben*—be	1450 *whiche*—swich
1430 *auȝt[e]*—owhte	1442 *shrewed[e]*—shrewede	*auȝt[e]*—owhte
1432 *Soþe*—soth	1446 *fals[e]*—false	1451 *whiche*—swich
swyfte—swyft	*al*—alle	*auȝt[e]*—owht
1435 *is*—nis	1447 *whiche*—which	1453 *al*—alle
1436 *effectis*—effect	1449 *auȝten*—owhten	1454 *haþ*—MS. haþe
1437 *oute*—owt	*rycchesse*—rychesses	1455 *sene*—1-scene

NOUIMUS QUANTOS DEDERAT.

[The sixte Metur.]

WE han wel knowen how many greet[e] harmes *and* destrucc*i*ouns weren doū by þe Emperoure Nero. ¶ He letee brenne þe citee of Rome *and* made slen þe senato*u*rs. and he cruel somtyme slou3 hys broþer. *and* he was maked moyst wiþ þe blood of hys modir. þat is to seyn he let sleen *and* slitten þe body of his modir to seen where he was conceiued. *and* he loked[e] on euery half vpon hir colde dede body. ne no tere ne wette his face. but he was so hard herted þat he my3t[e] ben domesman or Iuge of hire dede beaute. ¶ And 3itte neuerþeles gouerned[e] þis Nero by Ceptre al þe peoples þat phebus þe sonne m'ay seen comyng from his outerest arysyng til he hidde his bemes vndir þe wawes. ¶ þat is to seyne. he gouerned[e] alle þe peoples by Ceptre im-pe*r*ial þat þe so*n*ne goþ aboute from est to west ¶ And eke þis Nero goueyrende by Ceptre. alle þe peoples þat ben vndir þe colde sterres þat hy3ten þe seuene triones. þis is to seyn he gouerned[e] alle þe poeples þat ben vndir þe p*a*rties of þe norþe. ¶ And eke Nero gouerned[e] alle þe poeples þat þe violent wynde Nothus scorchiþ *and* bakiþ þe brennynge sandes by his drie hete. þat is to seyne. alle þe poeples in þe souþe. [but yit ne myhte nat al his heye power torne the woodnesse of this wykkyd nero / Allas it is greuous fortune it is]. as ofte as wicked swerde is ioygned to cruel venym. þat is to sein. venimous cruelte to lordshipe.

We know what ruin Nero did. 1459
He burnt Rome, he slew the conscript fathers, murdered his brother, and spilt his mother's blood.
He looked unmoved upon his mother's corpse, and passed judgment upon her beauty.
1467
Yet this parricide ruled over all lands, illumined by the sun in his diurnal course, and controlled the frozen regions of the pole.
1472

1475
He governed, too, the people in the torrid zone.

1478
But yet Nero's power could not tame his ferocious mind.
It is a grievous thing when power strengthens the arm of him whose will prompts him to deeds of cruelty.

1458 *greet[e]*—grete
1460 *letee*—let
1461 *somtyme slou3*—whilom slow
1463 *let*—lette
1464 *where*—wher
1465 *half*—halue
1466 *my3t[e]*—myhte
1467 *hire*—hyr
1468 *neuerþeles*—natheles *gouerned[e]*—gouernede
1469 *al*—alle
1469 *from*—fram *outerest*—owtereste
1470 *hidde*—hide
1471 *seyne*—seyn
1472 *goþ*—MS. goþe, C. goth
1473 *goueyrende*—gouernyd
1474 *triones*—tyryones
1475 *gouerned[e]*—gouernede
1476 *parties*—party *norþe*—north
1476 *gouerned[e]* — gouerncde
1477 *wynde*—wynd *scorchiþ*—scorklith
1479 *seyne*—seyn *souþe*—sowth
1479-81 [*but*—*it is*]—MS. has: but ne how greuous fortune is
1482 *swerde*—swerd

TUM EGO SCIS INQUAM.

[The seuende prose.]
B. Thou knowest that I did not covet mortal and transitory things.
I only wished to exercise my virtue in public concerns, lest it should grow feeble by inactivity.

Þanne seide I þus. þou wost wel þiself þat þe couetise of mortal þinges ne hadden neuer lordshipe of me. but I haue wel desired matere of þinges to done. as who seiþ. I desired[e] to han matere of gouernaunce ouer comunalites. ¶ For vertue stille ne sholde not elden. þat is to seyn. þat list þat or he wex

1490 olde ¶ His uertue þat lay now ful stille. ne sholde nat perisshe vnexcercised in gouernaunce of comune.

P. A love of glory is one of those things that may captivate minds naturally great, but not yet arrived at the perfection of virtue.

¶ For whiche men myȝten speke or writen of his goode gouernement. ¶ Philosophie. ¶ For soþe quod she. and þat is a þing þat may drawen to gouernaunce swiche hertes as ben worþi and noble of hir nature. but naþeles it may nat drawen or tollen swiche hertes as ben y-brouȝt to þe ful[le] perfeccioun of vertue. þat is

But consider how small and void of weight is that glory.

to seyn couetyse of glorie and renoun to han wel administred þe comune þinges. or doon goode decertes

1500 to profit of þe comune. for se now and considere how litel and how voide of al prise is þilke glorie. ¶ Certeine þing is as þou hast lerned by demonstracioun of astronomye þat al þe envyronynge of þe erþe aboute ne halt but þe resoun of a prykke at regard of þe gretnesse of heuene. þat is to seye. þat yif þat þer were maked comparisoun of þe erþe to þe gretnesse of

Astronomy teaches us that this globe of earth is but a speck compared with the extent of the heavens, and is as nothing if compared with the magnitude of the celestial sphere.

1507 heuene. men wolde Iugen in alle þat erþe [ne] helde no space ¶ Of þe whiche litel regioun of þis worlde þe ferþe partie is enhabitid wiþ lyuyng beestes þat we knowen. as þou hast þi self lerned by tholome þat prouiþ it. ¶ yif þou haddest wiþ drawen and abated in þi þouȝte fro þilke ferþe partie as myche space as þe see and [the] mareys contenen. and ouergon and as myche space as þe regioun of droughte ouerstreccheþ.

Ptolemy shows that only one-fourth of this earth is inhabited by living creatures.

Deduct from this the space occupied by seas, marshes, lakes, and deserts, and there remains but a small proportion left for the abode of man.

1487 desired[e]—desyre
1489 wex olde—wnx old
1492 whiche—which
speke—spekyn
1496 tollen—MS. tellen, C. tollen

1497 ful[le]—fulle
1501 al prise—alle prys
1503 seye—seyn
1507 wolde—woldyn
alle—al
[ne]—from C.

1510 lerned—ylerned
1512 þouȝte—thowht
myche—moche
1513 [the]—from C.
1514 myche space—moche spaces

FAME IS CIRCUMSCRIBED.

þat is to seye saudes *and* desertes wel vnneþ sholde
*þer dwellen a ryȝt streite place to þe habitacioun of
men. *and* ȝe þan þat ben environed *and* closed wiþ
inne þe leest[e] prikke of þilk prikke þenke ȝe to
manifesten ȝoure renou*n* *and* don ȝoure name to ben
born forþe. but ȝoure glorie þat is so narwe *and* so
streyt yþronge*n* in to so litel boundes. how myche
conteinþe it in largesse *and* in greet doynge. And also
sette þis þer to þat many a naciou*n* dyuerse of tonge
and of maneres. *and* eke of resou*n* of hir lyuyng ben
enhabitid in þe cloos of þilke litel habitacle. ¶ To þe
whiche naciou*n*s what for difficulte of weyes. *and* what
for diu*er*site of langages. *and* what for defaute of
vnusage entercomunynge of marchau*n*dise. nat only þe
names of singler men ne may [nat] strecchen. but eke
þe fame of Citees ne may nat strecchen. ¶ At þe
last[e] Certis in þe tyme of Marcus tulyus as hym
self writeþ in his book þat þe renou*n* of þe comune of
Rome ne hadde nat ȝitte passed ne cloumben ou*er* þe
mou*n*taigne þat hyȝt Caucasus. *and* ȝitte was þilk
tyme rome wel wexen *and* gretly redouted of þe parthes.
and eke of oþer folk enhabityng aboute. ¶ Sest þou
nat þan how streit *and* how compressed is þilke glorie
þat ȝe trauailen aboute to shew *and* to multiplie. May
þan þe glorie of a singlere Romeyne strecchen þider
as þe fame of þe name of Rome may nat clymben ne
passen. ¶ And eke sest þou nat þat þe maners of
diuerse folk *and* eke hir lawes ben discordau*n*t amonge
hem self. so þat þilke þing þat sommen iugen worþi of
preysynge. oþer folk iugen þat it is worþi of torment.
¶ and þer of comeþ þat þouȝ a man delite hy*m* in

1515
[* fol. 14 b.]

And do you, who are confined to the least point of this point, think of nothing but of blazing far and wide your name and reputation ? What is there great in a glory so circumscribed ?

1522

Even in this contracted circle, there is a great variety of nations,

to whom not only the fame of particular men, but even of great cities, cannot extend.

1529

In the time of Marcus Tullius the fame of Rome did not reach beyond Mount Caucasus.

1535

How narrow, then, is that glory which you labour to propagate. Shall the glory of a Roman citizen reach those places where the name even of Rome was never heard ? Customs and Institutions differ in different countries. What is praiseworthy in one is blame-worthy in another.

1545

1515 *seye*—seyn	1520 *narwe*—narwh	1533 *hadde*—hadden
1516 *streite*—streyt	1521 *streyt*—streyte	*ȝitte*—omitted
1517 þan—thanne	*myche*—mochel	1534 *hyȝt*—hyhte
1518 *inne*—in	1522 *conteinþe*—coueyteth	þilk—thikke
leest[e]—leste	1525 *habitacle*—MS. habit-	1535 *wexen*—waxen
þilk—thilke	ache, C. habytacule	1536 *Sest þou*—sestow
þenke ȝe—thinken ye	1529 [*nat*]—from C.	1538 *shew*—shewe
1520 *born forþe*—MS. borne,	1531 *last*[e]—laste	1539 *singlere*—singler
C. born, forth	1532 *writeþ*—writ	1545 *comeþ*—comth it

It is not the interest of any man who desires renown to have his name spread through many countries. He ought, therefore, to be satisfied with the glory he has acquired at home. But of how many personages, illustrious in their times, have the memorials been lost through the carelessness and neglect of writers. But writings do not preserve the names of men for ever.

*p*reysyng of his renou*n*. he ne may nat i*n* no wise bryngen furþe ne spreden his name to many manere peoples. ¶ And þerfore euery man*er* man au3te to ben paied of hys glorie þat is puplissed among hys owen ney3bores. ¶ And þilke noble renou*n* shal be restreyned wiþ-inne þe boundes of o maner folk but how many a man þat was ful noble in his tyme. haþ þe nedy *and* wrecched for3etynge of writers put oute of mynde *and* don awey. ¶ Al be it so þat certys þilke writynges profiten litel. þe whiche writynges longe *and* derke elde doþ aweye boþe hem *and* eke her autou*rs*. but

1557

But perhaps you suppose that you shall secure immortality if your names are transmitted to future ages. If you consider the infinite space of eternity you will have no reason to rejoice in this supposition. If a *moment* be compared with 10,000 years, there is a proportion between them, though a very small one. But this number of years, multiplied by whatever sum you please, vanishes when compared with the infinite extent of eternity. There may be comparison between finite things, but none between the infinite and finite. Hence it is, that Fame (however lasting), compared with eternity, will seem absolutely nothing.

3e men semen to geten 3ow a p*er*durablete whan 3e þenke þat in tyme comyng 3oure fame shal lasten. ¶ But naþeles yif þou wilt maken com*p*arisou*n* to þe endeles space of eternite what þing hast þou by whiche þou maist reioysen þe of lo*n*g lastyng of þi name. ¶ For if þer were maked comparysou*n* of þe abidyng of a mome*n*t to ten þousand wynter. for as myche as boþe þo spaces ben endid. ¶ For 3it haþ þe moment some porciou*n* of hit al þou3 it a litel be. ¶ But naþeles þilke self noumbre of 3eres. and eke as many 3eres as þer to may be multiplied. ne may nat certys be comparisou*n*d to þe p*er*durablete þat is een[de]les. ¶ For of þinges þat han ende may be mad comparisou*n* [but of thinges that ben w*ith*-owtyn ende to thinges þat han ende may be maked no com*p*arysou*n*]. ¶ And for þi is it al þou3 renou*n* of as longe tyme as euer þe lyst to þinken were þou3t by þe regard of eternite. þat is vnstaunchable *and* infinit. it ne sholde nat oonly semen litel. but pleinliche ry3t nou3t. ¶ But 3e men certys ne konne

1547 *furþe*—forth
   manere—maner
1548 *þerfore*—ther-for
   au3te—owhte
1549 *paied*—apayed
   hys owen—hiso owne
1550 *ney3bores*—nessheboures
   be—ben
1552 *haþ*—MS. haþe [put owt
1553 *put* (MS. *putte*) *oute*—

1556 *derke*—derk
   doþ aweye—MS. doþe, C.
      doth a-wey
   her autours—hir actorros
1557 *3e*—yow
   semen—semetn
1558 *comyng*—to comynge
1559 *wilt*—wolt
1560 *whiche*—which
1563 *myche*—mochel

1564 *þo*—tho
   haþ—MS. haþe
   some—som
1566 *self*—sclue
1567 *be* (2)—ben
1568 *een[de]les*—endeles
1569 *mad* — MS. made, C.
      maked
   [*but — comparysoun*] —
1573 *by*—to   [from C.

don no þing aryȝt. but ȝif it be for þe audience of poeple.
and for ydel rumours. and ȝe forsaken þo grete worþi-
nesse of conscience and of vertue. and ȝe seken ȝoure
gerdouns of þe smale wordes of strange folke. ¶ Haue
now here and vndirstonde in þe lyȝtnesse of whiche
pride and veyne glorie. how a man scorned[e] festiualy
and myrily swiche vanite. somtyme þere was a man þat
had[de] assaied wiþ striuyng wordes an oþer man. ¶ þe
whiche nat for vsage of verrey vertue. but for proude
veyne glorie had[de] taken vpon hym falsly þe name
of a philosopher. ¶ þis raþer man þat I speke of
þouȝt[e] he wolde assay[e] where he þilke were a philosopher or no. þat is to seyne yif he wolde han suffred
lyȝtly in pacience þe wronges *þat weren don vnto
hym. ¶ þis feined[e] philosophre took pacience a
litel while. and whan he hadde receiued wordes of
outerage he as in stryuynge aȝeine and reioysynge of
hym self seide at þe last[e] ryȝt þus. ¶ vndirstondest
þou nat þat I am a philosophere. þat oþer man answered[e] aȝein ful bityngly and seide. ¶ I had[de]
wel vndirstonden [yt]. yif þou haddest holden þi tonge
stille. ¶ But what is it to þise noble worþi men.
For certys of swyche folk speke .I. þat seken glorie wiþ
vertue. what is it quod she. what atteiniþ fame to
swiche folk whan þe body is resolued by þe deeþ. atte
þe last[e]. ¶ For yif so be þat men dien in al. þat is
to seyne body and soule. þe whiche þing oure resoun
defendiþ vs to byleuen þanne is þere no glorie in no
wyse. For what sholde þilke gloric ben. for he of
whom þis glorie is seid to be nis ryȝt nouȝt in no wise.
and ȝif þe soule whiche þat haþ in it self science of

1590

1600

1605

Margin notes:
But yet you do good from no other view than to have the empty applause of the people, foregoing the pleasures of a good conscience in order to have the praises of other people. This silly vanity was once thus ingeniously and pleasantly rallied. A certain man, who had assumed the name of a philosopher through a love of vain-glory, was told by a man of humour that he could prove he was a philosopher by bearing patiently the injuries offered him. [* fol. 15.]

After counterfeiting patience for a while, the sophist said to the other, 'You must surely confess that I am a philosopher.'
'I might have believed it,' said the other, 'had you held your tongue.'
What advantage is it to great and worthy men to be extolled after death?
If body and soul die, then there can be no glory; nor can there be when he (to whom it is ascribed) does not exist.

1580 *whiche*—swych
1581 *scorned*[e]—scornede
1582 *swiche*—swych
    somtyme—whilom
1583 *had*[de]—hadde
1584 *whiche*—which
    proude—prowd
1586 *speke*—spak
1587 *þouȝt*[e]—thowhte
1587 *assay*[e]—assaye
1589 *seyne*—seyn
1590 *feined*[e]—feynede
1592 *aȝeine*—ayein
1593 *last*[e]—laste
    vndirstondest þou—vn-dyrstondow
1594 *answered*[e]—answerde
1595 *had*[de]—hadde
1596 [yt]—from C.
1601 *last*[e]—laste
1602 *seyne*—seyn
1604 *for* (2)—whan
1605 *þis*—thilke
    seid—MS. seide, C. seyd
    nouȝt—nawht
1606 *haþ*—MS. haþe

DEATH PUTS AN END TO RENOWN.

But if the soul is immortal when it leaves the body, it takes no thought of the joys of this world.

goode werkes vnbounden fro þe prisoun of þe erþe wendeþ frely to þe heuene. dispiseþ it nouȝt þan alle erþely occupaciouns. *and* beynge in heuene reioiseþ þat it is exempt from alle erþely þinges [as wo seith / 1611 thanne rekketh the sowle of no glorye of renoun of this world].

QUICUMQUE SOLAM MENTE.

[The 7th Metre.] Let him who seeks fame, thinking it to be the sovereign good, look upon the broad universe and this circumscribed earth; and he will then despise a glorious name limited to such a confined space.

Who so þat wiþ ouerþrowyng þouȝt only sekeþ glorie of fame. *and* weniþ þat it be souereyne good ¶ Lete hym loke vpon þe brode shewyng contreys of þe heuen. *and* vpon þe streite sete of þis erþe. *and* he shal be ashamed of þe encres of his name. þat may nat fulfille þe litel compas of þe erþe. ¶ O what 1619 couciten proude folke to liften vpon hire nekkes in

Will splendid titles and renown prolong a man's life?

ydel *and* dedely ȝok of þis worlde. ¶ For al þouȝ [þat] renoune y-spradde passynge to ferne poeples goþ by dyuerse tonges. and al þouȝ grete houses *and* kyn- 1623 redes shyne wiþ clere titles of honours. ȝit napeles

In the grave there is no distinction between high and low. Where is the good Fabricius now? Where the noble Brutus, or stern Cato?

deeþ dispiseþ al heye glorie of fame. *and* deeþ wrappeþ to gidre þe heye heuedes *and* þe lowe *and* makeþ egal *and* euene þe heyest[e] to þe lowest[e]. ¶ where wonen now þe bones of trewe fabricius. what is now brutus or stiern Caton þe þinne fame ȝit lastynge 1629 of hir ydel names is markid wiþ a fewe lettres. but

Their empty names still live, but of their persons we know nothing.

al þouȝ we han knowen þe faire wordes of þe fames of hem. it is nat ȝeuen to knowe hem þat ben dede *and* consumpt. Liggiþ þanne stille al vtterly vnknowable

Fame cannot make you known.

ne fame ne makeþ ȝow nat knowe. and yif ȝe wene to lyuen þe lenger for wynde of ȝoure mortal name. 1635 whan o cruel day shal rauyshe ȝow. þan is þe secunde deeþ dwellyng in ȝow. *Glosa.* þe first deeþ he clepiþ

1608 *nouȝt þan*—nat thanne
1610 *from*—fro
1610—1612 [*as —— world*]—from C.
1615 *Lete*—Lat
loke—looken
1616 *sete*—Cyte
1617 *be*—ben

1619 *vpon*—vp
1620 *and dedely*—in the dedly
1621 *y-spradde*—ysprad
[*þat*]—from C.
ferne—MS. serue, C. ferne
goþ—MS. goþe, C. goth
1622 *and* (2)—or
1623 *shyne*—shynen

1623 *clere*—cler
1624 *al*—alle
1626 *heyest*[*e*]—heyeste
lowest[*e*]—loweste
1628 *stiern*—MS. sciern, C. stierne
1632 *consumpt*—consumpte
1634 *lenger*—longere

here þe depa*r*tynge of þe body a*nd* þe soule. ¶ and
þe secunde deeþ he clepeþ as here. þe styntynge of
þe renoune of fame.*

It will be effaced by conquering Time, so that death will be doubly victorious.
* The next three chapters are from the Camb. MS.

[SET NE ME INEXORABILE CONTRA.]

BVt for-as-mochel as thow shalt nat wenen q*uo*d she
þat I bere vntretable batayle ayenis fortune // yit
som-tyme it by-falleth þat she desseyuable desscrueth
to han ryht good thank of men // And þat is whan she
hire self opneth / *and* whan she descoue*r*eth hir frownt /
and sheweth hir maneres pa*r*-auenture yit vndir-
stondesthow nat þat .I. shal seye // it is a wondyr þat .I.
desyre to telle / *and* forthi vnnethe may I. vnpleyten my
sentense wi*th* wordes for I. deme þat contraryos fortune
*p*rofiteth more to men than fortune debonayre // For
al-wey whan fortune semeth debonayre than she lyeth 1650
falsly in by-hetynge the hope of welefulnesse // but forsothe *con*traryos fortune is alwey sothfast / whan she
sheweth hir self vnstable thorw hyr chau*n*gynge // the
amyable fortune desseyueth folk / the contrarye fortune
techeth // the amyable fortune byndeth wi*th* the beaute
of false goodys the hertes of folk þat vsen he*m* / the
contrarye fortune vnbyndeth he*m* by þ*e* knowynge of
freele welefulnesse // the amyable fortune maysthow sen
alwey wyndyngu *and* flowynge / *and* euere mysknowynge
of hir self // the contrarye fortune is a-tempre *and* re-
streynyd *and* wys thorw excersyse of hir aduersyte // at
the laste amyable fortune wi*th* hir flaterynges draweth
mys wandrynge men fro the souereyne good // the contraryos fortune ledith ofte folk ayein to sothfast goodes /
and haleth hem ayein as wi*th* an hooke / weenesthow
thanne þat thow owhtest to leten this a lytel thing / þat
this aspre *and* horible fortune hath discoueryd to the /
the thowhtes of thy trewe frendes // For-why this ilke for- 1668

*[The viij prose.]
'But do not believe,' said Philosophy, 'that I am an implacable enemy to Fortune. This inconstant dame sometimes deserves well of men, when she appears in her true colours. And what I say may perhaps appear paradoxical. That is, that adverse fortune is more beneficial than prosperous fortune.*

The latter lies and deceives us, the former displays her natural inconstancy.

That deceives us, this instructs us; that, by a fallacious show of good, enslaves the mind; this, by the knowledge of her fickleness, frees and absolves it.

The one is wavering and incapable of reflection, the other is staid and wise through experience of adversity.

Lastly, prosperous fortune leads men astray. Adversity teaches them wherein real happiness consists.

It renders us no inconsiderable service in enabling us to recognize our true friends.

1637 þe (1)—omitted. 1639 renoune—renoun.

1669 tune hath departyd *and* vncoueryd to the bothe the
certeyn vysages *and* ek the dowtos visages of thy
felawes // wha*n* she departyd awey fro the / she took
1672 awey hyr frendes *and* lafte the thyne frendes // now

At what price would you not have bought this knowledge in your prosperity?

wha*n* thow were ryche *and* weleful as the semede / wit*h*
how mochel woldesthow han bowht the fulle knowynge of this // þat is to seyn the knowynge of thy

Complain not, then, of loss of wealth, since thou hast found infinitely greater riches in your true friends.

verray freendes // now pleyne the nat thanne of Rychesse
.I.-lorn syn thow hast fowndyn the moste p*re*syos kynde
of Rychesses þat is to seyn thy verray frendes.

QUOD MUNDUS STABILI FIDE.

[The vii*j* Met*ur*.]
This world, by an invariable order, suffers change. Elements, that by nature disagree, are restrained by concord.

THat þ*e* world wit*h* stable feith / varieth acordable
chaungynges // þat the contraryos qualite of element₃
holden amonge hem self aliau*n*ce p*er*durable / þat phebu*s*
the sonne wit*h* his goldene chariet / bryngeth forth the
rosene day / þat the mone hath comma*un*dement ouer the

1684 nyhtes // whiche nyhtes hesp*er*us the eue sterre hat browt //

The sea is thus kept within its proper bounds.

þat þ*e* se gredy to flowen constreyneth wit*h* a certeyn ende
hise floodes / so þat it is nat l[e]ueful to strechche hise

1687 brode termes or bowndes vp-on the erthes // þat is to seyn

This concord is produced by love, which governeth earth and sea, and extends its influence to the heavens.

to couere alle the erthe // Al this a-cordau*n*ce of thinges
is bownden wit*h* looue / þat gouerneth erthe *and* see / *and*
hath also comma*un*dement₃ to the heuenes / *and* yif
this looue slakede the brydelis / alle thinges þat now

*If this chain of love were broken all things would be in perpetual strife, and the world would go to ruin.
Love binds nations together, it ties the nuptial knot, and dictates binding laws to friendship.
Men were truly blest if governed by this celestial love!*

louen hem to gederes / wolden maken a batayle contynuely *and* stryuen to fordoon the fasou*n* of this worlde /
the which they now leden in acordable feith by fayre
moeuynges // this looue halt to gideres poeples Ioygned
wit*h* an hooly bond / *and* knytteth sacrement of maryages of chaste looues // And loue enditeth lawes to
trewe felawes // O weleful were mankynde / yif thilke
loue þat gouerneth heuene gouerned[e] yowre corages /

EXPLICIT LIBE*R* 2*us*.

1690 *hath*—H. he hath

INCIPIT LIBER 3us

IAM CANTUM ILLA FINIERAT.

By this she hadde endid hire songe / whan the swetnesse of hire ditee hadde thorw perced me þat was desirous of herkninge / and .I. astoned hadde yit streyhte myn Eres / þat is to seyn to herknè the bet / what she wolde seye // so þat a litel here after .I. seyde thus // O thow þat art souereyn comfort of Angwissos corages // So thow hast remounted and norysshed me with the weyhte of thy sentenses and with delit of thy syngynge // so þat.I. trowe nat now þat .I. be vnparygal to the strokes of fortune / as who seyth. I. dar wel now suffren al the assautes of fortune and wel deffende me fro hyr // and tho remedies whyche þat thow seydest hire byforn weren ryht sharpe Nat oonly þat .I. am nat agrysen of hem now // but .I. desiros of herynge axe gretely to heeren tho remedyes // than seyde she thus // þat feelede .I. ful wel quod she // whan þat thow ententyf and stylle rauysshedest my wordes // and .I. abood til þat thow haddest swych habyte of thy thowght as thow hast now // or elles tyl þat .I. my self had[de] maked to the the same habyt / which þat is a moore verray thinge // And certes the remenaunt of thinges þat ben yit to seye / ben swyche // þat fyrst whan men tasten hem they ben bytynge / but whan they ben resseyuyd with-inne a whyht than ben they swete // but for thow seyst þat thow art so desirous to herkne hem // wit[h] how gret brennynge woldesthow glowen / yif thow wystest whyder .I. wol leden the // whydyre is þat quod .I. // to thilke verray welefulnesse quod she // of whyche thynge herte dremeth // but for as moche as thy syhte is ocupied and distorbed / by Imagynasyon of herthely thynges / thow mayst nat yit sen thilke selue welefulnesse // do quod .I. and shewe

[The fyrste prose.] Philosophy now ended her song. I was so charmed that I kept a listening as if she were still speaking.
At last I said, O sovereign comforter of dejected minds, how much hast thou refreshed me with the energy of thy discourse, so that I now think myself almost an equal match for Fortune and able to resist her blows. I fear not, therefore, thy remedies, but earnestly desire to hear what they are.

1713

P. When I perceived that, silent and attentive, you received my words, I expected to find such a state of mind in you, or rather, I created in you such an one. What remains to be said is of such a nature that when it is first tasted it is pungent and unpleasant, but when once swallowed it turns sweet, and is grateful to the stomach. But because you say you would now gladly hear, with what desire would you burn if you could imagine whither I am going to lead you?
B. Whither is that, I pray?
P. To that true felicity, of which you seem to have but a faint foretaste.

1702 *streyhte*—R. strenghed | 1718 *had*[*de*]—H. hade
1712 *am nat*—H. nam nought |

[sidenote: But your sight is clouded with false forms, so that it cannot yet behold this same felicity.
B. Show me, I pray, that true happiness without delay.
P. I will gladly do so at your desire, but I will first describe that false cause (of happiness), so that you may be better able to comprehend the exact model.

* Here the Add. MS. begins again.
[The fyrst metur.]
He who would sow seed must first clear the ground of useless weeds, so that he may reap an abundant harvest. Honey tastes all the sweeter to a palate disgusted by offensive flavours. The stars shine all the clearer when the southern showery blasts cease to blow. When Lucifer has chased away the dark night, then Phœbus mounts his gay chariot.
So you, beholding the false felicity, and withdrawing your neck from the yoke of earthly affections, will soon see the sovereign good.
[The 2ᵈᵉ prose.] Philosophy, with a serious air, and appearing to re-collect herself, and to rouse up all her faculties, thus began.
All the cares and desires of men seek one end— happiness.
[* fol. 15 b.]*

me / what is thilke verray welefulnesse / .I. preye the wi*th*-howte tarynge // þat wole .I. gladly don q*uod* she / for the cause of the // but .I. wol fyrst marken the by wordes / *and* I wol enforcen me to enformen the // thilke false cause of blysfulnesse þat thow more knowest / so þat whan thow hast fully by-holden thilke false goodes *and* torned thyne eyen to þat oother syde / thow mowe knowe the clernesse of verray blysfulnesse //]

*QUI SERERE INGENIUM.

¶ Who so wil sowe a felde plentiuous. lat hym first delyuer it of þornes *and* kerue asondre wiþ his hooke þe bushes *and* þe ferne so þat þe corne may come*n* heuy of eres a*nd* of greins. hony is þe more swete yif mouþes han firste tastid sauoures þat ben wikke. ¶ þe sterres shynen more agreably whan þe wynde Nothus letiþ his ploungy blastes. *and* aftir þat lucifer þe day sterre haþ chased awey þe derke ny3t. þe day þe feirer lediþ þe rosene horse of þe sonne. ¶ Ry3t so þou byholdyng first þe fals[e] goodes. bygynne to wiþdrawe þi nek[ke] fro þe 3ok of erþely affecc*i*ouns. *and* afterwarde þe verrey goodes sholle*n* entre i*n* to þi corage. 1750

TUNC DEFIXO PAULULUM.

Þ̵O fastned[e] she a lytel þe sy3t of hir eyen a*nd* wiþ-drow hir ry3t as it were in to þe streite sete of hir þou3t. *and* bygan to speke ry3t þus. Alle þe cures q*uo*d she of mortal folk whiche þat trauaylen hem i*n* many manere studies gon certys by diu*er*se weies. ¶ But naþeles þei enforced hem *to come*n* oonly to on

---

1734 *wol*—H. shalle
1739 *wil*—wole
  felde—feeld
1740 *delyuer*—delyuere
  of—fro
  hooke—hook
1741 *bushes*—busses
  ferne—fern
  corne—korn
1743 *firste*—fyrst

1743 *wikke*—wyckyd
1744 *wynde*—wynd
  his—hise
1745 *haþ*—MS. habe
1746 *feirer*—fayrere
1747 *horse*—hors
  Ry3t—And Ryht
1748 *fals*[e]—false
  bygynne—bygyn
  wiþdrawe—with drawen

1748 *nek*[ke]—nekke
1749 *afterwarde* — affterward
1750 *entre*—entren
1751 *fastned*[e]—fastnede
  wiþdrow — MS. wiþdrowen, C. with drowh
1752 *sete*—Cyte
1756 *enforced*—enforscn

ende of blisfulnesse [And blysfulnesse] is swiche a goode þat who so haþ geten it he ne may ouer þat no þing more desiire. and þis þing for soþe is þe souereyne good þat conteiniþ in hym self al manere goodes. to þe whiche goode yif þere failed[o] any þing. it my3t[e] nat ben souereyne goode. ¶ For þan were þere som goode out of þis ilke souereyne goode þat my3t[e] ben desired. Now is it clere and certeyne þan þat blisfulnesse is a perfit estat by þe congregacioun of alle goodes. ¶ þe whiche blisfulnesse as I haue seid alle mortal folke enforcen hem to geten by dyuerse weyes. ¶ For-whi þe couetise of verray goode is naturely y-plaunted in þe hertys of men. ¶ But þe myswandryng errour myslediþ hem in to fals[e] goodes. 1769 ¶ of þe whiche men some of hem wenen þat souereygne goode is to lyue wiþ outen nede of any þing. and trauuilen hem to ben habundaunt of rycchesse. and some oþer men demen. þat souerein goode be forto be ry3t digne of reuerences. and enforcen hem to ben reuerenced among hir ney3bours. by þe honours þat þei han.ygeten ¶ and some folk þer ben þat halden þat ry3t hey3e power to be souereyn goode. and enforcen hem forto regnen or ellys to ioignen hem to hem þat regnen. ¶ And it semeþ to some oþer folk þat noblesse of renoun be þe souerein goode. and hasten hem to geten glorious name by þe artes of werre or of pees. and many folke mesuren and gessen þat souerein goode be ioye and gladnesse and wenen þat it be ry3t blisful [thynge] to ploungen hem in uoluptuous delit. ¶ And þer ben folk þat enterchaungen þe causes and þe endes

Margin notes:
True happiness is that complete good which, once obtained, leaves nothing more to be desired. It is the sovereign good, and comprehends all others. It lacks nothing, otherwise it could not be the supreme good. Happiness is, therefore, that perfect state, in which all other goods meet and centre. It is the object which all men strive after. A desire of the true good is a natural instinct, but error misleads them to pursue false joys. Some, imagining the supreme good to consist in lacking nothing, labour for an abundance of *riches*; others, supposing that this good lies in the *reverence* and *esteem* of their fellow men, strive to acquire honourable positions. There are some, again, who place it in supreme *power*, and seek to rule, or to be favoured by the ruling powers. There are those who fancy *fame* to be the height of happiness, and seek by the arts of war or peace to get renown. Many there are who believe nothing to be better than *joy* and *gladness*, and think it delightful to plunge into luxury.

1757 [*And blysfulnesse*] — *goode*—good [from C.
1758 *so—so* þat
haþ—MS. haþe
1759 *souereyne*—souereyn
1760 *al*—alle
goode—good
1761 *þere*—ther
failed[*e*]—faylyde
my3t[*e*]—myhte
souereyne goode—souereyn good
1762 *þan*—thanne
þere—ther
1762 *goode*—good
souereyne—souereyn
1763 *goode*—good
my3t[*e*]—myhte
1764 *certeyne*—certein
1766 *seid* — MS. acide, C. *folke*—foolk [scyd
1767 *goode*—good
1769 *fals*[*e*]—false
1770 *souereygne goode is* — souereyn good be
1771 *lyue wiþ outen*—lyuen with owte
1772 *rycchesse*—Rychesses
1773 *some*—som
goode be—good ben
1774 *be*—ben
1775 *ney3bours*—neashebors
1776 *halden*—holden
1777 *hey3e*—heyh
to—omitted
goode—good
1780 *goode*—good
1781 *or*—*and*
1782 *folke*—folk
goode—good
1783 *be*—by
1784 [*thynge*]—from C.

Some there are who use these causes and ends Interchangeably, as those who desire riches as a means of getting power; or who desire power in order to get money or renown. In all they do they have a particular end in view. Nobility and popular favour are sought after by some in order to become famous. By others, wives and children are only desired as sources of pleasure. Friendship must not be reckoned among the goods of fortune, but among those of virtue, for it is a very sacred thing. All else are desired either for the power or pleasure they afford.	of þise forseide goodes as þei þat desire*n* rycchesse to han power *and* delices. Or ellis þei desiren power forto han moneye or for cause of renou*n*. ¶ In þise þinges *and in* swyche oþer þinges is tour*n*ed al þe entenc*i*ou*n* of desirynges *and* [of] werkes of men. ¶ As þus. ¶ Noblesse *and* fauo*ur* of poeple whiche þat ʒiueþ as it semeþ a manere clernesse of renou*n*. ¶ and wijf *and* children þat men desiren for cause of delit *and* mirinesse. ¶ But forsoþe frendes ne shollen nat ben rekkened among þe goodes of fortune but of vertue. for it is a ful holy mane*r*e þing. alle þise oþer þinges forsoþe ben taken for cause of power. or ellis for cause of delit. ¶ Certis now am I redy to referen þe goodes of þe body to þise forseide þinges abouen. ¶ For it semeþ þat strengþo *and* gretnesse of body ʒeuen power *and* worþinesse. ¶ and þat beaute *and* swiftenesse ʒeuen
1802 The goods of the body fall under the same predicament. Strength and a good stature seem to give power and worthiness. Beauty and swiftness give glory and fame; and health gives delight. In all these happiness alone is sought. What a man most wishes for, that he esteems the supreme good, which, as we have defined, is happiness. Thou hast now before thee a view of human felicity (falsely so called), that is, riches, honours, power, glory, and delight, which last Epicurus	noblesse *and* glorie of renou*n*. *and* hele of body semeþ ʒiuen delit. ¶ In alle þise þing*us* it semeþ oonly þat blisfulnesse is desired. ¶ For-whi þilke þing þat euery man desireþ moost ouer alle þinges. he demiþ þat be þe souereyne goode. ¶ But I haue diffined þat blisfulnesse is þe souereyne goode. for whiche euery wyʒt demiþ þat þilke estat þat he desireþ ouer alle þinges þat it be þe blisfulnesse. ¶ Now hast þou þan byforne [thy eyen] almost al þe p*ur*posed forme of þe welfulnesse of mankynde. þat is to seyne rycchesse. hono*ur*s. power. glorie. *and* delitʒ. þe whiche delit oonly considered Epicurus Iuged *and* establissed. þat delit is þe souereyne goode. for as myche as alle oþer þinges as hym þouʒt[e] by-refte awey ioie *and* myrþe from þe herte. ¶ But I retou*r*ne aʒcyne to þe studies of meen.

1786 *rycchesse*—rychesses 1787 *delices*—delytes 1789 *oþer*—oothre *al*—alle 1790 [*of*]—from C. 1794 *shollen*—sholden 1795 *þe*—tho 1796 *oþer*—oothre 1801 *swiftenesse*—sweftnesse 1803 ʒ*iuen*—MS. ʒiueþ, C.	yeuen 1806, 1807 *souereyne goode*— souereyn good 1807 *whiche*—whych 1809 *þe*—omitted [forn *þan byforne*—thanne by- 1810 [*thy eyen*]—from C.; MS. *has* ʒeuen aʒeyne *almost*—almest *welfulnesse*—welefulnesse	1811 *seyne rycchesse*—seyn Rychesses 1814 *souereyne goode*—souereyn good *myche*—moche *oþer*—oothre 1815 *þouʒt*[*e*]—thowhte *from*—fram 1816 *aʒeyne*—aycin

of whiche men þe corage alwey rehersiþ *and* sechkeþ þe ‖ considered as the sovereign good.
souereyne goode of alle be it so þat it be wiþ a derke ‖ I now return to the inclinations and pursuits of
memorie [but he not by whiche paath]. ¶ Ryȝt as a ‖ mankind.
dronke man not nat by whiche paþe he may retourne ‖ 1820
home to hys house. ¶ Semeþ it þanne þat folk folyen ‖ Their minds are bent upon the chief good, and
and erren þat enforcen hem to haue nede of no þing ‖ are ever seeking it with a dark-
¶ Certys þer nys non oþer þing þat may so weel *per-* ‖ ened understanding, like a
fourny blisfulnesse as an estat plenteu*ous* *of alle ‖ drunken man, [* fol. 16.]
goodes þat ne haþ nede of none oþer þing. but þat it is ‖ who cannot find his way home.
suffisant of hy*m* self. vnto hym self. and foleyen ‖ Do they go astray who strive to keep themselves from
swyche folk þanne. þat wenen þat þilk þing þat is ‖ want? By no means.
ryȝt goode. þat it be eke ryȝt worþi of honour *and* of ‖ No state is happier than that in
reuerence. ¶ Certis nay. for þat þing nys neyþer foule ‖ which a man is above want, and independent of
ne worþi to ben dispised þat al þe entenc*i*oun of mortel ‖ others. Are they guilty of
folke trauaille forto geten it. ¶ And power auȝt[e] ‖ folly that seek esteem and reverence?
nat þat eke to be rekened amonges goodes what ellis. ‖ No; for that is not contemptible
for it nys nat to wene þat þilke þing þat is most ‖ for which all men strive.
worþi of alle þinges be feble *and* wiþ out strengþe *and* ‖ Is not power to be reckoned amongst
clernesse of reno*un* auȝte þat to ben dispised. ¶ Certys ‖ desirable goods? Why not? For
þer may no man forsake þat al þing þat is ryȝt excellent ‖ that is not an insignificant good which invests a
and noble. þat it ne semeþ to be ryȝt clere *and* re- ‖ man with authority and command.
nomed. ¶ For certis it nediþ nat to seie. þat blisful- ‖ Fame also is to be regarded, for
nesse be anguissous ne dreri ne subgit to greua*n*ces ne ‖ everything excellent is also shining
to sorwes. syn þat in ryȝt litel þing*us* folk seken to ‖ and renowned. We hardly need
haue *and* to vsen þat may deliten hem. ¶ Certys þise ‖ say that happiness is not an unjoyous and
ben þe þinges þat men wolen *and* desyren to geten. ‖ melancholy state, for in the pursuit
and for þis cause desiren þei rycches. dignites. regnes. ‖ of the smallest matters men seek
glorie *and* delices ¶ For þerby wenen þei to han suffi- ‖ only pleasure. Hence it is that
saunce honour power. reno*un* *and* gladnesse. ¶ þanne ‖ mankind seek riches, &c., be-
is it goode. þat men seken þus by so many dyuerse ‖ cause by them they hope to get independence,
studies. In whiche desijr it may lyȝtly be shewed. ‖ honour, &c. However varied

---

1818 *souereyne goode*—souereyn good	1823 *perfourny*—performe	1832 *be*—ben
of—omitted	1825 *haþ*—MS. haþe	1834 *out*—owte
alle—al	*none*—non	1835 *auȝte*—owhte
derke—dirkyd	1827 *þilk*—thilke	1836 *al*—alle
1819 [*but—paath*]—from C.	1828 *goode*—good	1837 *be*—ben
1820 *dronke*—dronken	1829 *foule*—fowl	*clere*—cleer
paþe—paath	1830 *al*—welneyh alle	1843 *rycches*—Rychesses
1821 *home*—hym	1831 *trauaille*—trauaylen	1846 *goode*—good
	auȝt[e]—owhte	1847 *be*—ben

| their desires, happiness is their sole pursuit. However various men's opinions are respecting happiness, all agree in pursuing it as the end of their actions and desires. | how grete is þe strengþe of nature. ¶ For how so þat men han dyuerse sentences *and* discordyng algates men accordyn alle in lyuynge þe ende of goode. | 1850 |

[The 2de Metur.]
I will now sing of Nature's laws, by which the universe is governed.

QUANTAS RERUM FLECTAT.

IT likeþ me to shew[e] by subtil songe wiþ slakke *and* delitable sou*n* of strenges how þat nature my3ty enclineþ *and* flitteþ gouernement3 of þinges ¶ *and* by whiche lawes she p*ur*ueiable kepiþ þe grete worlde. *and* 1855 how she bindynge restreineþ alle þing*us* by a bonde þat

(j) The Punic lion submits to man, and dreads the keeper's lash;

may nat be vnbounden. ¶ Al be it so þat þe lions of þe contree of pene beren þe fair[e] cheines. *and* taken metes of þe handes of folk þat 3euen it hem. *and* 1859 dreden her sturdy maystres of whiche þei ben wont to

yet, if he once taste blood,

suffren [betinges]. yif þat hir horrible mouþes ben bibled. þat is to sein of bestes devoured. ¶ Hir corage of tyme passeþ þat haþ ben ydel *and* rested. repaireþ

his savage instincts revive,

a3ein þat þei roren greuously. *and* remembren on hir 1864 nature. *and* slaken hir nekkes from hir cheius vn-

and his keeper falls a victim to his fury.

bounden. and hir maistre first to-teren wiþ blody toþe assaieþ þe woode wraþþes of hem. ¶ þis is to sein þei

(i)}
if the caged bird though daintily fed, gets a sight of the pleasant grove where she was wont to sing,

freten hir maister. ¶ And þe Iangland brid þat syngiþ on þe heye braunches. þis is to sein in þe wode *and* after is inclosed in a streit cage. ¶ al þou3 [þat] þe 1870 pleiyng besines of men 3eueþ hem honied[e] drinkes *and* large metes. wiþ swete studie. ¶ 3it naþeles yif þilke brid skippynge oute of hir streite cage seeþ þe

she will spurn her food, and pine for the beloved woods.

agreable shadewes of þe wodes. she defouleþ wiþ hir fete hir metes yshad *and* sekeþ mournyng oonly þe

(ii)]
The sapling, bent down by a mighty

wode *and* twitriþ desirynge þe wode wiþ hir swete voys. ¶ þe 3erde of a tree þat is haled adou*n* by my3ty

---

1848 *grete*—gret
1849 *algates*—Allegates
1850 *goode*—good
1851 *shew[e]*—shewe
1854 *whiche*—MS. swiche, C. whyche
worlde—world
1856 *be*—ben
vnbounden—vnbownde

1857 *fair[e]*—fayre
1860 [*betinges*]—from C.
1862 *passeþ*—passed
1864 *from*—fram
vnbounden—vnbownde
1865 *to-teren*—to-torn
toþe—toth
1867 *Iangland*—Iangclynge
1869 *streit*—streyht

1870 *pleiyng*—MS. pleinyng, C. pleyynge
besines—bysynesse
honied[e]—honyede
1872 *oute*—owt
1873 *agreable*—agreables
1874 *fete*—feet
1875 *twitriþ*—twiterith

strengþe bowiþ redely þe croppe adoun. but yif þat þe hande of hym þat it bente lat it gon aȝein. ¶ An oon þe crop lokeþ vp ryȝt to heuene. ¶ þe sonne phebus þat failleþ at euene in þe westrene wawes retorniþ aȝein eftsones his cart by a priue paþe þere as it is wout aryse. ¶ Alle þinges seken aȝein in to hir propre cours. and alle þinges reioisen hem of hir retournynge aȝein to hir nature ne noon ordinaunce nis bytaken to þinges but þat. þat haþ ioignynge þe endynge to þe bygynnynge. *and* haþ makid þe cours of it self stable þat it chaungeþ nat from hys propre kynde. 1887

VOSQUE TERRENA ANIMALIA.

*C*Ertis also ȝe men þat ben erþeliche bestes dremen alwey [yowre bygynnynge] al þouȝ it be wiþ a þinne ymaginacioun. *and* by a maner þouȝt al be it nat clerly ne perfitly ȝe looken from a fer til þilk verray fyn of blisfulnesse. and þerfore þe naturel entencioun ledeþ ȝow to þilk verray good ¶ But 1893 many manere errours mistourniþ ȝow þer fro. ¶ Considere now yif þat be þilke þinges by whiche a man weniþ to gete hym blysfulnesse. yif þat he may comen to þilke ende þat he weneþ to come by nature ¶ For yif þat moneye or honours or þise oþer forseide þinges bryngen to men swiche a þing þat no goode ne faille hem. ne semeþ faille. ¶ Certys þan wil I graunt[e] þat þei ben maked blisful. by þilke þinges þat þei han 1901 geten. ¶ but yif so be þat þilke þinges ne mowe nat perfourmen þat þei by-heten *and* þat þer be defaute of many goodes. ¶ Sheweþ it nat þan clerely þat fals beaute of blisfulnesse is knowe *and* a-teint in þilke þinges. ¶ First *and* forward þou þi self þat haddest

Side notes:
hand, will resume its natural position as soon as the restraining force is removed.
[Hij] Though the sun sets in the western main at eve, yet by a secret path he takes his wonted jonrney toward the east.
All things pursue their proper course, obedient to the source of order.
Hence, throughout the world entire stability is found, for all things, having fulfilled their appointed course, return from whence they came.
[The 3ᵈᵉ prose.] [* fol. 16 b.]
O earthly animals, you have an indistinct perception of your beginning, and you have ever the true end of telicity in view, but your natural instincts are perverted by many errors.
Can men obtain the end they have in view by the means they usually employ in the pursuit of happiness?
If riches and honours and the like make men happy, so that they shall want for nothing, then happiness may be procured by these acquisitions.
But if these things cannot make good what they promise, if there still be something to be desired, then they are delusions, and the felicity after all is a counterfeit.

1877 *croppe*—crop
1878 *hande*—hand
bente—bent
1880 *failleþ*—falleth
1881 *cart*—carte
a—omitted
paþe—paath
1883 *of*—MS. of of
1885 *haþ*—MS. haþe

1885 *ioignynge*—Ioyned
1886 *haþ*—MS. haþe [from C.
1889 [*yowre bygynnynge*]— *al*—MS. as, C. Al
1891 *from*—fram *til þilk*—to thylke
1892 *þe*—omitted
1893 *þilk*—thylke
1895 *be*—by

1896 *gete*—geten
1899 *swiche*—swych
goode—good
1900 *wil*—wole
graunt[*e*]—graunte
1904 *many*—manye
clerely—clerly
fals—false
1905 *knowe*—knowen

In your prosperity were you never annoyed by some wrong or grievance?

haboundaunces of rycchesses nat long agon. ¶ I axe ʒif þat in þe haboundaunce of alle þilk[e] rycchesses þou were neuer anguissous or sory in þi corage of any wrong or greuaunce þat by-tidde þe on any syde.

B. I must confess that I cannot remember ever being wholly free from some trouble or other.
P. That was because something was absent which you did desire, or something present which you would fain be quit of.
B. That's quite true.
P. Then you did desire the presence of the one and the absence of the other?
B. I confess I did.
P. Every man is in need of what he desires.
B. Certainly he is.
P. If a man lack anything can he be supremely happy?
B. No.
P. Did you not in your abundance want for somewhat?
B. What then if I did?
P. It follows that riches cannot put a man beyond all want, although this was what they seemed to promise. Money may part company with its owner, however unwilling he may be to lose it.
B. I confess that's true.
P. It ought to be confessed when every day we see might prevailing over right. From whence springs so much litigation, but from this, that men seek to re-

¶ Certys quod I it remembreþ me nat þat euere I was so free of my þouʒt. þat I ne was al-wey in anguyshe of somwhat. þat was þat þou lakkedest þat þou noldest han lakked. or ellys þou haddest þat þou noldest han had. ryʒt so is it quod I þan. desiredest þou þe presence of þat oon *and* þe absence of þat oþer. I graunt[e] wel quod .I. for soþe quod she þan nediþ þer somwhat þat euery man desireþ. ʒe þer nediþ quod I. ¶ Certis quod she *and* he þat haþ lakke or nede of a wyʒt nis nat in euery way suffisaunt to hym self. no quod .I. *and* þou quod she in alle þe plente of þi rycchesse haddest þilke lak of suffisaunce. ¶ what ellis quod .I. ¶ þanne may nat rycchesse maken þat a man nis nedy. ne þat he be suffisaunt to hym self. *and* þat was it þat þei byhyʒten as it semeþ. ¶ and eke certys I trowe þat þis be gretly to consydere þat moneye ne haþ nat in hys owen kynde þat it ne may ben bynomen of hem þat han it maugre hem. ¶ I by-knowe it wel quod I ¶ whi sholdest þou nat by-knowen it quod she. whan euery day þe strenger folke by-nymen it fram þe febler maugre hem. ¶ Fro whennes comen ellys alle þise foreine compleintes or quereles of pletyngus. ¶ But for þat men axen aʒeine her moneye þat haþ be by-nomen hem by force or by gyle. *and* alwey maugre hem. ¶ Ryʒt so it is quod I. þan quod she haþ a man nede to seken hym foreyne helpe by whiche he may defende hys moneye. who may say nay

---

1908 þilk[e]—thylke
1913 þat——lakkedest—And was nat þat quod she for þat the lacked som-what
1915 had—MS. hadde, C. had
1917 graunt[e]—graunte
1919 haþ—MS. haþe
    a wyʒt—awht
1921 alle—al

1922 rycchesse—Rychesses
    lak—lakke
1923 rycchesse—Rychesses
1927 haþ—MS. haþe
    owen—owne
1930 strenger folke by-nymen — strengers folk by-nemyn
1931 fram—fro

1931 febler—febelere
    Fro—For
1933 aʒeine—ayeyn
1934 haþ—MS. haþe
    be—ben
1936 haþ—MS. haþe
    helpe—help
1937 say—sey

RICHES BRING ANXIETIES.

quod .I. ¶ Certis quod she *and* hym nediþ no helpe
yif he ne hadde no moneye þat he myȝt[e] leese. ¶ þat
is doutles quod .I. þanne is þis þing turned in to þe con- 1940
trarie quod she ¶ For rycchesse þat men wenen sholde
make suffisau*n*ce. þei maken a man raþer han nede of
foreine helpe. ¶ whiche is þe manere or þe gise quod
she þat rycches may dryuen awey nede. ¶ Riche folk
may þei neiþer han hungre ne þrest. þise ryche men
may þei feele no colde on hir lymes in wynter. ¶ But
þou wilt answere þat ryche men han y-nouȝ wher wiþ
þei may staunchen her hunger. *and* slaken her þrest
and don awey colde. ¶ In þis wise may nede be con-
forted by rycchesses. but certys nede ne may nat al
outerly be don awey. for þouȝ þis nede þat is alwey
gapyng *and* gredy be fulfilled wiþ rycchesses. *and* axe
any þing ȝit dwelleþ þanne a nede þat myȝt[e] ben fulfilled. ¶ I holde me stille *and* telle nat how þat litel
þing suffiseþ to nature. but certys to auarice ynouȝ ne
suffiseþ no þinge. *¶ For syn þat rychesse ne may nat
al don awey nede. but rychesse maken nede. what may
it þanne be þat ȝe wenen þat rychesses mowen ȝeue*n*
ȝow suffisau*n*ce. 1959

Sidenotes:
cover their own of which they have been unjustly deprived?
B. Nothing is more true.
P. Then a man needs the assistance of others in order to keep his riches. If he had no money to lose he would not stand in need of this help?
B. That is beyond all doubt.
P. Then the very reverse of what was expected (from riches) takes place? For riches add to a man's necessities. Tell me how do riches drive away necessity? Are not rich men liable to hunger, thirst, and cold? You will say that the rich have wherewithal to satisfy these wants. By riches indigence may be alleviated, but they cannot satisfy every want. [* fol. 17.] Even if gaping and greedy necessity be filled with riches, yet some cravings will remain. A little suffices for nature, but avarice never has enough.

QUAMUIS FLUENTER DIUES.

Al were it so þat a ryche couetous man hadde riuer
fletynge alle of golde ȝitte sholde it neuer staunche
hys couetise. ¶ And þouȝ he hadde his nekke I-charged
wiþ p*re*ciouse stones of þe rede see. *and* þouȝ he do
erye his feldes plentiuou*s* wiþ an hundreþ oxen neuere
ne shal his bytyng bysynesse forleten hym while he

Sidenotes:
If riches, then, add to our wants, why should you think that they can supply all your necessities? [The 3*de* Meter.] The rich man, had he a river of gold, would never rest content. Though his neck be loaded with precious pearls, and his fields be covered with in-

---

1938 *nediþ no helpe*—nedede non help
1939 *myȝt[e]*—myhte
1940 *doutles*—dowteles
1941 *rycchesse*—Rychesses
1943 *helpe*—help
  whiche—whych
1944 *rycches*—Rychesse
  dryuen—dryue
1945 *hungre*—hungyr
  þrest—thurst
1946 *þei*—the
  colde—coold
in—on
1947 *wilt answere* — wolt Answeren
  y-nouȝ—y-now
1948 *þrest*—thurst
1949 *colde*—coold
1950 *nat*—omitted
1951 *outerly*—vtrely
1953 *myȝt[e] ben*—myhte be
1957 *rychesse*—Ryehesses
1960 *riuer*—a Ryuer
1961 *alle*—al
  golde—gold
  ȝitte—yit
  staunche—staunchyn
1962, 1963 *þouȝ*—thow
1964 *erye*—Ere
  hundreþ—hundred
1965 *while*—whyl

| numerable herds, yet shall unquiet care never forsake him; and at his death his riches shall not bear him company.
¹ Read *dignitates*.

[The 4ᵗʰᵉ prose.] It may be said that *dignities* confer honour on their possessors. But have they power to destroy vice or implant virtue in the heart?'
So far from expelling vicious habits, they only render them more conspicuous. Hence arises the indignation when we see dignities given to wicked men.
Hence Catullus' resentment against Nonius, whom he calls the botch, or impostume of the State. | lyueþ. ne þe ly3t[e] rychesses ne shal nat beren hym compaignie whanne he is dede. 1967

SET DIGNITATIBUS.¹

Bvt dignitees to whom þei ben comen make þei hym honorable *and* reuerent. han þei nat so grete strengþe þat þei may putte vertues in þe hertis of folk. þat vsen þe lordshipes of hem. or ellys may þei don awey þe vices. Certys þei [ne] ben nat wont to don awey wikkednesses. but þei ben wont raþer to shew[en] wikkednesses. *and* þer of comeþ it þat I haue ry3t grete desdeyne. þat dignites ben 3euen ofte to wicked men. ¶ For whiche þing catullus clepid a consul of Rome þat hy3t nonius postum. or boch. as who seiþ he clepiþ hym a congregacioun of uices in his brest as a postum is ful of corrupcioun. al were þis nonius set in a chayere of dignitee. Sest þou nat þan how gret vylenye

1980

The deformities of wicked men would be less apparent if they were in more obscure situations. Would you free yourself from peril by accepting a magistracy along with Decoratus a buffoon and informer?

1987

Honours do not render undeserving persons worthy of esteem.

If you find a man endowed with wisdom you | dignitees don to wikked men. ¶ Certys vnworþines of wikked men sholde ben þe lasse ysen yif þei nere renomed of none honours. ¶ Certys þou þi self ne my3test nat ben brou3t wiþ as many perils as þou my3test suffren þat þou woldest bere þi magistrat wiþ decorat. þat is to seyn. þat for no peril þat my3t[e] bifallen þe by þe offence of þe kyng theodorik þou noldest nat ben felawe in gouernaunce with decorat. whanne þou say[e] þat he had[de] wikkid corage of a likerous shrewe *and* of an acusor. ¶ Ne I ne may nat for swiche honours Iugen hem worþi of reuerence þat I deme *and* holde vnworþi to han þilke same honours. ¶ Now yif þou saie a man þat were fulfilled of wisdom. certys þou

| 1966 *ly3t[e]*—lyhte
shal—shol
1967 *dede*—ded
1968 *make*—maken
1969 *grete*—gret
1972 [*ne*]—from C.
ben—be
1972, 1973 *wikkednesses*—wykkydnesse
1973 *to*—omitted
shew[en]—shewen
1974 *comeþ*—comth | 1974 *grete desdeyne*—gret desdaign
1976 *whiche*—which
1977 *hy3t*—hyhte
nonius—MS. vonnus, C. nomyus
boch—MS. boþe, C. boch
clepiþ—clepyd
1979 *nonius*—MS uonnus, C. nomyus
set—MS. sette, C. set
1980 *Sest þou*—Sesthow | 1980 *þan*—thanne
vylenye—fylonye [ynesse
1981 *vnworþines*—vnworth-
1982 *ben*—be
ysen—MS. ysene, C. I-sene
1984 *many*—manye
1985 *bere*—heren
1986 *my3t[e]*—myhte
1987 *þe* (2)—omitted
1988 *whanne*—whan
1989 *say[e]*—saye
had[de]—hadde |

ne myȝtest nat demen þat he were vnworþi to þe
honour. or ellys to þe wisdom of whiche he is fulfilled.
No quod .I. ¶ Certys dignitees quod she appertienen
properly to vertue. and uertue transporteþ dignite anon
to þilke man to whiche she hir self is conioigned.
¶ And for as moche as honours of poeple ne may nat
maken folk digne of honour. it is wel seyn clerly þat
þei ne han no propre beaute of dignite. ¶ And ȝit men
auȝten take more hede in þis. ¶ For if it so be þat he
is most out cast þat most folk dispisen. or as dignite ne
may nat maken shrewes worþi of no reuerences. þan
makeþ dignites shrewes more dispised þan preised. þe
whiche shrewes dignit[e] schoweþ to moche folk ¶ and
for soþe nat vnpunissed. þat is forto sein. þat shrewes
reuengen hem aȝeinward vpon dignites. for þei ȝelden
aȝein to dignites as gret gerdoun whan þei byspotten
and defoulen dignites wiþ hire vylenie. ¶ And for as
moche as þou mow[e] knowe þat þilke verray reuerence
ne may nat comen by þe shadewy transitorie dignitees.
vndirstonde now þis. yif þat a man hadde vsed and
hadde many manere dignites of consules and were
comen perauenture amonges straunge naciouns. sholde
þilke honour maken hym worshipful and redouted of
straunge folk ¶ Certys yif þat honour of poeple were
a naturel ȝifte to dignites. .it ne myȝte neuer cesen
nowher amonges no maner folke to done hys office.
¶ Ryȝt as fire in euery contre ne stinteþ nat to enchaufen and *to ben hote. but for as myche as forto
be holden honorable or reuerent ne comeþ nat to folk of

74   DIGNITIES DO CONFER ESTEEM.   [BOOK 3.
                                                                                     [MET. 4.

opinions of men, and vanish when they come among those who do not esteem them, that is, among foreign nations.

hir propre strengþe of natu*re*. but only of þe fals[e] opinioun of folk. þat is to sein. þat wenen þat dignites maken folk digne of hono*ur*. An on þerfore whan þat þei comen þer as folk ne knowen nat þilke dignites.

2027 her hono*ur*s vanissen awey *and* þat on oon. but þat is

Do they always endure in those places that gave birth to them?

a-mong straung folk. maist þou sein. but amo*n*gus hem þat þei weren born duren þilk[e] dignites alwey.

The Prætorate was once a great honour, but now it is only an empty name and a heavy expense.

¶ Certys þe dignite of þe prouostrie of Rome was somtyme a grete power. now is it no þing but an ydel name. *and* þe rente of þe senatorie a gret charge. *and*

What is more vile than the office of the superintendency of provisions?

yif a whi3t somtyme hadde þe office to taken he[de] to þe vitailes of þe poeple as of corne *and* what oþer þinges he was holden amonges grete. but what þing is more

That which hath no innate beauty must lose its splendour or value according as popular opinion varies concerning it.

nowe out cast þanne þilke prouostrie ¶ And as I haue seid a litel here byforne. þat þilke þing þat haþ no propre beaute of hym self resceyueþ somtyme pris *and* shinynge *and* somtyme lesiþ it by þe opinioun of

If dignities cannot confer esteem, if they become vile through filthy shrews, if they lose their lustre by the change of times, if they become worthless by the change of popular opinion, what beauty do they possess which should make them desirable, or what dignity can they confer on others?

vsaunces. ¶ Now yif þat dignites þanne ne mowen nat maken folk digne of reuerence. *and* yif þat dignites wexen foule of hir wille by þe filþe of shrewes. ¶ and yif þat dignites lesen hir shynynge by chaungyng of tymes. and yif þei wexen foule by estimacioun of poeple. what is it þat þei han in hem self of beaute þat au3te ben desired. as who seiþ none. þanne ne mowen þei 3iuen no beaute of dignite to none oþer. 2047

QUAMUIS SE TIRIO.

[The 4the Metur.] Nero, though invested with the purple and adorned with pearls, was hated by all men.

Al be it so þat þe proude nero wiþ al his woode luxurie kembed hym *and* apparailed hym wiþ faire purpers of Tirie *and* wiþ white perles. Algates 3itte throf he

---

2023 *fals[e]*—false
2024 *þat* (2)—omitted
2027 *her*—hyr
   vanissen—vanesshen
2028 *a-mong*—amonges
   straung—straunge
   but—no
2029 *þat*—ther
   duren þilk[e] — ne duren nat thylke
2030 *somtyme*—whylom

2031 *grete*—gret
2032 *þe* (2)—omitted
2033 *somtyme*—whylom
   þe—MS. þe þe
2034 *corne*—corn
   what—omitted
2035 *more nowe*—now more
2036 *cast*—MS. caste, C. cast
2037 *seid*—MS. seide, C. seyd
   here byforne—her by-forn
   haþ—MS. haþe

2042 *filþe*—felthe
2043 *þat*—omitted
2046 *au3te*—owhte
   none—non
2047 *þei*—MS. 3e, C. they
   none—non
2048 *al* (2)—alle
2049 *kembed*—kembde
   apparailed—MS. apparail en, C. a-paraylede
2050 *3itte*—yit

hateful to alle folk ¶ þis is to seyn þat al was he by-
hated of alle folk. ¶ ʒitte þis wicked Nero hadde gret
lordship *and* ʒaf somtyme to þe dredeful senatours þe
vnworshipful setes of dignites. ¶ vnworshipful setes
he clepiþ here fore þat Nero þat was so wikked ʒaf þo
dignites. who wolde þanne resonably wenen þat blysfulnesse were in swiche hono*ur*s as ben ʒeuen by vicious
shrewes.

AN UERO REGNA.   [The 5th prose.]

Bvt regnes *and* familarites of kynges may þei maken a
man to ben myʒty. how ellys. ¶ whanne hir
blysfulnesse dureþ p*er*petuely but certys þe olde age of
tyme passeþ. *and* eke of p*re*sent tyme now is ful of en-
saumples how þat kynges þat han chaunged in to
wrechednesse out of hir welefulnesse. ¶ O a noble þing
and a cler þing is power þat is nat founden myʒty to
kepe it self. ¶ And yif þat power of realmes be auctour
and maker of blisfulnesse. yif þilke power lakkeþ on
any side. amenusiþ it nat þilke blisfulnesse *and* bryngeþ
in wrechednesse. but yif al be it so þat realmes of mankynde stretchen broode. ʒit mot þer nede ben myche
folk ouer whiche þat euery kyng ne haþ no lordshipe
ne coma*u*ndement ¶ and certys vpon þilke syde þat
power failleþ whiche þat makiþ folk blisful. ryʒt on þat
same side nou*n*power entriþ vndirneþ þat makeþ hem
wreches. ¶ In þis manere þanne moten kynges han
more porcio*un* of wrechednesse þan of welefulnesse.
¶ A tyraunt þat was kyng of sisile þat had[de] assaied
þe p*er*il of his estat shewid[e] by similitude þe dredes
of realmes by gastnesse of a swerde þat heng ouer þe
heued of his familier. what þing is þan þis power þat

Yet he had lord-ship, and gave to the senators the dishonoured seats of dignity. Who then can think that felicity resides in honours given by vicious shrews?

P. Do kingdoms and a familiarity with princes make a man mighty?
B. Why should they not if they are durable?
P. Past ages, as well as the pre-sent, furnish us with many ex-amples of princes who have met with dismal re-verses of fortune.
O then how noble and glorious a thing is power that is too weak to preserve itself!
If dominion brings felicity, then misery will follow if it be de-fective.
But human rule has its limits, therefore wher-ever power ceases there impotence enters, bringing misery along with it.
Kings, therefore, have a larger por-tion of misery than of felicity.
Dionysius of Sicily, conscious of this condition, exhibited the fears and cares of royalty by the terror of a naked sword hanging

---

2053 *lordship*—lorshippe
  ʒaf *somtyme*—yaf whylom
  dredeful—reuerenc̉
2055 *fore*—for; ʒaf—yaf
2060 *myʒty*—MS. vnmyʒty,
  C. myhty
2063 *passeþ*—passed
  of (2)—omitted

2063 *kynges þat han* —
  kynges ben
2066 *kepe*—kepen
2067 *maker*—makere
2069 *yif*—yit
  realmes—the Reaumes
2070 *stretchen*—strechchen
  myche—moche

2071 *haþ*—MS. haþe
2073 *whiche*—whych
2074 *vndirneþ*—vndyr-nethe
2077 *had[de]*—hadde
2078 *shewid[e]*—shewede
2079 *realmes*—Reaumes
  swerde—swerd
  heng—MS. henge, C. heng

may nat don awey þe bytynges of besines ne eschewe þe prikkes of drede. and certys ȝit wolden þei lyuen *in sykernesse. but þei may nat. and ȝit þei glorifien hem in her power ¶ Holdest þou þan þat þilk[e] man be myȝty þat þou seest þat he wolde don þat he may nat don. ¶ And holdest þou þan hym a myȝty man þat haþ enuironed hise sydes wiþ men of armes or seruauntes *and* dredeþ more [hem] þat he makeþ agast. þen þei dreden hym. *and* þat is put in þe handes of hise seruauntȝ. for he sholde seme myȝty but of familiers [or] seruauntȝ of kynges. ¶ what sholde I telle þe any þing. syn þat I my self haue shewed þe þat realmes hem self ben ful of gret feblenesse. þe whiche familiers certis þe real power of kynges in hool estat *and* in estat abated ful [ofte] þroweþ adoun. ¶ Nero constreined[e] his familier *and* his maistre seneca to chesen on what deeþ he wolde deien. ¶ Antonius comaundid[e] þat knyȝtis slowen wiþ her swerdis Papinian his familier whiche Papinian had[de] ben long tyme ful myȝty a-monges hem of þe courte. and ȝit certis þei wolde boþe han renounced her power. of whiche [two] senek enforced[e] hym to ȝiuen to Nero his rychesses. *and* also to han gon in to solitarie exil. ¶ But whan þe grete weyȝt. þat is to sein of lordes power or of fortune draweþ hem þat sholden falle. neyþer of hem ne myȝt[e] do þat he wolde. what þing is þanne þilke power þat þouȝ men han it þat þei ben agast. ¶ *and* whan þou woldest han it þou nart nat siker. ¶ And yif þou woldest forleten it þou mayst nat eschewen it. ¶ But wheþir swiche men ben frendes at nede as ben consciled by fortune *and* nat by vertue. Certys swiche

over the head of his friend and flatterer Damocles. What then is this thing called [° fol. 13.] Power, which cannot do away with care or fear? Men would live in security but cannot, and yet they glory in their power. Is he powerful who cannot do what he wishes? Is he a mighty man who goes surrounded with an armed guard, to terrify those whom he himself fears, and whose power depends solely upon his numerous retinue? Why need I enlarge upon the favourites of princes having thus displayed the imbecility of kings! Their prosperity is affected by the caprice of their fortunate masters as well as by the adversity to which

2098

they are incident. Nero only allowed his master Seneca to choose the manner of his death. Antonius (Caracalla) commanded Papinian to be slain by the swords of his soldiers. Yet both would have given np all they possessed. Seneca begged for poverty and exile. But relentless fortune precipitated them to destruction, and did not permit them to choose their fate. What then is Power, which terrifies its possessors, and which cannot be got rid of at pleasure? No advantage is to be gained by friend-

2081 *besines*—bysynesse
2083 ȝit—yif
glorifien—gloryfye
2084 *þilk[e]*—thylke
2087 *haþ*—MS. haþe
enuironed—enuyrownede
2098 *[hem]*—from C.
2089 *þen*—than
2091 *[or]*—from C.
2092 *realmes*—Reaimes

2093 *feblenesse*—feblesse
2094 *real*—Ryal
2095 *[ofte]*—from C.
constreined[e] — *con-*
2096 *his* (1)—hyr [streynede
seneca—Senck
2097 *comaundid[e]* — com-
2098 *her*—hyr [aundede
2009 *whiche*—which
had[de] ben long — þat

hadde ben longe
2100 *courte*—court
wolde—wolden
2101 *[two]*—from C.
enforced[e]—enforcede
2102 *ȝiuen*—yeuen
his—hyse
2104 *weyȝt*—weyhte
2105 *sholden*—sholen
2106 *myȝt[e]*—myhte

GLORY IS DECEPTIVE.

folk as weleful fortune makeþ frendes. contrarious for- *ship based on prosperity instead of virtue.*
tune makeþ hem enmyse. ¶ And what pestilence is *Adversity will turn this sort of*
more myȝty forto anoye a wiȝt þan a familier enemy. *friendship into enmity. And what greater plague can there*

QUI SE UALET[1] ESSE POTENTEM. [¹ Read *volet*] *be than the enmity of thy familier friend?*

Who so wolde ben myȝty he mot daunten hys cruel *[The 5th Metur.] He who would*
corage. ne put[te] nat his nekke ouercomen vndir *obtain sovereign power must ob-*
þe foule reines of lecherie. for al be it so þat þi lord- *tain conquest over himself, and*
ship[e] strecche so fer þat þe contre Inde quakiþ at þi *not yield to his passions. Though*
comaundement. or at þi lawes. *and* þat þe leest isle in *your dominion extended from India to Thule, yet if*
þe see þat hyȝt tile be þral to þe ¶ ȝit yif þou mayst *thou art tormented by care*
nat puten awey þi foule derk[e] desijres *and* dryuen *thou hast no real power.*
oute fro þe wreched compleyntes. Certis it nis no
power þat þou hast. 2123

GLORIA UERO QUAM FALLAX.
[The 6th prose.]

Bvt glorie how deceiuable *and* how foule is it ofte. for *How deceptive and deformed a*
whiche þing nat vnskilfully a tregedien þat is to *thing is glory! Well did the*
sein a maker of dites þat hyȝten tregedies cried[e] *and* *Tragedian exclaim—*
seide. ¶ O glorie glorie q*uod* he. þou nart no þing *ὦ δόξα δόξα μυρίοισι δὴ βροτῶν, οὐδὲν*
ellys to þousandes of folkes. but a gret sweller of eres. *γέγωσι βίοτον ὠγκωσας μέγαν,*
for many[e] han had ful gret renoun by þe fals[e] op- *for the undeserving have been crowned with*
pinioun of poeple. and what þing may ben þouȝt fouler *glory and renown by popular and*
þen swiche preisynge for þilk[e] folk þat ben preised *erring opinion. What can be more infamous*
falsly. þei moten nedes han shame of hir preisynges. *than renown founded on the*
and yif þat folk han geten hem þank or preysyng by *prejudices of the vulgar?*
her desertes. what þing haþ þilk pris echid or en- *Those that are undeservedly*
cresed to þe conscience of wise folk þat mesuren hire *praised ought to blush for shame.*
good. not by þe rumour of þe poeple. but by þe soþe- *If a wise man gets well-merited*
fastnesse of conscience. *and* yif it seme a fair þing a *praise it does not add to his felicity.*
man to han encresid *and* sprad his name. þan folweþ *If it be a good thing to spread*

2115 *wolde ben*—wole be
2116 *put[te]*—putte
2117 *lordship[e]*—lordshype
2119 *comaundement* — co-
 maundementȝ
 leest isle—last Ile
2120 *hyȝt*—hyhte
2121 *puten*—putten
 derk[e]—dyrke

2122 *oute*—owt
2124 *foule*—fowl
2125 *whiche*—whych
2126 *maker*—makere
 cried[e]—cryde
2127 *he*—she
2128 *sweller*—swellere
2129 *many[e]*—manye
 had—MS. hadde, C. had

2129 *fals[e]*—false
2130 *fouler*—fowlere
2131 *þen*—thanne
 þilk[e]—thylke
2133 *or*—of
2134 *haþ*—MS. haþe
 þilk—thylke

abroad one's fame, it must be dishonourable not to do so.
But a good name cannot penetrate everywhere, and the most illustrious names must be unknown to the greatest part of the world.

The favour of the people is worth but little as it is seldom judicious and never permanent.
[* fol. 18 b.]

How empty and transitory are titles of nobility!

Gentility is wholly foreign to renown, and to those who boast of noble birth.

Nobility is fame derived from the merits of one's ancestors.

If praise can give nobility they are noble who are praised.

Then if thou hast no nobility of thy own, thou canst not derive any splendour from the merits of others.

If there be any good in nobleness of birth, it consists alone in this, that it imposes an obligation upon its possessors not to degenerate from the virtues of their ancestors.

[The 6th Metre.]
All men have the same origin. They have one father and one king, who gave the moon her horns, and adorned the sun with his rays. The same gave the earth to man

it. þat it is demed to ben a foule þinge yif it ne be ysprad ne encresed. but as I seide a litel her byforne. þat syn þer mot nedes ben many folk to whiche folk þe renoun of a man ne may nat comen. it byfalleþ þat he þat þou wenest be glorious *and* renomed. semiþ in þe nexte *p*arties of þe erþe to ben wiþ out glorie. *and* wiþ out renou*n*. ¶ and certis amonges þise þinges I ne trowe nat þat þe *p*ris *and* grace of þe poeple nis neiþer worþi *to ben remembrid ne comeþ of wise iugement. ne is ferm *p*erdurably. ¶ But now of þis name of gentilesse. what man is it þat ne may wel seen how veyne *and* 2150 how flittyng a þing it is. ¶ For if þe name of gentilesse be referred to renou*n* *and* clernesse of linage. þan is gentil name but a for[e]ine þing. þat is to sein to hem þat glorifien hem of hir linage. ¶ For it semeþ þat gentilesse be a maner *p*reysynge þat comeþ of decert of aunc*e*stres. ¶ And yif *p*reysynge makeþ gentilesse þan moten þei nedes be gentil þat ben *p*reysed. For whiche þing it folweþ. þat yif þou ne haue no gentilesse of þi self. þat is to sein pris þat comeþ of þi deserte foreine gentilesse ne makeþ þe nat gentil. ¶ But certis yif þer be any goode in gentilesse. I trowe it be i*n* al oonly þis. þat it semeþ as þat a maner necessitee be imposed to gentil men. for þat þei ne sholden nat outraien or forliuen fro þe uertues of hire noble kynrede. 2163

OMNE HOMINU*M* GENUS IN TERRIS.

A*l* þe linage of men þat ben i*n* erþe ben of semblable burþe. On al one is fadir of þinges. On alone minyst[r]eþ alle þinges. ¶ He ʒaf to þe sonne hys bemes. he ʒaf to þe moone hir hornes. he ʒaf þe men to þe erþe. he ʒaf þe sterres to þe heuene. ¶ he encloseþ

2139 *foule þinge*—fowl thing
2140 *ne—and*
byforne—byforn
2144 *parties*—partye
erþe—Erthes
out—owte
2145 *out*—owhte
2148 *ferm*—ferme
2149 *veyne*—veyn
2150 *if*—yif
2154 *comeþ of*—comth of the
2157 *whiche*—which
2158 *pris*—preys
comeþ—comth
2160 *goode*—good
in (2)—omitted
2161 *maner*—manere
2166 *hys*—hyse
2167 *hir*—hyse

SENSUAL PLEASURES FULL OF ANXIETY.

wiþ membres þe soules þat comen fro hys heye sete. ¶ þanne comen alle mortal folk of noble seed. whi noysen ȝe or bosten of ȝoure eldris ¶ For yif þou look[e] ȝoure bygynnyng. and god ȝoure auctour *and* ȝoure makere. þau is þer no forlyued wyȝt but ȝif he norisse his corage vnto vices *and* forlete his propre burþe. 2175

and adorned the sky with stars. He breathed into man the breath of life. All men spring from this illustrious source. Why then do they boast of pedigree? He alone is ignoble who submits to vice and forgets his noble origin.

QUID AUTEM DE CORPORIBUS.[1]

[1 Read *corporis voluptatibus*.]

[The 7the prose.]

But what shal I seie of delices of body. of whic[h]e delices þe desiringes ben ful of anguisse. *and* þe fulfillinges of hem ben ful of penaunce. ¶ How grete sekenesse *and* how grete sorwes vnsuffrable ryȝt as a manere fruit of wickednesse ben þilke delices wont to bryngen to þe bo[d]ies of folk þat vsen hem. ¶ Of whiche delices I not what ioye may ben had of hir moeuyng. ¶ But þis woot I wel þat who so euere wil remembreu hym of hys luxuries. he shal wel vndirstonde. þat þe issues of delices ben sorowful *and* sory. ¶ And yif þilke delices mowen make folk blisful. þan by þe same cause moten þise bestes ben clepid blisful. ¶ Of whiche bestes al þe entencioun hasteþ to fulfille hire bodyly iolyte. and þe gladnesse of wijf [*and*] children were [an] honest þing. but it haþ ben seid. þat it is ouer myche aȝeins kynde þat children han ben founden tormentours to hir fadres I not how many. ¶ Of whiche children how bitynge is euery condicioun. It nedeþ nat to tellen it þe þat hast or þis tyme assaied it. *and* art ȝit now anguyssous. In þis approue I þe sentence of my disciple Euridippus. þat seide þat he þat haþ no children is weleful by infortune. 2197

But what shall I say with respect to sensual pleasures, the desire of which is full of anxiety, and the enjoyment of them full of repentance? What diseases and intolerable pains (the merited fruits of vice) are these delights wont to bring upon those who enjoy them! I am unable to see what joy is to be found in the gratification of them. The remembrance of criminal indulgence brings with it bitter remorse. If such things make men happy, then may brutes attain to felicity, since by their instinct they are urged to satisfy their bodily delights. A wife and children do not always bring happiness, for some have found tormentors in their own offspring. I approve of this opinion of Euripides, that he who is childless is happy in his misfortune.

2169 *fro hys*—fram hyse
2170 *seed*—sede
2171 *bosten*—MS. voseen, C. bosten
2172 *look[e]*—loke
2173 *is*—nis
2176 *delices*—delites
body—bodye
2177 *anguisse*—Angwyssh
2178 *grete*—gret

2179 *sekenesse*—sykenesse
grete sorwes—gret soruwes
2180 *fruit*—frut
2182 *had* — MS. hadde, C. had
2183 *wil*—wole
2184 *hys*—hyse
2185 *sorowful*—sorwful
sory—sorye
2186 *make*—makyu

2189 [*and*]—from C.
2190 [*an*]—from C.
haþ—MS. haþe
seid—MS. seide, C. seyd
2191 *myche*—mochel
2192 *many*—manye
2196 *Euridippus* — Eurydyppys; read Euripides
2197 *haþ*—MS. haþe

[The 7de Metur.]
Pleasure leaves a pain behind it.
2199

The bee gives us agreeable honey, but try to hold it, and it quickly flies, leaving its sting behind.

HABET HOC UOLUPTAS.

Euery delit haþ þis. þat it anguisseþ hem wiþ prikkes þat vsen it. ¶ It resembliþ to þise flying flyes þat we clepen been. þat aftre þat þe bee haþ shed hys agreable honies he fleeþ awey *and* styngeþ þe hertes of hem þat ben ysmyte wiþ bytynge ouer longe holdynge. 2202

[The 8the prose.]
It appears then that happiness is not to be found in the above-mentioned external things.

[° fol. 19.]
These false ways are perplexed with many evils, as I shall presently show thee.
Do you want to amass wealth, then you must take it from your neighbours.
Would you shine in dignities, then you must beg for them and disgrace yourself by a humiliating supplication.
If power be your ambition, you expose yourself to the snares of inferiors.
Do you ask for glory, to be distracted by vexations and so lose all security.
Do you prefer a voluptuous life? Think then that all men will despise him who is a thrall to his body.
They build upon a weak foundation that place bodily delights above their own reason.
Can you surpass the elephant in bulk, or the bull in strength?

NICHIL IGITUR DUBIUM EST.

Now nis it no doute þan þat þise weyes ne ben a maner mysledyng to blisfulnesse. ne þat þei ne mowe nat leden folke þider as þei byheten to leden hem. ¶ But wiþ how grete harmes þise *forseide weyes ben enlaced. ¶ I shal shewe þe shortly. ¶ For whi yif þou enforcest þe to assemble moneye. þou most byreuen hym his moneye þat haþ it. and yif þou wilt shynen wiþ dignites. þou most bysechen *and* supplien hem þat ȝiuen þo dignitees. ¶ And yif þou coueitest by honour to gon by-fore oþer folk þou shalt defoule þi self by humblesse of axing. yif þou desiryst power. þou shalt by awaites of þi subgitȝ anoyously be cast vndir many periles. axest þou glorie þou shalt ben so destrat by aspre þinges þat þou shalt forgone sykernesse. ¶ And yif þou wilt leden þi lijf in delices. euery whiȝt shal dispisen þe *and* forleten þe as þou þat art þral to þing þat is ryȝt foule *and* brutel. þat is [to] sein seruaunt to þi body. ¶ Now is it þan wel yseen how lytel *and* how brutel possessioun þei coueiten þat putten þe goodes of þe body abouen hire owen resoun. ¶ For mayst þou sourmounten þise olifuntȝ in gretnesse or weyȝt of body. Or mayst þou ben strenger þan þe bole. Mayst þou ben swifter þan þe tigre. biholde þe

2198 *Euery*—MS. Ouery, C. Every
2199, 2200 *ha*þ—MS. haþe
  shed hys—shad hyse
2203 *nis*—is
2204 *mysledyng* — mysledynges
2205 *folke*—folk
2208 *enforcest* — MS. enforced, C. enforcest
22 9 *ha*þ—MS. haþe

2209 *wilt*—wolt
2211 ȝiuen—yeuen
2212 *gon*—MS. gone, C. gon
  by-fore—byforn
  shalt—shal
2213 *by*—thorw
2214 *by*—be
  be—ben
2216 *destrat*—MS. destralle, C. destrat
  forgone—forgoon

2217 *wilt*—wolt
2218 *whiȝt*—wyht
2219 *foule*—fowl
  [*to*]—from C.
2220 *yseen*—seen
2221 *brutel*—brotel
2222 *owen*—owne
2224 *weyȝt*—weyhty
  strenger—strengere
2225 *swifter*—swyftere
  biholde—by-hold

spaces *and* þe stablenesse *and* þe swyfte cours of þe *Art thou swifter than the tiger? Behold the immense extent of the heauens and*
heuene. *and* stynte somtyme to wondren on foule *cease to admire vile or lesser things.*
þinges. þe whiche heuene certys nis nat raþer for þise
þinges to ben wondred vpon. þan for þe resou*n* by *Admire what is still more admirable, the consummate wisdom that gouerns them.*
whiche it is gouerned. but þe shynynge of þi forme þat
is to seien þe beaute of þi body. how swiftly passyng is
it *and* how transitorie. ¶ Certis it is more flittynge *How fleeting is beauty! It fades sooner than the vernal flowers.*
þan þe mutabilite of floures of þe som*er* sesou*n*. For so
as aristotil telleþ þat yif þat men hadden eyen of a *For, as Aristotle says, if a man were lynx-eyed and could look into the entrails of Alciblades (so fair outwardly) he would find all foul and loathsome.*
beest þat hiȝt lynx. so þat þe lokyng of folk myȝt[e]
perce*n* þoruȝ þe þinges þat wiþstonden it. who so lokid
þan in þe entrailes of þe body of alcibiades þat was
ful fayr in þe sup*er*fice wiþ oute. it shulde seme ryȝt
foule. *and* for þi yif þou semest faire. þi nature ne *Thy nature does not make thee seem beautiful, but the imperfect view of thy admirers.*
makiþ nat þat. but þe desceinau*n*ce of þe fieblesse of þe
eyen þat loken. ¶ But p*r*eise þe goodes of þi body as
moche as euer þe list. so þat þou know[e] algates þat *Prize bodily perfections as much as you will, yet a three days' fever will destroy them.*
what so it be. þat is to seyn of þe goodes of þi body
whiche þat þou wondrest vpon may ben destroied or
dessolued by þe hete of a feuere of þre dayes. ¶ Of
alle whiche forseide þinges I may reduce*n* þis shortly in
a som*m*e. ¶ þat þise worldly goodes whiche þat ne *Worldly goods do not give what they promise, do not comprise every good, are not the paths to felicity, nor can of themselves make any one happy.*
mowen nat ȝiuen þat þei byheten. ne ben nat p*er*fit by
þe congregac*iou*n of alle goodes. þat þei ne ben nat
weyes ne paþes þat bryngen men to blysfulnesse ne
maken men to ben blysful.

HEU Q*VE* MISEROS TRAMITE.

[The 6*th* Met*ur*.]

Allas whiche folie *and* whiche ignorau*n*ce myslediþ *Alas! how through folly and ignorance do men stray from the path of true happiness!*
wandryng wrecches fro þe paþe of verrey good.
¶ Certis ȝe ne seken no golde in grene trees. ne ȝe ne

2227 *stynte*—stynt
2228 *whiche*—whych
2230 *whiche*—wych
2231 *seien*—seyn
2234 *as*—omitted
2235 *hiȝt*—hyhte
  myȝt[*e*]—myhte
2237 *alcibiades*—MS. alcidi-
2238 *fayr*—fayre   [ades

2238 *þe*—omitted
  shulde—sholde
2239 *foule*—fowl
  faire—fayr
  ne—omitted
2240 *desceinaunce of þe fleblesse*—deceyuable or the feblesse
2243 *moche*—mochel

2242 *know*[*e*]—knowe
2243 *þe*—omitted
  þi body whiche—the body whych
2247 *a*—omitted
2252 *whiche* (both)—whych
2253 *paþe*—pnath
  good—goode
2254 *golde*—gold

Ye do not seek gold upon trees nor diamonds from the vine. Ye lay not your nets to catch fish upon the lofty hills. The hunter goes not to the Tyrrhene waters to hunt the roe. Men know where to look for white pearls, and for the fish that yields the purple dye.

gadren [nat] precious stones in þe vines. ne ȝe ne hiden nat ȝoure gynnes in heyȝe mountaignes to kachen fisshe of whiche ȝe may maken ryche festes. and yif ȝow lykeþ to hunte to roos. ȝe ne gon nat to þe foordes of þe water þat hyȝt tyrene. and ouer þis men knowen wel þe crikes and þe cauernes of þe see yhidd in þe floodes. and knowen eke whiche water is most plentiuous of white perles. and knowen whiche water habundeþ

2263 most of rede purpre. þat is to seyen of a maner shel-fisshe with whiche men dien purpre. and knowen whiche strondes haboundeu most of tendre fisshes or of sharpe fisshes þat hyȝten echynnys. but folk suffren hem self to ben so blynde þat hem ne recchiþ nat to knowe where þilk[e] goodes ben yhidd whiche þat þei coueiten but ploungen hem in erþe and seken þere þilke goode þat sourmounteþ þe heuene þat bereþ þe sterres. ¶ what *preyere may I make þat be digne to þe nice þouȝtis of men. but I preye þat þei coueiten rycches and honours so þat whan þei han geten þo false goodes wiþ greet trauayle þat þerby þei mowe knowen þe verray goodes. 2275

They know where the most delicate of the finny race abound and where the fierce sea-urchin is to be found. But where the Sovereign Good abides blinded mortals never know, but plunge into the earth below to look for that which has its dwelling in the heavens. [fol. 19 b.] What doom do the silly race deserve? May they pursue such false joys, and having obtained them, too late find out the value of the true.*

HACTENUS MENDACIS FORMAM.

IT suffisiþ þat I haue shewed hider to þe forme of false wilfulnesse. so þat yif þou look[e] now clerely þe ordre of myn entencioun requeriþ from hennes forþe to shewen þe verray wilfulnesse. ¶ For quod .I. (b) [I.] se wel now þat suffisaunce may nat comen by richesse. ne power by realmes. ne reuerence by dignitees. ne gentilesse by glorie. ne ioye by delices. and (p) hast þou wel knowen quod she þe cause whi it is. Certis me semeþ

[The 9ne prose.] P. I have been describing the form of counterfeit happiness, and if you have considered it attentively I shall proceed to give you a perfect view of the true. B. I now see that there is no sufficiency in riches, no power in royalty, no esteem in dignities, nor nobility in re-

2256 heyȝe—the hyye
  kachen—kachche
2257 fisshe—fyssh
2258 hunte—honte
  roos—Rooes
2259 hyȝt—hyhte
2260 crikes—brykes
  yhidd—MS. yhidde, C. I-hyd
2261, 2262 whiche—whych

2263 shelfisshe—shelle fysh
2264, 2265 whiche—whych
2264 dien—deyen
2265 of—with
2266 echynnys—MS. ethynnys, C. Echynnys
2268 yhidd—MS. yhidde, C. I-hydd
2270 goode—good
2271 make—maken

2273 rycches—Rychesse
2277 wilfulnesse—welefulnesse
  look[e]—loke
  clerely—clerly [nesse
2279 wilfulnesse—weleful-
  For—For-sothe
  [I.]—from C.
2280 richesse—Rychesses
2281 realmes—Reames

THE INSUFFICIENCY OF WORLDLY BLISS.

q*uod* .I. þat .I. se hem ry3t as þou3 it were þoru3 a litel
clifte. but me were leuer knowen hem more openly of
þe. Certys q*uod* she þe resou*n* is al redy ¶ For
þilk þing þat symply is on þing wiþ outen o*n*y
diuisiou*n*. þe errour *and* folie of mankynde departeþ
and diuidiþ it. *and* misledi*þ* it *and* transporteþ from
verray *and* perfit goode. to goodes þat ben false *and*
inperfit. ¶ But seye me þis. wenest þou þat he þat haþ
nede of power þat hym ne lakkeþ no þing. Nay q*uod*
.I ¶ Certis q*uod* she þou seist ary3t. For yif so be
þat þer is a þing þat in any p*a*rtie be fieble of power.
Certis as in þat it most[e] nedes be nedy of foreine
helpe. ¶ Ri3t so it is q*uod* .I. Suffisaunce and power
ben þa*n* of on kynde ¶ So semeþ it q*uod* I. ¶ And
demyst þou q*uod* she þat a þing þat is of þis mancre.
þat is to seine suffisau*n*t *and* my3ty au3t[e] to ben dispised. or ellys þat it be ry3t digne of reuerences abouen
alle þinges. ¶ Certys q*uod* I it nys no doute þat it
nis ry3t worþi to ben reuerenced. ¶ Lat vs q*uod* she þan
adden reuerence to suffisaunce *and* to power ¶ So þat
we demen þat þise þre þinges ben alle o þing. ¶ Certis
q*uod* I lat vs adden it. yif we willen grau*n*ten þe soþe.
what demest þou þan q*uod* she is þat a dirke þing *and*
nat noble þat is suffisau*n*t reue*r*ent *and* my3ty. or ellys
þat is ry3t clere *and* ry3t noble of celebrete of renou*n*.
¶ Considere þan q*uod* she as we han grau*n*tid her byforne. þat he þat ne haþ ne[de] of no þing *and* is most
my3ty *and* most digne of hono*ur* yif hym nediþ any
clernesse of renou*n* whiche clernesse he my3t[e] nat
grau*n*ten of hym self. ¶ So þat for lakke of þilke
clerenesse he my3t[e] seme febler on any syde or þe

nown, nor joy in carnal pleasures.
I have a glimpse of the cause of all this, but I should like a more distinct view. P. The cause is obvious—for that which is by nature one and indivisible human ignorance separates and divides, and reverses the true order of things. Does that state which needs nothing stand in need of power?
B. I should say no. P. Right! That which wants power needs external aid. B. That is true! P. Sufficiency and power therefore are of one nature. B. It seems so indeed.
2297
P. Are power and sufficiency to be despised? Are they not rather worthy of universal respect? B. They are doubtless highly estimable. P. Add respect to sufficiency and power, and consider all three as one and the same thing. B. I see no objection to that view. P. But can that be obscure and ignoble which possesses three such attributes? is it not noble and worthy of a shining reputation? He who is most powerful and worthy of renown—if he lack fame which he cannot give to himself, must (by this defect) seem in some measure more weak and abject. He that is sufficiently mighty and esteemed will have necessarily

---

2287 *þilk*—thylke
on—o
2290 *goode*—good
2291 *seye*—sey
haþ—MS. haþe
2294 *fleble*—febler
2295 *most[e]*—mot
2296 *helpe*—help
2297 *on*—o

2298 *demyst þou*—demesthow
2299 *seine*—seyn
au3t[e]—owhte
2300 *reuerences*—Reuerence
2302 *nis ry3t*—is ryht
2304 *alle*—al
2305 *willen*—wolen
2306 *dirke*—dyrk
2308 *clere*—cler

2308 *of celebrete*—by cele-
bryte
2310 *haþ*—MS. haþe
2312 *whiche*—whych
my3t[e]—myhte
2314 *clerenesse*—clerness:
my3t[e]—myhte
febler—the febelere

an illustrious name. *B.* I cannot deny it, for reputation seems inseparable from the advantages you have just mentioned.
P. Therefore Renown differs in no wise from

2320

the three above-mentioned attributes. And if any one then stands in need of no external aid, can have all he wants, and is illustrious and respected—is not his condition very agreeable and pleasant?
B. I cannot conceive how such a one can have grief or trouble. *P.* It must then be a state of happiness; and we may also affirm that sufficiency, power, nobility, differ only in name, but

2330

not in substance. *B.* It is a necessary consequence. *P.* The depravity of mankind then divides that which is essentially indivisible; and, seeking for a part of that which has no parts, they miss the entire thing [* fol. 20.] which they so much desire.

2338

B. How is that? *P.* He that seeks riches in order to avoid poverty, is not solicitous about power; he prefers meanness and obscurity, and denies himself many natural pleasures that he may not lessen his heaps of pelf.

more outcaste. *Glosa.* þis is to seyne nay. ¶ For who so þat is suffisaunt myȝty *and* reuerent. clernesse of renoun folweþ of þe forseide þinges. he haþ it alredy of hys suffisaunce. boice. I may nat q*u*od I denye it. ¶ But I mot graunten as it is. þat þis þing be ryȝt celebrable by clernesse of renou*n and* noblesse. ¶ þan folweþ it q*u*od she þat we adden clernesse of renou*n* to þe pre forseide þinges. so þat þer ne be amonges hem no difference. *and* þis is a consequente q*u*od .I. þis þing þan q*u*od she þat ne haþ no nede of no foreine þing. *and* þat may don alle þinges by his strengþes. *and* þat is noble *and* honourable. nis nat þat a myrie þing *and* a ioyful. *boice.* but wenest q*u*od I þat any sorow myȝt[e] comen to þis þing þat is swiche. ¶ Certys I may nat þinke. *P.* ¶ þanne moten we graunt[e] q*u*od she þat þis þing be ful of gladnesse yif þe forseide þinges be soþe. ¶ And also certys mote we graunten. þat suffisaunce power noblesse reuerence *and* gladnesse ben only dyuerse bynames. but hir substaunce haþ no diuersite. *Boice.* It mot nedely be so q*u*od .I. *P.* þilke þinge þan q*u*od she þat is oon *and* simple i*n* his nature. þe wikkednesse of men departiþ it *diuidiþ it. *and* whan þei enforcen hem to gete p*a*rtie of a þing þat ne haþ no part. þei ne geten hem neiþer þilk[e] partie þat nis none. ne þe þing al hole þat þei ne desire nat. .b. In whiche manere q*u*od .I. *p.* þilke man q*u*od she þat sekeþ rychesse to fleen pouerte. he ne trauayleþ hym nat to for to gete power for he haþ leuer ben dirk *and* vile. *and* eke wiþdraweþ from hym selfe many naturel deliȝ for he nolde lesen þe moneye þat he haþ as-

2315 *seyne*—seyn	2331 *also certys*—certes also	2341 *rychesse*—Rychesses
2317 *haþ*—MS. haþe	2333 *haþ*—MS. haþe	*fleen*—MS. sleen, C. flen
2324 *haþ*—MS. haþe	2334 *nedely*—nedly	2342 *leuer*—leuer
2325 *his*—hyse	2335 *þinge*—thing	2343 *vile*—vyl
2326 *myrie*—mery	2337 *gete*—geten	*selfe*—self
2327 *wenest*—whennes	2338 *haþ*—MS. haþe	2344 *deliȝ*—delices
2328 *sorow myȝt[e]* — sorwe myhte	*þilk[e]*—thilke	*lesen*—lese
	2339 *none*—non	*haþ*—MS. haþe
2329 *graunt[e]*—graunte	*hole*—hool	
2331 *be*—ben	2340 *whiche*—whych	

sembled. but certis in þis manere he ne getiþ hym nat suffisaunce þat power forletiþ. *and* þat moleste prekeþ. *and* þat filþe makeþ outcaste. *and* þat derknesse hideþ. and certis he þat desireþ only power he wastiþ *and* scatriþ rychesse *and* dispiseþ delices *and* eke honour þat is wiþ out power. ne he ne preiseþ glorie no þing. ¶ Certys þus seest þou wel þat many þing*us* failen to hym. for he haþ somtyme faute of many necessites. *and* many anguysses biten hym ¶ *and* whan he may nat don þo defautes awey. he forleteþ to ben myȝty. *and* þat is þe þing þat he most desireþ. *and* ryȝt þus may I make semblable resou*n*s of honou*rs and* of glorie *and* of delices. ¶ For so as euery of þise forseide þinges is þe same þat þise oþer þinges ben. þat is to sein. al oon þing. who so þat euer sekeþ to geten þat oon of þise *and* nat þat oþer. he ne geteþ nat þat he desireþ. Boice. ¶ what seist þou þan yif þat a man coueiteþ to geten alle þise þinges to gider. P. Certys q*uo*d she .I. wolde seie þat he wolde geten hym souereyne blisfulnes. but þat shal he nat fynde in þo þinges þat .I. haue shewed þat ne mowe nat ȝeuen þat þei byheten. boice. Certys no q*uo*d .I. ¶ þan q*uo*d she ne sholden men nat by no weye seken blysfulnesse in swiche þinges as men wenen þat þei ne mowe ȝeuen but o þing senglely of alle þat men seken. I graunt[e] wel q*uo*d .I. ne no soþer þing ne may nat ben said. P. ¶ Now hast þou þan q*uo*d she þe forme *and* þe causes of false welefulnesse. ¶ Now turne a*nd* flitte þe eyen of þi þouȝt. for þere shalt þou seen an oon þilk verray blysfulnesse þat I haue byhyȝt þee. *b.* Certys q*uo*d .I. it is cler *and* opyn. þouȝ þat it were to a blynde man. *and* þat shewedest þou me [ful wel] a

He who lacks power, is pricked with trouble, and rendered an outcast and obscure by his sordid ways, does not possess sufficiency. He who only aims at power squanders his riches, and despises delights and honours unaccompanied by power. Such a one must be subject to many anxieties. And when he cannot get rid of these evils he ceases to have what he most desired—power. In the same way honour, glory, and pleasure, are all inseparable; he that seeks one without the other will fail to obtain his desires.
B. What then if a man should desire to gain them all at once?
P. He would then indeed 2361 desire perfect felicity—but can he ever expect to find it in the acquisitions above mentioned, which do not perform what they promise?
B. No, surely!
P. Then happiness is not to be sought in these things which are falsely supposed capable of satisfying our desires?
B. I confess it, and nothing can be more truly affirmed than this. Turn your mind's eye upon the reverse of all this *false felicity* and you will perceive *the true happiness.*
B. It is very clear, and I had a complete view of it when you explained to me the causes of its counterfeit.

2346 *prekeþ*—prykketh
2347 *derknesse*—dyrkenesse
2349 *scatriþ*—schatereth
delices—delycȝ
2350 *wiþ out*—with owte
2351 *many*—manye
2352 *haþ*—MS. haþe

2352 *faute*—defaute
2353 *may*—ne may
2354 *don*—MS. done, C. don
2356 *make*—maken
2357 *forseide*—MS. sorseide
2363 *souereyne*—souereyn
2365 *mowe*—mowen

2369 *wenen*—wene
mowe—mowen
2370 *graunt*[e]—graunte
soþer—sothere
2371 *said*—MS. ssaide, C. sayd
2376 [*ful wel*]—from C.

IN SEEKING SUPREME FELICITY [BOOK 3. PROSE 9.

True felicity consists in a state of sufficiency, of power, and honour—as well as of a shining reputation and every desirable pleasure: and I must confess that true felicity is that which is bestowed by these advantages, as they are in reality all one and the same.
P. O my nursling, how happy are

2385

you in this conviction, provided you add but one limitation.
B. What is that?
P. Thinkest thou that any thing in this world can confer this happiness? (the sovereign good).
B. I think not; for nothing can be desirable beyond such a state of perfection.
P. These imperfect things above mentioned only confer the shadow of the supreme good, or at most only an imperfect felicity, but they cannot bestow true and perfect happiness.
B. I quite agree with you.
P. Then, knowing the difference between true and false felicity you must now learn where to look for

2401

this supreme felicity.
P. But, as Plato [* fol. 20 b.] says that even in the least things the Divine assistance ought to be implored, what ought we do, to render us worthy of so important a discovery as the true source and seat of the sovereign good?

lytel her byforne. whan þou enforcedest þe to shewe me þe causes of þe false blysfulnesse ¶ For but yif I be bygiled. þan is þilke þe verray perfit blisfulnesse þat perfitly makiþ a man suffisaunt. myȝty. honourable noble. and ful of gladnesse. and for þou shalt wel knowe þat I haue wel vndirstonden þise þinges wiþ inne myne herte. I knowe wel þilke blisfulnesse þat may verrayly ȝeuen on of þe forseide þinges syn þei ben al oon .I. knowe douteles þat þilke þing is þe fulle of blysfulnesse. P. O my nurry quod she by þis oppinioun quod she I sey[e] þat þou art blisful yif þou putte þis þer to þat I shal seine. what is þat quod .I ¶ Trowest þou þat þer be any þing in þis erþely mortal toumblyng þinges þat may bryngen þis estat. Certys quod I trowe it nat. and þou hast shewed me wel þat ouer þilke goode þer is no þing more to ben desired. P. þise þinges þan quod she. þat is to seyne erþely suffisaunce and power. and swiche þinges eyþer þei semen likenesse of verray goode. or ellys it semeþ þat þei ȝeuen to mortal folk a maner of goodes þat ne ben nat perfit. ¶ But þilke goode þat is verray and perfit. þat may þei nat ȝeuen. boice. I. accorde me wel quod .I. þan quod she for as moche as þou hast knowen whiche is þilke verray blisfulnesse. and eke whiche þilke þinges ben þat lien falsly blisfulnesse. þat is to seyne. þat by desceit semen verray goodes. ¶ Now byhoueþ þe to knowen *whennes and where þou mowe seek[e] þilke verray blisfulnesse. ¶ Certys quod I þat desijr I gretly and haue abiden longe tyme to herkene it. ¶ But for as moche quod she as it likeþ to my disciple plato in his book of in thimeo. þat in ryȝt lytel þinges men sholde bysechen þe helpe of god. ¶ what iugest þou þat be

2377 *buforne*—by-forn
2378 *blysfulnesse* — MS. blyndenesse, C. blysfulnesse
2385 *of*—omitted
2386 *nurry*—norye
2387 *sey*[e]—seye

2388 *seine*—seyn
2389 *þis*—thise
2390 *nat*—nawht
2393 *seyne*—sey
2395 *ȝeuen*—yeue
2397 *goode*—good
2399 *whiche*—which

2401 *seyne*—seyn
2402 *knowen*—knowe
2403 *seek*[e]—seke
2405 *herkene*—herknen
2407 *sholde*—sholden
2408 *bysechen*—by-shechen
helpe—help

THE DIVINE AID IS TO BE INVOKED.

[now] to doue so þat we may deserue to fynde þe sete of þilke souereyne goode. *B.* ¶ Certys qu*o*d .I. I. deme þat we shulle clepen to þe fadir of alle goodes. ¶ For wiþ outen hym nis þer no þing founden ary3t. þou seist a-ry3t qu*o*d she. and bygan on-one to syngen ry3t þus.

O QUI PERPETUA.

O þou fadir creatour of heuene *and* of erþes þat gouernest þis worlde by p*er*durable resou*n* þat comaundist þe tymes for to gon from tyme þat age had[de] bygy*n*inyn*g*. þou þat dwellest þi self ay stedfast *and* stable *and* 3iuest alle oþer þinges to ben moeued. ne forein causes necesseden þe neuer to compounc werke of floterynge mater. but only þe forme of souereyne goode y-set wiþ inne [þe] wiþ outen envie þat moeued[e] þe frely. þou þat art alþerfairest beryng þe faire worlde in þi þou3t. formedest þis worlde to þe likkenesse semblable of þat faire worlde in þi þou3t. þou drawest alle þinges of þi souereyne ensampler. *and* comaundedist þat þis worlde p*er*fitlyche ymaked haue frely *and* absolut hyse p*er*fit parties. ¶ þou byndest þe element3 by noumbres proporcionables. þat þe colde þinges mowen accorde wiþ þe hote þinges. *and* þe drye þinges wiþ þe moyst þinges. þat þe fire þat is purest ne fleye nat ouer heye. ne þat þe heuynesse ne drawe nat adou*n* ouer lowe þe erþes þat ben plounged in þe watres. ¶ þou knyttest to-gidre þe mene soule of treble kynde moeuyng alle þinges. *and* diuidest it by membres accordynge. ¶ And whan it is þus diuided it haþ assembled a moeuyng in two roundes. ¶ It goþ to tour*n*e

*B. Let us invoke the Father of all things. You are right, said Philosophy, and thus she sang:—
O Father and Maker of heaven and earth, by whose eternal reason the world is governed, and by whose supreme command Time flows from the birth of ages, Thou, firm and unchanged thyself, makest all things else to move! Thy sovereign will to floating matter gave its various forms, impelled by no exterior causes, but by the idea of the 2419 Best in thy great mind conceived void of malice. Fairest thyself bearing the world's figure in thy thought, thou didst create the world after that prototype, and dost draw all things from the image of the fair Supreme, and dost command that this world should have perfect parts. By harmonious measures thou dost bind fast the elements, so that there is no discordance between things cold and hot, or between the moist and the dry. That the fire may not fly too high, and that weight may not press the earth and water lower than they are now placed, thou didst join the Middle Soul (of a three-fold nature) moving all things, and then by agreeing*

2409 [*now*]—from C.
2410 *souereyne goode*—verray good
2411 *shulle*—shollen
to—omitted
2413 *on-one*—anon
2415 *worlde*—world
2416 *from——age*—from syn þat age
had[de]—hadde
2417 *stedfast*—stedcfast

2418 *oþer*—oothre
2419 *forein*—foreyne *werke*—werk
2420 *souereyne goode*—souereyn good
2421 *y-set*—MS. y-sette, C. Iset
wiþ inne—with in
[*þe*]—the
wiþ outen—with owte
moeued[*e*]—moeuede

2422 *alþerfairest* — alderfayrest
2422-2 & 26 *worlde*—world
2423 *likkenesse*—lyknesse
2426 *and absolut*—C. omits
2427 *hyse*—hys
2430 *fire*—fyr
fleye—fle
2431 *drawe*—drawen
2435 *haþ*—MS haþe
2436 *goþ*—MS. goþe

numbers didst resolve it. When that is done, cut into two orbs, it moves about returning to itself, and then encompassing the profound mind doth by that fair idea turn the heaven. Thou by such causes dost raise all souls and lesser lives, and adaptest them to their light vehicles. Thou sowest them in heaven and earth, and they return to thee by thy kind law like a recoiling flame. O Father, elevate our souls and let them behold thy august throne. Let them behold the fountain of all good. Dispel the mists of sense, remove the weights of earth-born cares, and in thy splendour shine (in our minds). For thou art ever clear, and to the [The 10th prose.] good art peace and rest. He who looks on thee beholds beginning support, guide, path and goal, combined! Now that thou hast had a faithful representation of future felicity as well as of the true happiness, I shall show thee in what the Perfection of Happiness consists. Our best plan will be to inquire whether there be in nature such a good as thou hast lately defined, lest we be deceived by the vanity of Imagination and be carried beyond the truth of the matter subjected to our inquiry.

aȝein to hym owen self. *and* environeþ a fulle deep þouȝt. *and* tourniþ þe heuene by semblable ymage. þou by euenlyk causes enhau*n*sest þe soules *and* þe lasse liues *and* ablynge hem heye by lyȝt[e] cartes. þou sewest hem in to heuene *and* in to erþe. *and* whan þei ben conuertid to þe by þi benigne lawe. ¶ þou makest hem retorne aȝeine to þe by aȝein ledyng fijr. ¶ O fadir yif þou to þi þouȝt to stien vp in to þi streite sete. *and* graunte [hym] to environne þe welle of good. *and* þe lyȝte yfounde graunte hym to ficchen þe clere syȝtes of hys corage in þe. ¶ And scatre þou *and* to-breke [thow] þe weyȝtes *and* þe cloudes of erþely heuynesse. *and* shyne þou by þi bryȝtnes. for þou art clernesse þou art peisible to debonaire folke. ¶ þou þi self art bygynnynge. berere. ledere. paþ *and* ter*m*e to loke on þe [þat] is oure ende. *Glose.* 2452

QUONIAM IGITUR QUI SCIT.[1] [¹ Read que sit.]

For as moche þan as þou hast seyn. whiche is þe forme of goode þat nys nat perfit. *and* whiche is þe forme of goode þat is perfit. now trowe I þat it were goode to shewe in what þis perfeccio*un* of blisfulnesse is set. *and* in þis þing I trowe þat we sholden first enquere forto witen yif þat any swiche manere goode as þilke goode þat þou hast diffinissed a lytel her byforne. þat is to seine souereyne goode may be founden in þe nature of þinges. For þat veyne ymaginacio*un* of þouȝt ne desceiue vs nat. *and* putte vs oute of þe soþefastnesse of þilke þinge þat is su*m*myttid to vs. þis is to seyne. but it may nat ben denoyed þat þilke goode ne is. ¶ and þat it nis ryȝt as a welle of alle goodes. ¶ For

2437 *owen*—C. omits
2438 *tourniþ*—MS. tourniþe
2439 *euenlyk*—eueno lyke
2440 *lyȝt[e]*—lyhte
2442 *benigne*—bygynnynge
2444 *yif*—yiue
   þi streite—the streyte
2445 [*hym*]—from C.
2446 *lyȝte*—lyht

2448 [*thow*]—from C.
2449 *bryȝtnes*—bryhtnesse
2451 *paþ*—MS. paþe; paath
2452 [*þat*]—that
2453 *whiche*—which [good
2454 · 55 · 56 · 58 · 59 *goode*—
2456 *whiche*—whych
2457 *set*—MS. sette, C. set
2460 *seine*—seyn

2460 *souereyne goode*—souereyn good
   be founden—ben fownde
2461 *veyne*—veyn
2463 *þis is to seyne*—C. omits
2464 *denoyed*—MS. deuoyded, C. denoyed
   goode—good
2465 *of*—MS. of of

al þing þat is cleped inperfit. is proued inperfit by þe amenusynge of perfeccioun. or of þing þat is perfit. and her of comeþ it. þat in euery þing general. yif þat. þat men seen any þing þat is inperfit * certys in þilke general þer mot ben somme þing þat is perfit. ¶ For yif so be þat perfeccioun is don awey. men may nat þinke nor seye fro whennes þilke þing is þat is cleped inperfit. ¶ For þe nature of þinges ne token nat her bygynnyng of þinges amenused and inperfit. but it proccdiþ of þingus þat ben al hool. and absolut. and descendeþ so dounc in to outerest þinges and in to þingus empty and wiþ oute fruyt. but as I haue shewed a litel her byforne. þat yif þer be a blisfulnesse þat be frele and vein and inperfit. þer may no man doute. þat þer nys som blisfulnesse þat is sad stedfast and perfit. b. þis is concludid quod I fermely and soþefastly. P. But considere also quod she in wham þis blisfulnesse enhabiteþ. þe commune acordaunce and conceite of þe corages of men proueþ and graunteþ þat god prince of alle þingus is good. ¶ For so as no þing ne may ben þouȝt bettre þan god. it may nat ben douted þan þat [he þat] no þing is bettre. þat he nys good. ¶ Certys resoun sheweþ þat god is so goode þat it proueþ by verray force þat perfit goode is in hym. ¶ For yif god ne is swiche. he ne may nat ben prince of alle þinges. for certis som þing possessyng in hym self perfit goode sholde ben more þan god. and [it] sholde seme þat þilke þing were first and elder þan god. ¶ For we han shewed apertly þat alle þinges þat ben perfit. ben first or þinges þat ben inperfit. ¶ And for þi for as moche as [that] my resoun or my proces ne go nat awey wiþoute an ende. we ouȝt[e] to graunten þat þe soucreyne god is ryȝt ful of

The sovereign good does exist, and is the source of all other good. When we say that a thing is imperfect we [⁴ fol. 21.] assert that there is something else of its kind perfect. Nature takes not her origin from things diminished and imperfect; but, proceeding from an entire and absolute substance, descends into the remotest and most fruitless things. If there be an imperfect and fading felicity there must also be one stable and perfect. But now consider wherein this felicity resides. That God is the governor of all things is proved by the universal opinion of all men. For since nothing may be conceived better 2482 than God, then He who has no equal in goodness must be good. Reason clearly demonstrates (1)that God is good, and (2) that the sovereign good exists in him. If it were not so He could not be the Ruler of all things, for there would be some other being excelling him who possesses the supreme good and who must have existed before Him. And we have already shown that the perfect precedes the imperfect; wherefore, that our reasonings may not run on with infinity, we must confess that the Supreme God is full of perfect and consummate good.

2466 al þing—alle thing
2468 her of comeþ—ther of comht
2470 somme—som
2471 don—MS. done, C. don
2473 token—took
2475 hool—hoole
2476 dounc—down
2477 wiþ oute fruyt—with owten frut
2490 stedfast—stvdefast
2491 fermely—MS. feunely, C. fermely
soþefastly—sothfastly
2496 [he þat]—from C.
is bettre—nis bettre
2488-89-91 goode—good
2489 swiche—swych
2492 [it]—from C.
seme—semen
2493 elder—elders
2495 [that]—from C.
2496 proces—processes
2497 ouȝt[e]—owen

And as we have seen that the perfect good is true happiness, it follows that the true felicity resides in the Supreme Divinity. But let us see how we can firmly and irrefragably prove that the Supreme God contains in his own nature a plenitude of perfect and consummate good. If you think that God has received this good from without, then you must believe that the giver of this good is more excellent than God the receiver. But we have concluded that there is nothing more excellent than God. But if this supreme good is in Him by nature, and is nevertheless of a different substance, we cannot conceive, since God is the author of all things, what could have united these two substances differing one from another. Lastly, a thing which essentially differs from another cannot be the same with that from which it is supposed to differ. Consequently, what in its nature differs from the chief good cannot be the supreme good. But it would be impious and profane thus to conceive of God, since nothing can excel Him in goodness and worth.

souereyne perfit goode. and we han establissed þat þe souereyne goode is verrey blisfulnesse. þan mot it nedes ben [þat verray blysfulnesse is] yset in souereyne god. B. þis take I wel quod .I. ne þis ne may nat be wiþseid in no manere. ¶ But I preie þe quod she see now how þou mayst preuen holily and wiþ-outen corrupcioun þis þat I haue seid. þat þe souereyne god is ryȝt ful of souereyne goode. [In whych manere quod I.] wenest þou ouȝt quod she þat þis prince of alle þinges haue ytake þilke souereyne good any where þan of hym self. **2508** ¶ of whiche souereyne goode men proueþ þat he is ful ryȝt as þou myȝtest þinken. þat god þat haþ blisfulnesse in hym self. and þat ilke blisfulnesse þat is in hym were diuers in substaunce. ¶ For yif þou wene þat god haue receyued þilke good oute of hym self. þou mayst wene þat he þat ȝaf þilke good to god. be more goode þan is god. ¶ But I am byknowen and confesse and þat ryȝt dignely þat god is ryȝt worþi abouen alle þinges. ¶ And yif so be þat þis good be in hym by nature. but þat it is diuers from [hym] by wenyng resoun. syn we speke of god prince of alle þinges feyne who so feyne may. who was he þat [hath] conioigned þise diuers þinges to-gidre. and eke at þe last[e] se wel þat o þing þat is diuers from any þing. þat þilke **2522** þing nis nat þat same þing. fro whiche it is vndirstonden to ben diuers. þan folweþ it. þat þilke þing þat by hys nature is dyuers from souereyne good. þat þat þing nys nat souereyne good. but certys þat were a felonous corsednesse to þinken þat of hym. þat no þing nis more worþe. For alwey of alle þinges. þe nature

---

2408 *goode*—good
2409 *souereyne goode*—souc-
 reyn good
2500 [*þat*——*is*]—from C.
 yset—MS. ysette, C. set
2501 *be*—ben
 wiþseid — MS. wiþseide,
 C. withseid
2503 *wiþ-outen*—with-owte
2504 *seid*—MS. seide, C. seyd
2505 *souereyne goode*—souc-

2505 [*In*——*I*]—from C.
2506 *ouȝt*—awht
2507 *þan of*—owt of
2508 *whiche*—whych
 souereyne goode—souereyn
 good
2509 *haþ*—MS. habe
2510 *þal ilke*—thilke
2511 *were*—weren
2514 *goode*—worth

2517 *from*—fro
 [*hym*]—from C.
2518 *feyne*—faigne
2519 *feyne*—feigne
 [*hath*]—from C.
2520 *last[e]*—laste
2521 *o*—a
2522 *whiche*—whych
2524 *from*—fro
2527 *nis*—is

THERE CANNOT BE TWO CHIEF GOODS.

of hem ne may nat ben better þan his bygynnyng. ¶ For whiche I may concluden by ryȝt uerray resoun. þat þilke þat is bygynnyng of alle þinges. þilke same þing is good in his substaunce. *B.* þou hast seid ryȝt-fully q*uod* .I. *P.* But we han graunted q*uod* she þat soucreyne good is blysfulnes. þat is soþe q*uod* .I. þan q*uod* she mote we nedes graunten *and* confessen þat þilke same souereyne goode be god. ¶ Certys *q*uod* .I. I ne may nat denye ne wiþstonde þe resou*ns* pur-posed. and I see wel þat it folweþ by strengþe of þe premisses. ¶ Loke nowe q*uod* she yif þis be proued [yit] more fermely þus. ¶ þat þer ne mowen nat ben two souereyne goodes þat ben diuerse amo[n]ges hem self. þat on is nat þat þat oþer is. þan [ne] mowen neiþer of hem ben p*er*fit. so as eyþer of hem lakkiþ to oþir. but þat þat nis nat p*er*fit men may seen apertly þat it nis nat soucreyne. þe þinges þan þat ben soucreynely goode ne mowen by no wey ben diuerse. ¶ But I haue wel conclude þat blisfulnesse *and* god ben [the] souereyne goode. For whiche it mot nedes be þat souereyne blisfulnesse is souerey[ne] dyuynite. ¶ No þing q*uod* I nis more soþefast þan þis ne more ferme by resou*n*. ne a more worþi þing þan god may nat ben concluded. *P.* vpon þise þinges þan q*uod* she. ryȝt as þise geometriens whan þei han shewed her p*ro*posiciou*ns* ben wont to bryngen in þinges þat þei clepen porismes or declaraciou*ns* of forseide þinges. ryȝt so wil I ȝeue þe here as a corolarie or a mede of corowne. For whi. for as moche as by þe getynge of blisfulnesse men ben maked blysful. *and* blisfulnesse is diuinite. ¶ þan is it manifest *and* open þat by þe gety*n*g of diuinite men ben makid blisful. ryȝt as by þe getynge of iustice . . .

In fact, nothing can exist whose nature is better than its origin. We may therefore conclude that the Author of all things is really and substantially the supreme Good. *B.* Most rightly said! *P.* But you have owned that true felicity is the sovereign good; then you must also [* fol. 21 *b.*] grant that God is that true felicity. *B.* Your conclusions follow from your premises. *P.* Let us see whether we cannot prove this more convincingly by considering it in this view, that there cannot be two sovereign goods which differ in themselves. For it is plain that of the goods that differ one cannot be what the other is; wherefore neither of them 2545 can be perfect where one wants the other. That which is not perfect cannot be the supreme good. Neither can the chief good be essentially different. But it has been shown that God and happiness are the chief good, wherefore the sovereign felicity and the Supreme Divinity are one and the same. Following then the examples of geometricians who deduce their consequences from their propositions, I shall deduce to thee something like a corollary as follows:—Because by the attainment of felicity men become happy, and

---

2529 *better*—bettre
2530 *whiche*—whych
2531 *seid*—MS. seide, C. seyd
2533 *soþe*—soth
2534 *mote*—moten
2539 [*yit*]—from C.
2541 *is* (1)—nis

2541 *oþer*—othre
[*ne*]—from C.
2516 *conclude*—concluded
2547 [*the*] from C.
goode—good   *be*—ben
2549 *soþefast*—sothfast
ferme — MS. forme, C.

ferme
2552 *proposiciouns* — MS. proporsiouns, C. propo-siciouns
2553 *porismes* — MS. poeis-mes, C. porysmes
2554 *wil*—wole

as felicity is the same as Diuinity itself, therefore by the attainment of Diuinity men are made happy. But as by the participation of justice or of wisdom men become just or wise, so by partaking of Diuinity they must necessarily, and by parity of reason, become gods. Every happy man then is a god. But by nature there is only *One*; but by participation of Diuine essence there may be many gods. But as happiness seems to be an assemblage of many things, ought we not to consider whether these several things constitute conjointly the body of happiness, or whether there is not some one of these particular things that may complete the substance or essence of it, and to which all the rest have a relation? *B.* Illustrate this matter by proper examples. *P.* As you grant that happiness is a good, you may say the same of all the other goods; for perfect sufficiency is identical with supreme felicity; so is supreme power, likewise high rank, a shining reputation, and perfect pleasure. What say you, then; are all these things, sufficiency, power, and the rest, to be considered as constituent parts of felicity? or are they to be referred to the sovereign good as their source and principal?

and by þe getyng of sapience þei ben maked wise. ¶ Ryȝt so nedes by þe semblable resou*n* whan þei han getyn diuinite þei ben maked goddys. þan is euery blisful man god. ¶ But certis by nature. þer nys but oon god. but by þe participaciou*n*s of diuinite þere ne letteþ ne disturbeþ no þing þat þer ne ben many goddes. ¶ þis is qu*o*d .I. a faire þing *and* a precious. ¶ Clepe it as þou wolt. be it corolarie or porisme or mede of coroune or declarynges ¶ Certys qu*o*d she no þing nis fairer. þan is þe þing þat by resou*n* sholde ben added to þise forseide þinges. what þing qu*o*d .I. ¶ So qu*o*d she as it semeþ þat blisfulnesse conteniþ many þinges. it were forto witen wheþir [þat] alle þise þinges maken or conioignen as a maner body of blysfulnesse by diuersite of parties or [of] me*m*bris. Or ellys yif any of alle þilke þi*n*gus be swyche þat it acomplise by hy*m* self þe substaunce of blisfulnesse. so þat alle þise oþer þinges ben referred and brouȝt to blisfulnesse. þat is to seyne as to þe chief of hem. ¶ I wolde qu*o*d I þat þou makedest me clerly to vndirstonde what þou seist. *and* þat þou recordest me þe forseide þinges. ¶ Haue I nat iuged qu*o*d she. þat blisfulnesse is goode. ȝis forsoþe qu*o*d .I. *and* þat souereyne goode. ¶ Adde þan qu*o*d she þilke goode þat is maked blisfulnes to alle þe forseide þinges. ¶ For þilke same blisfulnesse þat is demed to ben souereyne suffisaunce. þilke self is souereyne power. souereyne reuerence. souereyne clernesse or noblesse *and* souereyne delit. what seist þou þan of alle þise þinges. þat is to seyne. suffisance power *and* þise oþer þinges. ben þei þan as membris of blisfulnesse. or ben þei referred *and* brouȝt to souereyne good. ¶ Ryȝt as alle þinges þat ben brouȝt to þe chief of hem.

2563 *oon*—o
2564 *letteþ*—let
2566 *faire*—fayr
2567 *porisme*—MS. pousme, C. porisme
2572 [*þat*]—from C.
2573 *maner*—manere *by*—be

2574 [*of*]—from C.
2575 *swyche*—swych
2576 *oþer*—oothre
2577 *seyne*—seyn
2578 *chief*—chef
2581 *goode ȝis*—good ys
2582 *souereyne goode*—souereyn good

2583 *goode*—good
2585 *self*—selue
2588 *þise*—C. omits *seyne*—seyn
2590 *oþer*—oothre
2591 *brouȝt*—MS. wrouȝt, C. browht

b. I vndirstonde wel quod .I. what þou purposest to
seke. but I desijr[e] to herkene þat þou shewe it me.
p. Take now þus þe discressioun of þis questioun quod
she. yif al þise þinges quod she weren membris to
felicite. þan weren þei diuerse þat oon fro þat oþer.
¶ And swiche is þe nature of parties or of membris.
þat dyuerse membris compounen a body. ¶ Certis
quod I it haþ wel ben shewed her byforne. þat alle þise
þinges ben alle on þing. þan ben þei none membris quod
she. for ellys it sholde seme þat blisfulnesse were
conioigned *al of one membre alone. but þat is a þing
þat may nat ben doon. þis þing quod .I. nys nat
doutous. but I abide to herkene þe remenaunt of þe
questioun. þis is open and clere quod she. þat alle oþer
þinges ben referred and brouȝt to goode. ¶ For þerfore is suffisaunce requered. For it is demed to ben
good. and forþi is power requered. for men trowen also
þat it be goode. and þis same þing mowe we þinken and
coueiten of reuerence and of noblesse and of delit. þan
is souereyne good þe soume and þe cause of alle þat
auȝt[e] be desired. forwhi þilke þing þat wiþ-holdeþ no
good in it self ne semblaunce of goode it ne may nat
wel in no manere be desired ne requered. and þe contrarie. For þouȝ þat þinges by hir nature ne ben nat
goode algates yif men wene þat þei ben goode ȝit ben
þei desired as þouȝ [þat] þei were verrayly goode. and
þerfore is it þat men auȝten to wene by ryȝt þat bounte
be souereyne fyn and þe cause of alle þinges þat ben to
requeren. ¶ But certis þilke þat is cause for whiche
men requeren any þing. ¶ it semeþ þat þilke same
þing be most desired. as þus yif þat a wyȝt wolde ryde
for cause of hele. he ne desireþ nat so mychel þe

B. I see what you are aiming at, and I am desirous to hear your arguments.
P. If all these things were members of felicity, they would differ one from another, for it is the property of diverse parts to compose one body. But it has been well shown that all these things are the same and do not differ, therefore they are not parts, for if they were, happi- [* fol. 22.] *ness might be made up of one member—which is absurd and impossible.*
B. This I doubt not, but I desire to hear the sequel.
P. All the things above-mentioned must be tried by

2607
Good, as the rule and square.
Sufficiency, power, &c., are all desir-ed, because they are esteemed a good. Good is the cause why all things are desired. For that which contains no good, either in reality or appearance, can never be desired. On the contrary, things not essen-tially good are desired because they appear to be real goods. Hence, Good is esteemed as the cause and end of all things that we desire. That which is the cause of our de-siring any thing is itself what we chiefly want. If a man desire to ride on account of health—it is not the ride he wants so much as its salutary effects.

2593 *desijr[e] to herkene*—de-sire for to herkne
2594 *Take*—tak
2596 *fro*—from
2597 *swiche*—swhych
2600 *on þing*—othing
2602 *one*—on
2603 *ben doon*—be don

2604 *herkene*—herknen
2605 *clere*—cler
oþer—oothre
2606 *goode*—good
2609 *goode*—good
mowe—mowen
2617 [*þat*]—from C.
were verrayly — weeren

verraylyche
2618 *þerfore*—therfor
auȝten—owhten
2619 *alle*—alle the
2620 *whiche*—whych
2623 *mychel*—mochel

GOD A HAVEN OF REST.

*Since all things are sought after for the sake of Good, they cannot be more desirable than the good itself. It has been shown that all the aforesaid things are only pursued for the sake of happiness—hence it is clear that good and happiness are essentially the same.
B. I see no cause to differ from you.
P. It has been proved that God and happiness are identical and inseparable.
B. That is true. Therefore the substance of God is also the same as that of the Supreme Good.

[The 10th Metur.] Come hither, all ye that are captives—bound and fettered with the chains of earthly desires;—come to this source of goodness, where you shall find rest and security.
[Chaucer's gloss upon the Text.' Not the gold of Tagus or of Hermus, nor the gems of India, can clear the mental sight from vain delusions, but rather darken it.
Such sources of our delight are found in the earth's gloomy caverns,—but the bright light that rules the heavens dispels the darkness of the soul.
He who has seen this light will confess that the beams of the sun are weak and dim.*

moeuyng to ryden as þe effect of his heele. Now þan syn þat alle þinges ben requered for þe grace of good. þei ne ben [nat] desired of alle folk more þan þe same good ¶ But we han graunted þat blysfulnesse is þat þing for whiche þat alle þise oþer þinges ben desired. 2629 þan is it þus þat certis only blisfulnesse is requered *and* desired ¶ By whiche þing it sheweþ clerely þat good *and* blisfulnesse is al oone *and* þe same substaunce. ¶ I se nat qu*od* I wher fore þat men myȝt[en] discorden in þis. *p. and* we han shewed þat god *and* verrey blysfulnesse is al oon þing ¶ þat is soþe q*uod* .I. þan mowe we conclude sikerly þat þe substaunce of god is set in þilke same good *and* in noon oþer place. 2636

NUNC OMNES PARITER ETC.

O Comeþ alle to-gidre now ȝe þat ben ycauȝt *and* ybounde wiþ wicked[e] cheines by þe deceiuable delit of erþely þinges inhabytynge in ȝoure þouȝt. here shal ben þe reste of ȝoure laboures. here is þe hauene stable in peisible quiete. þis al oone is þe open refut to 2642 wreches. *Glosa.* þis is to seyn. þat ȝe þat ben combred *and* deceyued wiþ worldly affecc*i*ou*n*s comeþ now to þis souereyne good þat is god. þat is refut to hem þat wolen come to hym. *Textus.* ¶ Alle þe þinges þat þe ryuere Tagus ȝiueþ ȝow wiþ his golden[e] grauels. or ellys alle þe þynges þat þe ryuere herm*us*. ȝiueþ wiþ his rede brynke. or þat yndus ȝiueþ þat is nexte þe hote partie of þe worlde. þat medeleþ þe grene stones (smaragde) wiþ þe white (margarits). ne sholde nat cleren þe lokynge of ȝoure þoȝt. but hiden raþer ȝoure blynde corages wiþ i*n*ne hire dirkenesse ¶ Alle þat likeþ ȝow here *and* excitiþ *and* moeueþ ȝoure þouȝtes.

2624 *moeuyng*—moeuynge
2626 [*nat*]—from C.
2629 *oþer*—oothre
2630 *clerely*—clerly
   good and blisfulnesse—of
   good *and* of blysfulnesse
2631 *oone*—oon
2632 *myȝt*[*en*]—myhten
2634 *oon*—oo

2634 *soþe*—soth
2635 *mowe*—mowen
2636 *set*—MS. sette, C. set
2638 *wicked*[*e*]—wyckyde
2639, 2640 *here*—her
2640 *hauene* — MS. heuene, C. hauene
2641 *al oone*—allone
2643 *worldly*—worldely

2645 *come*—comyn
2646 *golden*[*e*] *grauels* — goldene gra*u*ayles
2647 *þynges*—MS. rynges, C. thinges
   hermus—MS. herin*us*, C. herynus
2648 *nexte*—next
2649 *worlde*—world

þe erþe haþ noryshed it in hys lowe caues. but þe
shynyng by þe whiche þe heuene is gouerned *and*
whennes þat it haþ hys strengþe þat chaseþ þe derke
ouerþrowyng of þe soule. ¶ And who so euer may
knowen þilke ly3t of blisfulnesse. he shal wel seiue þat
þe white bemes of þe sonne ne ben nat cleer. 2659

ASSENCIOR INQ*UAM* CUNCTA. Boice.

[The 11 prose.]

I assent[e] me q*uod* .I. For alle þise þinges ben
strongly bounden wiþ ry3t ferme rosou*n*s. how
mychel wilt 'þou preisen it q*uod* she. yif þat þou
knowe what þilke goode is. I wol preise. it q*uod* I by
price wiþ outen ende. ¶ yif it shal bytyde me to
knowe also to-gidre god þat is good. ¶ certys q*uod* she
þat shal I do þe by verray resou*n*. yif þat þo þinges þat
I haue conclude[d] a litel her by *forne dwellen oonly
in hir first[e] grauntyng. Boice. þei dwellen graunted 2668
to þe q*uod* .I. þis is to seyne as who seiþ .I. graunt þi
forseide conclusiou*n*s. ¶ Haue I nat shewed þe q*uod*
she þat þe þinges þat ben requered of many folke. ne
ben nat verray goodes ne p*er*fit. for þei ben diu*er*se þat
oon fro þat oþer. *and* so as eche of hem is lakkyng to
oþer. þei ne han no power to bryngen a good þat is ful
and absolute. ¶ But þan atte arst ben þei verray good
whan þei ben gadred to-gidre al in to a forme *and* in
to oon wirchyng. so þat þilke þing þat is suffisaunce.
þilk same be power *and* reuerence. *and* noblesse *and* 2678
mirþe. ¶ And forsoþe but alle þise þinges ben alle o
same þing þei ne han nat wher by þat þei mowen ben
put iu þe nou*m*bre of þinges. þat au3ten ben requered
or desired. *b*. ¶ It is shewed q*uod* .I. ne her of may
þer no man douten. *p*. þe þinges þan q*uod* she þat ne

B. I assent, and am convinced by the force of your arguments.
P. But how greatly would you value it, did you fully know what this good is ?
B. I should value it infinitely if at the same time I might attain to the knowledge of God, who is the sovereign good.

P. I shall elucidate this matter by incontrovertible reasons if thou wilt grant me those things which I have before laid down as conclusions.
B. I grant them all.
P. Have I not shown that the things which the majority of mankind so eagerly [* fol. 22 b.] pursue are not true and perfect goods, for they differ from one another; and because where one of them is absent the others cannot confer absolute happiness (or good) ? Have I not shown, too, that the true and chief good is made up of an assemblage of all the goods in such a way, that if sufficiency is an attribute of this good, it must at the same time possess power, reverence, &c. If they be not one and the same, why should they be classed among desirable things ?
While these things differ from one another they are not goods;

2654, 2656 *haþ*—MS. haþe
2654 *hys*—hy*s*e
2656 *chaseþ þe derke* — es-chueth the dyrke
2657 *euer*—C. omits
2658 *seine*—scyn
2660 *assent[e]*—assente
2662 *mychel*—mochel

2663 *goode*—good
2664 *price*—prys
2669 *is*—omitted *seyne*—scyn
2671 *folke*—folkes
2673 *oþer*—oothre *eche*—ech
2675 *absolute*—absolut

2675 *atte arst*—at erste
2676 *al*—alle *a*—O
2677 *to*—omitted *wirchyng*—wyrkynge
2678 *þilk*—thilke
2681 *put*—MS. putte, C. put *au3ten*—owhten

but as soon as they become one then they are made goods.—
Do not they owe their being good to their unity?
B. So it appears.
P. Do you confess that everything that is good becomes such by the participation of the sovereign good or no?
B. It is so.
P. Then you must own that unity and good are the same (for the substance of those things must be the same, whose effects do not naturally differ). B. I cannot gainsay it.
P. Do you not perceive that everything which exists is permanent so long as it preserves its unity— but as soon as it loses this, it is dissolved and annihilated?

2700

B. How so?
P. In the animal creation as long as the soul and the body are united and conjoined in one, this being is called an animal or beast, but when the union is dissolved by the separation of these, the animal perishes and is no longer a beast. The same may be said of man and all other things; they subsist while unity is preserved, but as soon as that is destroyed the things themselves lose their existence.
B. I believe we should find this true in every case.
P. Is there anything which acts naturally that forgoes this desire of existence and wishes for death and corruption?

ben none goodes whan þei ben diuerse. and whan þei bygynnen to ben al o þing. þan ben þei goodes. ne comiþ it hem nat þan by þe getynge of unite þat þei ben maked goodes. b. so it semeþ quod .I. but alle þing þat is good quod she grauntest þou þat it be good by participacioun of good or no. ¶ I graunt[e] it quod .I. ¶ þan mayst þou graunt[en] it quod she by sembleable resoun þat oon and good ben o same þing. ¶ For of þinges [of] whiche þat þe effect nis nat naturely diuerse nedys þe substaunce mot ben o same þinge. I ne may nat denye it quod I. ¶ Hast þou nat knowen wel quod she. þat al þing þat is haþ so longe his dwellyng and his substaunce. as longe is it oone. ¶ but whan it forletiþ to ben oone it mot nedis dien and corrumpe to-gidre. ¶ In whiche manere quod .I. ¶ Ryȝt as in beestes quod she. whan þe soule and þe body ben conioigned in oon and dwellen to-gidre it is cleped a beest. and whan hire vnite is destroied by disseueraunce þat oon fram þat oþir. þan sheweþ it wel þat it is a dede þing. and þat it is no lenger no beste. and þe body of a wyȝt while it dwelleþ in oon forme by coniunccioun of membris it is wel seyn þat it is a figure of mankynde. and yif þe partyes of þe body ben [so] diuide[d] and disseuered þat oon fro þat oþir þat þei destroien vnite. þe body forletiþ to ben þat it was byforne. ¶ And who so wolde renne in þe same manere by alle þinges he sholde seen þat wiþ outen doute euery þinge is in his substaunce as longe as it is oon. and whan it forletiþ to ben oon it dieþ and perissiþ. boice. whan I considre quod I many þinges I see noon oþer. ¶ Is þer any þing þanne quod she þat in as moche as it lyueþ naturely. þat forletiþ þe appetit or talent of

2684 *none*—no
2685 *al o*—alle oon
2686 *comiþ*—comth
2689 *graunt[e]*—graunte
2690 *mayst þou graunt[en]*—mosthow graunten
2692 [*of*]—from C.

2695 *al*—alle
haþ—MS. haþe
2696, 2697 *oone*—oon
2698 *whiche*—which
2703 *dede*—ded
lenger—lenȝere
beste—beest

2704 *while*—whil
oon—oo
2706 [*so*] *diuide[d]*—so deuydyd
2709 *so*—omitted
2713 *many*—manye

hys beynge. *and* desireþ to come to deeþ *and* to cor-rupcioun. ¶ yif I considere q*uo*d I þe beestes þat han any manere nature of willynge or of nillynge I ne fynde no þing. but yif it be constreyned fro wiþ out forþe. þat forletiþ or dispiseþ to lyue *and* to duren or þat wole his þankes hasten hy*m* to dien. ¶ For euery beest trauayleþ hy*m* to defende *and* kepe þe sauuac*i*oun of lijf. *and* escheweþ deeþ *and* destrucc*i*oun. *b.* but certys I doute me of herbes *and* of trees. þat is to seyn þat I am in a doute of swiche þinges as herbes or trees þat ne han no felyng soule. ne no naturel wirchynges seruyng to appetite as beestes han wheþer þei han appetite to dwellen *and* to duren. ¶ Certis q*uo*d she ne þer of þar þe nat doute. ¶ Now look vpon þise herbes *and* þise trees. þei waxen firste in swiche place as be*n* couenable to hem. in whiche place þei ne mowen nat sone dien ne dryen as longe as hire nature may defenden he*m*. ¶ For some of hem waxen in feldes *and* some in mountaignes. *and* oþir waxen in mareis. [*A leaf lost here, and supplied from C.*] 2735 [*and* oothre cleuyn on Roches / *and* soume waxen plenty-uos in sondes / *and* yif þat any wyht enforce hym to beryn hem in to oother places / they wexen drye // For nature yeueth to euery thing þat / þat is conuenient to hym *and* trauaylith þat they ne dye nat as longe as they han power to dwellyn *and* to lyuen // what woltow seyn of this / þat they drawen alle hyr norysshynges by hyr rootes / ryht as they haddyn hyr Mowthes I.-plounged wit*h* in the erthes / *and* shedyn by hyr maryes (i. medull*us*) hyr wode *and* hyr bark / *and* what woltow seyn of this þat thilke thing / þat is ryht softe as the marye (i. sapp) is / þat is alwey hidd in the feete al wit*h* inne *and* þat it is defendid fro wit*h* owte by the stidefastnesse of wode // *and* þat the vttereste bark is put ayenis the des-

B. I do not find any creature endowed with volition, which, of itself and without self and without constraint, renounces or despises life and self-preservation or willingly hastens to destruction. But with regard to herbs and trees, I am doubtful whether I ought to have the same opinion of them, for they have no sensitive soul, nor any natural volition like animals. P. There is no cause for doubt in respect to these. Herbs and trees first choose a convenient place to grow in, where, agreeably to their respective natures, they are sure to thrive, and are in no danger of perishing; for some grow on plains, some on mountains, &c.; and if you try to transplant them, they forthwith wither and die. To everything that vegetates, nature gives what is needful for its subsistence, and takes care that they should not perish before their time. Need I tell you that plants are nourished by their roots (which are so many mouths hid in the earth), and diffuse strength throughout the whole plant, as through their marrow? And further, it is admirably contrived that the pith, the most tender part of plants, is hid in the middle of the trunk, surrounded with hard and solid wood, and with an outer coat of bark to ward off the storms and weather.

2718 *willynge*—wylnynge
or—and
2719 *þing*—beest
out forþe—owte forth

2720 *lyue*—lyuen
2723 *of lijf*—of hys lyf
2726 *soule*—sowles
2727 *appetite*—appetites

2729 *look*—loke
2730 *waxen firste*—wexen
2733, 2734 *some*—som [fyrst
2734 *oþir*—oothre

Admire, too, the diligence of nature in propagating plants by a multiplicity of seeds, which are as a foundation for a building, not to remain for a time, but as it were for ever. Things inanimate incline to what is most suitable to their beings, and to preserve continuance. For why should the flame mount upwards by lightness, and the earth tend towards its centre by gravity (weight), unless these motions were agreeable to their respective natures? Whatever is agreeable to the nature of a thing preserves it. So what is contrary to its nature destroys it. Dense bodies, such as stones, resist an easy separation of parts; whereas the particles of liquid or flowing things, such as air and water, are easily separated and soon reunited. Fire avoids and utterly refuses any such division. I am not now treating of the voluntary motion of a conscious soul, but of the natural intention and instinct. We swallow our meat without thinking of it, and we draw our breath in sleep without perception. The love of life in animals is not derived from an intellectual will, but from natural principles implanted in them. For the will, induced by powerful reasons,

tempraunce of the heuene / as a defendowr myhty to suf-
2751 fren harm / and thus certes maystow wel sen / how gret is
the diligence of nature / For alle thinges renouelen and
puplisen hem with seed. I.-multiplyed / ne ther nis no man
þat ne wot wel þat they ne ben ryht as a foundement and
edyfice for to duren / nat only for a tyme / but ryht as forto
duren perdurablely by generacyoun // and the thinges ek
þat men wenen ne hauen none sowles / ne desire they nat ech
of hem by sem[b]lable resoun to kepyn þat that is hirs / þat
is to seyn þat is acordynge to hyr nature in conseruacioun
of hyr beynge and endurynge // For wher for elles berith
2761 lythnesse the flaumbes vp / and the weyhte presseth the
erthe a-doun // but For as moche as thilke places and
thilke moeuynges ben couenable to euerich of hem //
and forsothe euery thing kepith thilke þat is acordynge
and propre to hym // ryht as thinges þat ben contraryes
and enemys corompen hem // and yit the harde thinges
as stoones clyuen and holden hyr partyes to gydere
ryht faste and harde / and deffenden hem in withstond-
enge þat they ne departe nat lyhtly a twyne // and the
things þat ben softe and fletynge as is water and Eyr
2771 they departyn lyhtly // and yeuen place to hem þat
brekyn or deuyden hem // but natheles they retornen
sone ayein in to the same thinges fro whennes they ben
arraced // but fyr [fleetħ] and refuseth alle deuysyoun /
ne I. ne trete nat heere now of weleful moeuynges of the
sowle þat is knowynge // but of the naturel entencioun
of thinges // As thus ryht as we swolwe the mete þat we
resseyuen and ne thinke nat on it / and as we drawen
owre breth in slepynge þat we wite it nat whil we slepyt //
For certes in the beestys the loue of hyr lyuynges ne of
2781 hyr beeinges ne comth nat of the wilnynges of the sowle //
but of the bygynnyngis of nature // For certes thorw
constreynynge causes / wil desireth and embraceth ful

2753 *puplisen*—H. publisshen)
2755 *edyfice*—MS. edyfíte

2755 *a tyme*—H. oon) tyme
2758 *that*—H. omits
hirs—H. his

2774 [*fleeth*]—from H.
2775 *weleful*—H. wilfulle
2779 *slepyt*—H. slepen

ofte tyme / the deth þat nature dredith // that is to seyn as thus that a man may ben constreynyd so by som cause that his wil desireth and taketh the deth which þat nature hateth *and* dredeth ful sore // And som tyme we seeth the contrarye / as thus that the wil of a wight / destorbeth *and* constreyneth þat þat nature desireth / and requereth al-wey // that is to sein the werk of gen*er*acioun / by the whiche gen*er*acioun only / dwelleth *and* is sustenyd the longe durablete of mortal thinges // And thus this charite and this Loue þat eu*er*y thing hath to hym self ne comth nat of the moeuynge of the sowle / but of the entencioun of nature // For the pu*r*uyance of god hat yeuen to thinges þat ben creat of hym / this þat is a ful gret cause / to lyuen *and* to duren / for which they desiren naturelly hyr lyf as longe as euer they mowen // For w[h]ych thou maist nat drede by no manere / that alle the thinges / that ben anywhere / that they ne requeren naturelly / the ferme stablenesse of p*er*durable dwellynge / and ek the eschuynge of destruccyoun // B // now confesse I. wel q*uod* I. that I. see wel now certeynly / wi*th* owte dowtes / the thinges that whylom semeden vncerteyn to me / P. // but q*uod* she thilke thyng þat desireth to be *and* to dwellyn p*er*durablely / he desireth to ben oon // For yif þat that oon weere destroied // certes beinge ne shulde ther non dwellyn to no wiht // that is soth q*uod* I. // Thanne q*uod* she desirin alle thinges oon // .I. assente q*uod* .I. // *and* I haue shewyd q*uod* she that thilke same oon is thilke that is good // B // ye forsothe q*uod* I. // Alle thinges thanne q*uod* she requyren good // And thilke good thanne [þow] maist descryuen ryht thus // Good is thilke thing þat euery wyht desireth // Ther ne may be thowht q*uod* .I. no moore verray thing / for either alle thinges ben referred *and* browht to nowht / *and* floteryn wi*th* owte gou*er*nour

sometimes chooses and embraces death, although nature dreads and abhors it. And, on the contrary, we see that concupiscence (by which alone the human race is perpetuated) is often restrained by the will. Self-love possessed by every creature is not the 2791 product of volition, but proceeds from a natural impression or intention of nature. Providence has implanted in all created things an instinct, for the purpose of self-preservation, by which they desire to prolong existence to its utmost limits. Doubt not, therefore, that everything which 2799 exists desires existence and avoids dissolution. B. You have made those things perfectly plain and intelligible, which before were obscure and doubtful. P. That which desires to subsist desires also to retain its unity for if this be taken away it cannot continue to exist. 2807 B. That is very true! P. All things then desire one thing— unity. B. They do. P. Unity then is the same as good. B. Yes. P. Thus all things desire good —and it is one 2813 and the same good that all creatures desire. B. Nothing is more true. For either all things must be reduced to nothing (or have no relation

---

2788 *seeth*—H. seen
teil—H. wille
2792 *And*—H. as

2796 *hat*—H. haue
2800 *the*—H. þo
2806 *perdurablely*—H. per-

durably
2807 *destroied*—H. destrued
2811 *thilke* (1)—H. ilke

despoiled of oon / as of hir propre heued / or elles yif ther be any thinge / to which þat alle thinges tenden and hyen / that thing moste ben the souereyn good of alle goodes / P /. thanne seyde she thus // O my norry quod she I haue gret gladnesse of the // For thow hast fichched in thin herte the myddel sothtfastnesse // that is to seyn the prykke // but this thing hath ben descouered to the / in that thow seydyst þat thow wystest nat a lytel her by-forn // what was that quod I. // That thow ne wystest nat quod she whych was the ende of thinges // and Certes that is the thing þat euery wiht desireth // and for as mochel as we han gaderid / and comprehendyd that good is thilke thing that is desired of alle / thanne moten we nedes confessun / that good is the fyn of alle thinges.

QUISQUIS PROFUNDA MENTE.

WHo so that sekith soth by a deep thoght And coueyteth nat to ben deseyuyd by no mys-weyes // lat hym rollen and trenden with Inne hym self / the Lyht of his inward syhte // And lat hym gadere ayein enclynynge in to a compas the longe moeuynges of hys thowhtes / And lat hym techen his corage that he hath enclosed and hyd / in his tresors / al þat he compaseth or sekith fro with owte // And thanne thilke thing that the blake cloude of errour whilom hadde y-couered / shal lyhten more clerly thanne phebus hym self ne shyneth // Glosa // who so wole seken the dep[e] grounde / of soth in his thowht / and wol nat be deceyuyd by false proposiciouns / that goon amys fro the trouthe // lat hym wel examine / and rolle with inne hym self the nature and the propretes of the thing // and lat hym yit eft sones examine and rollen his thowhtes by good deliberacioun

TRUTH INTUITIVE.

or that he deme // and lat hym techen his sowle that it 2849
hat by naturel pryncyplis kyndeliche y-hyd with in
it self alle the trowthe the whiche he ymagynith to ben [Chaucer's gloss]
in thinges with owte // And thanne alle the dyrknesse of
his mysknowynge shal seen more euydently to [þe]
syhte of his vndyrstondynge thanne the sonne ne semyth 2854
to [þe] syhte with owte forth / For certes the body *For when the body enclosed the soul*
bryngynge the weyhte of foryetynge / ne hath nat chasyd *and cast oblivion o'er its powers*
owt of yowre thowhte al the clernesse of yowre knowyng // *it did wholly exterminate the heaven-born light.*
For certeynly the seed of sooth haldith *and* clyueth *The germs of truth were latent within,*
with in yowre corage / *and* it is a-waked *and* excited by *and were fanned into action*
the wynde *and* by the blastes of doctryne // For where *by the gentle breath of learning.*
for elles demen ye of yowre owne wyl the ryhtes whan 2861
ye ben axed // but yif so were þat the noryssynges of *Were not truth implanted in the*
resoun ne lyuede .I.-plowngyd in the depthe of yowre *heart, how could man distinguish*
herte // this [is] to seyn how sholden men demen þe *right from wrong?*
sooth of any thing þat weere axed / yif ther neere a
Roote of sothfastnesse þat weere yplowngyd *and* hyd in 2866
the nature[l] pryncyplis / the whiche sothfastnesse
lyued with in the depnesse of the thowght // *and* yif *So, if what Plato taught is true,*
so be þat the Muse *and* the doctryne of plato syngyth *'to learn is no other than to remember what had*
sooth // al þat euery whyht lerneth / he ne doth no *been before forgotten.'*
thing elles thanne but recordeth as men recordyn thinges
þat ben foryetyn. 2872

TUM EGO PLATONI INQUAM.

[The .12. prose.]

Thanne seide I thus // I acorde me gretly to plato / for *B. I am quite of Plato's opinion,*
thow remenbrist *and* recordist me thise thinges yit] *for you have now a second time recalled these things*
* þe seconde tyme. þat is to seyn. first whan I lost[e] my **[Addit. MS. 10,340, fol. 23.]*
memorie by þe contagioūs coniunccioun of þe body wiþ *to my remembrance which had been forgotten,*
þe soule. *and* eftsones afterward whan I lost[e] it con- *first by the contagious union of*
founded by þe charge *and* by þe burden of my sorwe. *soul and body, and afterwards by*
¶ And þan sayde she þus. ¶ If þou look[e] quod she *the pressure of my afflictions.*
firste þe þinges þat þou hast grauntcd it ne shal nat *P. If you will reflect upon the con-*

2863 *depthe*—H. depe 2867 *nature[l]*—H. naturelle 2879 *look[e]*—looke
2864 [*is*]—from H. 2875, 2877 *lost[e]*—loste 2890 *firste*—fyrst
sholden—H. shulde 2878 *burden*—burdene

cessions you have already made, you will soon call to mind that truth, of which you lately confessed your ignorance.
B. What is that?
P. It was, by what power the world is governed.
B. With regard to that, I own I confessed my ignorance, but though I now remotely see what you infer, yet I wish for further explanation from you.
P. You acknowledged a little while ago that this world was governed by God?
B. I still cling to this opinion, and will give you my reasons for this belief. The discordant elements of this world

2895

would never have assumed their present form unless there had been a wise Intelligence to unite them; and even after such a union, the joining of such opposites would have disunited and ruined the fabric made up of them, had not the same conjoining hand kept them together. The order that reigns throughout nature could not proceed so regularly and uniformly if there were not a Being, unchangeable and stedfast, to order and dispose so great a diversity of changes. This Being, the creator and ruler of all things, I call God.
P. As thy sentiments on these

ben ryȝt feer þat þou ne shalt remembren þilke þing þat þou seidest þat þou nistest nat. what þing quod I. ¶ by whiche gouerment quod she þat þis worlde is gouerned. Me remembriþ it wel quod I. and I confesse wel þat I ne wist[e] it nat ¶ But al be it so þat I se now from afer what þou purposest ¶ Algates I desire ȝit to herkene it of þe more pleynely. ¶ þou ne wendest nat quod she a litel here byforne þat men sholden doute þat þis worlde is gouerned by god. ¶ Certys quod I ne ȝitte doute I it nauȝt. ne I nil neuer wene þat it were to doute. as who seiþ. but I wot wel þat god gouerneþ þis worlde. ¶ And I shal shortly answere þe by what resouns I am brouȝt to þis. ¶ þis worlde quod I of so many dyuerse and contrarious parties ne myȝten neuer han ben assembled in o forme. but yif þere ne were oon þat conioigned so many[e diuerse] þinges. ¶ And þe same diuersite of hire natures þat so discordeden þat oon fro þat oþer most[e] departen and vnioignen þe þinges þat ben conioigned. yif þere ne were oon þat contened[e] þat he haþ conioigned and ybounde. ne þe certein ordre of nature ne sholde. nat brynge furþe so ordinee moeuynge. by places. by tymes. by doynges. by spaces. by qualites. yif þere ne were oon þat were ay stedfast dwellynge. þat ordeyned[e] and disposed[e] þise diuersites of moeuynges. ¶ and þilke þinge what so euer it be. by whiche þat alle þinges ben maked and ylad. I clepe hym god þat is a worde þat is vsed to alle folke. þan seide she. syn þou felest þus þise þinges quod she. I trowe þat I haue lytel more to done. þat þou myȝty of

2883 *whiche*—which
gouerment—gouernement
worlde—wordyl
2885 *wist[e]*—wiste
2887 *pleynely*—pleynly
2888 *here byforne*—her byforn
2889 *worlde is*—world nis
2890 *ȝitte doute* — yit ne dowte
nil—nel
2892 *wot*—MS. wote, C. wot

2892, 2894 *worlde*—world
2893 *answere*—answeren
2894 *many*—manye
2895 *myȝten*—myhte
2896 *þere*—ther
many[e]—manye
2897 [*diuerse*]—from C.
hire—hir
2899 *most[e]*—moste
2900 *þere*—ther
contened[e]—contenede
haþ—MS. haþe

2902 *furþe*—forth
ordinee moeuynge—ordene moeuynges
2904 *þere*—ther
stedfast—stidefast
2905 *ordeyned[e]*—ordeynede
disposed[e]—disponede
2907 *whiche*—which
ben—be
ylad—MS. yladde, C. I-ladd
2908 *worde*—word
folke—foolk

wilfulnesse hool *and* sounde ne se eftsones þi contre. ¶ But lat vs loken þe þinges þat we han *purposed* her-byforn. ¶ Haue I nat noumbred *and* seid q*uod* she þat suffisaunce is in blisfulnesse. *and* we han accorded þat god is *and* þilke same blisfulnesse. ¶ yis forsoþe q*uod* I. *and* þat to gouerne þis worlde q*uod* she. ne shal he neuer han nede of none helpe fro wiþoute. for ellys yif he had[de] nede of any helpe. he ne sholde not haue [no] ful suffisau*n*ce. ȝis þus it mot nedes be q*uod* I. ¶ þan ordeyneþ he by hym self al oon alle þinges q*uod* she. þat may nat ben denied q*uod* I. ¶ And I haue shewed þat god is þe same good. ¶ It remembreþ me wel q*uod* I. ¶ þan ordeineþ he alle þinges by þilke goode q*uod* she. Syn he whiche we han accorded to ben good gouerneþ alle þing*us* by hym self. *and* he is a keye *and* a stiere by whiche þat þe edifice of þis worlde is ykept stable *and* wiþ oute corumpynge ¶ I accorde me gretly q*uod* I. *and* I ape*r*ceiuede a litel here byforn þat þou woldest seyne þus. Al be it so þat it were by a þinne suspeciou*n*. I trowe it wel q*uod* she. ¶ For as I trowe þou leedest nowe more ententifly þine eyen to loken þe verray goodes ¶ but naþeles þe þinges þat I shal telle þe ȝit ne sheweþ nat lasse to loken. what is þat q*uod* I. ¶ So as men trowen q*uod* she *and* þat ryȝtfully þat god gouerneþ alle þinges by þe keye of his goodnesse. ¶ And alle þise same þinges as I [haue] tauȝt þe. hasten hem by naturel entenciou*n* to comen to goode þer may no man doute*n*. þat þei ne ben gouerned uoluntariely. *and* þat þei ne conuerten [hem] nat of her owe*n* wille to þe wille of hire ordenou*r*. as þei þat ben accordyng *and* enclinynge to her gouernour

points are so just
I have but little
more to do—for
thou mayest be
happy and secure,
and revisit thy
own country. But
let us reflect a
little more upon
these matters.
Did we not agree
that *Sufficiency* is
of the nature of
true happiness?
And have we not
seen that God is
that true felicity,
and that He needs
no external aid
nor instruments?
For if he should,
he would not be
self-sufficient.
And he directs all
things by himself
alone?
B. It cannot be
gainsaid.
P. I have shown
that God is the
chief good; God
must,therefore,direct and order all
things by *good*,
since he governs
them by himself,
whom we have
proved to be the
supreme good,
2928
and he is that
helm and rudder,
by which this machine of the world
is steadily and securely conducted.
B. I entirely agree
to this, and partly
anticipated your
remarks. P. I
believe it; for your
eyes are now more
intent upon these
great truths relating to true
felicity; but what
I am going to say is
not less open to
your view.
B. What is that?
P. As we believe
that God governs
all things by his
goodness, and that
all things have a
natural tendency
towards the *good*,
can it be doubted
but that they all
voluntarily sub-

2911 *wilfulnesse* — welefulnesse
2912 *han*—ha
2913 *seid*—MS. seide, C. seyd
2916 *worlde*—world
2917 *none helpe*—non help
2918 *had[de]*—hadde
helpe—help
2919 [*no*]—from C.
2920 *al oon*—allone
2921 *ben denied*—be denoyed
2924, 2926 *whiche*—which
2925 *ben*—be
2926 *worlde*—world
2928 *gretly*—gretely
here—her
2929 *seyne*—seye
2931 *nowe*—now
2932 *naþeles*—nat[h]les
2935 *ryȝtfully*—MS. on ryȝtfully
2936 [*haue*]—from C.
2938 *goode*—good
2939 [*hem*]—from C.
2940 *nat*—omitted
her—hir
owen—owne
wille (both)—wil
hire—hyr
2941 *her*—hyr

[* Fol. 23 b.]
mit to the will
and control
of their ruler?
B. It cannot be
otherwise. There
would be no safety
for those who
obey, if the discord
of a portion were
allowed. P. Is
there anything
that follows the

2948

dictates of nature
that seeks to
counteract the will
of God? B. No.
P. If there should
be any such, it
could not pre-
vail against
him, who is su-
premely happy
and consequently
omnipotent.
Then there is
nothing that
either will or can
withstand this
supreme good?
B. Nothing,
certainly.
P. It is then the
supreme good that

2958

governs and
orders all things
powerfully and
benignly.
B. I am delighted
with your conclu-
sions, but much
more with your
language; so that
fools may be
ashamed of their
objections to the
divine govern-
ment.
[Chaucer's gloss.]
P. You have read
the Poets' fables,

2966

how the Giants
stormed heaven—
how they were re-
pulsed and
punished accord-
ing to their
deserts; but may
we not compare
our reasons to-
gether, for by so
doing some clear
spark of truth may
shine forth: ?

and her kyng. ¶ It mot nedys be so q*uo*d. I. *¶ For
þe realme ne sholde not seme blisful ʒif þere were a ʒok
of mysdrawynges in diuerse parties ne þe sauynge of
obedient þinges ne sholde nat be. þan is þere no þing
q*uo*d she þat kepiþ hys nature? þat enforceþ hym to
gone aʒeyne god. ¶ No quod. I. ¶ And if þat any þing
enforced[e] hym to wiþstonde god. myʒt[e] it auayle at
þe laste aʒeyns hym þat we han graunted to ben al
myʒty by þe ryʒt of blisfulnesse. ¶ Certis q*uo*d I al
outerly it ne myʒt[e] nat auaylen hym. þan is þere no
þing q*uo*d she þat eyþer wol or may wiþstonde to þis
souereyne good. ¶ I trowe nat q*uo*d. I ¶ þan is
þilke þe souereyne good q*uo*d she þat alle þingus
gouerneþ strongly *and* ordeyneþ hem softly. þan seide I
þus. I delite me q*uo*d I nat oonly in þe endes or in þe
sommes of [the] resouns þat þou hast concludid *and*
proued. ¶ But þilke wordes þat þou vsest deliten me
moche more. ¶ So at þe last[e] fooles þat somtyme
renden greet[e] þinges auʒten ben asshamed of hem
self. ¶ þat is to seyne þat we fooles þat reprehenden
wickedly þe þingus þat touchen goddes gouernaunce we
auʒten ben asshamed of oure self. As I þat seide god
refuseþ oonly þe werkes of men. *and* ne entremetiþ nat
of hem. p. þou hast wel herd q*uo*d she þe fables of þe
poetes. how þe geauntes assailden þe heuene wiþ þe
goddes. but for soþe þe debonaire force of god disposed[e]
hem so as it was worþi. þat is to seyne distroied[e] þe
geauntes. as it was worþi. ¶ But wilt þou þat we
ioygnen togedre þilke same resouns. for perauenture of
swiche coniuncciou*n* may sterten vp some faire sperkele
of soþe ¶ Do q*uo*d I as þe list. wenest þou q*uo*d she

2943 *realme*—Reaume
seme—semen
2945 þere—ther
2947 *goneaʒeyne*—goonayein
2948 *enforced[e]*—enforcede
myʒt[e]—myhte
auayle—auaylen
2949 *aʒeyns*—a-yenis
2951 *outerly*—owtrely
myʒt[e]—myhte
auaylen — MS. aualcyne,

C. auaylen
hym—hem
þere—ther
2952 *wol*—wole
wiþstonde—with-stondyn
þis *souereyne* — his soue-
2955 *softly*—softtely [reyn
2957 *sommes*—somme
[*the*]—from C.
2959 *last[e]*—laste
2960 *greet[e]*—grete

2960, 2963 *auʒten*—owhten
2961 *seyne*—seyn
2965 *of hem*—of it
herd—MS. herde, C. herd
2967 *disposed[e]*—de-posede
2968 *seyne distroied[e]*—seyn
destroyede
2971 *swiche*—swych
some—som
2972 *soþe*—soth
list—liste

þat god ne is almyȝty. no man is in doute of it. Certys *B. As you plense.*
quod I no wyȝt ne defendiþ it if he be in hys mynde. *P. Is God omnipotent? B. No one doubts it.*
but he quod she þat is al myȝty þere nis no þing þat he *P. If he is almighty, there are,*
ne may do. þat is soþe quod I. May god done yuel *then, no limits to his power?*
quod she. nay for soþe quod. I. ¶ þan is yuel no þing *B. He can doubtless do all things.*
quod she. ¶ Syn þat he ne may not done yuel þat *P. May God do evil? B. No.*
may done alle þinges. scornest þou me quod. I. or ellys *P. Is evil nothing, since God, who is almighty, cannot*
pleyest þou or decciuest þou me. þat hast so wouen me *do it? B. Dost thou mock*
wiþ þi resouns. þe house of didalus so entrelaced. þat it *me or play with me, leading me*
is vnable to ben vnlaced. þou þat oþer while entrest *with thy arguments into an inextricable laby-*
þere þou issest *and* oþer while issest þere þou entrest. *rinth, and enclosing me in a won-*
ne fooldest þou nat to gidre by replicacioun of wordes a *derful circle of Divine Simplicity?*
maner wondirful cercle or envirounynge of symplicite *For thou didst first begin with*
deuyne. ¶ For certys a litel her byforne whan þou by- *happiness, and didst say that it*
gunne atte blisfulnesse þou seidest þat it is souereyne *was the sovereign good, and that it*
good. *and* seidest þat it is set in souereyne god. *and* þat *resided in God; then, that God was*
god is þe ful[le] blisfulnesse. for whiche þou ȝaf[e] me *that Good and the*
as a couenable ȝifte. þat is to seyne þat no wyȝt nis *perfection of happiness; and,*
blisful. but yif he be good al so þer wiþ *and* seidest *hence, thou didst infer that nobody could be happy*
eke þat þe forme of goode is þe substaunce of god. *and* *unless he became likewise a God.*
of blisfulnesse. *and* seidest þat þilke same oone is þilke *Again, thou saidst that the very form*
same goode þat is requered *and* desired of al þe kynde *of good was the substance whereof*
of þinges. *and* þou proeuedest in disputynge þat god *God and happiness were composed,*
gouerneþ alle [the] þinges of þe worlde by þe gouerne- *and that it was the object and*
mentys of bountee. *and* seydest þat alle þinges wolen *desire of all things in nature. Thou didst prove that*
ybeyen to hym. and seidest þat þe nature of yuel nis *God rules the world by his goodness, and that all*
no þing. *and* þise þinges ne shewedest þou nat wiþ no *things willingly obeyed him; and*
resouns ytake fro wiþoute but by proues in cercles *and* *that evil has no existence. These*
homelyche knowen. ¶ þe whiche proeues drawen to hem *truths you established by forcible*
self hir feiþ *and* hir accorde eueriche [of] hem of oþer. þan *and natural arguments, and by no strained and far-*
seide she þus. I ne scorne þe nat ne pleye ne desseyue *fetched reasons.*

2973 *is* (1)—be
 man—omitted
 is (2)—nis
2974 *defendiþ*—dowteth
2975 *þers*—ther
2976 *do*—C. omits
 soþe—soth
 done—don
2978, 2979 *done*—don
2980 *wouen*—MS. wonnen, C.

wouen
2981 *house*—hows
2983 *þere (both)*—ther
2987 *atte*—at
2988 *set*—MS. sette, C. set
1999 *ful[le]*—fulle
 whiche—which
 ȝaf[e]—yaue
2990 ȝifte—yift
 seyne—seyn

2992, 2994 *goode*—good
2993 *oone*—oon
2994 *al*—alle
2996 [*the*]—from C.
2998 *ybeyen*—obeyen
2999 *no* (2)—none
3000 *ytake*—I-taken
3001 *homelyche*—hoomlich
3002 *eueriche*—euerich
 [*of*]—from C.

GOD IS LIKE A SPHERE.

P. I have not deluded you, for by the Divine aid we have accomplished our chief task. I have proved to you that it is an essential property of the Divine nature not to go out of itself, nor to receive into itself anything extraneous. Parmenides says of the Deity that God is like a well-rounded sphere.

þe. but I haue shewed to þe þinge þat is grettest ouer alle þinges by þe ȝifte of god þat we some tyme prayden ¶ For þis is þe forme of [the] deuyne substaunce. þat is swiche þat it ne slydeþ nat in to outerest foreine þinges. ne ne rec[e]yueþ no strange þinges in hym. but ryȝt as parmaynws seide in grek of þilke deuyne substaunce. he seide þus þat þilke deuyne substaunce torneþ þe worlde and þilke cercle moeueable of þinges while þilke dyuyne substaunce kepiþ it self wiþ outen 3012

[* fol. 24.] He causes the moving globe to revolve, but is himself immovable. If I have chosen my arguments from within range of our discussion, do not let that surprise you, for, as Plato has taught us, there ought to be an alliance between the words and the subject of discourse.

moeuynge. þat * is to seyne þat it ne moeuiþ neuere mo. and ȝitte it moeueþ alle oþer þinges. but na-þeles yif I [haue] stered resouns þat ne ben nat taken fro wiþ oute þe compas of þe þinge of whiche we treten. but resouns þat ben bystowed wiþ inne þat compas þere nis nat whi þat þou sholde[st] merueylen. sen þou hast lerned by þe sentence of plato þat nedes þe wordes moten ben cosynes to þo þinges of whiche þei speken. 3020

FELIX QUI POTERIT. ET CETERA.

[The .12. Metur.] Happy is he that hath seen the lucid spring of truth! Happy the man that hath freed himself from terrestrial chains! The Thracian poet, consumed with grief for the loss of his wife, sought relief from music. His mournful songs drew the woods along; the rolling rivers ceased to flow; the savage beasts became heedless of their prey; the timid hare was not aghast at the hound. But the

Blisful is þat man þat may seen þe clere welle of good. blisful is he þat may vnbynde hym fro þe bonde of heuy erþe. ¶ þe poete of trace [orpheus] þat somtyme hadde ryȝt greet sorowe for þe deeþ of hys wijf. aftir þat he hadde maked by hys wepely songes þe wodes meueable to rennen. and hadde ymaked þe ryueres to stonden stille. and maked þe hertys and hyndes to ioignen dredles hir sides to cruel lyouns to herkene his songe. and had[de] maked þat þe hare was nat agast of þe hounde whiche þat was plesed by hys songe. so þat whane þe most[e] ardaunt loue of hys wijf brende þe

---

3004 þe þinge—the the thing
3005 ȝifte—yift
    some tyme prayden — whilom preyeden
3006 [the]—from C.
3007 swiche—swich
3009 parmaynws — a parmanides
3011 worlde—world
3012 while—whil
    wiþ outen—with owte

3013 seyne—seyn
3014 ȝitte—yit
    oþer—oothre
3015 [haue]—from C.
3016 whiche—which
3017 wiþ inne—with in
3020 cosynes—MS.conceyued, C. cosynes
    þo—þe
    whiche—which
3022 vnbynde—vnbyndyn

3022 bonde—bondes
3023 [orpheus]—from C.
    somtyme—whilom
3024 sorowe—sorwe
3029 dredles—dredeles
    to herkene—forto herknen
3029 had[de]—hadde
3030 þat (2)—omitted
3031 most[e]—moste

THE POWER OF MUSIC.

entrailes of his brest. ne þe songes þat hadde ouer
comen alle þinges ne my3ten nat assuage hir lorde
orpheus. ¶ He pleyned[e] hym of þe godes þat weren
cruel to hym. he wente hym to þe houses of helle *and*
þere he tempred[e] hys blaundissyng songes by re- 3036
sounyng of hys strenges. ¶ And spak *and* song in
wepynge alle þat euer he hadde resceyued *and* laued
oute of þe noble welles of hys modir calliope þe goddesse. *and* he song wiþ as mychel as he my3t[e] of
wepynge. *and* wiþ as myche as loue þat doubled[e] his
sorwe my3t[e] ;eueu hym *and* teche hym in his seke
herte. ¶ And he commoeuede þe helle *and* requered[e]
and sou3te by swete preiere þe lordes of soules in helle 3044
of relesynge. þat is to seyne to 3elden hym hys wif.
¶ Cerberus þe porter of helle wiþ his þre heuedes was
cau3t *and* al abaist for þe new[e] songe. *and* þe þre god-
desses furijs *and* vengerisse of felonies þat tourmenten
and agasten þe soules by anoye wexen sorweful *and* sory 3049
and wepen teres for pitee. þan was nat þe heued of
Ixione ytourmented by þe ouerþrowing whele. ¶ And
tantalus þat was destroied by þe woodnesse of longe
þrust dispiseþ þe flodes to drynke. þe fowel þat hy3t
voltor þat etiþ þe stomak or þe giser of ticius is so fulfilled of his songe þat it nil etyn ne tyren no more.
¶ Atte þe laste þe lorde *and* Iuge of soules was moeued
to misericordes *and* cried[e] we ben ouer comen q*uo*d
he. yif[e] we to orpheus his wijf to bere hym compaignye he haþ welle I-bou3t hir by his faire songe *and*

*songs that did all
things tame, could
not allay their
master's ardent
love. He bewailed
the cruelty of the
gods above, and
descended to
Pluto's realm.*

*There he struck
his tuneful strings
and sang, ex-
hausting all the
harmonious art
imparted to him
by his mother
Calliope.
In songs dictated
both by grief and
love, he implored
the infernal
powers to give
him back his
Eurydice.*

*Cerberus, Hell's
three-headed
porter, stood
amazed;
the Furies, tor-
mentors of guilty
souls, did weep;*

*Ixion, tormented
by the revolving
wheel, found rest;
Tantalus, suffer-
ing from a long
and raging thirst,
despised the
stream;
and the greedy
vulture did cease
to eat and tear the
growing liver of
Tityus. At length
Pluto himself re-
lented, crying
out, 'We are
overcome! Let
us give him back
his wife, he hath
well won her by
his song.*

3032 *hadde*—hadden
3033 *assuage*—asswagen
  lorde—lord
3034 *pleyned*[e]—pleynede
  godes—heuene goodes
3035 *wente*—MS. wenten, C.
  wente
3036 *tempred*[e] *hys*—tem-
  prede hise
3037 *of hys*—C. omits
  spak—MS. spakke, C. spak
  song—MS. songe, C. soonge
3038 *alle*—al
3039 *oute*—owt
  goddesse—goddes
3040 *song* — MS. songe, C.

*soonge
mychel*—mochel
3041 *myche*—moche
  doubled[e]—dowblede
3042 *my3t*[e]—myhte
  3euen—yeue
  teche—thechen
  in——*herte*—omitted
3043 *commoeuede*—MS. comaunded, C. commoeuede
3044 *sou3te*—by-sowhte
3045 *3elden*—yilden
3046 *his*—hise
3047 *cau3t*—MS. cau3te, C.
  cawht
  new[e] *songe*—newe song

3049 *anoye* ——*sorweful*—
  anoy woxen soruful
3050 *þan*—tho ne
3051 *whele*—wheel
3053 *þrust*—thurst
  hy3t—hihte
3054 *fulfilled*—fulfyld
3055 *songe*—song
3056 *Atte*—At
  lorde—lord
3057 *cried*[e]—cryde
3058 *yif*[e]—yiue
3059 *haþ*—MS. haþe
  welle—wel
  faire—C. omits
  songe—song

But we will lay this injunction upon him. Till he escape the infernal bounds, he shall not cast a backward look.' But, who shall give a lover any law? Love is a greater law than may be given to any earthly man. Alas! having left the realms of night, Orpheus cast a look behind and lost his too-much-loved Euridice. This fable belongs to all you, whose minds would view the Sovereign Good.		his ditee. but we wil putte*n* a lawe in þis. *and* couenaunt in þe ʒifte. þat is to seyne. þat til he be out of helle yif he loke byhynden hym [þ*at*] hys wijf shal come*n* aʒeine to vs ¶ but what is he þat may ʒeue a lawe to loueres. loue is a gretter lawe *and* a strongere to hym self þan any lawe þat men may ʒeuen. ¶ Allas whan Orpheus *and* his wijf were al most at þe termes of þe nyʒt. þat is to seyne at þe last[e] boundes of helle. Orpheus loked[e] abakwarde on Erudice his wijf *and* lost[e] hir *and* was deed. ¶ þis fable apperteineþ to ʒow alle who so euer desireþ or sekiþ to lede his pouʒte
3071		in to þe souereyne day. þat is to seyne to clerenes[se]
For he who fixes his thoughts upon earthly things and low, must lose the noble and heaven-imparted Good.		of souereyne goode. ¶ For who so þat euere be so ouer come*n* þat he fycche hys eyen in to þe put[te] of helle. þat is to seyne who so setteþ his pouʒtes in erþely þinges. al þat euer he haþ drawen of þe noble good
3076		celestial he lesiþ it whan he lokeþ þe helles. þat is to seyne to lowe þinges of þe erþe.

EXPLICIT LIBER TERCIUS.

[* fol. 24 b.] **INCIPIT LIBER QUARTUS.**

HEC CUM PHILOSOPHIA DIGNITATE UULT*US*.

[The 1ᵐᵉ prose.]
When P. with grace and dignity had poured forth her songs, I, not quite quit of my load of grief, interrupted her as she was continuing her discourse.

Whanne philosophie hadde songe*n* softly *and* delitably þe forseide þinges kepynge þe dignitee of hir cheere in þe weyʒte of hir wordes. I þan þat ne hadde nat al out*er*ly forʒeten þe wepyng *and* mournyng

3082 þat was set in myne herte for-brek þe entenc*i*oun of hir

All your discourses, O my conductress to the

þat entended[e] ʒitte to seyne oþer þinges. ¶ Se q*uod* I. þou þat art gideresse of verray lyʒte þe þinges þat þou

---

3060 *wil putten*—wol putte
3062 *byhynden*—by-hynde
   [þ*at*]—from C.
3063 *to*—vn-to
3064 *gretter*—gret
3066 *were al most*—weren almest
3067 *last*[*e*]—laste
3068 *loked*[*e*] *abakwarde* —

lokede abacward
3069 *lost*[*e*]—loste
3070 þouʒ*te*—thowht
3071 *clerenes*[*se*]—clernesse
3072 *souereyne goode*—souereyn god
3073 *put*[*te*]—putte
3074 *setteþ*—sette
3075 *haþ*—MS. haþe

3078 *softly*—softely
3080 *cheere in*—cheere *and*
3082 *set*—MS. sette, C. set
   myne—Myn
   for-brek—MS. for-breke, C. Forbrak
3083 *entended*[*e*]—entendede
3084 *lyʒte*—lyht

hast seid [me] hider to ben to me so clere *and* so shew- <small>true light! have been very clear and</small>
yng by þe deuyne lokyng of hem *and* by þi resou*n*s þat <small>unanswerable, both by the divine testimony which</small>
þei ne mowe nat ben ouercomen. ¶ And þilke þi*ngus* <small>they carry along with them, and</small>
þat þou toldest me. al be it so þat I hadde som tyme <small>by thy irrefragable arguments.</small>
fo[r]ȝeten hem for [the] sorwe of þe wronge þat haþ ben <small>Through the oppression of grief I had forgotten</small>
don to me. ȝit naþeles þei ne were nat alouterly vn- <small>these truths, but was not wholly</small>
knowen to me. but þis same is namly a gret cause of <small>ignorant of them. The principal</small>
my sorwe. þat so as þe gouernoure of þinges is goode. <small>cause of my trouble is this—</small>
yif þat yuelys mowen ben by any weyes. or ellys yif <small>that, whilst the absolute Ruler of</small>
þat yuelys passen wiþ outen punyssheinge. þe whiche <small>all things is goodness itself, evil exists and is al-</small>
þinge oonly how worþi it is to ben wondred vpon. þou <small>lowed to pass unpunished. This,</small>
considerest it weel þi self certeynly. but ȝitte to þis <small>to say the least, is astonishing.</small>
þing þere is an oþer þing y-ioigned more to ben ywon- 3097
dred vpon. ¶ For felonie is emperisse *and* flowreþ ful of <small>Moreover, while vice flourishes</small>
rycchesse. and vertues nis nat al oonly wiþ outen medes. <small>*virtue* is not only unrewarded, but</small>
but it is cast vndir *and* fortroden vndir þe feet of fe- <small>trampled under foot by base and</small>
lonous folk. *and* it abieþ þe tourmentes in sted of <small>profligate men, and suffers the</small>
wicked felou*n*s ¶ Of al[le] whiche þing þer nis no wyȝt <small>punishment due to impiety. Here is cause for</small>
þat [may] merueyllen ynouȝ ne compleyne þat swiche <small>wonderment, since such things</small>
þinges ben don in þe regne of god þat alle þinges woot. <small>are possible under the government of an omniscient and</small>
and alle þinges may *and* ne wool nat but only goode <small>omnipotent God, who wills nothing</small>
þinges. ¶ þan seide she þus. certys quod she þat were <small>but what is the best.</small>
a grete meruayle *and* an enbaissynge wiþouten ende. 3107
and wel more horrible þan alle monstres yif it were as <small>P. It were indeed, not only marvellous, but</small>
þou wenest. þat is to sein. þat in þe ryȝt ordeyne house <small>also horribly monstrous, if, in</small>
of so mochel a fader *and* an ordenour of meyne. þat þe <small>the well-regulated family of so great a master, the</small>
vesseles þat ben foule *and* vyle sholde ben honou*r*ed <small>worthless vessels should be</small>
and heried. and þe precious uesseles sholde ben de- <small>honoured and the precious ones be</small>
fouled *and* vyle. but it nis nat so. For yif þe þinges <small>despised:—but it is not so. For if</small>

3095 *seid*—MS. seide, C. scid
[*me*]—from C.
3096 þi—the
3097 *mowe*—mowen
3098 *som tyme*—whilom
3099 [*the*]—from C.
wronge—wrong
haþ—MS. haþe
3090 *don*—MS. done, C. don
were—weeren
3091 *namly*—namely
3092 *goode*—good
3093 *wiþ outen*—with owte

3095 *þinge*—thing
3097 *þere*—ther
ben ywondred—be wondryd
3098 *flowreþ*—MS. folwep, C. flowrith
3099 *rycchesse*—Rychesses
vertues—vertu
wiþ outen—with owte
3101 *in sted*—in stide
3102 *wicked*—wikkede
al[le]—alle
þing—thinges

3103 [*may*]—from C.
3104 *don*—MS. done, C. doon
3105 *wool*—wole
goode—good
3107 *grete*—gret
enbaissynge—enbasshinge
3108 *alle*—al
3109 *ordeyne house*—ordence hows
3111, 3113 *ryle*—vyl
3112 *heried*—he heryed
sholde—sholden
3113 *þe*—tho

þat I haue concluded a litel here byforne ben kept hoole *and* vnraced. þou shalt wel knowe by þe auctorite of god. of þe whos regne I spoke þat certys þe good[e] folk ben alwey my3ty. *and* shrewes ben alwey yuel *and* feble. ne þe vices ben neuere mo wiþ outen peyne! ne þe vertues ne ben nat wiþ outen mede. and þat blisfulnesses comen alwey to goode folke. *and* infortune comeþ alwey to wicked folke. ¶ And þou shalt wel knowe many[e] þinges of þis kynde þat sholle cessen þi pleyntes. *and* stedfast þe wiþ stedfast saddenesse. ¶ And for þou hast seyn þe forme of þe verray blisfulnesse by me þat [haue] somtyme I-shewed it þe. And þou hast knowen in whom blysfulnesse is set. alle þinges I treted þat I trowe ben nessessarie to put[te] furþe ¶ I shal shewe þe. þe weye þat shal brynge þe a3eyne vnto þi house *and* I shal ficche feþeres in þi þou3t by whiche it may arysen in hey3te. so þat al tribulacioun don awey. þou by my gidyng & by my paþe *and* by my sledes shalt mowen retourne hool *and* sounde in to þi contre. 3132

SUNT ETENIM PENNE. ET CETERA.

I Haue for soþe swifte feþeres þat surmounten þe hey3t of þe heuene whan þe swifte þou3t haþ cloþed it self. in þo feþeres it dispiseþ þe hat[e]ful erþes. *and* surmounteþ þe hey3enesse of þe greet[e] eyir. *and* it seiþ þe cloudes by-hynde hir bak *and* passeþ þe hey3t of þe regioun of þe fire þat eschaufiþ by þe swifte moeuyng of

3139 þe firmament. til þat she a-reisiþ hir in til þe houses þat

---

3114 *here byforne*—her byform
kept—MS. kepte, C. kept
3116 *good[e]*—goode
3117 *alwey* (2)——*feble*—alwey owt cast *and* feble
3118, 3119 *wiþ outen*—with owte
3119 *vertues*—vertuus
3122 *many[e]*—manye
sholle cessen—shollen cesen
3123 *stedfast*——*stedfast*—strengthyn the with stidfast

3124 *seyn*—MS. seyne, C. seyn
3125 [*haue*]—from C. *somtyme*—whilom
3126 *set*—MS. sette, C. I-set
3127 *put[te] furþe*—putten forth
3128 *weye*—wey
brynge—bryngen
þi house—thin hows
3129 *ficche*—tycchen
3130 *arysen*—areysen
don—MS. done, C. ydoñ
3131 *paþe*—paath
shalt mowen—shal mowe

3132 *sounde*—sownd
3133 *hey3t of þe heuene*—beyhte of heuene
3134 *haþ*—MS. haþe
3136 *hey3enesse——eyir*—Rounduesse of the grete ayr
seiþ—seth
3137 *hir*—his
3138 *fire*—Fyr
eschaufiþ—MS. eschaufiþe
3139 *she*—he
hir—hym

beren þe sterres. *and* ioygneþ hir weyes wiþ þe sonne
phebus. *and* felawshipeþ þe weye of þe olde colde
saturnus. and she ymaked a knyȝt of þe clere sterre.
þat is to seyne þat þe soule is maked goddys knyȝt by
þe sekyng of treuþe to comen to þe verray knowlege of
god. and þilke soule renne[þ] by þe cercle *of þe sterres
in alle þe places þere as þe shynyng nyȝt is depeynted.
þat is to seyne þe nyȝt þat is cloudeles. for on nyȝtes þat
ben cloudeles it semeþ as þe heuene were peynted wiþ
dyuerse ymages of sterres. *and* whan þe soule haþ gon
ynouȝ she shal forleten þe last[e] poynt of þe heuene.
and she shal pressen *and* wenden on þe bak of þe swifte
firmament. and she shal ben maked perfit of þe drede-
fulle clerenesse of god. ¶ þere haldeþ þe lorde of kynges
þe ceptre of his myȝt *and* attempereþ þe gouernementes
of þis worlde. *and* þe shynynge iuge of þinges stable in
hym self gouerneþ þe swifte carte. þat is to seyne þe
circuler moeuyng of [the] sonne. *and* yif þi weye ledeþ
þe aȝeyne so þat þou be brouȝt þider. þan wilt þou seye
now þat þat is þe contre þat þou requeredest of whiche þou
ne haddest no mynde. but now it remenbreþ me wel
here was I born. here wil I fastne my degree. here wil
I dwelle. but yif þe lyke þan to loken on þe derkenesse
of þe erþe þat þou hast for-leten. þan shalt þou seen þat
þise felonous tyrauntes þat þe wrecched[e] poeple dredeþ
now shule ben exiled from þilke faire contre.

3142

3161

3140 *hir*—his
3141 *weye*—wey
þe——*saturnus*—MS. saturnus þe olde colde
3142 *saturnus*—saturnis
she—he
3143 *soule*—thowght
3144 *treuþe*—trowthe
knowlege—knolcche
3145 *soule*—thoght
3146 *depeynted*—painted
3149-50 *and whan*——*she snal*

——*and* whanne he hath I-doon there I-nowh he shal
3149 *haþ*—MS. haþe
3150 þe *last*[*e*]——*heuene*—the laste heuene
3151-2 *she*—he
3152-3 *of þe*——*of god*—of the worshipful lyht of god
3153 *þere haldeþ*—ther halt
3155 *þis worlde*—the world
3156 *carte*—cart or wayn

3157 [*the*]—from C.
3159 *whiche*—which
3161 *here* (1, 2, 3)—her
born—MS. borne, C. born
wil (1)—wol
wil (2)—wole
3162 *lyke*—liketh
derkenesse—dyrknesses
3164 *wrecched*[*e*]—wrecchede
3165 *shule*—shollen
from—fro

TUNC EGO PAPE INQUAM, ET CETERA.

[The 2ᵒ prose.]
B Ah! thou promisest me great things indeed!—but without delay, satisfy the expectations you have raised.
P. You must first be convinced that the good are always strong and powerful and the wicked destitute of strength. These assertions do mutually demonstrate each other. For since good and evil are contrary, if good be powerful evil must be impotent. And if the frailty of evil is known, the strength and stability of good must also be known to you. But to convince you I shall proceed to prove it from both these principles, establishing these truths, by arguments drawn first from one of these topics and then from the other. Two things are necessary to every action—the Will and the Power; if either be wanting, nothing can be effected. A man can do nothing without the concurrence of his will, and if power falleth the will is of no effect. Hence, if you see a person desirous of getting what he cannot procure, you are sure he lacks power to obtain it. And if you see another do what he had a mind to do, can you doubt

þAnne seide I þus. [owh] I wondre me þat þou byhetest me so grete þinges. ne I ne doute nat þat þou ne mayst wel performe þat þou by-hetest. but I preie þe oonly þis. þat þou ne tarie nat to telle me þilke þinges þat þou hast meoued. first quod she þou most nedes knowen. þat good[e] folk ben al wey strong[e] and myȝty. and þe shrewes ben feble and desert and naked of alle strengþes. and of þise þinges certys eueryche of hem is declared and shewed by oþer. ¶ For so as good and yuel ben two contraries. yif so be þat goode be stedfast. þan sheweþ þe fieblesse of yuel al openly. and yif þou knowe clerely þe freelnesse of yuel. þe stedfastnesse of goode is knowen. but for as moche as þe fey of my sentence shal be þe more ferme and haboundaunt. I wil goon by þat oon wey and by þat oþer and I wil conferme þe þinges þat ben purposed now on þis side and now on þat syde. ¶ Two þinges þer ben in whiche þe effect of alle þe dedes of man kynde standiþ. þat is to seyn. wil and power. and yif þat oon of þise two fayleþ þere nis no þing þat may be don. for yif þat wil lakkeþ þere nys no wyȝt þat vndirtakeþ to done þat he wol not don. and yif power fayleþ þe wille nis but in ydel and stant for nauȝt. and þer of comeþ it þat yif þou se a wyȝt þat wolde geten þat he may nat geten. þou mayst nat douten þat power ne fayleþ hym to hauen þat he wolde. ¶ þis is open and clere quod I. ne it may nat ben denyed in no manere. and yif þou se a wyȝt quod she. þat haþ don þat he wolde don þou nilt nat douten þat he ne haþ had power to done it. no quod. I. and in þat. þat euery wyȝt may. in þat þat men may holden

3166 [owh]—from C.
3171 good[e]—goode
strong[e]—stronge
3172 desert—dishert
3173 eueryche—euerich
3175 goode—good
3176 stedfast—stidefast
3177 freelnesse—frelenesse
stedfastnesse — stidefast-

nesse
3178 goode—good
3180 oon—oo
wil (2)—wole
3183-6 þere—ther
3185 don—MS. done, C. don
3186 done—don
3187 wille—wil
3188 comeþ—comht

3189 mayst — MS. mayste, C. mayst
3191 clere—cler
3192 denyed—denoyed
3193-4 haþ—MS. ha þe
3193 don (both)—MS. done, C. doon
3194 had—MS. hadde, C. had
done—doon

hym myȝty. as who seiþ in as moche as a man is myȝty to done a þing. in so moche men halden hym myȝty. and in þat þat he ne may. in þat men demen hym to ben feble. I confesse it wel quod I. Remembriþ þe quod she þat I. haue gadred and shewed by forseide resouns þat al þe entencioun of þe wil of mankynde whiche þat is lad by diuerse studies hastiþ to comen to blisfulnesse. ¶ It remembreþ me wel quod I þat it hath ben shewed. and recordeþ þe nat þan quod she. þat blisfulnesse is þilke same goode þat men requeren. so þat whan þat blisfulnesse is requered * of alle. þat goode [also] is requered and desired of al. It recordeþ me wel quod I. for haue it gretly alwey ficche[d] in my memorie. alle folk þan quod she goode and eke badde enforcen hem wiþ oute difference of entencioun to comen to goode. þat is a uerray consequence quod I. and certeyne is quod she þat by þe getyng of goode ben men ymaked goode. þis is certeyne quod. I. ¶ þan geten goode men þat þei desiren. so semeþ it quod I. but wicked[e] folk quod she yif þei geten þe goode þat þei desiren þei [ne] mowen nat ben wicked. so is it quod . I. ¶ þan so as þat oon and þat oþer [quod she] desiren good. and þe goode folk geten good and nat þe wicked folk ¶ þan nis it no doute þat þe goode folk ne ben myȝty and þe wicked folk ben feble. ¶ who so þat euer quod I douteþ of þis. he ne may nat considre þe nature of þinges. ne þe consequence of resoun. and ouer þis quod she. ¶ yif þat þer ben two þinges þat han o same purpos by kynde. and þat one of hem pursueþ and performeþ þilke same þinge by naturel office. and þat oþer ne may nat done þilk naturel office. but folweþ by oþer manere þan is couenable to nature ¶ Hym þat

that he had the power to do it ?
B. No, surely.
P. A man, then, is esteemed powerful in respect of what he is able to do, and weak in relation to what he is unable to perform.
B. That is true.
P. Do you remember that I proved that the will of man. following different pursuits, seeks happiness only ?
Do you recollect too, that it has been shown that happiness is
(* fol. 25 b.)
the supreme good of men—and all desire this good, since all seek happiness ?
All men, then, good and bad, seek to acquire good ?
And it is certain that when men obtain good they become good ?
3212
B. It is most certain.
P. Do good men, then, get what they desire ?
B. It seems so.
P. If evil men obtain the good, they can be no longer evil ?
B. It is so.
P. Since then both parties pursue the good, which only the virtuous obtain, we must believe that good men are powerful, and that the wicked are weak and feeble ?
B. None can doubt this, save such as either consider not rightly the nature of things, or are incapable of comprehending the force of any reasoning.
P. If two beings have the same end in view—

3196 *as moche*—so moche
3197 *done*—doon
moche—mochel
halden—halt
3201 *whiche*—which
3202 *lad*—MS. ladde, C. lad
3203 *it hath ben*—MS. I herde

þe, C. it hath ben
3205-6 *goode*—good
3206 [*also*]—from C.
3207 *al*—alle
It——I—it nerecordeth me nat quod I
3210-12(1)-15 *goode*—good

3214 *wicked*[*e*]—wikkede
3215 [*ne*]—from C.
3216 *mowen*—mowe
3217 [*quod she*]—from C.
3218 *wicked*—wilke (? wikke)
3220 *wicked*—wikkede
3226 *þilk*—thilke

| and one of them accomplishes his purpose by the use of natural means, while the other not using legitimate means does not attain his end—which of these two is the most powerful? *B.* Illustrate your meaning more clearly. *P.* The motion of walking is natural to man? And this motion is the natural office of the feet? Do you grant this? *B.* I do. *P.* If, then, he who is able to use his feet walks whilst another lacking this power creeps on his hands—surely he that is able to move naturally upon his feet is more powerful than he who cannot. *P.* The good and bad seek the supreme good: the good by the natural means of virtue—the wicked by gratifying divers desires of earthly things (which is not the natural way of obtaining it). Do you think otherwise? *B.* The consequence is plain, and that follows from what has been granted— that the good are powerful, while the wicked are feeble. *P.* You rightly anticipate me; for it is a good sign, as physicians well know, when Nature exerts herself and resists the malady. But, as you are so quick of appre- | acomplisiþ hys purpos kyndely. and ȝit he ne acomplisiþ nat hys owen purpos. wheþer of þise two demest þou for more myȝty. ¶ yif þat I coniecte quod .I. þat þou wilt seye algates. ȝit I desire to herkene it more pleynely of þe. þou nilt nat þan denye quod she þat þe moeuementȝ of goynge nis in men by kynde. no for soþe quod I. ne þou ne doutest nat quod she þat þilke naturel office of goynge ne be þe office of feet. I ne doute it nat quod .I. þan quod she yif þat a wyȝt be myȝty to moeue and goþ vpon hys feet. and anoþer to whom þilke naturel office of feet lakkeþ. enforceþ hym to gone crepynge vpon hys handes. ¶ whiche of þise two auȝte to ben holden more myȝty by ryȝt. knyt furþe þe remenaunt quod I. ¶ For no wyȝt ne douteþ þat he þat may gone by naturel office of feet. ne be more myȝty 3243 þan he þat ne may nat ¶ but þe souereyne good quod she þat is euenlyche purposed to þe good folk and to badde. þe good folke seken it by naturel office of uertues. and þe shrewes enforcen hem to geten it by dyuerse couetise of erþely þinges. whiche þat nis no naturel office to geten þilke same souereyne goode. trowest þou þat it be any oþer wyse. nay quod .I. for þe consequence is open and shewynge of þinges þat I haue graunted. ¶ þat nedes goode folk moten ben myȝty. and shrewes feble and vnmyȝty. ¶ þou rennest aryȝt byfore me quod she. and þis is þe iugement þat is to seyn. ¶ I iuge of þe ryȝt as þise leches ben wont forto hopen of seke folk whan þei aperceyuen þat nature is redressed and wiþstondeþ to þe maladie. ¶ But for I see þe now al redy to þe vndirstandynge I shal shewe þe more þilke and continuel resouns. ¶ For loke now |

3229 *owen*—owne
3231 *wilt*—wolt
    herkene—herkne
3232 *pleynely*—pleynly
    denye—denoye
3233 *moeuementȝ* — Moeuement
3237 *goþ*—MS. goþe

hys—hise
3238 *gone*—goon
3239 *hys*—hise
    whiche—which
3240 *more*—the Moore
    furþe—forth
3242 *gone*—gon
3245 *good*—goode

3246 *uertues*—vertuus
3247 *whiche*—which
3248 *goode*—good
3253 *byfore*—by-forn
3254 *forto*—to
3255 *seke*—sike

how gretly shewiþ þe feblesse *and* infirmite of wicked folke. þat ne mowen nat come to þat hire naturel entenci*oun* ledeþ hem. *and* ȝitte almost þilk naturel entenci*oun* constreineþ hem. ¶ and what were to deme þan of shrewes. yif þilke naturel helpe hadde for-leten hem. ¶ þe whiche naturel helpe of entenci*oun* goþ alwey byforne hem. *and* is so grete þat vnneþ it may be ou*er*comen. ¶ Considre þan how gret defaute of power *and* how gret feblesse þere is in grete felonous folk as who seiþ þe gretter þi*n*ges þat ben coueited *and* þe desire nat accomplissed of þe lasse myȝt is he þat coueiteþ it *and* may nat acomplisse. ¶ And forþi philosophie seiþ þus by souereyne good. ¶ Sherewes ne requere nat lyȝt[e] modes ne veyne gaines whiche þei ne may nat folwen ne holden. but þei fayle*n* of þilke some of þe heyȝte of þinges þat is to seyne souereyne good. ne þise wrecches ne comen nat to þe effect of souereyne good. *þe whiche þei enforcen hem oonly to gete*n* by nyȝtes *and* by dayes. ¶ In þe getyn[g] of whiche goode þe strengþe of good folk. is ful wel ysen. For ryȝt so as þou myȝtest demen hym myȝty of goynge þat goþ on hys feet til he myȝt[e] come to þilke place fro þe whiche place þere ne lay no wey forþer to be gon. Ryȝt so most þou nedes demen hym for ryȝt myȝty þat getiþ *and* atteiniþ to þe ende of alle þinges þat ben to desire. by-ȝonde þe whiche ende þat þer nis no þing to desire. ¶ Of whiche power of good folk men may conclude þat wicked men semen to ben bareyne *and* naked of alle strengþe. For whi forleten þei vertues *and* folwen vices. nis it nat for þat þei ne knowen nat þe goodes.

hension, I shall continue this mode of reasoning. The weakness of the wicked is conspicuous—they cannot attain the end to which their natural disposition prompts and almost compels them; what would become of them without this natural prompting, so powerful and irresistible? Consider how great is the impotence of the wicked. (The greater the things desired, but unaccomplished, the less is the power of him that desires, and is unable to attain his end.) The wicked seek after no trivial things —which they fail to obtain; but they aspire in vain to the sovereign good, which they endeavour [* fol. 26.] day and night to obtain. The good attain the end of their desires, and therein their power is manifested. For as you deem him a good walker that goes to the end of his journey, so you must esteem him powerful that attains his desires, beyond which there is nothing to desire. Wicked men, then, are destitute of those powers which the good so amply possess. Wherefore do they leave virtue, and follow vice? Is it because they are ignorant of good?

3275

3259 *wicked*—wikkede
3260 *come*—comyn
3261 *þilk*—thilke
3262 *deme*—demen
3263-4 *helpe*—help
3264 *whiche*—which
  goþ—MS. goþe
3265 *grete*—gret
  vnneþ—vnnethe
  be ouercomen—ben ouercome
3267 *þere*—ther

grete—wikkede
3268 *þinges*—thing
  ben—is
3271 *Sherewes ne requere*—
  ne shrewes ne requeren
3272 *lyȝt[e]*—lyhte
  veyne—veyn
  nat—omitted
3276 *whiche*—which
3277 *getyn[g]*—getinge
  whiche goode—which good
3278 *ysen*—MS. and C. yseue

3279 *goþ*—MS. goþe
3280 *myȝt[e]*—mylite
3281 *þere*—ther
  lay—laye
  forþer—forthere
  be—ben
3283 *desire*—desired
3284 *þat*—omitted
3285 *whiche*—the which
  þat—þat the
3286 *ben*—be

THE WICKED HAVE NO REAL EXISTENCE. [BOOK 4. PROSE 2.

What is more weak and base than the blindness of ignorance? Or do they know the way they ought to follow, but are led astray by lust and covetousness? And so, indeed, weak-minded men are overpowered by intemperance, for they cannot resist vicious temptations. Do they willingly desert Good and turn to Evil? If they do so, they not only cease to be powerful, but even cease to exist. For those who neglect the common end of all beings, cease to exist. You may marvel that I assert that the wicked, the majority of the human race, have no existence—

¶ But what þing is more feble *and* more caitif þan is þe blyndenesse of ignoraunce. or ellys þei knowen ful wel whiche þinges þat þei auȝten to folwen ¶ but lecherye *and* couetise ouerþroweþ hem mysturned. ¶ and certis so doþ distemperaunce to feble men. þat ne mowen nat wrastle aȝeins þe vices ¶ Ne knowen þei nat þan wel þat þei foreleten þe good wilfully. *and* turnen hem vilfully to vices. ¶ And in þis wise þei ne forleten nat oonly to ben myȝty. but þei forleten al outerly in any wise forto ben ¶ For þei þat forleten þe comune fyn of alle þinges þat ben. þei for-leten also þerwiþ al forto ben. and *per*auenture it sholde semen to som folk þat þis were a meruelle to seyne þat shrewes whiche þat contienen þe more partie of men ne ben nat. ne han no

3304 beynge. ¶ but naþeles it is so. *and* þus stant þis þing

but it is, however, most true. That the wicked are bad I do not deny—but I do not admit that they have any real existence. You may call a corpse a dead man, but you cannot with propriety call it a man. So the vicious are profligate men, but I cannot confess they absolutely exist. That thing exists that preserves its rank, nature, and constitution, but when it loses these essentials it ceases to be. But, you may say that the wicked have a power to act, nor do I deny it; but their power is an effect of weakness. They can do evil, but this they could

for þei þat ben shrewes I denye nat þat þei ben shrewes. but I denye *and* sey[e] symplely and pleynly þat þei [ne] ben nat. ne han no beynge. for ryȝt as þou myȝtest seyn of þe careyne of a man þat it were a ded man. ¶ but þou ne myȝtest nat symplely callen it a man. ¶ So graunt[e] I wel for soþe þat vicious folk ben wicked. but I ne may nat graunten absolutely *and* symplely þat þei ben. ¶ For þilk þing þat wiþ holdeþ ordre *and* kepiþ nature. þilk þing is *and* haþ beynge. but þat þing þat faileþ of þat. þat is to seyne he þat forletiþ naturel ordre he for-letiþ þilk beyng þat is set in hys nature. but þou wolt sein þat shrewes mowen. ¶ Certys þat ne denye I nat. ¶ but certys hir power ne descendeþ nat of strengþe but of feblesse. for þei mowen don wickednesses. þe whiche þei ne myȝten nat don yif þei myȝten dwelle in þe forme *and*

3291 *auȝten to folwen* — owhten folwe
3293 *doþ*—MS. doþe, C. doth
3294 *wrastle*—wrastlen
3295 *vilfully*—wilsfully
3297 *outerly*—owtrely
3301 *seyne*—seyen
3304-5 *denye*—denoye

3305 *sey[e] symplely* — seye sympeli
3306 [*ne*]—from C.
3307 *seyn*—seyen
3309 *graunt[e]*—graunte
3311-12 *þilk*—thilke
3312 *haþ*—MS. haþe
3313 *þat* (1)—what

3313 *seyne*—seyn
3314 *þilk*—thilke
3315 *set*—MS. sette, C. set
3316 *denye*—denoye
3318 *don*—MS. done, C. don
3319 *myȝten* (1)—myhte
 dwelle—dwellin

BOOK 4.
PROSE 2.] POWER, AN ATTRIBUTE OF THE CHIEF GOOD. 117

in þe doynge of goode folke. ¶ And þilke power *not do, if they retained the power of doing good. This power, then, clearly shows their impotence. For as evil is nothing, it is clear that while the wicked can only do evil they can do nothing. That you may understand the force of this power, I have proved that nothing is more powerful than the sovereign good. B. That is true. P. And that supreme good can do no evil? B. Certainly not. P. Is there any one who thinks that man can do all things? B. No sane man can think so. P. But men may do evil. B. I would to God they could not. P. Since he that can do good, can*
shewoþ ful euydently þat þei ne mowen ry3t nau3t.
¶ For so as I haue gadered *and* proued a lytel her byforn þat yuel is nau3t. *and* so as shrewes mowen oonly
but shrewednesse. þis conclusiou*n* is al clere. ,þat
shrewes ne mowen ry3t nat to han power. and for as
moche as þou vndirstonde whiche is þe strengþe þat is
power of shrewes. I haue diffinised a lytel here byforn
þat no þing nis so my3ty as souereyne good ¶ þat is
soþe quod .I. [*and* thilke same souereyn good may don
non yuel // Certes no q*uod* I] ¶ Is þer any wy3t þan
q*uod* she þat weniþ þat men mowen don alle þinges.
No man q*uod* .I. but yif he be out of hys witte. ¶ but
certys sherewes mowen don̄ yuel q*uod* she. ¶ 3e wolde
god q*uod* I þat þei ne my3te*n* don none. þat q*uod* she
so as he þat is my3ty to done oonly but good[e] þinges
may don alle þinges. and þei þat ben my3ty to done 3336
yuel[e] þinges ne mowen nat alle þinges. þan is þis open *do all things, and he that has power to do evil cannot do all things, therefore the evil-doers are less powerful. Let me add too that power is one of the things to be desired, and that all such things are to be referred to the chief good (the perfection of their nature). But the power of doing evil has no relation to that Good, therefore it is not desirable; but as [* fol. 25 b.] all power is desirable, it is clear that the ability to do evil is not power. It clearly follows from this reasoning,*
þing *and* manifest þat þei þat mowe*n* don yuel ben of
lasse power. and 3itte to p*r*oue þis conclusiou*n* þere
helpeþ me þis þat I haue shewed here byforne. þat al
power is to be noumbred amonge þinges þat men au3ten
requere. *and* haue shewed þat alle þinges þat au3ten ben
desired ben referred to good ry3t as to a manere hey3te
of hyr nature. ¶ But for to mowen don yuel *and*
felonye ne may nat ben referred to good. þan nis nat
yuel of þe nou*m*bre of þinges þat au3te*n*. *be desired. but
al power au3t[e] ben desired *and* requered. ¶ þan is
it open *and* cler þat þe power ne þe moeuyng of shrewes
nis no powere. *and* of alle þise þinges it sheweþ wel þat

3320 *goode*—good
3324 *shrewednesse* — shrewednesses
    clere—cleer
3325 *nat*—*power* — nawht
    he han no power
3326 *whiche*—which
    þat is—of this
3327 *here*—her
3328 *nis*—is
3329 *soþe*—soth

3329, 3330 [*and thilke* —— *quod I*]—from C..
3334 *don*—MS. done, C. don
    none þat—non thanne
3335 *done*—doon
    good[*e*]—goode
3336 *don*—MS. done, C. don
    done—don
3337 *yuel*[*e*]—yuele
    þis—it
3338 *don*—MS. done, C. don

3339 *3itto*—3it
    þere—ther
3340 *shewed here byforne*—
    I shewed her by-forn
    al—alle
3341 *amonge*—among
3344 *don*—MS. done, C. don
3346 *au3ten be*—owhte ben
3347 *al*—alle
    au3t[*e*]—owhte

þe goode folk ben certeynly myȝty. and þe shrewes ben douteles vnmyȝty ¶ And it is clere *and* open þat þilke sentence of plato is uerray *and* soþe. þat seyþ þat oonly wisemen may [doon] þat þei desiren. *and* shrewes mowen haunten þat hem lykeþ. but þat þei desiren þat is to seyne to comen to souereyne good þei ne han no power to acomplissen þat. ¶ For shrewes don þat hem list whan by þo þinges in whiche þei deliten þei wenen to atteyne to þilke good þat þei desiren. but þei ne geten ne atteynen nat þer to. ¶ for vices ne comen nat to blisfulnesse. 3360

QUOS UIDES SEDERE CELSOS.

Who so þat þe couertures of her veyn apparailes myȝt[e] strepen of þise proude kynges þat þou seest sitten on heyȝe in her chayeres glyterynge in shynynge purpre envyroned wiþ sorweful armures manasyng wiþ cruel mouþe. blowyng by woodnesse of herte. ¶ He sholde se þan þat ilke lordes beren wiþ inne hir corages ful streyte cheynes for leccherye tormentiþ hem on þat oon syde wiþ gredy venyms *and* troublable Ire þat araiseþ in hem þe floodes of troublynges tourmentiþ vpon þat oþer side hir þouȝt. or sorwe halt hem wery or yeauȝt. or slidyng *and* disseyuyng hope tourmentiþ hem. And þerfore syn þou seest on heed. þat is to seyne oon tyraunt bere so many[e] tyrauntis. þan ne doþ þilk tyraunt nat þat he desiriþ. syn he is cast doune wiþ so many[e] wicked lordes. þat is to seyn wiþ so many[e] vices. þat han so wicked lordshipes ouer hym. 3377

3351 *clere*—cler
3352 *soþe*—soth
  þat seyþ—MS. but siþe, C.
  þat seyth
3353 [*doon*]—from C.
3355 *seyne*—seyn
3357 *whiche*—which
3361-63 *her*—hir
3362 *myȝt[e]*—myhte

3363 *heyȝe*—heygh
3364 *sorweful*—sorwful
3365 *mouþe*—Mowth
3366 *se*—seen
  ilke—thilke
3368 *on*—in
3369 *hem*—hym
3371 *disseyuyng* — deceyuynge

3373 *seyne*—seyn
  bere—beeren
3373-75-76 *many[e]*—manye
3373 *tyrauntis*—tyranyes
3374 *doþ*—MS. doþe
  þilk—thilke
3375 *doune*—down
  wicked—wikkede
3376 *wicked*—wikkedly

VIDES NE IGITUR QUANTO.

Sest þou nat þan in how gret filþe þise shrewes ben ywrapped. *and* wiþ whiche cleernesse þise good folk shynen. In þis sheweþ it wel þat to good folk ne lakkeþ neuer mo hir medes. ne shrewes ne lakken neuer mo tourmentis. for of alle þinges þat ben ydou þilke þing for whiche any þing is doon. it semeþ as by ryȝt þat þilke þing be þe mede of þat. as þus. ¶ yif a man renneþ in þe stadie or in þe forlonge for þe corone. þan lieþ þe mede in þe corone for whiche he renneþ. ¶ And I haue shewed þat blisfulnesse is þilke same good for whiche þat alle þing*us* ben don. þan is þilke same good p*ur*posed to þe werkes of mankynde ryȝt as a comune mede. whiche mede ne may ben disseuered fro good folk. for no wyȝt as by ryȝt fro þennes forþe þat hym lakkiþ goodnesse ne shal ben cleped good. For whiche þing folk of good[e] maneres her medes ne forsaken hem neuer mo. For al be it so þat sherewes waxen as wood as hem list aȝeynes good[e] folk. ȝitte neuer þe les þe corone of wise men ne shal nat fallen ne faden. ¶ For foreine shrewednesse ne bynymeþ nat fro þe corages of good[e] folk hire p*ro*pre honoure. but yif þat any wyȝt reioiseþ hem of goodnesse þat þei had[de] taken fro wiþoute. as who seiþ yif [þat] any wyȝt had[de] hys goodnesse of any oþer man þan of hym self. certys he þat ȝaf hym þilke goodnesse or ellys som oþer wyȝt myȝt[e] bynym[e] it hym. but for as moche as to euery wyȝt hys owen p*ro*pre bounte ȝcueþ hy*m* hys mede. þan at arst shal he faylen of mede whan he forletiþ to ben good. *and* at þe laste so as alle medes be*n* requered for men wenen þat þei ben

---

[The iij.ᵈᵉ prosa.]
See you not in how great and filthy a mire the wicked wallow? This is a proof that good folks do not go unrewarded, nor do the evil-doers escape punishment. Every action is done for a certain end, and that end is the reward of the action. But Happiness is that good for which all things are done. Therefore happiness is the reward which all the human race seek as the reward of their actions. This good is inseparable from the virtuous, therefore virtue can never want its reward. Evil men may rage as they please against the good, but the crown of the wise shall not fall nor fade. The wickedness of another cannot deprive a virtuous soul of its own honour. If a man pride himself on the possession of an advantage received from another, he may be deprived of it, either by the giver or by others. But, as the reward of the virtuous is derived from virtue, a man cannot lose this meed unless he ceases to be virtuous. Lastly, since a reward is desired because it is supposed to be a good, can we believe that he who is capable of good is deprived of the recompence?

3379 *whiche*—which
3390 *good*—goode
3381 *ne* (2)—omitted
3383 *whiche*—which
3385 *forlonge*—forlong
3386-88-90 *whiche*—which
3391 *forþe*—forth
3393 *whiche*—which
3393 *good[e]*—goode
3395 *wood*—woode
good[e]—goode
3396 *les*—leese
ne—omitted
3398 *good[e]*—goode
3399 *reioiseþ*—reioyse
hem—hym
3399 *þei had[de]*—he hadde
3400 [*þat*]—from C.
3401 *had[de]*—hadde
3402 *self*—MS. selk
3403 *myȝt[e] bynym[e]* — myhte be-nyme
3404 *owen*—owne
3406 *laste*—last

good[e]. who is he þat wolde deme þat he þat is ryȝt myȝty of goode were partles of mede. *and of what mede shal he be gerdoned. certys of ryȝt faire mede and ryȝt greet abouen alle medes. ¶ Remembre þe of þilk noble corolarie þat I ȝaf þe a lytel here byforne. and gadre it to gidre in þis manere. so as god hym self is blisfulnesse. þan is it clere and certeyn. þat alle good folk ben makid blisful for þei ben good[e]. and þilke folk þat ben blisful it accordiþ and is couenable to ben godde[s]. þan is þe mede of goode folk swiche. þat no day [ne] shal enpeyren it. ne no wickednesse shal endirken it. ne power of no wyȝt ne shal nat amenusen it þat is to seyn to ben maked goddes. ¶ and syn it is þus þat goode men ne faylen neuer mo of hire medes. ¶ certys no wise man ne may doute of þe vndepartable peyne of shrewes. ¶ þat is to seyn þat þe peyne of shrewes ne departiþ nat from hem self neuer mo. ¶ For so as goode and yuel and peyne and medes ben contrarie it mot nedes ben þat ryȝt as we seen by-tiden in gerdoun of goode. þat also mot þe peyne of yuel answere by þe contrarie partye to shrewes. now þan so as bounte and prowesse ben þe medes to goode folk. also is shrewednesse it self torment to shrewes ¶ þan who so þat euer is entecched and defouled wiþ yuel. yif shrewes wolen þan preisen hem self may it semen to hem þat þei ben wiþ outen partye of tourment. syn þei ben swiche þat þe [vtteriste wikkednesse / þat is to seyn wikkede thewes / which þat is the] outereste and þe w[or]ste kynde of shrewednesse ne defouliþ nat ne entecchiþ nat hem oonly but infectiþ and enuenemyþ hem gretely ¶ And al so loke on shrewes þat ben þe contrarie partye of goode men. how grete peyne felaw-shipeþ *and* folweþ hem. ¶ For þou hast lerned a litel here byforn þat al þing þat is *and* haþ beynge is oon. *and* þilke same oon is good. þan is þis consequence þat it semeþ wel. þat al þat is *and* haþ beynge is good. þis is to seyne. as who seiþ þat beynge *and* vnite *and* goodnesse is al oon. *and* in þis manere it folweþ þan. þat al þing þat faileþ to ben good. it styntiþ forto be. *and* forto haue any beynge. wher fore it is þat shrewes stynten forto ben þat þei weren. but þilke oþer forme of mankynde. þat is to seyne þe forme of þe body wiþ oute. shewiþ ȝit þat þise shrewes were somtyme men. ¶ wher fore whan þei ben peruerted *and* torned in to malice. certys þan han þei forlorn þe nature of man-kynde. but so as oonly bounte *and* prowesse may en-hawnse euery man ouer oþer men. þan mot it nedes be þat shrewes whiche þat shrewednesse haþ cast out of þe condicioun of mankynde ben put vndir þe merite *and* þe deserte of men. þan bitidiþ it þat yif þou seest a wyȝt þat be transformed in to vices. þou ne mayst nat wene þat he be a man. ¶ For ȝif he [be] ardaunt in auarice. *and* þat he be a rauynour by violence of foreine rychesse. þou shalt seyn þat he is lyke to a wolf. *and* yif he be felonous *and* wiþ out reste *and* exercise hys tonge to chidynges. þou shalt lykene hym to þe hounde. *and* yif he be a preue awaitour yhid *and* reioyseþ hym to rauysshe by wyles. þou shalt seyne hym lyke to þe fox whelpes. ¶ And yif he be dis-tempre *and* quakiþ for ire men shal wene þat he bereþ þe corage of a lyoun. *and* yif he be dredeful *and* fleynge *and* dredeþ þinges þat ne auȝten nat ben dred. men

Marginal glosses:
3443 pollutes them. But contemplate the punishment of the wicked. You have been taught that *unity* is essential to being and is good—and all that have this unity are good; what-soever, then, fails to be good ceases to exist. So that it appears that evil men must cease to be what they were. That they were once men, the outward form of the body, which still re-mains, clearly testifies. Where-fore, when they degenerate into wickedness they
3452 lose their human nature. But as virtue alone ex-alts one man above other men, it is evident that vice, which divests a man of his nature, must sink him below humanity. You cannot, therefore, esteem him to be a man whom you see thus trans-formed by his vices. The greedy robber, you will say, is like a *wolf*.
3461 He who gives no rest to his abusive tongue, you may liken to a *hound*. Does he delight in fraud and trick-ery? then is he like young *foxes*. Is he intemperate in his anger? then men will compare him to a raging *lion*. If he
3468 be a coward, he will be likened to

3439 *grete*—gret
3441 *al*—alle
  haþ—MS. haþe
3443 *al*—alle
  haþ—MS. haþe
3446 *al*—alle
3447 *haue*—han
3449 *stynten*—MS. styntent

3450 *were somtyme*—weeren whilom
3452 *forlorn*—MS. forlorne, C. forlorn
3453 *as*—omitted enhawnse—enhawsen
3455 *whiche*—which
  haþ—MS. haþe

3459 [*be*]—from C.
3461 *yhid*—MS. yhidde, C. I-hidd
3465 *seyne*—seyn
3468 *dredeful*—dredful
3469 *ben*—to ben
  dred — MS. dredde, C. dredd

122 HE WHO CEASES TO BE VIRTUOUS [BOOK 4. MET. 3.

a hart. If he be slow, dull, and lazy, then is he like an ass. Is he fickle and inconstant? Then is he like a bird. Doth he wallow in filthy lusts? Then doth he roll himself in the mire like a nasty sow. It follows, then, that he who ceases to be virtuous, ceases to be a man; and, since he cannot attain divinity, he is turned into a beast.

shal holde hym lyke to þe herte. *and* yif he be slowe *and* astoned *and* lache. he lyueþ as an asse. *and* yif he be lyʒt *and* vnstedfast of corage *and* chaungeþ ay his studies. he is lickened to briddes. ¶ *and* yif he be plounged in foule *and* vnclene luxuries. he is wiþholden in þe foule delices of þe foule soowe. ¶ þan folweþ it þat he þat forletiþ bountee *and* prowesse. he forletiþ to ben a man. syn he ne may nat passe in to þe condicio*u*n of god. he is tourned in to a beest. 3478

[* fol. 27 b.]

*V[E]LA NARICII DUCIS.

[The 3*ir* Met*ur*.] *Ulysses was driven by the eastern winds upon the shores of that isle where Circe dwelt, who, having entertained her guests with magic draughts, transformed them into divers shapes —one into a boar, another into a lion;*

Evius þe wynde aryueþ þe sayles of vlixes duc of þe contre of narice. *and* hys wandryng shippes by þe see in to þe isle þere as Circe þe fayre goddesse douʒter of þe sonne dwelleþ þat medlyþ to hir newe gestes drynkes þat ben touched *and* maked wiþ enchauntmentʒ. *and* after þat hir hande myʒty of þe herbes had[de] chau*n*ged hir gestes i*n* to dyuerse maneres. þat

3486 oon of hem is couered his face wiþ forme of a boor. þat oþer is chau*n*ged in to a lyou*n* of þe contre of marmorike. *and* his nayles *and* his teþe wexen. ¶ þat

some into howling wolves, and others into Indian tigers. oþer of hem is newliche chaunged in to a wolf. *and* howeliþ whan he wolde wepe. þat oþer goþ debonairly

But Mercury, the Arcadian god, rescued Ulysses from the Circean charms. Yet his mariners, having drunk of her infected drinks, were changed to swine, and fed on acorns. in þe house as a tigre of Inde. but al be it so þat þe godhed of mercurie þat is cleped þe bride of arcadie haþ had mercie of þe duc vlixes byseged wiþ diuerse yueles *and* haþ vnbounden hym fro þe pestilence of hys oosteresse algates þe rowers *and* þe maryners hadden by

3496 þis ydrawen in to hir mouþes *and* dronken þe wicked[e]

3470 *holde*—holden
lyke—lyk
herte—hert
slowe—slowh
3472 *vnstedfast*—vnstidefast
his—hise
3475 *þan*—MS. pat, C. thanne
3477 *passe*—passen
3479 *aryueþ*—aryuede
vlixes—MS. vluxies, C.

vlixes
3481 *Circe*—Circes
3483 *enchauntmentʒ* — enchauntmentʒ
3484 *hande*—hand
of—ouer
3485 *had[de]*—hadde
gestes — MS. goostes, C. gestes
3486 *boor*—boore
3488 *his* (1)—hise

his teþe—hise teth
3489 *newliche*—neweliche
3490 *goþ*—MS. goþe
3491 *house*—hows
3492 *bride*—bryd
haþ—MS. haþe
3493 *mercie*—MS. mercurie, C. mercy
3494 *haþ*—MS. haþe
3495 *oosteresse*—oostesse
3496 *wicked[e]*—wikkede

drynkes þei þat were woxen swyne hadden by þis
chau*n*ged hire mete of brede forto ete acorns of ookes. 3498
non of hir lymes ne dwelliþ wiþ he*m* hoole. but *All traces of the human form were*
þei han lost þe voys *and* þe body. Oonly hire þou3t *lost, and they were bereft of*
dwelleþ wiþ hem stable þat wepiþ *and* bywailiþ þe *speech. Their souls, unchanged,*
monstruous chaungynge þat þei suffren. ¶ O ouer ly3t *bewailed their dreadful fate.*
hand. as who seiþ. ¶ O feble *and* ly3t is þe hand of *O most weak, are*
Circes þe enchaunteresse þat chaungeþ þe bodies of folk *Circe's powers compared with the potency of*
in to bestes to regarde *and* to comparisou*n* of mutaciou*n* *vice, to transform the human shape!*
þat is makid by vices. ne þe herbes of circes ne ben nat *Circe's herbs may change the body,*
my3ty. for al be it so þat þei may chau*n*gen þe lymes *but cannot touch the mind, the inward strength of*
of þe body. ¶ algates 3it þei may nat chaunge þe *man.*
hertes. for wiþ inne is yhid þe strengþe *and* þe vigour 3509
of me*n* in þe secre toure of hire hertys. þat is to seyn
þe strengþe of resou*n*. but þilke uenyms of vices to- *But vice is more potent than*
drawen a man to hem more my3tily þan þe veny*m* of *Circe's poisonous charms.*
circes. ¶ For vices ben so cruel þat þei percen *and*
þoru3 passen þe corage wiþ inne. *and* þou3 þei ne anoye *Though it leaves the body*
nat þe body. 3itte vices wooden to distroien men by *whole, it pierces the inner man,*
wounde of þou3t. 3516 *and inflicts a deadly wound upon the soul.*

TUNC EGO FATEOR INQ*U*AM.

[*The ferthe prose.*]

þan seide I þus I confesse *and* am aknowe q*uod* I. ne *B. I confess that vicious men are*
I ne se nat þat men may seyn as by ry3t. þat *rightly called beasts. They retain the outward*
shrewes ne ben nat chaunged in to beestes by þe *form of man, but the qualities of*
qualite of hir soules. ¶ Al be it so þat þei kepen 3itte *their souls prove them to be beasts.*
þe forme of þe body of mankynde. but I nolde nat of *I wish, however, that the wicked*
shrewes of whiche þe þou3t cruel woodeþ alwey in to *were without the power to annoy*
destruccio*n* of good[e] men. þat it were leueful to hem *and hurt good men.*
to done þat. ¶ Certys q*uod* she ne it nis nat leueful *P. They have no power, as I shall*
to hem as I shal wel shewen þe in couenable place. *presently show you.*
¶ But naþeles yif so were þat þilke þat me*n* wene*n* ben 3526

3497 *were woxen swyne* — weeren wexen swyn
3498 *chau*n*ged* — Ichau*n*ged
brede — bred
forto — MS. and forto
ete acorns — eten akkornes
3499 *hoole* — hool
3501 *wepiþ* — MS. kepiþ, C. weepith
3502 *monstruous* — MS. monstronous, C. Moustruos
3504 *Circes* — MS. Cirtes
folk — folkys   [I-hydd
3509 *yhid* — MS. yhidde, C.
3515 *wooden* — MS. wolden, C. wooden
3518 *seyn* — sayn
3523 *good*[*e*] — goode
3524 *done* — don
3526 *ben* — be

| But were this power, which men ascribe to them, taken away from the wicked, they would be relieved of the greatest part of their punishment. The wicked are more unhappy when they have accomplished their evil designs than when they fail to do so. If it is a miserable thing to will evil, it is a greater unhappiness to have the power to execute it, without which power the wicked desires would languish without effect. Since, then, each of these three things (i. e. the will, the power, and the accomplishment of evil) hath its misery, therefore a threefold wretchedness afflicts those who both will, can, and do commit sin. | leueful for shrewes were bynomen hem. so þat þei ne my3ten nat anoyen or don harme to goode men. ¶ Certys a gret party of þe peyne to shrewes shulde ben allegged and releued. ¶ For al be it so þat þis ne seme nat credible þing perauenture to somme folk 3it mot it nedes be þat shrewes ben more wrecches and vnsely. whan þei may don and performe. þat þei coueiten [than yif they myhte nat complyssen þat they coueyten]. ¶ For yif so be þat it be wrecchednesse to wilne to don yuel : þan is it more wrecchednesse to mowen don yuel. wiþ oute whiche moeuyng þe wrecched wille sholde languisshe wiþ oute effecte. ¶ þan syn þat eueryche of þise þinges haþ hys wrecchednesse. þat is to seyne wil to done yuel. and moeuynge to done yuel. it mot nedes be. þat þei (shrewes) ben constreyned by þre vnselynesses þat wolen and mowen and performen felonyes and shrewednesses. ¶ I accorde me quod I. but I |
| 3544 B. I grant it—but still I wish the vicious were without this misfortune. [* fol. 28.] P. They shall be despoiled of it sooner than you wish perhaps, or than they themselves imagine. In the narrow limits of this life, nothing, however tardy it appears, can seem to an immortal soul to have a very long duration. The great hopes, and the subtle machinations of the wicked, are often suddenly frustrated, by which an end is put to their wickedness. If vice renders | desire gretely þat shrewes losten sone þilke vnselynesses. þat is to seyne þat shrewes were despoyled of moeuyng to don yuel. ¶ so shullen þei quod she. sonnere perauenture þen þou woldest *or sonnere þen þei hem self wenen to lakken mowynge to done yuel. ¶ For þere nis no þing so late in so short boundes of þis lijf þat is longe to abide. namelyche to a corage inmortel. Of whiche shrewes þe grete hope and þe heye compassyngus of shrewednesse is often destroyed by a sodeyne ende or þei ben war. and þat þing establiþ to shrewes þe ende of hir shrewednesse. ¶ For yif þat shrewednesse makiþe wrecches. þan mot he nedes be most wrecched þat lengest is a shrewe. þe whiche wicked shrewes wolde ydemen aldirmost vnsely and |

3527 *for*—to
3528 *my3ten*—myhte
  don—MS. done, C. doon
  harme—harm
3529 *gret*—MS. grete, C. gret
3533-36 *don*—MS. done, C. doon
3533-34 [*than——coueyten*]— from C.
3537 *moeuyng*—mowynge

3537 *wille*—wil
3539 *haþ*—MS. haþe
  seyne—seyn
3540 *done* (1)—doon
  moeuynge to done—Mowynge to don
  mot—MS. mote, C. mot
3544 *gretely*—gretly
3545 *seyne*—seyn
  were—weeren

3545 *moeuyng*—mowynge
3548 *wenen*—weene
  to lakken —— yuel—omitted
3549 *þere*—ther
  so (2)—the
3550 *longe*—long
3552 *shrewednesse* — shrewednesses
  often—ofte

caytifs yif þat hir shrewednes ne were yfinissed. at þe
leste weye by þe outerest[e] deeþ. for [yif] I haue concluded soþe of þe vnselynesse of shrewednesse. þan sheweþ
it clerely þat þilke shrewednesse is wiþ outen ende þe
whiche is certeyne to ben perdurable. ¶ Certys quod I
þis [conclusion] is harde *and* wonderful to graunte. ¶ But
I knowe wel þat it accordeþ moche to [the] þinges þat I
haue graunted her byforne. ¶ þou hast quod she þe ryʒt
estimacioun of þis. but who so euere wene þat it be an
harde þing to acorde hym to a conclusioun. it is 'ryʒt
þat he shewe þat somme of þe premisses ben fals. or
ellys he mot shewe þat þe colasioun of preposiciouns
nis nat spedful to a necessarie conclusioun. ¶ and yif it
be nat so. but þat þe premisses ben ygranted þer nis
nat whi he sholde blame þe argument. for þis þing þat
I shal telle þe nowe ne shal not seme lasse wondirful.
but of þe þinges þat ben taken al so it is necessarie as
who so seiþ it folweþ of þat whiche þat is purposed
byforn. what is þat quod I. ¶ certys quod she þat is
þat þat þise wicked shrewes ben more blysful or ellys
lasse wrecches. þat byen þe tourmentes þat þei han
deserued. þan yif no peyne of Iustice ne chastied[e]
hem. ne þis ne seye I nat now for þat any man myʒt[e]
þenk[e] þat þe maneres of shrewes ben coriged *and*
chastised by veniaunce. *and* þat þei ben brouʒt to þe
ryʒt wey by þe drede of þe tourment. ne for þat þei
ʒeuen to oþer folk ensample to fleyen from vices. ¶ But
I vndirstonde ʒitte [in] an oþer manere þat shrewes
ben more vnsely whan þei ne ben nat punissed al be it
so þat þere ne ben had no resoun or lawe of correccioun.
ne none ensample of lokynge. ¶ And what manere

*men wretched,
the longer they
are vicious the
longer must they
be miserable. And
they would be in-
finitely wretched
if death did not
put an end to
their crimes. It
is clear, as I haue
already shown,
that eternal
misery is infinite.
B. This conse-
quence appears to
be just, but diffi-
cult to assent to.
P. You think
rightly; but if
you cannot assent
to my conclusion
you ought to show
that the premises
are false, or that
the consequences
are unfairly de-
duced; for if the
premises be
granted, you can-
not reject the in-
ferences from
them. What I
am about to say
is not less wonder-
ful, and it follows
necessarily from
the same pre-
mises.
B. What is that?
P. That the wick-
ed who have been
punished for
their crimes, a*re
happier than if
justice had allow-
ed them to go
unpunished. I do
not appeal to
popular argu-
ments, that
punishment cor-
rects vice, that
the fear of chas-
tisement leads
them to take the
right path, and
that the suffer-
ings of evil-doers
deter others from
vice, but I believe
that guilty men,
unpunished, be-
come much more
unhappy in
another way.*

3574

3588

3558 *shrewednes* — shrewednesse '
yfinissed—fynyshed
3559 *weye*—wey
outerest[e]—owtterysto
[*yif*]—from C.
3560 *soþe*—soth
3561 *clerely*—cleerly
3563 [*conclusion*]—from C.

3563 *harde*—hard
3564 [*the*]—from C.
3567 *harde*—hard
3568 *fals*—false
3573 *nowe*—now
3575 *who so seiþ*—ho seyth
whiche—which
3578 *byen*—a-byen
3579 *chastied[e]*—chastysede

3580 *myʒt[e]*—myhte
3581 *þenk[e]*—thinke
3584 *ʒeuen*—MS. ʒeuene, C.
ʒeuen
fleyen—flen
3585 *ʒitte*—yif
[*in*]—from C.
3588 *none*—non

B. In what way do you mean?
P. Are not good people happy, and evil folk miserable?
B. Yes.
P. If good be added to the wretchedness of a man, will not he be happier than another whose misery has no element of good in it?
B. It seems so.
P. And if to the same wretched being another misery be annexed, does not he become more wretched than he whose misery is alleviated by the participation of some good?

3602
B. He does.
P. When evil men are punished they have a degree of good annexed to their wretchedness, to wit, the punishment itself, which as it is the effect of justice is good. And when these wretches escape punishment something more of ill (i.e. exemption from punishment) is added to their condition.
B. I cannot deny it.
P. Much more unhappy are the wicked when they enjoy an unmerited impunity than when they suffer a lawful chastisement. It is just to punish evildoers, and unjust that they should escape punishment.
[* fol. 28 b.]
B. Nobody denies that.
P. Everything, too, which is just

shal þat ben quod I. ouþer þan haþ ben told here
byforn ¶ Haue we nat graunted þan quod she þat
good[e] folk ben blysful. *and* shrewes ben wrecches.
ȝis quod I. [thanne quod she] ȝif þat any good were
added to þe wrecchenesse of any wyȝt. nis he nat more
blisful þan he þat ne haþ no medelyng of goode in hys
solitarie wrecchednesse. so semeþ it quod I. and what
seyst þou þan quod she of þilke wrecche þat lakkeþ alle
goodes. so þat no goode nis medeled in hys wrecchednesse. *and* ȝitte ouer alle hys wickednesse for whiche
he is a wrecche þat þer be ȝitte anoþer yuel anexid *and*
knyt to hym. shal not men demen hym more vnsely
þan þilke wrecche of whiche þe vnselynesse is re[le]ued
by þe *participacioun* of som goode. whi sholde he nat
quod I. ¶ þan certys quod she han shrewes whan þei
ben punissed somwhat of good anexid to hir wrecchednesse. þat is to seyne þe same peyne þat þei suffren
whiche þat is good by þe resou*n* of Iustice. And whan
þilke same shrewes ascapen wiþ outen tourment. þan
han þei somwhat more of yuel ȝit ouer þe wickednesse
þat þei han don. þat is to seye defaute of peyne.
whiche defaute of peyne þou hast graunted is yuel.
¶ For þe desert of felonye I ne may nat denye it quod
I. ¶ Moche more þan quod she ben shrewes vnsely
whan þei ben wrongfully delyuered fro peyne. þan
whan þei beþ punissed by ryȝtful vengeaunce. but þis is
open þing *and* clere þat it is ryȝt þat shrewes ben
punissed. *and* it is wickednesse *and* wrong þat þei
escapin vnpunissed. ¶ who myȝt[e] denye *þat quod I.
but quod she may any man denye. þat al þat is ryȝt nis
good. *and* also þe contrarie. þat alle þat is wrong nis

3589 *ouþer*—oother
 haþ—MS. haþe
 ben—be
 told—MS. tolde, C. told
3591 *good[e]*—goode
3592 *[thanne — she]*—from C.
3594 *blisful*—weleful
 haþ—MS. haþe
3594-97 *goode*—good

3598 *alle*—al
 whiche—which
3600 *knyt*—knytte
3601 *re[le]ued*—releued
3602 *goode*—good
3605 *seyne*—seyn
3606 *whiche*—which
3607 *outen*—owte
3609 *don*—MS. done
 seye—seyn

3610 *whiche*—which
3611 *desert*—deserte
3614 *beþ*—MS. beþe, C. ben
3615 *clere*—cler
3617 *myȝt[e]*—myhte
3618 *is ryȝt nis*—MS. nis ryȝt is
3619 *alle*—al
 nis wicked—is wykke

wicked. certys quod I þise þinges ben clerc ynouȝ. *and* is good; and, on the contrary,
þat we han concludid a litel here byforne. but I preye whatsoever is unjust is evil.
þe þat þou telle me yif þou accordest to leten no tour- *B. These are just inferences from our former premises. But is*
ment to þe soules aftir þat þe body is dedid by þe deþe.
þis [is] to seyn. vndirstondest þou ouȝt þat soules han *there any punishment for the soul after death of the body?*
any to*ur*ment after þe deþe of þe body. ¶ Certis quod *P. Yes, and great ones too. Some*
she ȝe *and* þat ryȝt grete. of whiche soules qu*o*d she I *punishments are rigorous and*
trowe þat somme ben tou*r*mentid by asprenesse of *eternal. Others have a corrective*
peyne. *and* somme soules I trowe be excercised by a *and purifying force, and are of*
pu*r*ging mekenesse. but my conseil nys nat to deter- *finite duration. But this is not*
myne of þis peyne. but I haue trauayled and told it *to our purpose.*
hider to. ¶ For þou sholdest knowe þat þe mowynge *I want you to see that the power of*
[.i. myght] of shrewes whiche mowynge þe semeþ to *the wicked is in reality nothing,*
ben. vnworþi nis no mowynge. *and* eke of shrewes of *that the wicked never go un-*
whiche þou pleynedest þat þei ne were nat punissed. *punished; that their licence to do*
þat þou woldest seen þat þei ne weren neuer mo wiþ *evil is not of long duration, and*
outen þe torment of hire wickednesse. *and* of þe licence *that the wicked would be more*
of mowynge to done yuel. þat þou preidest þat it *unhappy if it were longer, and in-*
myȝt[e] sone ben endid. *and* þat þou woldest fayne *finitely wretched, if it were to con-*
lerne. þat it ne sholde nat longe endure. *and* þat *tinue for ever.*
shrewes ben more vnsely yif þei were of lenger duryng.
and most vnsely yif þei weren perdurable. *and* after *After this I*
þis I haue shewed þe þat more vnsely ben shrewes *showed that evil men are more unhappy, having*
whan þei escapen wiþ oute ryȝtful peyne. þan whan þei *escaped punishment, than if*
ben punissed by ryȝtful uengeaunce. and of þis sentence *justly chastised. Wherefore when*
folweþ it þat þan be*n* shrewes constreyned atte laste wiþ *they are supposed to get off scot-free*
most greuous tourment. whan men wene þat þei ne ben *they suffer most grievously.*
nat ypunissed. whan I considre þi resou*n*s qu*o*d I. I. *B. Your reasoning appears convincing and con-*
ne trowe nat þat men seyn any þing more verrely. *and* *clusive. But your*
yif I tou*r*ne aȝeyn to þe studies of men. who is [he] to *arguments are opposed to current opinions,*
whom it sholde seme þat [he] ne sholde nat only leue*n* *and would hardly command assent,*
þise þinges. but eke gladly herkene he*m*. Certys qu*o*d *or even a hearing.*

3621 *here*—her
3623 *dedid*—endyd
   deþe—deth
3624 [*is*]—from C.
   ouȝt—awht
3625 *deþe*—deth
3626 *grete*—gret
3628 *be*—ben

3629 *determyne*—determenye
3630 *peyne*—peynes
   told—MS. tolde
3632 [*.i. myght*]—from C.
3632-34 *whiche*—which
3633 *eke*—ek
3635 *seen*—seyn
3637 *done*—don

3638 *myȝt*[*e*]—myhte
   fayne lerne—fayn lernen
3639 *endure*—dure
3645 *atte*—at the
   laste—MS. past, C. laste
3647 *resouns*—resoun
3649-50 [*he*]—from C.
3651 *eke*—ek

P. It is so. For those accustomed to the darkness of error cannot fix their eyes on the light of perspicuous truth, like birds of night which are blinded by the full light of day. They consider only the gratification of their lusts, they think there is happiness in the liberty of doing evil and in exemption from punishment. Do you attend to the eternal law written in your own heart. Conform your mind to what is good, and you will stand in no need of a judge to confer a reward upon you —for you have it already in the enjoyment of the best of things (*i.e.* virtue). If you indulge in vice, you need no other chastisement— you have degraded yourself into a lower order of beings. The multitude doth not consider this. What then? Shall we take them as our models who resemble beasts? If a man who had lost his sight, having even forgotten his blindness, should declare that his faculties were all perfect, shall we weakly believe that those who retain their sight are blind? The vulgar will not assent to what I am going to say, though supported by conclusive arguments—to wit, that persons are more unhappy that do wrong

she so it is. but men may nat. for þei han hire eyen so wont to derkenesse of erþely þinges. þat þei may nat liften hem vp to þe lyȝt of clere sopefastnes. ¶ But þei ben lyke to briddes of whiche þe nyȝt lyȝtneþ hyre lookyng. *and* þe day blyndeþ hem. for whan men loken nat þe ordre of þinges but hire lustes *and* talentȝ. þei wene þat oþir þe leue or þe mowynge to done wickednesse or ellys þe escap*in*g wiþ oute peyne be weleful. but *considere* þe iugement of þe *per*durable lawe. for if þou conferme þi corage to þe beste þinges. þou ne hast no nede to no iuge to ȝiue*n* þe *pr*is or meede. for þou hast ioigned þi self to þe most excellent þing. and yif þou haue enclined þi studies to þe wicked þinges. ne seek no foreyn wrekere out of þi self. for þou þi self hast þrest þe in to wicked þinges. ryȝt as þou myȝtest loken by dyuerse tymes þe foule erþe *and* þe heuene.

3668 *and* þat alle oþer þinges stynten fro wiþ oute. so þat þou [nere neyther in heuene ne in erthe] ne say[e] no þing more. þan sholde it semen to þe as by only resou*n* of lokynge. þat þou were in þe sterres. *and* now in þe erþe. but þe poeple ne lokeþ nat on þise þinges. what þan shal we þan approchen vs to hem þat I haue shewed þat þei ben lyke to þe bestes. (q. d. no*n*) ¶ And what wilt þou seyne of þis ¶ yif þat a man hadde al forlorn hys syȝt. *and* had[de] forȝeten þat he euer saw *and* wende þat no þing ne fayled[e] hym of *per*feccio*un* of ma*n*kynde. now we þat myȝten sen þe same þing wolde we nat wene þat he were bly*n*de (q. d. sic). ne also ne accordeþ nat þe poeple to þat I shal seyne. þe whiche þing is susteyned by a stronge foundement of resou*n*s. þat is to seyn þat more vnsely ben þei

3653 *derkenesse*—derknesse
3654 *clere sopefastnes*—cleer sothfastnesse
3655 *whiche*—which
3658 *oþir*—eyther *done*—don
3659 *escaping*—schapynge
3662 *to* (1)—of
3665 *foreyn*—foreyne
3666 *þrest*—thryst

3666 *wicked*—wikke
3669 [*nere——erthe*]—from C. *heuene*—C. heuenene *say*[*e*]—C. sayo
3672 *on*—in
3674 *lyke*—lyk q. d.—MS. quod
3675 *wilt þou seyne*—woltow seyn
3670 *forlorn*—MS. forlorne,

C. for-lorn *syȝt*—syhte *had*[*de*]—hadde
3677 *saw*—MS. sawe, C. sawh *fayled*[*e*]—faylede
3678 *sen*—MS. sene, C. sen
3679 *þing*—thinges q. d.—MS. quod
3681 *whiche*—which

þat don wrong to oþer folk. þen þei· þat þe wrong suffren. ¶ I wolde heren þilke *same resouns quod I ¶ Deniest þou quod she þat alle shrewes ne ben worþi to han tourment. nay quod I. but quod she I am certeyne by many resouns þat shrewes ben vnsely. it accordeþ quod I. þan [ne] dowtest þou nat quod she þat þilke folk þat ben worþi of tourment þat þei ne ben wrecches. It accordeþ wel quod I. yif þou were þan quod she yset a Iuge or a knower of þinges. wheþer trowest þou þat men sholde tourment[e] hym þat haþ don þo wronge. or hym þat haþ suffred þe wronge. I ne doute nat quod I. þat I nolde don suffissaunt satisfaccioun to hym þat had[de] suffred þe wrong by þe sorwe of hym þat had[de] don þe wronge. ¶ þan semeþ it quod she þat þe doar of wrong is more wrecche þan he þat haþ suffred þe wrong. þat folweþ wel quod [I]. þan quod she by þise causes and by oþer causes þat ben enforced by þe same roate þat filþe or synne by þe propre nature of it makeþ men wrecches. and it sheweþ wel þat þe wrong þat men don nis nat þe wrecchenesse of hym þat receyueþ þe wrong. but þe wrecchednesse of hym þat doþ þe wronge ¶ but certys quod she þise oratours or ₍aduocatȝ don al þe contrarie for þei enforcen hem to commoeue þe iuges to han pite of hem þat han suffred and resceyued þe þinges þat ben greuous and aspre. and ȝitte men sholden more ryȝtfully han pitee on hem þat don þe greuaunces and þe wronges. þe whiche shrewes it were a more couenable þing þat þe accusours or aduocatȝ not wroþe but pitous and debonaire ladden þe shrewes þat han don wrong to þe Iugement. ryȝt as men leden seke folk to þe leche. for þat þei sholden seken out þe maladies of synne by

than those who suffer wrong.
[* fol. 29.]
B. I would willingly hear your reasons.
P. Do you deny that every wicked man deserves punishment?
B. No, I do not.
P. I am satisfied that impious men are in many ways miserable.
B. They are so.
P. Then those that deserve punishment are miserable.
B. I admit it.
P. If you were a judge, upon whom would you inflict punishment?
upon the wrongdoer, or upon the injured?
B. I should not hesitate to punish the offender as a satisfaction to the sufferer.
P. Then you would deem the injuring person more unhappy than he who had been wronged?
B. That follows naturally.
P. From this then, and other reasons of like nature, it seems

3703

that vice makes men miserable, and an injury done to any man is the misery of the doer, and not of the sufferer.
But our advocates think differently—they try to obtain pity for those that have suffered cruelty and oppression; but the juster pity is really due to the oppressors, who ought, therefore, to be led to judgment as the sick are to the physician, not by angry but by merciful and kind accusers, so that,

3693 don—MS. done, C. don
oþer—oothre
3698 [ne]—from C.
3691 yset — MS. ysette, C. yset
wheþer—omitted
3692 tourment[e]—torment-
3692-3 haþ—MS. haþe [en
3693 wronge (2)—wrong
3695 had[de]—hadde
3696 had[de]—hadden
wronge—wrong
3697 doar—doere
3698 haþ—MS. haþe
3699 [I]—from C.
3700 ben—hen of
3700 roate—Roote
3703-4 but——wronge—omitted
3704 doþ—MS. doþe
3711 wroþe—wroth
3712 þe—tho
don—MS. done, C. don
3713 seke—ᴎyke

9

by the phylic of chastisement, they may be cured of their vices. I would not have the guilty defrauded by their advocates. Their duty is to accuse, and not to excuse offenders. Were it permitted the wicked to get a slight view of virtue's beauty, which they have forsaken, and could they be persuaded of the purifying effects of lawful chastisement, they surely would not consider punishment as an evil, but would willingly give themselves up to justice and refuse the defence of their advocates. The wise hate nobody, only a fool hates good men; and it is as irrational to hate the wicked. Vice is a sickness of the soul, and needs our compassion, and not our hate, for the distempers of the soul are more deplorable than those of the body, and have more claims upon our compassion.

tourmentʒ. and by þis couenaunt eyþer þe entent of þe defendours or aduocatʒ sholde fayle and cesen in al. or ellys yif þe office of aduocatʒ wolde bettre profiten to men. it sholde be tourned in to þe habit of accusacioun. þat is [to] s[e]yn þei sholden accuse shrewes. and nat 3720 excuse hem. and eke þe shrewes hem self. ʒit it were leueful to hem to seen at any clifte þe vertue þat þei han forleten. and sawen þat þei sholde putten adoun þe filþes of hire vices by [the] tourmentʒ of peynes. þei ne auʒten nat ryʒt for þe recompensacioun forto geten hem bounte and prowesse whiche þat þei han lost demen ne holden þat þilke peynes weren tourmentes to hem. 3727 and eke þei wolden refuse þe attendaunce of hir aduocatʒ and taken hem self to hire iuges and to hir accusours. for whiche it bytideþ [þat] as to þe wise folk þer nis no place ylete to hate. þat is to seyn. þat hate ne haþ no place amonges wise men. ¶ For no wyʒt wolde haten gode men. but yif he were ouer moche a fole. ¶ and forto haten shrewes it nis no resoun. 3734 ¶ For ryʒt so as languissing is maladie of body. ryʒt so ben vices and synne maladies of corage. ¶ and so as we ne deme nat þat þei þat ben seek of hire body ben worþi to ben hated. but raþer worþi of pite. wel more worþi nat to ben hated. but forto ben had in pite ben þei of whiche þe þouʒtes ben constreined by felonous 3740 wickednesse. þat is more cruel þan any languissinge of body.

[The ferthe Metur.]
What frenzy causes man to hasten on his fate, that is, by war or by strife. If death is desired he de-

QUID TANTOS IUUAT.

What deliteþ it ʒow to exciten so grete moewynges of hatredes and to hasten and bisien [the] fatal disposicioun of ʒoure deeþ wiþ ʒoure propre handes. þat is 3745 to seyn by batailes or [by] contek. for yif ʒe axen þe

3715 tourmentʒ—torment þe (2)—omitted
3719 [to] s[e]yn—to seyn
3722 sawen—sawh sholde—sholden
3723 [the]—from C.
3724 auʒten—owhte

3725-29 whiche—which
3729 bytideþ—MS. byndeþ, C. bytidith
[þat]—from C.
3730 ylete—I-leten
3731 haþ—MS. haþe
3732 wolde—nyl

3732 moche—mochel
3733 fole—fool
3736 seek—syke
3743 [the]—from C.
3745 [by]—from C.

THE FOLLY OF WAR.

deeþ it hastisiþ hym of hys owen wille. ne deeþ ne
tarieþ nat hys swifte hors. and [the] men þat þe ser-
pentȝ *and* þe lyouns. *and* þe tigre. *and* þe beere *and* þe
boore seken to sleen wiþ her teþe. ȝit þilke same men
seken to sleen eueryche of hem oþer wiþ swerde. loo for
her ma*n*ers ben * diuerse *and* discordaunt ¶ þei
moeuen vnryȝtful oostes *and* cruel batailes. *and* wilne
to *p*erisse by enterchaungynge of dartes. but þe resou*n*
of cruelte nis nat ynouȝ ryȝtful. wilt þou þan ȝelden a
couenable gerdou*n* to þe desertes of men ¶ Loue ryȝtfully goode folk! *and* haue pite on shrewes.   3756

lays not to come. Why do they who are exposed to the assaults of beasts of prey and venomous reptiles seek to slay each other with the sword. Lo! their manners and opinions do not [* fol. 29 b.] *accord, wherefore they engage in unjust wars, and fiercely urge on each other's destiny. But this is no just reason for shedding blood. Wouldst thou reward each as he deserves? Then love the good as they deserve, and have pity upon the wicked.*

HINC EGO UIDEO INQU*A*M. ET CETE*RA*.

[The fyfthe prose.]

Þus see I wel q*uod* I. eyþer what blisfulnesse or ellys
what vnselinesse is estab[l]issed in þe desertys of
goode men *and* of shrewes. ¶ but in þis ilke fortune
of peeple I see somwhat of goode. *and* somwhat of
yuel. for no wise man haþ nat leuer ben exiled pore
and nedy *and* nameles. þan forto dwellen in hys Citee
and flouren of rychesses. *and* be redoutable by honoure. 3763
and stronge of power for in þis wise more clerely *and*
more witnesfully is þe office of wise men ytretid whan
þe blisfulnes *and* [the] pouste of gouernours is as it
were yshad amonges poeples þat ben neyȝboures *and*
subgitȝ. syn þat namely prisou*n* lawe *and* þise oþer
tou*r*mentȝ of lawful peynes ben raþer owed to felonous
Citeȝeins. for þe whiche felonous Citeȝeins þo peynes   3770
ben establissed. þan for goode folk. ¶ þan I meruaile
me gretly q*uod* I. whi [þat] þe þinges ben so mys entrechaunged. þat tourmentȝ of felounes pressen *and*
confounden goode folk. *and* shrewes rauyssen medes of

B. I see plainly the nature of that felicity which attends the virtues of the good, and of the misery that follows the vices of the wicked. But in Fortune I see a mixture of good and evil. The wise man prefers riches, &c., to poverty, &c. And wisdom appears more illustrious, when wise men are governors and impart their felicity to their subjects; and when imprisonment, torture, &c., are inflicted only upon bad citizens.

Why, then, should things undergo so unnatural a change? Why should the worthy suffer and the vicious re-

---

3746 *hastisi*þ—hasteth
  owen wille—owne wyl
3747 [*the*]—from C.
3749 *boore*—boor
  teþe—teth
3750 *swerde*—swerd
3751 *her*—hir
3752 *wilne*—wylnen
3753 *enterchaungynge* — entrechaungynges
3760 *goode*—good
3761 *ha*þ—MS. haþe
  nat—omitted
  leuer—leuere
3762 *þan*—MS. þat, C. than
3763 *redoutable* — MS. re-
  dentable, C. redowtable
3764 *stronge*—strong
3764 *clerely*—clerly
3766 [*the*]—from C.
3767 *neyȝboures* — nesshe-
  bors
3769 *lawful*—laweful
3771 *goode*—good
3772 [*þat*]—from C.

THE OPERATIONS OF CHANCE.

ceive the reward of virtue? I should like to hear the reason of so unjust a distribution. I should not marvel so much if Chance were the cause of all this confusion. But I am overwhelmed with astonishment when I reflect, that God the director of all things thus unequally distributes rewards and punishments. What difference is there, then, unless we know the cause, between God's proceedings and the operations of Chance? P. It is not at all surprising that you think you see irregularities, when you are ignorant of that order by which God proceeds. But, forasmuch as God, the good governor, presides over all, rest assured that all things are done rightly and as they ought to be done.

vertue *and* ben i*n* hono*u*rs. *and* in grete estatis. and I desire eke to wite*n* of þe. what semeþ þe to ben þe resou*n* of þis so wro*n*gful a confusiou*n*   ¶ For I wolde wondre wel þe lasse yif I trowed[e] þat alle þise þinges were medeled by fortuouse hap.   ¶ But now hepeþ *and* encreseþ myne astonyenge god gouernour of þinges. þat so as god ȝeueþ ofte tymes to good[e] men goodes *and* myrþes. *and* to shrewes yuel and aspre þinges. *and* ȝcueþ aȝeynewarde to goode folk hardnesse. *and* to shrewes [he] graunteþ hem her wille *and* þat þei desiren. what difference þan may þer be bitwixen þat þat god doþ. *and* þe hap of fortune. yif men ne knowe nat þe cause whi þat [it] is. it nis no merueile qu*o*d she þouȝ þat men wenen þat þer be somwhat folysche and confus whan þe resou*n* of þe order is vnknowe.   ¶ But alle þouȝ þou ne know nat þe cause of so gret a disposiciou*n*. naþeles for as moche as god þe good[e] gouernour attempreþ *and* gouerneþ þe world. ne doute þe nat þat alle þinges ne ben doon aryȝt.   3793.

[* MS. arituri] (The fyfthe Metur.) He who knows not that the Bear is seen near the Pole, nor has observed the path of Boötes, will marvel at their appearance.

SI QUIS ARCTURI * SYDERA.

Who so þat ne knowe nat þe sterres of arctour ytou*r*ned neye to þe souereyne contre or point. þat is to seyne ytou*r*ned neye to þe souereyne pool of þe firmament *and* woot nat whi þe sterre boetes passeþ or

3798 gaderiþ his wey[n]es. *and* drencheþ his late flaumbes in þe see. *and* whi þat boetes þe sterre vnfoldiþ his ouer

The vulgar are alarmed when shadows terrestrial obscure the moon's brightness, causing the stars to be displayed.

swifte arisynges. þan shal he wo*n*dre*n* of þe lawe of þe heye eyre. *and* eke if þat he ne knowe nat why þat þe hornes of þe ful[le] moene waxen pale *and* infect by þe boundes of þe derke nyȝt ¶ and how þe moene dirk

3775 *grete*—gret
3776 *to witen*—forto weten
3778 *trowed[e]*—trowede
   alle—al
3779 *were*—weeren
   fortuouse—fortunous
3780 *myne*—myn
3781 *good[e]*—goode
3782 *yuel*—yuelis
3783 *hardnesse*—hardnesses

3784 [*he*]—from C.
   wille—wyl
3785 *difference*—MS. differ-
3786 *doþ*—MS. doþe   [ence
   hap—happe
3787 [*it*]—from C.
   it—ne it
3788 *confus*—confuse
3789 *alle*—al
3791 *good[e]*—goode

3793 *ne*—omitted
3794 *arctour*—MS. aritour
3795 *neye*—neygh
3796 *seyne*—seyn
   neye—nygh
3797-99 *boetes*—MS. boeres, C. boetes
3798 *his* (1)—hise
   wey[n]es—weynes
3802 *ful[le]*—fulle

and confuse discouereþ þe sterres. þat she had[de] ycouered by hir clere visage. þe co*m*mune errour moeueþ folk *and* makiþ wery hir bacines of bras by þikke strookes. þat is to seyne þat þer is a maner poeple þat hyȝt[e] coribandes þat wenen þat whan þe moone is in þe eclips þat it be enchau*n*tid. and þerfore forto rescowe þe moone þei betyn hire basines wiþ þikke strokes. ¶ Ne no man ne wondreþ whan þe blastes of þe wynde chorus betyn þe strondes of þe see by quakynge floodes. ne no man ne wondreþ whan þe weyȝte of þe snowe yhardid by þe colde. is resolued by þe brennynge hete of phebus þe sonne. ¶ For here seen men redyly þe causes. but þe * causes yhid þat is to seye in heuene trouble þe brestes of men. ¶ þe moeueable poeple is a-stoned of alle þinges þat comen selde *and* sodeynely in oure age. but yif þe troubly errour of oure ignora*n*ce departid[e] from vs. so þat we wisten þe causes whi þat swiche þinges bitiden. certys þei sholde*n* cesse to seme wondres.

Thinking the eclipse the result of enchantment, they sought to destroy the charms by the tinkling of brazen vessels or cymbals. Yet none marvel when the north-west wind renders the sea tempestuous; nor when vast heaps of congealed snow are melted by the warm rays of the sun, because the causes are apparent.

3813 Things whose causes are unknown disquiet the human mind.

[* fol. 30.]

The fickle mob stands amazed at every rare or sudden phenomenon. Fear and wonder, however, soon cease when ignorance gives place to certain knowledge.

3822

ITA EST INQUAM.

Þvs is it qu*od* I. but so as þou hast ȝeuen or byhyȝt me to vnwrappe*n* þe hidde causes of þinges ¶ and to discoueren me þe resou*n*s couered w*ith* dirknesses I preye þe þat þou diuise *and* Iuge me of þis matere. *and* þat þou do me to vndrestonde*n* it. ¶ For þis miracle or þis wondre troubleþ me ryȝt gretely. *and* þan she a litel [what] smylyng seide. ¶ þou clepest me qu*od* she to telle þing. þat is grettest of alle þinges þat mowen ben axed. ¶ And to þe whiche questiou*n* vnneþ[e]s is þere auȝt ynow to lauen it. as who seiþ. vnneþes is þer suffisauntly any þing to answere pe*r*fitly to þi questiou*n*. 3833

[The ayxte prose.' B. So it is. But as thou hast promised to unfold the hidden causes of things, and unveil things wrapt up in darkness; I pray thee deliver me from iny present perplexity, and explain the mystery I mentioned to you. P. You ask me to declare to you the most intricate of all questions, which I am afraid can scarce be answered.

3904 *had[de]*—hadde	3815 *here*—her	3824 *hidde*—hyd
3906 *bacines*—MS. batines þikke—MS. þilke, C. thilke	*redyly*—redely	3826 *preye*—precy
	3816 *yhid*—MS. yhidde, C. I-hid	*diuise*—deuyse
3907 *seyne*—seyn	*seye*—seyn	3827 *do*—don
3908 *hyȝt[e]*—hihte	3817 *trouble*—trowblen	3828 *gretely*—gretly
3809 *eclips*—eclypse	3820 *departid[e] from*—departede fro	3829 *[what]*—from C.
3812 *chorus*—MS. thorus, C. chorus		3832 *þere auȝt*—ther awht
3813 *snowe*—sonwh = snowh	3823 *byhyȝt*—by-hylite	

FIVE GREAT QUESTIONS.

For the subject is of such a kind, that when one doubt is removed, innumerable others, like the heads of the hydra, spring up. Nor would there be any end of them unless they were restrained by a quick and vigorous effort of the mind. The question whereof you want a solution embraces the five following points: 1. Simplicity, or unity of Providence. 2. The order and course of Destiny. 3. Sudden chance. 4. Prescience of God, and divine predestination. 5. Free-will. I will try to treat of these things:— Resuming her discourse as from a new principle,

3849

Philosophy argued as follows:— The generation of all things, every progression of things liable to change, and everything that moveth, derive their causes, order, and form from the immutability of the divine understanding. Providence directs all things by a variety of means. These means, referred only to the divine intelligence, are called Providence; but when contemplated in relation to the things which receive motion and order from them, are called Destiny. Reflection on the efficacy of the one and the other will soon

¶ For þe matere of it is swiche þat whan oon doute is determined *and* kut awey þer wexen oþer doutes wiþ-outen noumbre. ryȝt as þe heuedes waxen of ydre þe serpent þat hercules slouȝ. ¶ Ne þere ne were no manere no noon ende. but yif þat a wyȝt constreined[e] þo doutes. by a ryȝt lyuely *and* a quik fire of þouȝt. þat is to seyn by vigo*ur and* strengþe of witte. ¶ For in þis matere me*n* weren wont to maken questiou*n*s of þe simplicite of þe p*ur*ueau*n*ce of god *and* of þe ordre of destine. *and* of sodeyne hap. *and* of þe knowyng *and* predestinacio*un* deuine *and* of þe lyberte of fre wille. þe whiche þing þou þi self aperceiust wel of what weyȝt þei ben. but for as mochel as þe knowynge of þise þinges is a manere porcio*un* to þe medicine to þe. al be it so þat I haue lytel tyme to don it. ȝit naþeles I wole enforcen me to shewe somwhat of it. ¶ but al þouȝ þe norissinges of dite of musike deliteþ þe þow most suffren. *and* forberen a litel of þilk delite while þat I weue (contexo) to þe resou*n*s yknyt by ordre ¶ As it likeþ to þe q*uo*d I so do. ¶ þo spak she ryȝt a[s] by an oþer bygynnyn[ge] *and* seide þus. ¶ þe enge*n*drynge of alle þinges q*uo*d she *and* alle þe progressiou*n*s of muuable natu*re*. *and* alle þat moeueþ in any manere takiþ hys causes. hys ordre. *and* hys formes. of þe stablenesse of þe deuyne þouȝt [*and* thilke deuyne thowht] þat is yset *and* put in þe toure. þat is to seyne in þe heyȝt of þe simplicite of god. stablisiþ many manere gyses to þinges þat ben to don. ¶ þe whiche manere whan þat men loken it i*n* þilke pure clerenesse of þe deuyne intelligence. it is ycleped p*ur*ueau*n*ce ¶ but whan þilke manere is re-

---

3834 *swiche*—swych
oon—o
3835 *wiþouten noumbre*—with-owte nowmbyr
3836 *waxen*—wexen
3837 *þere*—ther
3838 *constreined*[*e*]—constreynede
3839 *lyuely*—lyfly
3840 *witte*—wit

3843 *hap*—happe
3845 *weyȝt*—wyht
3848 *wole*—wol
3850 *þow*—MS. now, C. þou
most suffren—MS. moste to souereyne ; C. most suffren
3851 *þilk*—thilke
3853 *þo*—so
spak—MS. spake, C. spak

3853 *a*[*s*]—as
3856 *alle*—al
3858 [*and*——*thowht*]—from C.
yset—MS. ysette, C. yset
3859 *toure*—towr
seyne—seyn
heyȝt—heyhte
3861 *don*—done
3862 *clerenesse*—klennesse

ferred by men to þinges þat it moeueþ *and* disponeþ þan of olde men. it was cleped destine. ¶ þe whiche þinges yif þat any wyȝt lokeþ wel in his þouȝt. þe strengþe of þat oon *and* of þat oþer he shal lyȝtly mowen seen þat þise two þinges ben diuers. ¶ For *pur*ueau*n*ce is þilke deuyne resou*n* þat is establissed in þe souereyne *pr*ince of þinges. þe whiche *pur*ueaunce disponiþ alle þinges. but destine is þe disposicio*un and* ordenaunce cleúynge to moeuable þinges. by þe whiche disposicio*un* þe *pur*ueaunce knyteþ alle þinges in hire ordres. ¶ For *pur*ueaunce enbraceþ alle þinges to hepe. al þouȝ þat þei ben dyuerse *and* al þouȝ þei ben wiþ outen fyn. but destynie departeþ *and* ordeyneþ alle þinges singlerly *and* diuideþ. in moeuynges. in places. in formes. in tymes. dep*ar*tiþ [as] þus. so þat þe vnfoldyng of tem*por*el ordenaunce assembled *and* ooned in þe lokyng of þe deuyne þouȝt ¶ Is *pur*ueaunce *and* þilke same assemblynge. *and* oonyng diuided *and* vnfolden by tymes. lat þat ben called destine. *and* al be *it so þat þise þinges ben dyuerse. ȝitte naþeles hangeþ þat oon on þat oþer. forwhi þe ordre destinal procediþ of þe simplicite of purueaunce. for ryȝt as a werkman þat ap*er*ceiueþ in hys þouȝt þe forme of þe þing þat he wil make moeueþ þe effect of þe werke. *and* lediþ þat he had[de] loked byforne in hys þouȝt symply *and* presently by temp*or*el þouȝt. ¶ Certys ryȝt so god disponiþ in hys p*ur*ueaunce singlerly *and* stably þe þinges þat ben to done. but he amynistreþ in many maneres *and* in dyuerse tymes by destyne. þilke same þinges þat he haþ disponed þan wheþir þat destine be excercised. eyþer by somme dyuyne spirites seruauntez to þe deuyne p*ur*ueaunce. or ellys by somme soule (anima

3880

[* fol. 30 b.]

3872 *cleuynge*—clvuynge
3875 *wiþ outen fyn* — Infynyte
3876 *singlerly*—syngulerly
3877 *in* (3)—MS. *and*, C. in
3878 *departiþ*—omitted [*as*]—from C.
3878 *so þat*—lat
3881 *on*—of
3886 *wil*—wol
3888 *had[de]*—hadde *symply*—symplely
3889 *þouȝt*—ordinaunce
3890 *singlerly*—syngulerly
3890 *stably*—stablely
3893 *haþ*—MS. haþe
3894 *eyþer*—owther *seruauntez* — MS. seruauncez
3895 *somme*—som

| he accomplishes what he has planned, conformably to that order and that time. So then, however Fate be exercised, it is evident that things subject to Destiny are under the control of Providence, which disposes Destiny. But some things under Providence are exempt from the control of Fate; being stably fixed near to the Divinity himself, and beyond the movement of Destiny. For even, as among several circles revolving round one common centre, that which is innermost approaches nearest to the simplicity of the middle points, and is, as it were, a centre, round which the outward ones revolve; whilst the outermost, revolving in a wider circumference, the further it is from the centre describes a larger space—but yet, if this circle or anything else be joined to the middle point, it is constrained to be immovable. By parity of reason, the further anything is removed from the first Intelligence, so much the more is it under the control of Destiny; and the nearer anything approaches to this Intelligence, the centre of all things, the more stable it becomes, and the less dependent upon Destiny. | mundi). or ellys by al nature scruynge to god. or ellys by þe celestial moeuyng of sterres. or ellys by þe vertue of aungels. or ellys by þe dyuerse subtilite of deueles. or ellys by any of hem. or ellys by hem alle þe destynal ordynau*n*ce is ywouen or accomplissed. certys it is open þing þat þe puruccaunce is an vnmoeueable *and* symple forme of þinges to done. *and* þe moeueable bonde *and* þe tempo*r*el ordynaunce of þinges whiche þat þe deuyne simplicite of puruеaunce haþ ordeyned to done. þat is destine. For whiche it is þat alle þinges þat ben put vndir destine ben certys subgit₃ to pu*r*ueaunce. to whiche pu*r*ueaunce destine it self is subgit *and* vndir. ¶ But somme þinges ben put vndir puruеaunce þat sou*r*mounten þe ordinaunce of destine. *and* þo ben þilke þat stably ben yfiсched ney to þe first godhed þei sou*r*mounten þe ordre of destinal moeuablite. ¶ For ry3t as cercles þat tou*r*nen aboute a same Centre or about a poynt. þilke cercle þat is inrest or moost wiþ-ynne ioineþ to þe symplesse of þe myddel *and* is as it were a Centre or a poynt to þat·oþer cercles þat tourne*n* aboute*n* hym. ¶ and þilke þat is outcrest compased by larger envyronnynge is vnfolden by larger spaces in so mochel as it is forþest fro þe mydel symplicite of þe poynt. and yif þer be any þing þat knytteþ *and* felaw-shippeþ hym selfe to þilke mydel poynt it is constreyned in to symplicite. þat is to seyn in to [vn]moeueablete. *and* it ceseth to ben shad *and* to fletin dyuersly. ¶ Ry3t so by semblable resou*n*. þilke þinge þat depаrtiþ firþest fro þe first þou3t of god. it is vnfolde*n* *and* sumittid to gretter bondes of destine. and in so moche is þe þing more free *and* loys fro destyne as it axeþ *and* |

3896 *al*—alle
3897 *moeuyng*—moeuynges
3900 *ywouen*—MS. ywonnen, C. ywouen
or—and
3902 *bonde*—bond
3904 *haþ*—MS. haþe
3905 *whiche*—which

3912 *as*—as of
3913 *about*—a-bowte
inrest—innerest
3917 *larger* (1)—a large
3918 *mochel*—moche
forþest—ferthere
3920 *selfe*—self
3921 *[vn]moeueablete* — vn-

moeuablete
3922 *ceseth* — MS. fleþe, C. cesith
3923 *þinge*—thing
3924 *of*—MS. to, C. of
3920 *lovs*—laus

holdeþ hym ner to þilke Centre of þinges. þat is to seyne god. ¶ and if þe þinge cleueþ to þe stedfastnesse of þe þou3t of god. *and* be wiþ oute moeuyng certys it sourmounteþ þe necessite of destyne. þan ry3t swiche comparisou*n* as [it] is of skilynge to vndirstondyng *and* of þing þat is engendred to þing þat is. *and* of tyme to eternite. *and* of þe cercle to þe Centre. ry3t so is þe ordre of moeucable destine to þe stable symplicite of pu*r*ueau*n*ce. ¶ þilke ordinau*n*ce moeueþ þe heuene *and* þe sterres *and* attempreþ þe elyment3 to gider amonges hem self. *and* transformeþ hem by enterchau*n*gable mutaciou*n*. ¶ and þilke same ordre neweþ a3ein alle þinges growyng *and* fallyng a-doune by sembleables progressiou*n*s of seedes *and* of sexes. þat is to sein. male *and* female. and þis ilke ordre co*n*streyneþ þe fortunes *and* þe dedes of men by a bonde of causes nat able to ben vnbou*n*den (indissolubili). þe whiche destinal causes whanne þei passen oute fro þe bygynnynges of þe vnmoeueable pu*r*ueau*n*ce it mot nedes be þat þei ne be nat mutable. *and* þus ben þe þinges ful wel ygouerned. yif þat þe symplicite dwelly*n*ge* in þe deuyne þou3t sheweþ furþe þe ordre of causes. vnable to be I-bowed. *and* þis ordre co*n*streyneþ by hys propre stablete þe moeucable þinges. or ellys þei sholde fleten folily for whiche it is þat alle þinges semen to be confus *and* trouble to vs men. for we ne mowe nat considere þilke ordinau*n*ce. ¶ Naþeles þe propre manere of euery þing dressynge hem to goode disponit hem alle. for þere nis no þinge don for cause of yuel. ne þilke þing þat is don by wicked[e] folk nis nat don for yuel þe whiche shrewes as I haue shewed [ful] plentiuously

And if we suppose that the thing in question is joined to the stability of the supreme mind, it then becomes immovable, and is beyond the necessity and power of destiny. As rensoning is to the understanding, as that which is produced to that which exists of itself, as time to eternity, as the circle to the centre, so is the movable order of Fate to the stable simplicity of Providence. Destiny rules nature. It controls the actions of men by an indissoluble chain of causes, and is, like their

3941

origin, immutable. Thus, then, are all things well conducted, since that invariable order of cause has its origin in the simplicity of the Divine mind, and by its inherent immutability ex-

[* fol. 31.]

ercises a restraint upon mutable things, and preserves them from irregularity. To those who understand not this order, things appear confused—nevertheless, the proper condition of all things directs and inclines it to their true good. For there is nothing done for the sake of evil, not eve by the wicked, who, in seeking for felicity, are led astray by crooked error.

3927 *ner*—nere
3928 *seyne*—seyn
  þinge cleueþ — thing clyueth
  stedfastnesse — stydefastnesse
3930 *swiche*—swych
3931 [*it*]—from C.
3932 *to* (2)—MS. of, C. to

3937 *enterchaungable*—MS. enterchau*n*gyngable, C. entrechaungeable
3939 *a-doune*—a-down
  sembleables—semblable
3942 *bonde*—bond
3943 *ben vnbounden*—be vnbou*n*do
3944 *oute*—owt

3948 *furþe*—forth
3949 *I-bowed*—MS. vnbounden, C. I-bowed
3950 *sholde*—sholden
3951 *whiche*—which
3952 *mowe*—mowen
3956 *wicked[e]*—wykkede
3957 [*ful*]—from C.

But the order proceeding from the centre of supreme goodness does not mislead any. But you may say, what greater confusion can there be than that both prosperous and adverse things should at times happen to good men, and that evil men should at one time enjoy their desires and at another be tormented by hateful things. Are men wise enough to discover, whether those whom they believe to be virtuous or wicked, are so in reality? Opinions differ as to this matter. Some who are deemed worthy of reward by one person, are deemed unworthy by another. But, suppose it were possible for one to distinguish

3975

with certainty between the good and the bad? Then he must have as accurate a knowledge of the mind as one has of the body. It is miraculous to him who knows it not, why sweet things are agreeable to some bodies, and bitter to others; why some sick persons are relieved by lenitives and others by sharper remedies. It is no marvel to the leech, who knows the causes of disease, and their cures. What constitutes the health of the mind, but goodness? And what are its maladies, but vice? Who is the preserver of good,

seken goode. but wicked errour mystourniþ hem. ¶ Ne þe ordre comynge fro þe poynt of souereyne goode ne declineþ nat fro hys bygynnynge. but þou mayst sein what vnreste may ben a wors confusiou*n* þan þat goode men han somme tyme aduersite. *and* somtyme prosperite. ¶ and shrewes also han now þinges þat þei desiren. *and* now þinges þat þei haten ¶ wheþer men lyuen now in swiche hoolnesse of þou3t. as who seiþ. ben men now so wise. þat swiche folk as þei demen to ben goode folk or shrewes þat it mot nedes ben þat folk ben swiche as þei wenen. but in þis manere þe domes of men discorden. þat þilke men þat somme folk demen worþi of mede. oþer folk demen hem worþi of to*ur*ment. but lat vs graunt[e] I pose þat som man may wel demen or knowen þe goode folk *and* þe badde. May he þan knowen *and* seen þilke inrest attemperaunce of corages. as it haþ ben wont to be said of bodyes. as who saiþ may a man speken *and* determine of attempe*r*aunce in corages. as men were wont to demen or speken of complexiou*n*s *and* attemperaunces of bodies (q' non). ne it [ne] is nat an vnlyke miracle to hem þat ne knowe*n* it nat. ¶ As who seiþ. but is lyke a merueil or a miracle to hem þat ne knowe*n* it nat. whi þat swete þinges [ben] couenable to some bodies þat ben hool *and* to some bodies bittre þinges ben couenable. *and* also whi þat some seke folk ben holpen wi*th* ly3t medicines [*and* some folk ben holpen wi*th* sharppe medicynes] but naþeles þe leche þat knoweþ þe manere *and* þe attemperaunce of heele *and* of maladie ne merucileþ of it no þing. but what oþer þing semeþ hele of corages but bounte *and* prowesse. *and* what oþer þing semeþ maladie of corages but vices. who is ellys kepere of good or

3958-9 *goode*—good
3960 *declineþ*—MS. eneclineþ, C. declynyth
3961 *wors*—worse
3962 *somme tyme*—somtyme
3965 *swiche*—swych
3967 *goode*—good

3967 *mot*—moste
3971 *graunt*[*e*]—graunte
3973 *inrest*—Innerysto
3974 *haþ*—MS. haþe
said—MS. saide, C. seyd
3975 *determine*—determinen
3978 [*ne*]—from C.

3978 *vnlyke*—vn-lyk
3979 *lyke*—lik
3981 [*ben*]—from C.
hool—hoole
3984 [*and*——*medicynes*]—from C.

dryuere awey of yuel but god gouernour *and* leecher of þou3tes. þe whiche god wha*n* he haþ by-holden from þe heye toure of hys purueaunce he knoweþ what is couenable to euery wy3t. *and* leneþ hem þat he wot [þat] is couenable to hem. Loo here of comeþ *and* here of is don þis noble miracle of þe ordre destinal. whan god þat alle knoweþ doþ swiche þing. of whiche þing [þat] vnknowyng folk ben astoned but forto constreine as who seiþ ¶ But forto comprehende *and* telle a fewe þinges of þe deuyne depnesse þe whiche þat mans resou*n* may vnderstonde. ¶ þilk man þat þou wenest to ben ry3t Iuste *and* ry3t kepyng of equite. þe contrarie of þat semeþ to þe deuyne purueaunce þat al woot. ¶ And lucan my familier telleþ þat þe victories cause liked[e] to þe goddes *and* causes ouercomen liked[e] to catou*n*. þan what so euer þou mayst seen þat is don in þis [world] vnhoped or vnwened. certys it is þe ry3t[e] ordre of þinges. but as to þi wicked[e] oppiniou*n* it is a confusiou*n*. but I suppose þat som man be so wel yþewed. þat þe deuyne Iugement *and* þe Iugeme*n*t of mankynde accorden hem to gidre of hym. but he is so vnstedfast of corage [þat] yif any aduersite come to hym he wolde for-leten perauenture to continue i*n*nocence by þe whiche he ne may nat wiþholden fortune. ¶ þan þe wise dispensac*i*ou*n* of god spareþ hym þe whiche manere aduersite * my3t[e] enpeyren. ¶ For þat god wil nat suffren hym to trauaile. to whom þat trauayl nis nat couenable. ¶ An oþe*r* man is perfit in alle uertues. *and* is an holy man *and* neye to god so þat þe purueaunce of god wolde demen þat it were a felony þat he were touched wiþ any aduersites. so þat he ne

or the driver away of evil, but God, the physician of souls, who knows what is necessary for men, and bestows it upon them? From this source spring that great marvel —the order of destiny— wrought by the wisdom of God, and marvelled at by ignorant men. But, now let us notice a few things concerning the depth of the Divine knowledge which human reason may comprehend. The man you deem just, may appear otherwise to the omniscient eye of Providence. When you see apparent irregularities—unexpected and unwished for—deem them to be rightly done. Let us suppose a man so well behaved, as to be approved of God and man— but not endowed with firmness of mind, so that the reverses of fortune will cause him to forgo his probity, since with it he cannot retain his prosperity. A wise Providence, knowing that adversity might destroy this man's integrity, averts from him that [* fol. 31 b.] adversity which he is not able to sustain. Another man is thoroughly virtuous, and approaches to the purity of the deity —him Providence deems it an injustice to oppress by adversity, and therefore exempts

---

3991 *haþ*—MS. haþe
3993 *wot*—MS. wote, C. wot
3994 [*þat*]—from C.
3995 *don*—MS. done, C. don
miracle—MS. mirache, C. myracle
ordre—MS. ordre of
3996 *a:le*—al
doþ—MS. doþe

3996 *whiche*—which
3997 [*þat*]—from C.
3999 *mans*—mannes
4000 *þilk*—thilke
4004 *liked*[*e*] (*both*)—lykede
4005 *is don*—MS. is to don
4006 [*world*]—from C.
ry3t(*e*)—ryhte
4007 *wicked*[*e*]—wykkede

4010 *vnstedfast*—vnstydefast
4011 [*þat*]—from C.
wolde—wol
4015 *manere*—man
my3t[*e*]—myhte
4016 *wil*—wol
4018 *neye*—negh

him even from bodily disease. Providence often gives the direction of public affairs to good men, in order to curb and restrain the malice of the wicked. To some is given a mixture of good and evil, according to what is most suitable to the dispositions of their minds. Upon some are laid moderate afflictions, lest they wax proud by too long a course of prosperity. Others suffer great adversities that their virtues may be exercised, and strengthened by the practice of patience. Some fear to be afflicted with what they are able to endure. Others despise what they are unable to bear; and God punishes them with calamities, to make them sensible of their presumption. Many have purchased a great name by a glorious death. Others by their unshaken fortitude, have shown that virtue cannot be overcome by adversity. These things are done justly, and in order, and are for the good of those to whom they happen. From the same causes it happens, that sometimes adversity and sometimes prosperity falls to the lot of the wicked. None are surprised to see bad men afflicted—they get

4036

wil nat suffre þat swiche a man be moeued wiþ any manere maladie. ¶ But so as seide a philosophre [the moore excellent by me]. þe aduersites comen nat (he seide in grec!) þere þat uertues han edified þe bodie of þe holy man. and ofte tyme it bitideþ þat þe somme of þinges þat ben to don is taken to good folk to gouerne. for þat þe malice habundaunt of shrewes sholde ben abatid. and god ȝeueþ and departiþ to oþer folk prosp[er]ites and aduersites ymedeled to hepe aftir þe qualite of hire corages and remordiþ som folk by aduersites. for þei ne sholden nat wexen proude by longe welefulnesse. and oþer folk he suffreþ to ben trauayled wiþ harde þinges. ¶ For þat þei sholden conferme þe vertues of corage by þe vsage and exercitacioun of pacience. and oþer folke dreden more þen þei auȝten þe wiche þei myȝt[en] wel beren. and þilke folk god lediþ in to experience of hem self by aspre and sorweful þinges. ¶ And many oþer folk han bouȝt honorable renoune of þis worlde by þe pris of glorious deeþ. and som men þat ne mowen nat ben ouer-comen by tourment han ȝeuen ensample to oþer folk þat vertue ne may nat be ouer-comen by aduersites. ¶ and of alle þise þinges þer nis no doute þat þei ne ben don ryȝtfully and ordeinly to þe profit of hem to whom we seen þise þinges bitide. ¶ For certys þat aduersite comeþ some tyme to shrewes. and some tyme þat þei desiren it comeþ of þise forseide causes and of sorweful þinges þat bytyden to shrewes. Certys no man ne wondreþ. For alle men wenen þat þei han wel deserued it. and þei ben of wicked merite of whiche

4021 *wil*—wol
swiche—swych
4022 *manere*—bodyly
4022-3 [*the*——*me*]—from C.
4023 þe *aduersites*——*nat* —omitted
4024 þere—omitted
4026 *don*—done
to (2)—MS. so
to good——*gouerne* — to gouerne to goode folk

4028 *oþer*—oothre
4030 *som*—some
4031 *sholden*—sholde
4033 *conferme*—couformen
4034 *corage*—corages
4036 *myȝt[en]*—myhten
4037 *hem*—hym
sorweful—sorwful
4038 *oþer*—oothre
4039 *worlde*—world
of (2)—of the

4041 *oþer*—othre
4046 *comeþ*—comth
some (both)—som
þat þei—MS. þei þat, C.
þat that they
4047 *comeþ*—comth
soruoful—sorwful
4050 *wicked*—wykkede
merite — MS. ucrite, C.
meryte

shrewes þe tourment som tyme agastep oþer to done
folies. and som tyme it amendeþ hem þat suffren þe
tourmentis. ¶ And þe prosperite þat is ȝeuen to
shrewes sheweþ a grete argument to good[e] folk what
þing þei sholde demen of þilk wilfulnesse þe whiche
prosperite men seen ofte serue to shrewes. in þe whiche
þing I trowe þat god dispensiþ. for perauenture þe nature
of som man is so ouerþrowyng to yuel and so vncouen-
able þat þe nedy pouerte of hys house-hold myȝt[e]
raþer egren hym to done felonies. and to þe maladie
of hym god puttiþ remedie to ȝiuen hym rychesse. and
som oþer man byholdiþ hys conscience defouled wiþ
synnes and makiþ comparisoun of his fortune and of
hym self ¶ and dredeþ perauenture þat hys blisfulnesse
of whiche þe vsage is ioyful to hym þat þe lesynge of
þilke blisfulnesse ne be nat sorweful to hym. and þerfore he wol chaunge hys maneres. and for he dredeþ
to lese hys fortune. he forletiþ hys wickednesse. to
oþer folk is welefulnesse yȝeuen vnworþily þe whiche
ouerþroweþ hem in to destruccioun þat þei han deserued. and to som oþer folk is ȝeuen power to
punissen. for þat it shal be cause of continuacioun and
exercisinge to good[e] folk. and cause of tourment to
shrewes. ¶ For so as þer nis none alyaunce bytwixe
good[e] folke and shrewes. ne shrewes ne mowen nat
accorden amonges hem self and whi nat. for shrewes
discorden of hem self by her vices þe whiche vices al to
renden her consciences. and don oft[e] tyme þinges þe
whiche þinges whan þei han don hem. þei demen þat
þo þinges ne sholde nat han ben don. for whiche þinge
þilke souereyne puruenunce haþ maked oft[e] tyme

4066

4051 oþer—oothre
done—don
4052 folies—felonies
4054 grete—gret
good[e]—goode
4055 sholde—sholden
þilk—thilke
4056 serue—seruen
whiche—which
4057 dispensiþ—MS. dispis-

iþ, C. dispensith
4059 myȝt[e]—myhte
4060 done—don
4061 rychesse—Rychesses
4065 whiche—which
4068 MS. wrongly inserts
welefulnesse after wick-
ednesse
4069-71 oþer—oothre
4073 good[e]—goode

4074 none—non
4075 good[e]—goode
4076 accorden—acordy
4078 don—MS. done, C. don
oft[e]—ofte
4079 don—MS. done, C. don
4080 sholde—sholden
whiche þinge—whichthing
4081 haþ—MS. huþe
oft[e]—ofte

pryre of. Hence arises a signal miracle brought about by Providence—that evil men have often made wicked men good.
For these latter having suffered injuries from the former, have become virtuous, in order that they might not resemble those whom they so detested.
It is only the Divine power that can turn evil to good, overruling it for his own purposes.
Nothing occurs by the caprice of chance in the realms of Divine Providence.
Since God is the governor of all things, it is not lawful to man to attempt to comprehend the whole of the Divine economy, or to explain it in words. Let it suffice to know that God orders all things for the best.

And while he retains things created after his own likeness conformably to his goodness, he banishes evil by the cause of destiny out of his empire.
So that those evils which you seem to see are only imaginary.
But you are exhausted and weary with the prolixity of my reasoning, and look for relief from the harmony of my verse.

[fair*e*] miracle so þat shrewes han maked oftyme shrewes to ben good[e] men. for whan þat som shrewes *seen þat þei suffren wrongfully felonies of oþer shrewes þei wexen eschaufed in to hat[e] of hem þat anoien hem. *and* retournen to þe fruit of uertue. when þei studien to ben vnlyke to he*m* þat þei han hated.

4088 ¶ Certys þis only is þe deuyne myȝt to þe whiche' myȝt yueles ben þan good. whan it vseþ þo yueles couenably *and* draweþ out þe effect of any good. as who seiþ þat yuel is good oonly by þe myȝt of god. for þe myȝt of god ordeyneþ þilk yuel to good. For oon ordre enbrasiþ alle þinges. so þat what wyȝt [þat] departiþ fro þe resou*n* of þe ordre whiche þat is assigned to hym. algates ȝit he slideþ in to an oþer ordre. so þat noþing nis leueful to folye in þe realme of þe deuyne purueaunce. as who seiþ no þing nis wiþouten ordinaunce in þe realme of þe deuyne purueaunce. ¶ Syn þat þe ryȝt strong[e] god gouerniþ alle þinges in þis worlde for it nis nat leueful to no man to co*m*prehenden by witte ne vnfolden by worde alle þe subtil ordinaunces *and* dis-

4102 posicio*uns* of þe deuyne entent. for oonly it auȝt[e] suffice to han loked þat god hym self makere of alle natures ordeyniþ and dressiþ alle þinges to good. while þat he hastiþ to wiþhalden þe þinges þat he haþ maked in to hys semblaunce. þat is to seyn forto wiþholden þinges in to good. for he hym self is good he chaseþ oute al yuel of þe boundes of hys communalite by þe ordre of necessite destinable. For whiche it folweþ þat yif þou loke þe p*ur*ueaunce ordeynynge þe þinges þat men wenen ben haboundaunt in erþes. þou ne shalt not seen in no place no þing of yuel. ¶ but I se now þat

4082 [*faire*]—from C.
 oftyme—omitted
4083 *good*[*e*]—goode
4085 *hat*[*e*]—hate
 anoien—anoyeden
4087 *studien*—omitted
 vnlyke—vnlyk
4089-90 *good*—goode
4092 *þilk*—thilko

4093 [*þat*]—from C.
4094 *þe* (2)—thilke
 whiche—which
4096 *realme*—Reame
4099 *strong*[*e*]—stronge
 worlde—world
4100 *no*—omitted
 witte—wit
4101 *worde alle*—word al

4102 *auȝt*[*e*]—owhte
4104 *good while*—goode wyl
4105 *haþ*—MS. haþe
4108 *of* (1)—fro
4109 *whiche*—which
4111 *ben haboundaunt*—ben outraious / or habowndant

LOVE TEMPERS ALL THINGS.

þou art charged wiþ þe weyȝte of þe questiou[n] *and* wery wiþ lengþe of my resou*n*. *and* þat þou abidest som swetnesse of songe. tak þa*n* þis drauȝt *and* wha*n* þou art wel refresshed *and* refet þou shalt ben more stedfast to stye in, to heyere questiou*n*s. 4117

Take, then, this draught, with which when refreshed, you may more strongly proceed to higher matters.

SI UIS CELSI IURA.

[*The syxte Metur.*]

Yif þou wolt demen in þi pure þouȝt þe ryȝtes or þe lawes of þe heye þund[ere]re. þat is to seyne of god. loke þou *and* bihold þe heyȝtes of souereyne heuene. ¶ þere kepen þe sterres by ryȝtful alliaunce of þinges hir olde pees. þe sonne ymoeued by hys rody fire. ne destourbiþ nat þe colde cercle of þe moone. ¶ Ne þe sterre yclepid þe bere. þat encliniþ hys rauyssynge courses abouten þe souereyne heyȝt of þe worlde. ne þe same sterre vrsa nis neuer mo wasshen in þe depe westerne see. ne coueitiþ nat to dyȝen hys flaumbes in þe see of [the] occian. al þouȝ he see oþer sterres y-plounged in to þe see. ¶ And hesperus þe sterre bodiþ *and* telliþ alwey þe late nyȝtes. And lucifer þe sterre bryngeþ aȝeyne þe clere day. ¶ And þus makiþ loue enterchaungeable þe p*er*durable courses. *and* þus is discordable bataile yput oute of þe contre of þe sterres. þis accordaunce attempreþ by euene-lyke manere[s] þe elementes. þat þe moyste þinges striuen nat wiþ þe drye þinges. but ȝiuen place by stoundes. and þat þe colde þinges ioynen hem by feiþ to þe hote þinges. *and* þat þe lyȝt[e] fyre arist in to heyȝte. *and* þe heuy erþes aualen by her weyȝtes. ¶ by þise same cause þe floury yere ȝeldeþ swote smellys in þe fyrste somer sesou*n* warmynge. *and* þe hote somer dryeþ þe cornes. *and*

If thou wouldst explore the laws of the high Thunderer, behold the lofty heavens, where, bound by fixed laws, the stars keep their ancient peace. There the rosy Sun does not invade the moon's colder sphere. Nor doth the Bear stray from his appointed bounds, to quench his light in the western main. Vesper always makes its wonted appearance at eve. 4128 *Lucifer ushers in the morn. So mutual love moves all things, and from the starry region banishes all strife. This concord in equal measures tempers the elements, so that the moist atoms war no more with the dry, nor heat with cold contends; but the aspiring flame soars aloft, while down the heavy earth descends. By these same causes the flowing year yields sweet smells in the warm springtide; the hot summer ripens the corn. Autumn comes crowned*

4115 *tak*—MS. take, C. tak
4116 *refet*—refect
shalt ben—shal be
stedfast—stydefast
4118 *þou wolt*—þou wys wilt
4119 *þund[ere]re* — thon-*seyne*—seyn [derere
4120 *bihold*—MS. biholde, C. byhold [rody
4122 *rody* — MS. redy, C.

4122 *fire*—Fyr
4123 *cercle*—clerke
4125 *courses*—cours
heyȝt—beyhte
4127 *westerne*—westrene
dyȝen—deeyn
4128 *[the]*—from C.
he see—MS. it sewe, C. he see
oþer—oothre

4131 *aȝeyne*—ayein
4133 *oute*—owt
4134 *euene-lyke manere*[s]—euenelyk maneres
4135 *striuen*—stryuynge
nat—omitted
4136 *but*—omitted
4138 *lyȝt[e] fyre arist*—lyhte fyr arysith
4140 *yere*—ȝer

with plenty, and winter wets the earth with showers. These changes give life and growth to all that breathe; and at last by death efface whatever has had birth. [* fol. 33 b.] Meanwhile the world's Creator, the Source of all, the Lawgiver, the wise Judge, sits above equitably directing all things. Those things which have been set in motion by him are also checked and forced to move in an endless round, lest they go from their source, and become chaotic.	autumpne comeþ aʒeyne heuy of apples. and þe fletyng reyne bydeweþ þe wynter. þis attemperaunce noryssiþ *and* brynggeþ furþe al þinge þat bredeþ lyfe in þis worlde. ¶ and þilk same attemperaunce rauyssyng hideþ *and* bynymeþ *and* drencheþ vndir þe last[e] deþe alle *þinges yborn. ¶ Amonges þise þinges sitteþ þe heye makere kyng *and* lorde. welle *and* bygynnynge. lawe *and* wise Iuge. to don eqnite *and* gouerniþ *and* encliniþ þe bridles of þinges. *and* þo þinges þat he stireþ to don by moeuynge he wiþdraweþ *and* arestiþ *and* affermiþ þe moeueable or wandryng þinges. ¶ For ʒif þat he ne clepiþ nat aʒein þe ryʒt goynge of þinges. *and* ʒif þat he ne constreyned[e] hem nat eftesones in to roundenesse enclined þe þinges þat ben now continued by stable ordinaunce. þei sholde departen from hir welle. þat is

4148

4157

| This love is common to all things, and all things tend to good; so, urged by this, they all revert to that First Cause that gave them being. | to sein from hir bygynnynge *and* failen. þat is to sein tournen in to nauʒt. ¶ þis is þe commune loue of alle þinges. *and* alle þinges axen to be holden by þe fyn of good. For ellys ne myʒten þei nat lasten yif þei ne come nat eftesones aʒeine by loue retourned to þe cause þat haþ ʒeuen hem beynge. þat is to seyn to god. 4162 |

[The seuende prose.]

IAM NE IGITUR UIDES.

| P. Do you see what follows from our arguments? B. What is it? P. That all fortune is good. B. How can that be? P. Since all fortune, whether prosperous or adverse, is for the reward of the good or the punishment of | Sest þou nat þan what þing folweþ alle þe þinges þat I hauc scid. what þing quod I. ¶ Certys qu*o*d she outerly þat al fortune is good. and how may þat be quod .I. ¶ Now vndirstand qu*o*d she so as [alle fortune wheyther so it be Ioyeful fortune / or aspre] fortune is ʒiuen eiþer by cause of gerdonynge or ellys of exercisynge of goode folk or ellys by cause to punissen. |

| 4142 *comeþ aʒeyne* — comth ayein 4143 *reyne*—reyn 4144 *furþe al þinge*—forth alle thing *brediþ lyfe*—herith lyf 4145 *worlde*—world *þilk*—thilke 4146 *last[e] deþe*—laste deth 4147 *yborn*—MS. yborne, C. I-born 4148 *lorde*—lord | 4149 *wise*—wys 4150 *stireþ*—sterith *don*—gon 4151 *þe*—omitted 4153 *clepiþ*—klepede 4154 *constreyned[e]* — constreynede *roundenesse* — Rowndnesses 4156 *sholde*—sholden 4158 *tournen*—torne *of*—to | 4150 *be*—ben 4161 *eftesones aʒeine* — eft sones ayein 4162 *haþ*—MS. haþe 4163 *þing*—thinge 4165 *outerly*—al owtrely *al*—alle 4166-7 *[alle——aspre]*—from C. 4160 *goode*—good |

PUNISHMENT IS BENEFICIAL.

or ellys to chastysen shrewes. ¶ þan is alle fortune good. þe whiche fortune is certeyne þat it be ciþer ryȝtful or profitable. ¶ For soþe þis is a ful verray resoun quod I. and yif I considere þe purueaunce *and* þe destine þat þou tauȝtest me a litel here byforne þis sentence is susteyned by stedfast resouns. but yif it like vnto þe lat vs noumbre hem amonges þilk[e] þinges of whiche þou seidest a litel here byforne þat þei ne were nat able to ben ywened to þe poeple. ¶ whi so quod she. for þat þe comune worde of men mysusiþ quod I. þis manere speche of fortune. *and* sein ofte tymes [þat] þe fortune of som wyȝt is wicked. wilt þou þan quod she þat I proche a litel to þe wordes of þe poeple so it seme nat to hem þat I be ouer moche departid as fro þe vsage of man kynde. as þou wolt quod I. ¶ Demest þou nat quod she þat al þing þat profitiþ is good. ȝis quod I. certis þilk þing þat exercisiþ or corigiþ profitiþ. I confesse it wel quod I. þan is it good quod she. whi nat quod I. but þis is þe fortune [quod she] of hem þat eiþer ben put in vertue *and* batailen aȝeins aspre þinges. or ellys of hem þat eschewen *and* declinen fro vices *and* taken þe weye of vertue. ¶ þis ne may nat I denye quod I ¶ But what seist þou of þe myrye fortune þat is ȝeuen to good folk in gerdoun deuiniþ ouȝt þe poeples þat it is wicked. nay forsoþe quod I. but þei demen as it soþe is þat it is ryȝt good. ¶ And what seist þou of þat oþer fortune quod she. þat al þouȝ it be aspre *and* restreiniþ þe shrewes by ryȝtful tourment. weniþ ouȝt þe poeple þat it be good. nay quod I. ¶ But þe poeple demiþ þat it be most wrecched of alle þinges þat may ben þouȝt. war now *and* loke wel quod she lest þat we in folwyng þe opynioun of poeple haue con-

the bad. all fortune is good which is either just or useful. But let us put this opinion among those positions which thou saidst were not commonly believed by the people. P? Why so? B. Because it is a common expression that the fortune of such a one is bad. P. Do you wish me to conform for awhile to the language of the people, lest we should seem to depart too much from the popular mode of expression? B. As you please. P. Is everything profitable that is good? B. Yes, certainly. P. That which exercises or corrects is profitable?

4186

B. It is. P. Therefore it is good? B. Yes. P. This is the fortune of the virtuous who combat with adversity, or of those who, relinquishing vice, pursue the path of virtue? B. It is. P. The vulgar regard that prosperity which is bestowed as a reward on the good to be beneficial, and they believe those calamities by which the wicked are punished as the most miserable things that can be imagined. But in following the popular opinion, let us beware of being involved in some new and incredible consequence.

4174 *here byforne*—her byforn
4175 *stedfast*—stydefast
4176 *noumbre*—nowmbren þilk[e]—thilke
4177 *here byforne*—her byforn
4178 *ywened*—weened
4179 *worde*—word
4180 [*þat*]—from C.
4181 *wicked*—wykkede
4182 *proche*—aproche
4185 *al*—alle
4186 *þilk*—thilke
4188 [*quod she*]—from C.
4191 *weye*—wey
4193 *deuiniþ*—demyth
4194 *ouȝt*—awht
4195 *soþe*—soth
4198 *ouȝt*—awht
4199 *be*—is

B. What is that?
P. We have decided that the fortune of the virtuous or of those growing up in virtue must needs be good—but that the fortune of the wicked must be most wretched.
B. That's true, though none dare acknowledge it.
P. Why so?
The wise man ought not to be cast down, when he has to wage war with Fortune, no more than the valiant man ought to be dismayed on hearing the noise of the [* fol. 83.] battle. The dangers of war enable the one to acquire more glory, and the difficulties of the other aid him to confirm and im-

4217

prove his wisdom. Thus virtue, in its literal acceptation, is a power that, relying on its own strength, overcomes all obstacles. You, who have made so much progress in virtue, are not to be carried away by delights and bodily lusts. You must engage in a fierce conflict with every fortune—with adversity, lest it dismay you—with prosperity, lest it corrupt you. Seize the golden mean with all your strength. All below or above this line is a contemptible and a thankless felicity. The choice of fortune lies in your own hands, but remember that even adverse fortune, unless it exercises the

fessed *and* concluded þing þat is vnable to be wened to be poeple. what is þat q*uod* I ¶ Certys q*uod* she it folweþ or comeþ of þinges þat ben graunted þat alle fortune what so euer it be. of hem þat eyþer ben i*n* possessiou*n* of vertue. [or in the encres of vertu] or ellys in þe purchasynge of vertue. þat þilke fortune is good. ¶ And þat alle fortune is ry3t wicked to hem þat dwellen in shrewednesse. as who seiþ. *and* þus weneþ nat þe poeple. ¶ þat is soþe q*uod* I. ¶ Al be it so þat noma*n* dar confesse*n* it ne byknowen it. ¶ whi so q*uod* she. For ry3t as no strong man ne semeþ nat to abassen or disdaigne*n* as *ofte tyme as he hereþ þe noise of þe bataile. ne also it ne semeþ nat to þe wyse man to beren it greuously as oft[e] as he is lad in to þe strif of fortune. for boþe to þat on man *and* eke to þat oþer þilke difficulte is þe matere to þat oon man of encrese of his glorious renou*n*. *and* to þat oþer man to conferme hys sapience. þat is to seine þe asprenesse of hys estat. ¶ For þerfore is it called uertue. for þat it susteniþ *and* enforceþ by hys strengþes þat it nis nat ouer-comen by aduersites. ¶ Ne certys þou þat art put in þe encrese or in þe hey3t of uertue ne hast nat comen to fleten wiþ delices *and* forto welken in bodyly lust. ¶ þou sowest or plauntest a ful egre bataile in þi corage a3eins euery fortune. for þat þe sorweful fortune ne confounde þe nat. ne þat þe myrye fortune ne corrumpe þe nat. ¶ Occupy þe mene by stedfast strengþes. for al þat euer is vndir þe mene. or ellys al þat ouer-passeþ þe mene despiseþ welefulnesses. ¶ As who seiþ. it is vicious *and* ne haþ no mede of hys trauaile. ¶ For it is set in 3oure hand. as who seiþ it lieþ in 3oure power what fortune 3ow is leuest. þat is to seyne good or yuel. ¶ For alle fortune

---

4204 *comeþ*—comth
4206 [*or*——*vertu*] from C.
4208 *wicked*—wykkede
4210 *soþe*—soth
4211 *confessen*—confesse
4212 *no strong*—the strange
4213 *abassen*—abayssen

4215 *of*[*e*]—ofte
4219 *seine*—seyn
4223 *hey3t*—heyhte
4224 *welken*—wellen
4226 *confounde* — MS. confounded, C. confownde
4227 *Occupy*—Ocupye

4228 *stedfast*—stydefast
4230 *haþ*—MS. haþe
4231 *set*—MS. sette, C. set
4232 *lieþ*—lith
4233 *seyne*—seyn

þat semeþ sharpe or aspre yif it ne exercise nat þe good *virtues of the good or chastiacs*
folk. ne chastisiþ þe wicked folk. it punisseþ.   4235 *the wicked, is a punishment.*

BELLA BIS QUENIS. ET CETERA.

[The seuende Metur.]

þE wrekere attrides ¶ þat is to seyne agamenon þat *Atrides carried on a ten years' war to*
wrou3t[e] and continued[e] þe batailes by ten 3ere *punish the licentious Paris.*
recouered[e] and purged[e] in wrekyng by þe destruc-
cioun of troie þe loste chambres of mariage of hys broþer 4239
þis is to seyn þat [he] agamenon wan a3ein Eleine þat
was Menelaus wif his broþer. In þe mene while þat *With blood he purchased*
þilke agamenon desired[e] to 3euen sailes to þe grek- *propitious gales for the*
ysshe nauye and bou3t[e] a3ein þe wyndes by blode. he *Grecian fleet, by casting off all*
vncloþed[e] hym of pite as fader. and þe sory prest *fatherly pity, and sacrificing his daughter*
3iueþ in sacrifiynge þe wreched kuyttyng of þrote of þe *Iphigenia to the vengeance of*
dou3ter. ¶ þat is to sein þat agamenon lete kuytten þe *Diana.*
þrote of hys dou3ter by þe prest. to maken alliaunce wiþ 4247
hys goddes. and for to haue wynde wiþ whiche he
my3t[e] wende to troie. ¶ Itakus þat is to sein vlixies *Ulysses bewailed his lost mates,*
bywept[e] hys felawes ylorn þe whiche felawes þe *devoured by Polyphemus,*
fiers[e] pholifemus ligginge in his grete Caue had[de] *but, having deprived the Cyclop of his sight, he*
freten and dreint in hys empty wombe. but naþeles *rejoiced to hear the monster's*
polifemus wood for his blinde visage 3eld to vlixies ioye *roar.*
by hys sorowful teres. þis is to seyn þat vlixes smot
oute þe eye of poliphemus þat stod in hys forhede. for 4255
whiche vlixes hadde ioie whan he saw poliphemus
wepyng and blynde. ¶ Hercules is celebrable for hys *Hercules is renowned for his many labours, so*
hard[e] trauaile he dawntede þe proude Centauris half *successfully overcome. He overthrew the proud*
hors half man. and he rafte þe despoylynge fro þe *Centaurs;*

4234 *sharpe*—sharp
4236 *seyne*—seyn
4237 *wrou3t[e]*—wrowhte
 continued[e]—continuede
 3ere—3er
4238 *purged[e]*—purgede
4240 *[he]*—from C.
 wan—MS. wanne, C. wan
4242 *desired[e]*—desirede
4243 *bou3t[e]*—bowhte
 blode—blod
4244 *vncloþed[e]*—vnclothede
 as—of
4245 *kuyttyng*—MS. knyt-

tyng, C. kuttynge
4246 *lete*—let
 kuytten—MS. knytten, C. kuttyn
4248 *haue*—han
4249 *my3t[e] wende*—myhte wenden
4250 *bywept[e]*—by-wepte
 ylorn—MS. ylorne, C. ylorn
4251 *fiers[e]*—feerse
 had[de]—hadde
4253 3eld—yald
4254 *sorowful*—sorwful

4254 *smot*—MS. smote, C. smot
4255 *oute*—owt
 stod—MS. stode, C. stood
 forhede—forhed
4256 *saw*—say
4258 *hard[e] trauaile*—harde trauayles
 dawntede—MS. dawnded, C. dawntede
4259 *half*—MS. hals
 rafte—byrafte
 fro—from

he slew the Nemean lion and wore his skin as a trophy of his victory; he smote the Harpies with his arrows; he carried off the golden apples of the Hesperides, and killed the watchful dragon; he bound Cerberus with a threefold chain; he gave the body of proud Diomede as food for the tyrant's horses;	cruel lyoun þat is to seyne he slouȝ þe lyoun *and* rafte hym hys skyn. he smot þe brids þat hyȝten arpijs [in þe palude of lyrne] wiþ certeyne arwes. he rauyssed[e] applis fro þe wakyng dragoun. *and* hys hand was þe more heuy for þe golde[ne] metal. He drouȝ Cerberus þe hound of helle by hys treble cheyne. he ouer-comer as it is seid haþ put an vnmeke lorde fodre to hys cruel hors ¶ þis is to sein. þat hercules slouȝ diomedes *and* made his hors
he slew the serpent Hydra; he caused Achelous to hide his blushing head within his banks;	to etyn hym. and he hercules slouȝ Idra þe serpent *and* brend[e] þe venym. and achelaus þe flode defouled[e] in his forhede dreint[e] his shamefast visage in his strondes. þis is to sein þat achelaus couþe transfigure
	4273 hym self in to dyuerse lykenesse. *and* as he fauȝt wiþ orcules at þe laste he turnid[e] hym in to a bole. and hercules brak of oon of hys hornes. *and* achelaus for
he left Antæus dead upon the [* fol. 33 b.] Lybian shore; he appeased Evander's wrath by killing Cacus;	shame hidde hym in hys ryuer. ¶ And [he] hercules *cast[e] adoun Antheus þe geaunt in þe strondes of libye. *and* kacus apaised[e] þe wraþþes of euander. þis is to sein þat hercules slouȝ þe Monstre kacus *and*
he slew the Erymanthean boar;	apaised[e] wiþ þat deeþ þe wraþþe of euander. ¶ And þe bristled[e] boor marked[e] wiþ scomes þe sholdres of
and bore the weight of Atlas upon his shoulders.	hercules. þe whiche sholdres þe heye cercle of heuene sholde preste. *and* þe laste of his labours was þat he
These labours justly raised him to the rank of a god.	sustened[e] þe heuene vpon his nekke vnbowed. *and* he descrued[e] eftsones þe heuene to ben þe pris of his
Go then, ye noble souls, and follow the path of this great example.	laste trauayle ¶ Goþ now þan ȝe stronge men þere as þe heye weye of þe grete ensample ledeþ ȝou. ¶ O nice
	4288 men whi nake ȝe ȝoure bakkes. as who seiþ. ¶ O ȝe

4260 *seyne*—seyn
4261 *smot*—MS. smote, C. smot
4262 [*in*——*lyrne*]—from C.
4263 *rauyssed*[*e*] — rauyssh-ede
4266 *seid* — MS. seide, C. sayd
haþ—MS. haþe
4267 *lorde*—lord
4269 *etyn*—freten
4270 *brend*[*e*]—brende

4270 *flode defouled*[*e*]—flood defowlede
4271 *forhede dreint*[*e*]—for-hed dreynte
4273 *lykenesse*—lyknesses
4274 *turnid*[*e*]—tornede
4275 *brak* — MS. brake, C. brak
hys—hise
4276 [*he*]—from C.
4278-80 *apaised*[*e*] — apay-sede

4281 *bristled*[*e*]—brystelede *marked*[*e*]—markede
4282 *cercle*—clerke
4283 *preste*—thriste
4285 *descrued*[*e*]—descruede
4286 *Goþ*—MS. Goþe *þere*—ther
4287 *weye*—way
4288 *nake* — MS. make, C. nake

slowe *and* delicat men whi fley 3e aduersites. *and* ne
fy3ten nat a3eins hem by vertue to wynnen þe mede of
þe heuene. for þe erþe ouer-come*n* 3cueþ þe sterres.
¶ þis is to seyne þat whan þat erþely lust is ouer-comen.
a man is maked worþi to þe heuene.

O ye slothful ones, wherefore do ye basely fly! 4291 He who conquers earth doth gain the heavens.

EXPLICIT LIBER QUARTUS.

INCIPIT LIBER QUINTUS.

DIXERAT ORACIONISQ*VE* CURSUM.

She hadde seid *and* tou*r*ned[e] þe cours of hir resoun to somme oþer þinges to ben tretid *and* to ben ysped. þan seide I. Certys ry3tful is þin amonestyng *and* ful digne by auctorite. but þat þou seidest som tyme þat þe questiou*n* of þe deuyne p*ur*ueaunce is enlaced wiþ many oþer questiou*n*s. I vndir-stonde wel *and* proue it by þe same þinge. but I axe yif þat þou wenest þat hap be any þing in any weys. *and* if þou wenest þat hap be any [thing] what is it. þan q*uo*d she. I haste me to 3elden *and* assoilen þe to þe dette of my byheste *and* to shewen *and* opnen þe wey by whiche wey þou maist come a3ein to þi contre. ¶ but al be it so þat þe þinges whiche þat þou axest ben ry3t profitable to knowe. 3itte ben þei diuers somwhat fro þe paþe of my purpos. And it is to douten þat þou ne be maked weery by mysweys so þat þou ne mayst nat suffise to mesuren þe ry3t weye. ¶ Ne doute þe þer-of no þing q*uo*d I. for forto knowen þilke þinges to-gidre in þe whiche þinges I delite me gretly. þat shal ben to me in stede of reste. Syn it nis nat to douten of þe þinges folwynge whan euery side of þi disputisou*n* shal be stedfast to me by vndoutous feiþ. þan seide she. þat manere wol I don

[The fyrste prose.] When Philosophy had thus spoken, and was about to discuss other matters I interrupted her. B. Thy exhortation is just and worthy of thy authority, but thou saidst that the question of the Divine Superintendence or Providence is involved with many others—and this I believe. I am desirous, however, of knowing whether there be such a thing as Chance, and what thou thinkest it is. P. I hasten to fulfil my promise and to show the road to your own country. But although these things you question me about are profitable to know, yet they lead us a little out of our way. And by straying from the path you may be too fatigued to return to the right road. B. Don't be afraid of that, for it will refresh me as much as rest to know these things in which I am delightfully

---

4289 *slowe* — MS. slou3, C. slowe
fley—flee
4292 *seyne*—seyn
4294 *seid*—MS. seide, C. seyd
þe—by
4297 *som tyme*—whilom
4298 þe (2)—thy

4300 þinge—thing
4302 [*thing*]—from C.
4303 3elden—yilden
assoilen—MS. assailen, C. assoylen
byheste—byhest
4304-6 *whiche*—which
4306 ben—MS. bene

4307 *paþe*—path
4312 *stede*—styde
4314 *disputisoun* — disputacioun
be—ben ben
stedfast—stydefast

150 — DEFINITION OF CHANCE. [BOOK 5. PROSE 1.]

*interested.
P. I will then comply with thy requests. If we define Chance to be an event produced by an unintelligent motion, and not by a chain or connection of causes, I should then affirm that Chance is nothing and an empty sound. What room is there for folly and disorder where all things are restrained by order, through the ordinance of God? For it is a great truth that nothing can spring out of nothing. Now, if anything arises without the operation of a cause, it proceeds from nothing. But if this is impossible, then there can be no*

4331

*such a thing as Chance, as we have defined it.
B. Is there nothing, then, that may be called Chance or Fortune? Is there nothing (hid from the vulgar) to which these words may be applied?
P. Aristotle defines this matter with much precision and [* fol. 34.] probability.
B. How?
P. So often as a man does anything for the sake of any other thing, and another thing than what he intended to do is produced by other causes, that thing so produced is called Chance. As if a man trench the ground for tillage*

þe. *and* bygan to spoken ry3t þus ¶ Certys q*uo*d she yif any wy3t diffinisse hap in þis manere. þat is to seyn. þat hap is bytidynge y-brou3t forþe by foelyshe moeuynge. *and* by no knyttyng of causes. ¶ I conferme þat hap nis ry3t nau3t in no wise. and I deme al outerly þat hap nis ne dwelliþ but a voys. ¶ As who seiþ. but an ydel worde wiþ outen any significac*i*oun of þing summittid to þat vois. for what place my3t[e] ben left or dwellynge to folie *and* to disordinau*n*ce. syn þat god lediþ *and* streyniþ alle þinges by ordre. ¶ For þis sentence is verray *and* soþe þat no þinge ne haþ his beynge of nou3t. to [the] whiche sentence none of þise olde folk ne wiþseide neuere al be it so þat þei ne vndirstoden ne moeueden it nau3t by god prince *and* gynner of wirkyng. but þei casten as a manere foundement of subgit material. þat is to seyn of [the] nature of alle resou*n*. *and* 3if þat ony þinge is woxen or comen of no causes. þan shal it seme þat þilke þinge is comen or woxen of nou3t. but yif þis ne may nat ben don. þan is it nat possible þat þere haþ ben any swiche þing as I haue diffinissid a litel here byforne. ¶ How shal it þan ben q*uo*d I. nis þer þan no þing þat by ry3t may be cleped eyþer hap*p*e or ellis auenture of fortune. or is þer ou3t al *be it so þat it is hidd fro þe poeple to whiche þise wordes ben couenable. Myn aristotul q*uo*d she. in þe book of his phisik diffinisseþ þis þing by short resou*n* and ney3e to þe soþe. ¶ In whiche manere q*uo*d I. ¶ As ofte q*uo*d she as men don any þing for grace of any oþer þing. *and* an oþer þinge ˏþan þilke þing þat men ententen to doon bytideþ by som[e] causes it is ycleped hap*p*e. ¶ Ry3t as a man dalf þe erþe by

---

4317 *seyn*—seyng
4318 *forþe*—forth
4322 *worde*—word
4323 *my3t*[e]—myhte
4324 *left*—lefte
4325 *streyniþ*—co*n*streynyth
4326 *soþe*—soþ
   no þinge—nothing
   haþ—MS. haþe

4327 [*the*]—from C.
4330 *gynner*—bygynnere
4331 [*the*]—from C.
4332 *3if*—MS. 3it, C. yif
   þinge—thing
4335 *þat—ben*—þat hap be
   haþ—MS. haþe
   swiche—swych
4338 *happe*—hap

4330 *hidd*—MS. hidde, C. hidd
4340 *whiche*—which
4342 *ney3e*—nehg
   whiche—which
4343 *don*—MS. done, C. don
4344 *þinge*—thing
4345 *som*[e]—some
4346 *happe*—hap

DEFINITION OF CHANCE.

cause of tyliengc of þe felde. *and* fond þere a gobet of golde by-doluen. þan wenen folk þat it is fallen by fortunous bytydyng. but for soþe it nis nat for nauȝt for it haþ hys propre causes of whiche causes þe cours vnforseyn and vnwar semiþ to han maked happe. ¶ For yif þe tilier in þe erþe ne delue nat in þe felde. and yif þe hider of þe golde ne hadde hidd þe golde in þilke place. þe golde ne had[de] nat ben founde. þise ben þan þe causes of þe abreggynge of fortune hap. þe whiche abreggynge of fortune hap comeþ of causes encountrynge *and* flowyng to-gidre to hem selfe. *and* nat by þe entencioun of þe doer. ¶ For neiþer þe hider of þe gold. ne þe deluer of þe felde ne vndirstanden nat þat þe golde sholde han be founde. but as I scide. it bytidde *and* ran to-gidre þat he dalf þere as þat oþer hadde hidd þe golde. Now may I þus diffinissen happe. ¶ Happe is an vnwar bytydyng of causes assembled in þinges þat ben don for som oþer þinge. but þilke ordre procedynge by an vneschewable byndynge to-gidre. whiche þat descendeþ fro þe wel of purueaunce þat ordeineþ alle þinges *in* hire places *and* in hire tymes makeþ þat þe causes rennen *and* assemblen to-gidre. 4368

and find gold, then this is believed to happen by chance, although it is not so. For if the tiller had not ploughed the field, and if the hider of the gold had not concealed it in that spot, the gold had not been found. These, then, are the causes of a fortuitous acquisition which proceeds from a conflux of encountering causes, and not from the intention of the doer. For neither the hider of the gold nor the husbandman intended or understood that the gold should be found. But it happened by the concurrence of these two causes that the one did dig where the other had hidden the money. Chance, then, is an unexpected event, by a concurrence of causes, following an action designed for a particular purpose. This concurrence of causes proceeds from that order which flows from the fountain of Providence and disposes all things as to place and time.

RUPIS ACHEMENIE.

[The fyrste Metur.]

Tigris [*and*] eufrates resoluen *and* spryngen of a welle in þe kragges of þe roche of þe contre of achemenye þere as þe fleenge [batayle] ficchiþ hire dartes retournid in þe brestes of hem þat folwen hem. ¶ And sone aftre þe same ryueres tigris *and* eufrates vnioygnen *and* de-

Where the flying Parthian doth pierce his pursuers with his shafts, there from the Achemenian heights flow the Tigris and Euphrates, but soon

---

4347 *of*(1)—to
 fond — MS. fonde, C. fownde
4348 *golde*—gold
 fallen—byfalle
4349 *for* (2)—of
4350 *haþ*—MS. haþe
 hys—hise
4351 *happe*—hap
4352 *tilier*—tylyere
 delue—dolue
4353 *hider*—hydere
 golde—gold
 hidd—MS. hidde

4353-4 *golde*—gold
4354 *had[de]*—hadde
4355 *fortune*—fortuit
 whiche—which
4356 *fortune*—fortuit
 comeþ—comth
4357 *flowyng*—MS. folwyng,
 C. flowyngo
 selfe—self
4358 *doer*—doere
 hider—hidere
4359 *deluer*—deluere
 felde—feeld
 vndirstanden—vndirstod-

4360 *golde*—gold
4361 *hidd* — MS. hidde, C. hyd
4362 *happe* (*both*)—hap
4365 *whiche*—which
4366 *descendeþ*—MS. defendeþ, C. descendith
 wel—welle
4369 [*and*]—from C.
 a—no
4371 [*batayle*]—from C.
4373 þe—the
 [en

their streams divide and flow into separate channels. But should they unite again, in the impetuous stream, boats, ships, and trees would be all intermingled, whirled about; and blind Chance seems to direct the current's course. But the sloping earth, the laws of fluids, govern these things. So though Chance seems to wander unrestrained, it is nevertheless curbed and restrained by Divine Providence.

[The .2de. prose.]
B. Is there any free-will in this chain of cohering causes? Or doth the chain of destiny constrain the motions of the human mind? P. There is a freedom of the will possessed by every rational being. A rational being has judgment to judge of and discern everything. Of himself he knows what he is to avoid or to desire. He seeks what he judges desirable, and he shuns what he deems should be avoided. A rational being possesses, then, the liberty of choosing and rejecting. This liberty is not equal in all beings. In heavenly substances, as spirits, &c., judgment is clear, and the will is incorruptible, and has a ready and efficacious power of doing things which are desired.

[* fol. 34 b.]

parten hire watres. and yif þei comen to-gidre *and* ben assembled *and* clepid to-gidre in to o cours. þan moten þilke þinges fletyn to-gidre whiche þat þe water of þe entrechaungyng flode bryngeþ þe shippes *and* þe stokkes araced wiþ þe flood moten assemble. *and* þe watres ymedlyd wrappiþ or implieþ many fortunel happes or maneres. þe whiche wandryng happes naþeles þilke enclinyng lowenes of þe erþe. *and* þe flowynge ordre of þe slidyng water gouerniþ. ¶ Ry3t so fortune þat semeþ as [þat] it fletiþ wiþ slaked or vngouerned[e] bridles. It suffriþ bridles þat is to seyn to ben gouerned *and* passeþ by þilke lawe. þat is to sein by þe deuyne ordinaunce. 4386

ANIMADUERTO INQUAM.

Þis vndirstonde I wel quod I. *and* accorde wel þat it is ry3t as þou seist. but I axe yif þer be any liberte or fre wil in þis ordre of causes þat clinen þus to-gidre in hem self. ¶ or ellys I wolde witen yif þat þe destinal cheine constreiniþ þe moeueuynge of þe corages of men. yis quod she þer is liberte of fre wille. ne þer ne was neuer no nature of resoun þat it ne hadde liberte of fre wille. ¶ For euery þing þat may naturely vsen resoun. it haþ doom by whiche it discerniþ *and* demiþ euery þing. ¶ þan knoweþ it by it self þinges þat ben to fleen. *and* þinges þat ben to desiren. *and* þilk þing þat any wy3t demeþ to ben desired þat axeþ or desireþ he *and* fleeþ [thilke] þing þat he troueþ ben to fleen. ¶ wher-fore in alle þinges þat resoun is. in hem also is libertee of willyng *and* of nillynge. . ¶ But I ne ordeyne nat. as who seiþ. I ne graunte nat þat þis liberteo be euene like in alle þinges. forwhi in þe souereyns deuynes substaunces. þat is to *seyn in spirit3 ¶ Iugement is

4374 *to-gidre*—to-gyderes
4376 *whiche*—which
4377 *flode*—flod
4378 *assemble*—assemblyn
4380 *enclinyng*—declynynge
4381 *lowenes*—lownesse

4383 [*þat*]—from C.
vngouerned[*e*]—vngouernede
4385 *þe*—thilke
4389 *or*—of
4390 *hem*—hym

4392 *yis*—MS. yif. C. yis
4392-94 *wille*—wil
4395 *whiche*—which
4397 *þilk*—thilke
4399 [*thilke*]—from C.

more clere *and* wil nat be corumped. *and* haþ my3t
redy to speden þinges þat ben desired. ¶ But þe soules
of men moten nedes ben more free whan þei loken hem
in þe speculacio*un* or lokynge of þe deuyne þou3t. *and*
lasse free whan þei sliden in to þe bodies. *and* 3it lasse
free whan þei ben gadred to-gidre *and* compr*ehendid* in
erþely membris. but þe last[e] seruage is whan þat þei
ben 3euen to vices. *and* han yfalle fro þe possessio*un* of
hire *propre* resoun ¶ For after þat þei han cast aweye
hir eyen fro þe ly3t of þé souereyn soþefastnesse to lowe
þinges *and* dirke ¶ Anon þei dirken by þe cloude of
ignoraunce *and* ben troubled by felonous talent3. to þe
whiche talent3 whan þei approchen *and* assenten. þei
hepen *and* encresen þe seruage whiche þei han ioigned
to hem self. and in þis manere þei ben caitifs fro hire
propre libertee. þe whiche þinges naþeles þe lokynge of
þe deuyne purueaunce seeþ þat alle þinges byholdeþ
and seeþ fro ete*r*ne. and ordeyneþ hem eueryche i*n* her
merites. as þei ben *pre*destinat. *and* it is seid in grek.
þat alle þinges he seeþ *and* alle þinges he hereþ. 4424

The souls of men must needs be more free when employed in the contemplation of the Divine Mind, and less so when they enter into a body, and still less free when enclosed and confined in earthly members; but the most extreme servitude is when they are given over to vice and wholly fallen from their proper reason. For at once they are enveloped by the cloud of ignorance and are troubled by pernicious desires, by yielding to which they aid and increase that slavery which they brought upon themselves, and thus even under the liberty proper to them, they remain captives. Yet the eye of Providence, beholding all things from eternity, sees all this and disposes according to their merit all things as they are predestinated. He, as Homer says of the sun, *sees of the sun, sees and hears all things.*

PURO CLARUM LUMINE.

HOmer wiþ þe hony mouþe. þat is to seyn. homer
wiþ þo swete dites syngeþ þat þe sonne is cleer by
pure ly3t. naþeles 3it ne may it nat by þe inferme ly3t
of hys bemes breke*n* or *per*cen þe inwarde entrailes of
þe erþe. or ellys of þe see. ¶ so ne seeþ nat god makere
of þe grete worlde to hym þat lokeþ alle þinges from on
heye ne wiþstandiþ nat no þinges by heuynesses of erþe.
ne þe ny3t ne wiþstondeþ nat to hy*m* by þe blake
cloudes. ¶ þilke god seeþ i*n* o strook of þou3t alle
þinges þat ben or weren or schullen come. ¶ and þilke

[The .2de. Metur.] The sweet-tongued Homer sings of the sun's pure light. Yet the sun's beams cannot pierce into the inner bowels of the earth, nor into the depths of the sea. But God, the world's maker, beholding from on high, has his vision impeded neither by earth nor cloud. At a glance he sees all events, present, past, and future.

4405 *haþ*—MS. haþe
4411 *last[e]*—laste
4412 *fro*—from
4415 *cloude*—clowdes
4419 *whiche*—which

4423 *seid*—MS. seide, C. seyd
4425 *mouþe*—Mowth
4428 *percen* — MS. perten, C. *per*cen
inwarde—inward

4430 *worlde*—world
on heye—an hegh
4431 *nat*—omitted
4434 *schullen come*—shollen comyn

154 GOD'S FOREKNOWLEDGE [BOOK 5. PROSE 3

God, then, that alone sees all things, may indeed be called the true Sun.

god for he lokeþ *and* seeþ alle þinges al oon. þou maist seyn þat he is þe verray sonne.   4436

[The .3de. prose.]

TAMEN EGO EN INQUAM.

B. I am distracted by a more difficult doubt than ever. God's foreknowledge seems to me inconsistent with man's freewill. For if God foresees all things, and cannot be deceived, then that which Providence hath foreseen must needs happen. If God from eternity doth foreknow not only the works, but the designs and wills of men, there can be no liberty of will—nor can there be any other action or will than that which a Divine and infallible Providence hath foreseen. For if things fall out contrary to such foreseeing, and are wrested another way, the prescience of God in regard to futurity would not be sure and unerring—it would be nothing but an uncertain opinion of them; but I take it to be impious and unlawful to believe this of God. Nor do I approve of the reasoning made use of by some. For they say that a thing is not necessarily to happen because God hath foreseen it, but rather because it is to happen it cannot be hid from the Divine Providence.

Þ An seide I now am I confounded by a more harde doute þan I was. what doute is þat quod she. ¶ For certys I coniecte now by whiche þinges þou art troubled. It semeþ quod I to repugnen *and* to contrarien gretly þat god knoweþ byforn alle þinges. *and* þat þer is any fredom of liberte. for yif so be þat god lokeþ alle þinges byforn. ne god ne may nat ben desseiuid in no manere. þan mot it nedes ben þat alle þinges bytyden þe whiche þat þe purueaunce of god haþ sein byforn to comen. ¶ For whiche yif þat god knoweþ by-forn nat oonly þe werkes of men. but also hir conseils *and* hir willes. þan ne shal þer be no liberte of arbitre. ne certys þer ne may ben noon oþer dede ne no wille but þilke whiche þe deuyne purueaunce 4451 þat ne may nat ben desseiued haþ feled byforn ¶ For yif þat þei myȝten wryþen awey in oþer manere þan þei ben purueyed. þan ne sholde þer ben no stedfast prescience of þinge to comen but raþer an vncerteyn oppinioun. þe whiche þinge to trowen on god I deme it felonie *and* vnleueful. ¶ Ne I ne proeue nat þilk same resoun. as who seiþ I ne allowe nat. or I ne preise nat þilke same resoun by whiche þat som men wenen þat þei mowen assoilen *and* vnknytten þe knot of þis questioun. ¶ For certys þei seyn þat þing nis nat to come for þat þe purueaunce of god haþ seyn it byforne. þat is to comen but raþer þe contrarie. ¶ And þat is þis þat for þat þe þing is to comen þat þerfore ne may it nat ben hyd fro þe purueaunce of god.

4435 *al oon*—alone
4437 *harde*—hard
4445 *haþ*—MS. haþe
4446 *whiche*—which
4450 *wille*—wil
   whiche—which þat

4451 *haþ*—MS. haþe
4453 *stedfast*—stydefast
4454-55 *þinge*—thing
4455 *on*—of
4456 *þilk*—thilke
4458 *whiche*—which

4459 *knot*—knotte
4461 *come*—comyn
   haþ—MS. haþe
4464 *hyd* — MS. hydde, C. hidde

*and in þis manere þis necessite slydiþ aȝein in to þe contrarie partie. ne it ne byhoueþ [nat] nedes þat þinges bytiden þat ben ypurueid. [but it by-houeth nedes / þat thinges þat ben to comyn ben yporueyid] but as it were ytrauailed. as who seiþ. þat þilke answere procediþ ryȝt as þouȝ men trauailden or weren bysy to enqueren þe whiche þing is cause of whiche þinges. as wheþer þe prescience is cause of þe necessite of þinges to comen. or ellys þat þe necessite of þinges to comen is cause of þe purueaunce. ¶ But I ne enforce me nat now to shewen it þat þe bytidyng of þinges y-wist byforn is necessarie. how so or in what manere þat þe ordre of causes haþ it self. al þouȝ þat it ne seme nat þat þe prescience brynge in necessite of bytydynge of þinges to comen. ¶ For certys yif þat any wyȝt sitteþ it byhoueþ by necessite þat þe oppinioun be soþe of hym þat coniectiþ þat he sitteþ. and aȝeinward. al so is it of þe contrarie. yif þe oppinioun be soþe of any wyȝt for þat he sitteþ it byhoueþ by necessite þat he sitte ¶ þan is here necessite in þat oon *and* in þat oþer. for in þat oon is necessite of sittynge. *and* certys in þat oþer is necessite of soþe but þerfore ne sitteþ nat a wyȝt for þat þe oppinioun of sittyng is soþe. but þe oppinioun is raþer soþe for þat a wyȝt sitteþ by-forn. and þus al þouȝ þat þe cause of soþe comeþ of [þe] syttyng. and nat of þe trewe oppinioun. Algates ȝitte is þer comune necessite in þat oon *and* in þat oþer. ¶ þus sheweþ it þat I may make semblable skils of þe purueaunce of god *and* of þinges to come. ¶ For al þouȝ for þat þat þinges ben to comen. þer-fore ben þei purueid. nat certys for þei ben purueid. þer-fore ne bytide þei nat. ȝit naþeles byhoueþ it by necessite þat eiþer þe þinges to comen ben ypurueied of god. or ellys þat þe þinges þat ben

[* fol. 35.] Now by this reason necessity appears to change sides. For it is not necessary that the things which are foreseen should happen, but it is necessary that the things which are to befall should be foreseen. As if the question was, which was the cause of the other— *prescience* the cause of the necessity of future events, or the *necessity* the cause of the prescience of future events? But I will prove that, however the order of causes may stand, the event of things foreseen is necessary, although prescience doth not seem to impose a necessity upon future things to fall out. For if a man sit— the belief in the sitting is true; and, on the other hand, if the opinion is true of his sitting, he must needs sit. In both cases there is a necessity—in the latter that the person sits—in the former, that the opinion concerning the other is true. But the man does not sit because the opinion of his sitting is true, but the opinion is true because the action of his being seated was antecedent in time. So that although the cause of truth arises from the sitting, there is a common necessity in both. Thus may we reason concerning Providence and future events.

4481

4486 [nat]—from C.
4487-8 [but———yporueyid]—from C.
4471 þinges—thing
4477 haþ—MS. hnþe
4480-82 soþe—soth

4486 soþe—sooth
4487 soþe—soth
4488 soþe—sooth
4489 soþe comeþ — sooth comth
[þe]—from C.

4490 comune—MS. comme, C. comune
4493 come—comyn
4494 to—omitted
4494-95 purueid—MS. purueide, C. purueyid

For allowing things are foreseen because they are to happen, and that they do not befall because they are foreseen, it is necessary that future events should be foreseen of God, or if foreseen that they should happen; and this alone is sufficient to destroy all idea of *free-will*. But it is preposterous to make the happening of temporal things the cause of eternal prescience, which we do in imagining that God foresees future events because they are to happen. And, moreover, when I know that anything exists, it is necessary for my belief that it should be. So 4513 also when I know that an event shall come to pass, it must needs happen. The event, therefore, of a thing foreseen must befall. Lastly, if a person judge a thing to be different to what it is — this is not knowledge, but a false opinion of it, and far from the true knowledge. If, therefore, a thing be so to happen that the event of it is neither necessary nor certain, how can any one foresee what is to happen? For as pure knowledge has no element in it of falsehood, so what is comprehended by true knowledge cannot be otherwise than as comprehended. Hence it is that true	purueied of god bitiden [.s.] by necessite. ¶ And þis þing oonly suffiseþ I-nouȝ to distroien þe fredome of oure arbitre. þat is to seyn of oure fre wille ¶ But now [certes] sheweþ it wel how fer fro þe soþe *and* how vp so doun is þis þing þat we seyn þat þe bytidinge of temporel þinges is þe cause of þe eterne prescience. ¶ But forto wenen þat god purueiþ [the] þinges to comen. for þei ben to comen. what oþer þing is it but forto wene þat þilke þinges þat bitiden som tyme ben causes of þilke souereyne purueaunce þat is in god. ¶ And her-to I adde ȝitte þis þing þat ryȝt as whan þat I woot þat o þing is it byhoueþ by necessite þat þilke self þing be. *and* eke þat whan I haue knowe þat any þinge shal bitiden so byhoueþ it by necessite þat þilk[e] same þing bytide. so folweþ it þan þat þe bytydynge of þe þinge Iwist by-forn ne may nat ben eschewed. ¶ And at þe last[e] yif þat any wyȝt wene a þing to ben oþer weyes þan it is. it nys nat oonly vnscience. but it is deceiuable oppinioun ful diuerse *and* fer fro þe soþe of science. ¶ wher-fore yif any þing be so to comen so þat þe bytydynge of it ne be nat certeyne ne necessarie. ¶ who may weten [byforn] þat þilke þing is to come. ¶ For ryȝt as science ne may nat be modelyd wiþ falsnesse. as who seiþ þat yif I woot a þing. it ne may nat be fals þat I ne woot it. ¶ Ryȝt so þilk þing þat is conceyued by science ne may [nat] ben noon oþer weyes þan [as] it is conceiued. For þat is þe cause whi þat science wantiþ lesynge. as who seiþ. whi þat witynge ne receyueþ nat lesynge of þat it woot. ¶ For it byhoueþ by necessite þat euery þinge [be] ryȝt as science comprehendiþ it to be. what shal 1 þan sein. ¶ In whiche manere knoweþ god byforn þe þinges to comen.

4498 [*.s.*]—from C.	4509 *o*—a	4519 [*byforn*]—from C.
4499 *fredome*—freedom	*self*—solue	4522 *fals*—false
4500 *wille*—wil	4510 þ*inge*—thing	4523 (*nat*]—from C.
4501 [*certes*]—from C.	4511 þ*ilk*[*e*]—thilke	*ben*—MS. by, C. ben
4504 *purueiþ*—MS. p*urueiþe*	4513 þ*inge*—thing	4524 þ*an* (*as*) *it is*—MS. þan
(*the*)—from C.	4514 *last*[*e*]—laste	it is be
4506 *bitiden*—bytydden	4515 *nys*—is	4527 [*be*]—from C.
som tyme—whilom	4518 *it*—hit	4529 *whiche*—which

¶ yif þei ne be nat certeyne. ¶ For yif þat he deme þat þei ben to comen vneschewably. *and* so may be þat it is possible þat þei ne shulle*n* *nat comen. god is desseiued. but nat only to trowen þat god is desseiued. but for to speke it wiþ mouþe it is a felonous sy*n*ne. ¶ But yif þat god woot þat ryȝt so as þinges ben to comen. so shulle þei comen. so þat he wit[e] egaly. as who seiþ indifferently þat þinges mowen ben don or ellys nat don. what is þilke prescience þat ne compre-hendiþ no certeyne þinge ne stable. or ellys what differ-ence is þer bytwixe þe prescience. *and* þilke iape-worþi dyuynynge of Tiresie þe diuino*ur* þat seide. ¶ Al þat I scie q*uod* he eyþer it shal be. or ellys it ne shal nat be. Or ellis how moche is worþe þe diuyne prescience more þan þe oppinion of mankynde yif so be þat it demeþ þe þinges vncerteyne as me*n* don. of þe whiche domes of men þe bytydynge nis nat certeyne. ¶ But yif so be þat noon vncerteyne þinge may ben in hym þat is ryȝt certeyne welle of alle þinges. þa*n* is þe bytydynge certeyne of þilke þinges whiche he haþ wist byforn fermely to come*n*. For whiche it folweþ þat þe fredom of þe co*n*seils *and* of þe werkes of mankynde nis non syn þat þe þouȝt of god seeþ alle þinges wi*th* outen errou*r* of falsnesse byndeþ *and* constreiniþ hem to a bitidynge by necessite. and yif [this] þi*n*g be on-is grauntid *and* receyued. þat is to seyn. þat þer nis no fre wille. þan sheweþ it wel how gret distruccio*un* *and* how grete damages þer folwen of þinges of mankynde. ¶ For in ydel ben þer þan p*ur*posed and byhyȝt medes of goode folk. *and* peynes to badde folk. syn. þat no moeuynge of free corage uoluntarie ne haþ nat deserued hem. þat is to seyn neiþer mede nor peyne. ¶ And it sholde seme þan þat þilke þinge is alþer worste whiche

knowledge cannot err, because every-thing must pre-cisely be what true knowledge [* fol. 35 b.] perceives it to be. What follows, then?

4534
How does God foreknow those uncertain con-tingencies? For if he thinks that a thing will inevitably hap-pen, which pos-sibly may not, he is deceived—but this is sheer blas-phemy.

4540
But if God dis-cerns that just as things are to come they shall come; if he knows that they may or may not come, what sort of prescience is this, which com-prehends nothing certain, nothing invariable? Or how does divine prescience differ from human opinion, if He hath an uncertain judgment of things, whereof the events are un-certain and un-fixed?

4551
But if there can be no uncer-tainty in his knowledge, who is the source of all certainty; the event of all things which he foreknows must be fixed and in-evitable. Whence it fol-lows that men have no free-dom in their designs and ac-tions; because the Divine Mind, endowed with an infallible fore-sight, constrains and binds them to a certain event.

4562

4534 *mouþe*—Mowth
4536 *shulle*—shullyn
wit[*e*]—wite
4538 *don*—MS. done, C. y-doon
4543 *moche*—mochel

4543 *worþe*—worth
4549 *haþ*—MS. haþe
4550 *whiche*—which
4551 *mankynde*—man-kynd
4554 [*this*]—from C.
4555 *grauntid*—ygraunted

4558 *medes of*—Mecdes to
4560 *haþ*—MS. haþe
4562 *alþer worste whiche*—alderworst which

Rewards and punishments now deemed just and equitable, will be considered most unjust, when it is allowed, that mankind are not prompted by any will of their own, to either virtue or vice, but in all their actions are impelled by a fatal necessity.	þat is nowe demed. for alþer moste iuste *and* moste ryȝtful. þat is to seyn þat shrewes ben punyssed. or ellys þat good[e] folk ben ygerdoned. þe whiche folk syn þat þe propre wille [ne] sent hem nat to þat oon ne to þat oþer. þat is to seyn. neþer to good[e] ne to harme. but constreineþ hem certeyne necessite of þinges to comen. ¶ þanne ne shollen þer neuer ben ne neuer
4570	weren vice ne vertue. but it sholde raþer ben confusioun
Nor would there be such things as virtue or vice, but such a medley of the one and the other as would be productive of the greatest confusion. And from this it will follow —that since all order comes of Divine Providence, and that there is no freedom of the human will, that also our vices must be referred to the author of all good —which is a most impious opinion. Then is it useless to hope for anything from God, or to pray to him. For why should men do either, when all they can desire is irreversibly predestined? Hope and prayer being thus ineffectual, all intercourse is cut off between God and man.	of alle desertes medlid wiþoute discresioun. ¶ And ȝitte þer folweþ an oþer inconuenient of þe whiche þer ne may ben þouȝt ne more felonous ne more wikke. *and* þat is þis þat so as þe ordre of þinges is yledd *and* comeþ of þe puruoaunce of god. ne þat no þing nis leueful to þe conseils of mankynde. as who seiþ þat men han no power to done no þing. ne wilne no þing. þan folweþ it þat oure vices ben refferred to þe mak[er]e of alle good. as who seiþ þan folweþ it. þat god auȝt[e] han þe blame of oure vices. syn he constreiniþ by necessite to don vices. þan nis þer no resoun to han hopen in god. ne forto preien to god. ¶ For what sholde any wyȝt hopen to god. or whi sholde he preien to god. syn þat þe ordenaunce of destine whiche þat ne may nat ben enclined. knytteþ *and* streiniþ alle þinges þat men may desiren. ¶ þan sholde þere be don awey þilke oonly alliaunce bytwixen god *and* men. þat is to
4588	seien to hopen *and* to preien. but by þe preis of ryȝt-
By reverent and humble supplication we earn divine grace, a most inestimable favour, and are able to associate with the Deity, and to unite ourselves to the inaccessible light.	fulnesse *and* of veray mekenesse we descrue þe gerdoun of þe deuyne grace whiche þat is inestimable. þat is to sein þat it is so grete þat it ne may nat ben ful ypreised. *and* þis is oonly þe manere. þat is to seyen hope *and* prayeres. for whiche it semeþ þat [men] mowen speken

4563 *nowe*—MS. newe, C. now *alþer moste iuste*—alder moost lust *moste*—most 4565-67 *good[e]*—goode 4566 *wille*—wil [*ne*]—from C. 4571 *wiþoute*—with-owten 4573 *þouȝt*—thoght	4574 *yledd*—MS. yledde, C. yled 4575 *comeþ*—comth 4577 *done*—doon 4578 *mak[er]e*—makere 4579 *auȝt[e]*—owhte 4584 *whiche*—which 4588 *preis*—prys *ryȝtfulnesse*— Rihtwesse-	nesse 4589 *deserue*—desseruyn 4590 *deuyne*—MS. deuynes, C. dyuyne 4500-93 *whiche*—which 4591 *grete*—gret 4593 [*men*]—from C. *speken*—spoke

wiþ god. *and* by resou*n* of supplicac*i*ou*n* ben conioigned *If men believe that hope and*
to þilk clernesse þat nis nat approched no raþer or *prayer have no power because of the necessity of*
þat men byseken it *and* emprenten it. And yif men *future events, by what other way*
ne wene [nat] þat [hope] ne p*r*eiers ne han no strengþes. *can we be united, and hold fast to*
by þe necessite of þinges to come*n* y-resceiued. what *the sovereign Lord of all things?*
þi*n*g is þer þan by whiche we mowen be conioygned 4599
and clyuen to þilke soue*r*eyne p*r*ince of þinges. ¶ For *Wherefore mankind must be dissevered and disunited from the*
whiche it byhoueþ by necessite þat þe lynage of ma*n*- *source of its existence, and* [* fol. 36.]
kynde a*s* *þou songe a litel here byforne ben depa*r*ted *shrink from its beginning.*
and vnioyned from hys welle *and* faylen of hys bygyn-
nynge. þat is to seien god. 4604

QUE NAM DISCORS

[*The .3de. Metur.*]

W hat discordable cause haþ to-rent *and* vnioigned þe *Say what discordant cause looses*
byndyng or þe alliaunce of þinges. þat is to seyne *the bonds of things?*
þe coniu*u*cc*i*ou*n* of god *and* of man. ¶ whiche god 4607 *What power doth*
haþ establissed so grete bataile bitwixe*n* þise two soþe-. *make these two great truths (i. e.*
fast or verray þinges. þat is to sein bytwixen þe p*ur*ue- *Providence and Free-will) contend, which when*
aunce of god *and* fre wille. þat þei ben synguler *and* *separate are plain*
diuided. ne þat þei ne wolen nat ben medeled ne *united appear dark and perplexed?*
coupled to-gidre. but þer nis no discorde to [tho] verray 4613
þinges. but þei cleuen certeyne al wey to hem self. but *The mind of man*
þe þou3t of man co*n*founded *and* ouerþrowen by þe dirke *encumbered by the earthly body, can never, with*
membris of þe body ne may nat by fir of his dirk[ed] *her cloudy sight, discover the*
lokynge. þat is to seyn by þe vigo*u*r of hys insy3t while *subtle and close bonds of things.*
þe soule is in þe body knowen þe þinne subtil knyt- 4617
tynges of þi*n*ges. ¶ But wherfore eschaufiþ it so by so *But why does man burn with ardour to learn*
grete loue to fynden þilke note[s] of soþe y-coue*r*ed. (*glosa*) *the hidden notes of truth?*
þat is to sein wherfore eschaufiþ þe þou3t of man by so *Why gropes he for he knows not what?*
grete desir to knowen þilke notificac*i*oun*s* þat ben yhidd *None seek to know what is*
vndir þe couertou*r*s of soþe. woot it ou3t þilke þinges *known.*

4595 *þilk*—thilke
4596 *emprenten*—impetrent
4597 [*nat*]—from C.
[*hope*]—from C.
4601 *whiche*—which
4602 *byforne*—by-forn
4605 *haþ*—MS. haþe
4606 *seyne*—seyn
4607 *whiche*—which

4608 *haþ*—MS. haþe
grete—gret
soþefast—soothfast
4610 *wille*—wil
4612 *discorde*—discord
[*tho*]—from C.
4613 *cleuen*—clyuen
4615 *dirk*[*ed*]—derkyd
4616 *while*—whil

4617 *knowen*—knowe
4619-21 *grete*—gret
note[*s*]—notes
4619 *soþe*—soth
4621 *yhidd*—MS. yhidde, C. lhyd
4622 *soþe*—sooth
þinges—thing

If he knows them not, what does he so blindly seek?	þat it anguissous desireþ to knowe. as who seiþ nay. ¶ For no man ne trauaileþ forto witen þinges þat he woot.
	4625 and þerfore þe texte seiþ þus. ¶ [*Glosa*] Si enim anima
Who wishes for things he hath never known? Or if he seek, where shall he find them? Or if he find, how shall he be sure that he has found what he sought for? The pure soul that sees the divine thought, knows all the secret chains of things.	ignorat istas subtiles connexiones. *res*ponde. vn*d*e est quod desiderat scire cum nil ignotum possit desiderare. ¶ But who traua[i]leþ to wyten þinges y-knowe. and yif þat he ne knoweþ hem nat. what sekiþ þilke blynde þouʒt. what is he þat desireþ any þinge of whiche he woot ryʒt nat. as who seiþ who so desiriþ any þing nedis som what he knoweþ of it. or ellys he ne coupe
	4633 nat desire it. or who may folwen þinges þat ne ben nat
Yet, though now hidden in its fleshly members, it hath some remembrance of its pure state—it retains the sums of things, but has lost their particulars. He who seeks truth is not in either circumstance (*i. e.* seeking for what he knows or knows not), he knoweth not all things, nor hath he wholly forgotten all.	ywist ¶ and þouʒ [þat] he seke þo þinges where shal he fynde*n* hem. what wyʒt þat is al vnknowynge *and* ignoraunt may knowe þe forme þat is yfounde. ¶ But whan þe soule byholdeþ *and* seeþ þe heye þouʒt. þat is to seyn god. þan knoweþ it to-gidre þe somme *and* þe singularites. þat is to seyn þe p*r*inciples a*nd* euery che by hym self. ·¶ But now while þe soule is hidd in þe cloude *and* in þe derknesse of þe membris of þe body. it ne haþ nat al forʒeten it selfe. but it wiþholdeþ þe
	4643 somme of þinges *and* lesiþ þe singularites. þan who so
But he ponders on what he knows, that he may add those things that he hath forgotten to those that he retains.	þat sekeþ soþenesse. he nis in neiþ*er* nouþir habit. for he not nat alle ne he ne haþ nat alle for-ʒeten. ¶ But ʒitte hym remembriþ þe somme of þinges þat he wiþ-holdeþ *and* axeþ counseil *and* tretiþ depelyche þinges ysein byforne. [*Glosa*] þat is to sein þe grete somme in hys mynde. [*textus*] so þat he mowe adden þe parties þat he͵haþ forʒeten. to þilke þat he haþ wiþholden.

4625 [*Glosa*]—from C.	4635 *what*—MS. þat, C. what	*selfe*—self
4630 *þinge*—thing	*vnknowynge*—vnkunnynge	4644 *nouþir habit* — nother
whiche—which	4639 *eueryche*—euerych	habite
4631 *woot*—not	4640 *while*—whil	4645 *alle* (*both*)—al
nat—nawht	þe—MS. þe þe	*haþ*—MS. haþe
4632 *coupe*—kowde	*hidd*—MS. hidde, C. hidde	4648 [*Glosa*]—from C.
4634 [*þat*]—from C.	4641 *derknesse*—derkenesse	4649 [*textus*]—from C.
where—wher	4642 *haþ*—MS. haþe	4650 *haþ* (*both*)—MS. haþe

TAMEN ILLA UETUS INQUIT HEC EST.

Þanne seide she. þis is quod she þe olde questioun of þe purueaunce of god. and marcus tulius whan he deuided[e] þe deuinaciouns. þat is to sein in hys booke þat he wroot of deuinaciouns. he moeued[e] gretly þis questioun. and þou þi self hast souȝt it mochel and outerly and long[e]. but ȝit ne haþ it nat ben determined ne yspedd fermely and diligently of any of yow. ¶ And þe cause of þis derkenesse and [of this] difficulte is for þat þe moeuynge of þe resoun of mankynde ne may nat moeuen to. þat is to sein applien or ioygnen to þe simplicite of þe deuyne prescience. ¶ þe whiche symplicite of þe deuyne prescience ȝif þat men [myhten thinken it in any manere/ þat is to seyn /þat yif men] myȝte þinken and comprehenden þe þinges as god seeþ hem. þan ne sholde þer dwellen outerly no doute. þe whiche resoun and cause of difficulte I shal assaie at þe laste to shewen and to speden. . ¶ whan I haue *firste [yspendyd / and] answered to þo resouns by whiche þou art ymoeued. ¶ For I axe whi þou wenest þat þilk[e] resouns of hem þat assoilen þis questioun ne ben nat spedeful ynouȝ ne sufficient þe whiche solucioun or þe whiche resoun for þat it demiþ þat þe prescience nis nat cause of necessite to þinges to comen. þan ne weneþ it nat þat fredom of wille be distourbed or ylett by prescience. for ne drawest þou nat argumentes from ellys where of þe necessite of þinges to comen. As who seiþ any oþer wey þan þus. but þat þilke þinge[s] þat þe prescience woot byforn [ne] mowen nat vnbitide. þat is to seyn þat þei moten bitide. ¶ But þan yif þat prescience ne putteþ no necessite to þinges to comen. as þou þi self

[The 4th prose.]
P. This is the old objection against Providence, so ably handled by Cicero in his *Book of Divination;* and you yourself have anxiously discussed it. But neither of you have offered a satisfactory solution of the difficulty. The cause of this mystery is that the human understanding cannot conceive the simplicity of the divine prescience, for if it were possible to comprehend this, every difficulty would at once disappear. I shall, therefore, try to explain and solve this difficult question. I ask, then, why you do not approve the [* fol. 36 b.] reasoning of such as think—that Prescience does not obstruct the liberty of the will, because it is not the necessitating cause of future events? Do you draw an argument of the necessity of future events, from any other topic than this,—that those things which are foreknown must of necessity happen? If divine prescience imposes no necessity upon future things, must not the issue of things be voluntary, and man's will free and unconstrained?

4655

4665

4675

4653 *deuided[e]*—deuynede
    booke—book
4654 *moeued[e]*—moeuede
4655 *souȝt*—I-sowht
4l 6 *lonȝ[e]*—longe
    haþ—MS. haþe
4657 *yspedd*—MS. yspedde,
    C. Isped
    fermely — MS. feruently,

C. fermely
4658 *derkenesse*—dirknesse
    [*of this*]—from C.
4662-3 [*myhten* —— *men*] —
    from C.
4663 *myȝte*—myhten
4667 *firste*—fyrst
4668 [*yspendyd and*]—from C.

4668 *þo*—the
    whiche—which
4660 *art*—MS. arte
    þilk[e]—thilke
4671 *spedeful*—spedful
4672 *whiche*—which
4674 *wille*—wyl
4677 *þinge[s]*—thinges

11

NECESSITY AND PRESCIENCE. [BOOK 5. PROSE 4.

For argument sake let us suppose there is no prescience, would, then, the events which proceed from free-will alone be under the power of necessity? B. No. P. Let us, then, admit Prescience, but that it imposes no necessity on what is to happen; the freedom of the will would still remain entire and absolute. But although Prescience, you may say, is not the necessary cause of future events, yet it is a sign that they shall necessarily happen, and hence it follows that, although there were no prescience, future events would still be an inevitable necessity. For the sign of a thing is not really the thing itself, but only points out what the individual is. Wherefore, it must be first proved that everything happens by necessity before we can conclude that prescience is a sign of that necessity. For if there be no necessity, prescience cannot be the sign of that which has no existence. The assertion that nothing happens but by necessity, must be proved by arguments drawn from causes connected and agreeing with this necessity, and not from signs or from guu causes.

hast confessed it *and* by knowen a litel her byforne. ¶ what cause [or what] is it. as who seiþ þere may no cause be. by whiche þat þe endes (exitus) uoluntarie of þinges my3ten be constreyned to certeyne bitydyng. ¶ For by grace of possessioun. so þat þou mowe þe better vndirstonde þis þat folweþ. ¶ I pose (inpossibile) þat þer ne be no prescience. þan axe I quod she in as moche as apperteniþ to þat. sholde þan þinges þat comen of frewille ben constreined to bytiden by necessite. Boicius. nay quod I. þan a3einward quod she. I suppose þat þere be prescience. but þat ne putteþ no necessite to þinges. þan trowe I þat þilk self fredom of wille shal dwellen al hool *and* absolut *and* vnbounden. but þou wolt sein þat al be it so þat prescience nis nat cause of þe necessite of bitidynge to þinges to comen. ¶ Algates 3itte it is a signe þat þe þinges ben to bytiden by necessite. by þis manere þan al þou3 þe prescience ne hadde neuer yben. 3it algate or at þe lest[e] wey. it is certeyne þing þat þe endys *and* þe bitydynges of þinges to comen sholde ben necessarie. ¶ For euery sygne sheweþ *and* signifieþ oonly what þe þing is ¶ but it ne makiþ nat þe þing þat it signifieþ. ¶ For whiche it byhoueþ firste to shewen þat no þing ne bitidiþ [þat it ne bytydith] by necessite. so þat it may apere þat þe prescience is signe of þis necessite ¶ or ellys yif þere nere no necessite. certys þilke prescience ne my3t[e] nat ben signe of þinge þat nis nat. ¶ But certys it is nowe certeyne þat þe preue of þis susteniþ by stedfast resoun ne shal nat ben ladd ne proued by signes ne by argumentys ytaken fro wiþ oute. but by causes couenable *and* necessarie ¶ But þou mayst sein how may it be þat þe þinges ne bitiden nat

---

4683 *whiche*—which
4685 *better*—betere
4688 *moche*—mochel
4689 *frewille*—free wyl
4691 *þat ne*—þat is ne
4692 *þat*—MS. þan
þilk self—thilke selue

4693 *wille*—wil
4699 *lest[e]*—leeste
4700 *sholde*—sholden
4703 *whiche*—which
firste—fyrst
4704 [*þat* — *bytydith*] — from C.

4707 *my3t[e]*—myhte
þinge—thing
4708 *nowe*—now
4709 *susteniþ*—ysustenyd
stedfast—stydefast
ladd—MS. ladde, C. lad

þat ben ypurueyed to comen. but certys ry3t as we trowen þat þo þinges whiche þat þe purueaunce woot by-forn to comen. ne ben nat to bitiden. but [þat] ne sholde we nat demen. but raþer al þou3 [þat] þei schal bitiden. 3it ne haue þei no necessite of hire kynde to bitiden. and þis maist þou ly3tly aperceyuen by þis þat I shal seyn. but we seen many þinges whan þei ben don by-forn oure eyen ry3t as men seen þe karter worken in þe tournynge and in attempryng or in adressyng of hys kartes or chariottes. ¶ and by þis manere as who seiþ mayst þou vnderstonde of alle manere oþir werkemen. ¶ Is þere þanne any necessite as who seiþ in oure lok-ynge [þat] constreineþ or compelliþ any of þilke þinges to ben don so. b. nay quod I ¶ For in ydel and in veyne were alle þe effect of crafte yif þat alle þinges weren moeued by constreynynge. þat is to séyn by con-streynynge of oure eyen or of oure sy3t. P. þise þingus þan quod she þat whan men don hem ne han non necessite þat men don hem. eke þo same þinges first or þei be don. þei ben to comen wiþ out necessite. for whi þer ben somme þinges to bytide of whiche þe endys and þe bitidynges of hem ben absolut *and quit of alle necessite. for certys I ne trowe nat þat any man wolde seyn þis. þat þo þinges þat men don now þat þei ne weren to bitiden. first or þei were ydon ¶ and þilk same þinges al þou3 þat men hadden ywyst hem by-forn. 3itte þei han fro bitidynges. for ry3t as science of þinges present ne bryngeþ in no necessite to þinges [þat men doon // Ryht so the prescience of thinges to comen ne bryngeth in no necessite to thinges] to bytiden but þou mayst seyn þat of þilke same it is ydouted. as wheþer þat of þilke þinges þat ne han non endes and

We see many things when they are done before our eyes; such as a charioteer driving his chariot, and other things of like nature. Now, is there any necessity which compels these things to be done ? B. No. For if all things were moved by com-pulsion—the efforts of art would be vain and fruitless. P. The things, then, which are done are under no necessity that they should be done ; then first before they were done, they were under no neces-sity of coming to pass; wherefore some things hap-pen, the event of which is uncon-strained by ne-cessity. These things therefore, although fore-known, have free events: for as the knowledge of present things imposes no ne-cessity upon things which are now done, so [* fol. 37.] neither does the foreknowledge of futurities necessi-tate the things which are to come. But you may doubt whether there can be any cer-tain prescience of things, of which the event is not necessitated: for here there seems to be an evident contradiction. If things are fore-known, you may contend they must necessarily happen; and if their event is not necessary,

4714 whiche—which
4715 [þat]—from C.
sholde—sholden
4716 demen—MS. denyen [þat]—from C.
4717 necessite—MS. necessi-
4721 hys—hise [tes
4725 [þat]—from C.
4727 veyne—veyn alle—al
crafte—craft [the
4729 þise—MS. þise þise, C.
4732 wiþ out—with-owte
4733 bytide—bytyden
4733 whiche—which
4737 were—weeren [I-doon ydon — MS. ydone, C. þilk—thilke
4741-2 [þat —— thinges] — from C.
4744 endes—issues

they cannot be foreseen, because true knowledge can comprehend nothing but what is absolutely certain. And if things uncertain in their events are foreseen as certain, this knowledge is nothing more than a false opinion. For it is very remote from true knowledge to judge of things otherwise than they really are. The cause of this error is that men imagine that their knowledge is wholly derived from the nature of the things known, whereas it is quite the reverse. Things are not known from their inherent properties, but by the faculties of the observer.

bytidynges necessaryes yif þer-of may ben any prescience ¶ For certys þei seme to discorde. for þou wenest þat yif þat þinges ben yseyn byforn þat necessite folweþ hem. and yif (*et* putas) necessite faileþ hem þei ne myȝten nat ben wist byforn. *and* þat no þinge ne may ben comprehendid by science but certeyne. *and* yif þo þinges þat ne han no certeyne bytidynges ben ypurucied as certeyn. it sholde ben dirkenesse of oppinioun nat soþefastnesse of science [*and* þou weenyst þat it be diuerse fro the hoolnesse of science / þat any man sholde deme a thing to ben oother weys thanne it is it self]. and þe cause of þis errour is. þat of alle þe þinges þat euery wyȝt haþ yknowe. þei wenen þat þo þinges ben y-knowe al oonly by þe strengþe *and* by þe nature of þe þinges þat ben ywyst or yknowe. *and* it is al þe contrarie. for alle þat euere is yknowe. it is raþer comprehendid *and*

4761
The roundness of a body affects the sight in one way, and the touch in another. The eye, from afar, darts its rays upon the object, and by beholding it comprehends its form. But the object is not distinguished by the touch unless the hand comes in contact with it and feels it all round. Man himself is surveyed in divers ways—by the senses, by the imagination, by reason, and by the intelligence (of the Deity). The senses take note of his material figure—the imagination considers the form alone, exclusive of the matter.

yknowen nat after his strengeþ *and* hys nature. but after þe faculte þat is to seyn þê power *and* [the] nature of hem þat knowen. *and* for þat þis shal mowe shewen by a short ensample þe same roundenes of a body .O. oþer weyes þe syȝt of þe eye knoweþ it. *and* oþer weyes þe touching. þe lokynge by castynge of his bemes waiteþ *and* seeþ fro afer alle þe body to-gider wiþ oute mouynge of it self. but þe touchinge cliuiþ *and* conioigneþ to þe rounde body (*orbi*) *and* moueþ abouten þe cnvironynge. *and* comprehendiþ by partics þe roundenesse. ¶ and þe man hym self oþer weies wyt byholdiþ hym. *and* oþerweyes ymaginacioun *and* oþer weyes resoun. *and* oþer weyes intelligence. ¶ For þe wit comprehendiþ fro wiþ outen furþe þe figure of þe body of þe man. þat is establissed in þe matere subiect. But þe ymaginacioun [comprehendith only the figure with owte the matere /

4746 *seme*—semyn
discorde—discorden
4749 *þat*—yif
4753-5 [*and* —— *self*]—from C.
4757 *haþ*—MS. haþe
4760 *alle*—al

4763 *mowe*—mowen
4764 *roundenes* — Rowndnesse
4765 *syȝt*—sihte
4767 *alle*—al
4769 *abouten*—abowte
4770 *roundenesse* — Rownd-

nesse
4774 *fro wiþ outen furþe*—with owte forth
4776-7 [*comprehendith* —— *ymaginacioun*]—from C.

Resoun surmounteth ymaginacioun] *and* comprehendeþ
by an vniuersel lokynge þe commune spece (*speciem*)
þat is in þe singuler peces. ¶ But þe eye of intelligence
is hey3er for it sourmounteþ þe environynge of þe
vniuersite *and* lookeþ ouer þat by pure subtilite of þou3t.
þilk same symple forme of man þat is perdurably in þe
deuyne þou3t. in whiche þis au3t[e] gretely to ben considered þat þe heyest strengþe to comprehenden þinges
enbraceþ *and* conteyneþ þe lower[e] strengþe [but the
lowere strengthe ne arysith nat in no manere to heyere
strengthe]. for wit ne may no þinge comprehende oute of
matere. ne þe ymagynacioun ne lokeþ nat þe vniuerseles
speces. ne resoun ne takeþ nat þe symple forme. so as
intelligence takeþ it. but þe intelligence þat lokeþ al
abouen whan it haþ comprehendid þe forme it knoweþ
and demeþ alle þe þinges þat ben vndir þat forme. but
she knoweþ hem vndir þilke manere in þe whiche it
comprehendiþ þilke same symple forme þat ne may
neuer be knowen to non of þat oþer. þat is to seyn to
non of þo þre forseide strengþes of þe soule. for it
knoweþ þe vniuersite of resoun *and* þe figure of þe ymaginacioun. *and* þe sensible material conseiued. *and* þou
wenest þat it be diuerse fro þe hoolnesse of science. þat
any man sholde deme a þing to ben oþerweyes þan it is
it self *and* þe cause of þis errour etc'. *vt supra*. by wit.
ne it ne vseþ nat nor of resoun ne of ymaginacioun ne
of wit wiþ oute forþe but it byholdeþ alle þinges so as I
shal seye. by a strok of þou3t formely wiþ oute discours
or collacioun ¶ Certys resoun whan it lokeþ any þing
vniuersel it ne vseþ nat of ymaginacioun nor of wit *and*
algates 3it [it] comprendiþ þe þinges ymaginable *and*
sensible. for resoun is she þat *diffinisseþ þe vniuersel

Reason transcends the imaginations, and examining existences in general discovers the particular species, but the eye of Intelligence soars still higher; for, going beyond the bounds of what is general, it surveys the simple forms themselves, by its own pure and subtle thought: in which this is chiefly to be considered, that the higher power of perception embraces the lower; but the inferior cannot attain to the energy of the superior: for the senses cannot go beyond the perception of matter; the imagination cannot comprehend existences in general, nor can the reason conceive the simple form. But the Intelligence looking-down (as from 4794 above) and having conceived the form, discerns all things that are below it, and comprehends what does not fall within the reach of the other faculties of the mind. Without the aid of those faculties Intelligence comprehends things formally (i.e. by beholding their simple forms) by one effort of mind. Reason, without the aid of Imagination and Sense, in considering things in general, comprehends all imaginable and sensible things. For instance, reason defines her general conceptions thus:—

[* fol. 37 b.]

4777 *comprehendeþ* — MS. comprehendynge
4778 *an*—omitted
4780 *hey3er*—heyere
4783 *whiche*—which
  au3t[e]—owhte
4784 *heyest*—heyiste
4785 *lower[e]*—lowere
4785-7 *[but —— strengthe]*— from C.
4787 *wit*—witte
  oute—owt
4791 *haþ*—MS. haþe
4793 *whiche*—which
4795-6 *non*—none
4796 *strengþes*—thinges
4798-4801 *and þou —— vt supra*—omitted
4805 *collacioun*—MS. callacioun, C. collacioun
4806 *wit*—witte

[BOOK 5.
MET. 4.

HOW OUR KNOWLEDGE OF

Man is a rational two-footed animal, which, though it be a general idea, yet every one knows that man thus defined is perceived both by the imagination and the senses, notwithstanding that in this instance reason does not make use of imagination or the senses, but of her own rational conception. The imagination also, although it derives its power of seeing and forming figures from the senses, yet in the absence and without the use of the senses it considers and comprehends all sensible things by its own imaginative power. Do not you see that men attain to the knowledge of things more by their own faculties, than by the inherent property of things?

[The 4the Metur.] Nor is it unreasonable that it should be so—for since every judgment is the act of the person judging; every one must needs do his own work by the help of his own faculties, and not by the aid of foreign power. Fallacious and obscure was the lore of the Stoics, who taught that images of things obvious to the senses were imprinted on the mind by external objects, and that the soul is at first like a mirror or a clean parchment, free from figures and letters.

of hir conseite ryȝt þus. ¶ Man is a resonable t[w]o-footid beest. and how so þat þis knowynge [is] vniuersel. ȝit nys þer no wyȝt þat ne woot weL þat a man is [a thing] ymaginable and sensible ¶ and þis same considereþ wel resoun. but þat nis nat by ymaginacioun. nor by witte. but it lokiþ it by [a] resonable concepcioun. ¶ Also ymaginacioun al be it so. þat it takeþ of wit þe bygynyngus to seen and to formen þe figures. algates al þouȝ þat wit ne ware not present. ȝit it envirouniþ and comprehendiþ alle þinges sensible. nat by resoun sensible of demynge. but by resoun ymaginatif. ¶ sest þou nat þan þat alle þe þinges in knowynge vsen more of hir faculte or of hir power. þan þei don of [the] faculte or of power of þinges þat ben yknowen. ne þat nis no wronge. for so as euery iugement is þe dede or þe doynge of hym þat demeþ. It byhoueþ þat euery wyȝt performe þe werke and hys entencioun nat of forein power? but of hys propre power.

QUONDAM PORTICUS ATTULIT.

Þ E porche þat is to sein a gate of þe toune of athenis þer as philosophres hadde hir congregacioun to dispoyten. and þilke porche brouȝt[e] somtyme olde men ful derke in hire sentences. þat is to sein philosophers þat hyȝten stoiciens. þat wenden þat ymages [and] sensibilites þat is to sein sensible ymaginaciouns. or ellys ymaginacioun of sensible þinges weren inprentid in to soules fro bodies wiþ oute forþe. ¶ As who seiþ þat þilke stoiciens wenden þat þe soule hadde ben naked of it self. as a mirour or a clene parchemyn. so þat alle fygures mosten [fyrst] comen fro þinges fro wiþ oute in to soules. and ben inprentid in to soules. Textus. Ryȝt as we ben wont some tyme by a swift poyntel to ficchen lettres emprentid in þe smoþenesse or in þe plainesse of

---

4810 [is]—from C.
4813 witte—wit
4821 don—MS. donc, C. doon
[the]—from C.
4822 yknowen—Iknowe

4822 no wronge—nat wrong
4824 werke—werk
4825 forein—foreyne
4827 hadde—hadden
dispoyten—desputen

4828 brouȝt[e]—browhte
4830 [and]—from C.
4837 inprentid—aprentyd
4838 some tyme—somtyme
swift—swyfte

þe table of wex. or in parchemyn þat ne haþ no figure [ne] note in it. *Glosa.* But now arguiþ bocce aȝeins þat oppinioun *and* seiþ þus. but yif þe þriuyng soule ne vnplitiþ no þing. þat is to sein ne doþ no þing by hys propre moeuynges. but suffriþ *and* lieþ subgit to þe figures *and* to þe notes of bodyes wiþ oute forþe. *and* ȝeldeþ ymages ydel *and* veyne in þe manere of a mirour. whennes þriueþ þan or whennes comeþ þan þilke knowyng in oure soule. þat discerniþ *and* byholdeþ alle þinges. and whennes is þilke strengþe þat byholdeþ þe syngulere þinges. or whennes is þe strengþe þat dyuydeþ þinges yknowe. *and* þilke strengþe þat gadereþ to-gidre þe þinges deuided. *and* þe strengþe þat cheseþ hys entrechaunged wey. for som tyme it heueþ vp þe heued. þat is to sein þat it heueþ vp þe entencioun to ryȝt heye þinges. *and* som tyme it discendiþ in to ryȝt lowe þinges. *and* whan it retourniþ in to hym self. it repreuiþ *and* destroieþ þe false þinges by þe trewe þinges. ¶ Certys þis strengþe is cause more efficient *and* mochel more myȝty to seen *and* to knowe þinges. þan þilke cause þat suffriþ and resceyueþ þe notes *and* þe figures inpressed in manere of matere algates þe passioun þat is to seyn þe suffraunce or þe wit in þe quik[e] body goþ byforne excitynge *and* moeuyng þe strengþes of þe þouȝte. ryȝt so as whan þat clerenesse smyteþ þe eyen *and* moeuiþ hem to seen. or ryȝt so as voys or soune hurtliþ to þe eres *and* commoeuiþ hem to herkne. þan is þe strengþe of þe þouȝt ymoeuid *and* excitid *and* clepeþ furþe þe semblable moeuynges þe speces þat it halt wiþ inne it self. *and* addiþ þo speces to þe notes *and* to þe þinges wiþ out forþe. *and* medeleþ þe ymages of þinges wiþ out forþe to þe forme[s] yhid wiþ inne hym self.

4845
4854
4860
4866
4872

But if the mind is passive in receiving the impressions of outward objects, whence proceeds the knowledge by which the mind comprehends all things?

Whence its force to conceive individual existences, to separate those things when known, to unite divided things, and to choose and change its path, soaring to the highest and descending to the lowest things—and returning to itself, to confute false things by the true?

This cause is more efficacious and powerful to see and to know things, than that cause which receives the characters impressed like servile matter.

Yet the sense in the living body excites and moves the mental powers; as when the light striking the eyes causes them to see, or as the voice rushing into the ear excites hearing.

Then is the force of thought excited; it calls forth the images within itself, and adds to them the outward forms, blending external images with the counterparts concealed within.

4840 *haþ*—MS. haþe
4843 *vnplitiþ*—vnpleyteth
  doþ—MS. doþe
4845 *þe*—tho
4853 *quik[e]*—qwyke
4863 *goþ*—MS. goþe
4864 *þouȝte*—thoȝht
4865 *clerenesse*—cleernesse
4866 *soune*—sown
4868 *furþe*—forth
4870 *out*—owte
4871 *out forþe*—owte forth
4872 *forme[s]*—formes
  yhid—I-hidde

QUOD SI IN CORPORIBUS SENCIENDIS.

*QUESTIO.

[* fol. 88.]

[The .5th prose.]
Although there are in objects certain qualities which strike externally upon the senses, and put their instruments in motion; although the passive impression upon the body precedes the action of the mind, and although the former rouses the latter to action, yet if in the perception of bodily things, the soul is not by the impression of external things made to know these things, but by its own power judgeth of these bodily impressions, how much more shall those pure spiritual beings (as God or angels) discern things by an act of their understanding alone, without the aid of impressions from external objects? For this reason, then, there are several sorts of knowing distributed among various beings. For sense (or sensation) destitute of all other knowledge is allotted to those creatures that have no motion, as shell-fish. But imagination is given to such brutes capable of motion, and having in some degree the power of desiring or refusing. Reason, however, is the attribute of man alone, as Intelligence is that of God.

But what [yif] þat in bodies to ben feelid þat is to scin in þe takynge of knowelechinge of bodyly þinges. and al be it so þat þe qualites of bodies þat ben obiect fro wiþ oute forþe mocuen and entalenten þe instrumentes of þe wittes. and al be it so þat þe passioun of þe body þat is to seyn þe witte [or the] suffraunce [goth to-forn the strengthe of the workynge corage./ the which passioun or suffraunce] clepiþ furþe þe dede of þe þou3t in hym self. and mocueþ and exiteþ in þis mene while þe formes þat resten wiþ in forþe. and yif þat in sensible bodies as I haue seid oure corage nis nat ytau3t or enprentid by passioun to knowe þise þinges. but demiþ and knoweþ of hys owen strengþe þe passioun or suffraunce subiect to þe body. Moche more þan þoo þinges þat ben absolut and quit fram alle talent3 or affeccïouns of bodies. as god or hys aungels ne folwen nat in discernynge þinges obiect from wiþ oute forþe. but þei accomplissen and speden þe dede of hir þou3t by þis resoun. ¶ þan þere comen many manere knowynges to dyuerse and differyng substaunces. for þe wit of þe body þe whiche witte is naked and despoyled of alle oþer knowynges. þilke witte comeþ to bestes þat ne mowen nat mocuen hem self here ne þere. as oystres and muscles and oþer swiche shelle fysshe of þe see. þat cliuen and ben norissed to roches. but þe ymaginacïoun comeþ to remuable bestes þat semen to han talent to fleen or to desiren any þinge. but resoun is al only to þe lynage of mankynde ry3t as intelligence is oonly þe deuyne nature. of whiche it folweþ þat þilke knowyng is more worþe þan [th]is[e] oþer. syn it knoweþ by hys

4885

4902

4973 [yif]—from C.
4878 [or the]—from C. suffraunce — MS. suffraunce, C. suffraunce
4970-80 [goth——suffraunce] —from C.

4883 seid—MS. seide, C. seyd
4887 quit—quite
4888 hys—hise
4889 discernynge — MS. discryuyng, C. discernynge from—fro

4893-94 witte—wit
4895 mowen—mowe here ne þere—her and ther
4901 whiche—which
4902 [th]is[e] oþer — thise oothre

propre nature nat only hys subiect. as who seiþ it ne knoweþ nat al oonly þat apperteiniþ proprely to hys knowynge. but it knoweþ þe subgitȝ of alle oþer knowynges. but how shal it þan be yif þat wit *and* ymaginacioun stryuen aȝeins resonynge *and* sein þat of þilke vniuersel þinges. þat resoun weneþ to seen þat it nis ryȝt nauȝt. for wit *and* ymaginacioun seyn þat þat. þat is sensible or ymaginable it ne may nat ben vniuersel. þan is eiþer þe iugement of resoun [soth]. ne þat þer nis no þinge sensible. or ellys for þat resoun woot wel þat many þinges ben subiect to wit *and* to ymaginacioun. þan is þe consepcioun of resoun veyn *and* fals whiche þat lookeþ *and* comprehendiþ. þat þat is sensible *and* synguler as uniuersele. and ȝif þat resoun wolde answeren aȝein to þise two þat is to sein to wit *and* to ymaginacioun. *and* seiu þat soþely she hir self. þat is to seyn þat resoun lokeþ *and* comprehendiþ by resoun of vniuersalite. boþe þat þat is sensible *and* þat þat is ymaginable. *and* þat þilke two þat is to seyn wit *and* ymaginacioun ne mowen nat strecchen ne enhaunsen hem self to knowynge of vniuersalite for þat þe knowyng of hem ne may excedẹn nor sourmounten þe bodyly figure[s] ¶ Certys of þe knowyng of þinges men auȝten raþer ȝeue credence to þe more stedfast *and* to þe more perfit iugement. In þis manere stryuynge þan we þat han strengþe of resonynge *and* of ymaginynge *and* of wit þat is to seyn by resoun *and* by ymaginacioun *and* by wit. [*and*] we sholde raþer preise þe cause of resoun. as who seiþ þan þe cause of wit or ymaginacioun. semblable þinge is it þat þe resoun of mankynde ne weneþ nat þat þe deuyne intelligence byholdeþ or knoweþ þinges to comen. but ryȝt as þe resoun of mankynde knoweþ hem. for þou arguist *and* seist þus. þat

Hence His (i. e. God's) *knowledge exceeds all other, comprehending both what belongs to His own nature, and what is comprehended by all inferior creatures. But how shall it be then, if sense and imagination oppose reason, affirming that the general idea of things, which reason thinks it so perfectly sees, is nothing? For what falls under the cognisance of the senses and imagination cannot be general. But if reason should answer to this—that in her idea of what is general she comprehends whatever is sensible and imaginable; but as to the senses and imagination, they cannot attain to the knowledge of what is general, since their knowledge is confined to material figures; and therefore in all real knowledge of things we must give the greatest credit to that faculty which has a more steadfast and perfect judgment of things. In a controversy of this kind ought not we, who possess faculties of reason, &c., to side with reason and espouse her cause? The case is entirely similar when human reason thinks the Divine Intelligence cannot behold future events in any other way than she herself is capable of perceiving them. For thus you argue:—*

4921

4907 *aȝeins*—ayein
4908 *vniuersel*—vniuersels
4911 [*soth*]—from C.
4914 *fals whiche*—false which
4917 *wit*—witte
4918 *soþely*—soothly
4923 *knowynge*—knowy
4926 *ȝeue*—yeuen
4926 *stedfast*—stidefast
4930 [*and*]—from C.
4931 *or*—and of

What things are not necessitated cannot be foreknown; therefore there is no prescience of these things, for, if there were, everything would be fixed by an absolute necessity. If it were possible to enjoy the intelligence of the Deity, we should then deem it right that

sense and imagination should yield to reason, and also judge it proper that human reason should submit to the Divine Intelligence. Let us, therefore, strive to elevate ourselves to the height of the supreme intelligence—there shall reason see what she cannot discover in herself; and that is in what manner the prescience of God sees and defines all things; although they have no certain event; and she will see that this is no mere conjecture, but rather simple, supreme, and unlimited knowledge.

[The 5ᵗʰᵉ Metur.]
Various are the shapes of created beings. Some creep along the ground and trace the dust in furrows as they go; others with nimble wings float through the air; some with their feet impress the ground, or tread lightly o'er the meads, or seek the shady grove.

yif it ne seme nat to men þat somme þinges han certeyne *and* necessarie bytidynges. þei ne mowen nat ben wist byforn certeynely to bytiden. þan nis [ther] no prescience of þilke þinges. *and* yif we trowen þat prescience ben in þise þinges. þan is þer no þinge þat it ne bitidiþ by necessite. but certys yif we myȝten han þe iugement of þe deuyne þouȝt as we *ben pa*rsoners of resou*n*. ryȝt so as we han demed. it byhoueþ þat yma-

4944 ginaci*oun and* wit ben byneþe resou*n*. ryȝt so wolde we deme*n* þat it were ryȝtful þing þat ma*n*s resou*n* auȝt[e] to su*m*mitten it self *and* to ben byneþe þe deuyne þouȝt. for whiche þat yif we mowen. as who seiþ. þat yif þat we mowe*n* I conseil[e] þat we enhanse vs in to þe heyȝt of þilke souereyne i*n*telligence. for þere shal resou*n* wel seen þat þat it ne may nat by-holden in it self. and certys þat is þis in what manere þe prescience of god seeþ alle þinges *certeins and* difinissed al þouȝ þei ne han no certein issues or by-tydynges. ne þis is non oppinio*un* but it is raþer þe simplicite of þe souerey*n.* science þat nis nat enclosed nor yshet wiþinne no boundes.

QUAM UARIIS FIGURIS.

Þ̵E bestes passen by þe erþes by ful dyuerse figures for somme of hem han hir bodies strauȝt *and* crepen in þe dust *and* drawen after hem a trais or a forghe contynued. þat is to sein as addres or snakes. and oþer bestes by [the] wandryng lyȝtnesse of hir wenges beten þe wyndes *and* ouer-swymme*n* þe spaces of þe longe eyer by moist flee[y]nge. and oþer bestes gladen hem to diggen her traas or her stappes i*n* þe erþe wiþ hir goynge or wiþ her feet. or to gone eyþe[r]

4965 by þe grene feldes or [elles] to walken vnder þe wodes.

4938 [*ther*]—from C.
4939 *trowen*—trowe
4942 *parsoners*—parsoneres
4945 *mans*—mannes
4946 *auȝt*[*e*]—owte
4947 *whiche*—which
4948 þat *yif*—yif þat

4949 *heyȝt*—heihte
þere—ther
4952 þouȝ—MS. þouȝt
4955 *no*—none
4957 *somme*—som
4959 *forghe contynued* — forwh Ikonntynued

4959 *addres*—nadris
4960 [*the*]—from C.
4963 *hem*—hem self
stappes—steppis
4964 *or to gone*—*and* to gon
eyþe[*r*]—eyther
4965 [*elles*]—from C.

DEFINITION OF ETERNITY.

and al be it so þat þou seest þat þei alle discorden by dyuerse formes. algate hire [faces] enclini[n]g heuieþ hire dulle wittes. Onlyche þe lynage of man heueþ heyest hys heyʒe heued *and* stondeþ lyʒt wiþ hys vpryʒt body *and* byholdeþ þe erþe vndir hym. [and] but-ʒif þou erþely man wexest yuel oute of þi witte. þis figure amonesteþ þe þat axest þe heuene wiþ þi ryʒt[e] visage. *and* hast areised þi forhede to beren vp on heye þi corage so þat þi þouʒt ne be nat yheuied ne put lowe vndir foot. sen þat þi body is so heye areised. 4975

Though we see an endless variety of forms, yet all are prone; to the earth they bend their looks, increasing the heaviness of their dull sense. Man alone doth raise aloft his noble head; light and erect he spurns the earth. Thou art admonished by this figure then, unless by sense deceived, that whilst taught by thy lofty mien thou shouldst elevate thy mind lest it sink below its proper level.

PROSA VLTIMA.

[The 6ᵗᵉ prose and the laste.]

QUONIAM IGITUR UTI PAULO ANTE.

BEr-fore þan as I haue shewed a litel her byforne þat al þinge þat is ywist nis nat knowen by hys nature propre. but by þe nature of hem þat compr*e*henden it. ¶ Lat vs loke now in as moche as it is leueful to vs. as who seiþ lat vs loken now as we mowen whiche þat þe estat is of þe deuyne substaunce so þat we mowen [ek] knowen what his science is. þe comune iugement of alle creatures resonables þan is þis þat god is eterne. lat vs considere þa*n* what is eternite. For certys þat shal shewen vs to-gidre þe deuyne nature *and* þe deuyne science ¶ Eternite þan is p*er*fit possessiou*n and* al togidre of lijf interminable *and* þat sheweþ more clerely by þe co*m*parisou*n* or collaciou*n* of tempo*r*el þinges. for al þing þat lyueþ in tyme it is present *and* procediþ fro preteritʒ in to fut*u*res. þat is to sein. fro tyme passed in to tyme comynge. ne þer nis no þing establissed *in* tyme þat may enbracen to-gidre al þe space of hys lijf. for certys ʒit ne haþ it nat taken þe tyme of þe morwe. *and* it haþ lost þat of ʒister-day. and certys in þe lijf

Since everything which is known is not, as I have shown, perceived by its own inherent properties, but by the faculties of those comprehending them, let us now examine the disposition of the Divine nature. All rational creatures agree in affirming that God is eternal. And eternity is a full, total, and perfect possession of a life which shall never end. This will appear more clearly from a comparison with temporal things. Temporal existence proceeds from the past to the present, and thence to the future. And there is nothing under the law of time, which can at once comprehend the whole space of its existence. Having lost yesterday it does not as yet enjoy to-morrow; and as for to-day it consists only in the present transitory moment.

4967 [*faces*]—from C.
algate—algates
enclini[n]g—enclynyd
4968 Onlyche—Oonly
heyest—heyeste
4970 erþe—erthes
4971 oute—owt
witte—wit

4972 ryʒt[e]—ryhte
hast—MS. haþe, C. hast
4973 forhede—forehcuyd
on heye—a heygh
4974 foot sen—foote syn
4977 al þinge — alle thinges
4979 moche—mochel
4980 loken—loke

4980 whiche—which
4981 [ek]—from C.
4987 clerely—clcerly
4989 al—alle
4993-4 haþ—MS. haþe
4993 þe (2)—to
4994 þat—the tyme

of þis day ȝe ne lyuen no more but ryȝt as in þis moeueable *and* transitorie moment. þan þilke þinge þat suffriþ temporel condicio*un*. a[l]þoughe þat [it] bygan neuer to be. ne þoughe it neue*re* cese forto be. as aristotle demde of þe worlde. and al þouȝ þat þe lif of it be strecchid wiþ infinite of tyme. ȝit al*gates nis it no swiche þing þat men myȝten trowen by ryȝt þat it is eterne. for al þouȝ þat it comprehende *and* embrace þe space of life infinite. ȝit algates ne [em]braceþ it nat þe space of þe lif alto-gidre. for it ne haþ nat þe *futures* þat ne ben nat ȝit. ne it ne haþ no lenger þe *preterit*ȝ þat ben ydon or ypássed. but þilke þing þan þat haþ *and* comprehendiþ to-gidre alle þe plente of þe lif interminable. to whom þere ne failiþ nat of þe *future*. *and* to whom þer nis nat of þo *preterit* escapid nor ypassed. þilk[e] same is ywitnessed or yproued by ryȝt to ben eterne. and it byhoueþ by necessite þat þilke þinge be alwey p*re*sent to hym self *and* compotent. as who seiþ alwey p*re*sent to hym self a*nd* so myȝty þat al by ryȝt at hys plesaunce. *and* þat he haue al present þe infinit of þe moeuable tyme. wherfore som men trowe*n* wrongefully þat whan þei heren þat it semid[e] to plato þat þis worlde ne had[de] neuer bygynnynge of tyme. ne þat it neue*re* shal haue faylynge. þei wenen i*n* þis manere þat þis worlde ben maked coeterne wiþ his makere. as who seiþ. þei wenen þat þis worlde *and* god ben maked to-gidre eterne. and it is a wrongful wenynge. for oþer þing is it to ben yladd by lif interminable as plato graunted[e] to þe worlde. *and* oþer þing is it to embracen to-gidre alle þe presence to þe lif interminable. þe whiche þing it is clere *and* manifest

---

Whatever, therefore, is subjected to a temporal condition, as Aristotle thought of the world, may be without beginning and without end; and although its duration may extend [* fol. 39.] to an infinity of time, yet it cannot rightly be called eternal: for it doth not comprehend at once the whole extent of its infinite duration, having no knowledge of things future which are not yet arrived. For what is eternal must be always present to itself and master of itself, and have always with it the infinite succession of time. Therefore some philosophers, who had heard that

5011

Plato believed that this world had neither beginning nor end, falsely concluded, that the created universe was coeternal with its Creator. But it is one thing to be conducted through a life of infinite duration, which was Plato's opinion of the world, and another thing to comprehend at once the whole extent of this duration as present which, it is manifest, can only belong to the Divine mind. Nor ought it to seem to us that God is prior to and more ancient than his creatures by the space of

---

4997 a[l]þoughe—al-thogh
  [it]—from C.
4999 worlde—world
5001 swiche—swych
5002 eterne – from C., MS.
  eternite
5003 life—lyf
5004-5-6 haþ—MS. haþe
5006 ydon—MS. ydone, C. I-

doon
5007 alle—al
5008-9 nat—nawht
5010 þilk[e]—thilko
  or—and
5014 by—be
5016 semid[e]—semede
5017 worlde—world
  had[de]—hadde

5018 haue—han
5019-20 worlde—world
5022 yladd—MS. yladde, C. l-lad
5023 worlde—world
5024 embracen—enbrace
  alle—al
  presence to—present of
5025 clere—cleer

GOD IS ETERNAL.

þat it is propre to þe deuine þou3t. ne it ne sholde nat semen to vs þat god is elder þan þinges þat ben ymaked by quantite of tyme. but raþer by þe proprete of hys symple nature. for þis ilke infinit[e] moeuyng of temporel þinges folwiþ þis presentarie estat of þe lijf inmoeueable. *and* so as it ne may nat contrefeten it ne feynen it ne ben euene lyke to it. for þe inmoeueablete. þat is to seyn þat is *in* þe eternite of god. ¶ it faileþ *and* falleþ in to moeuynge fro þe simplicite of [the] presence of god. *and* disencresiþ to þe infinite quantite of future *and* of preterit. *and* so as it ne may nat han togidre al þe plente of þe lif. algates 3itte for as moche as it ne cesiþ neuere forto ben in som manere it semeþ somde[l] to vs þat it folwiþ *and* resembliþ þilke þing þat it ne may nat attayne to. ne fulfille. *and* byndeþ it self to som manere presence of þis litel *and* swifte moment. þe whiche presence of þis lytele *and* swifte moment. for þat it bereþ a manere ymage or lykenesse of þe ay dwellynge presence of god. it grauntep to swiche manere þinges as it bitidiþ to þat it semeþ hem þat þise þinges han ben *and* ben *and* for [þat] þe presence of swiche litel moment ne may nat dwelle þer-for [it] rauyssid[e] *and* took þe infinit[e] wey of tyme. þat is to seyn by successioun. *and* by þis manere it is ydon. for þat it sholde continue þe lif in goynge of þe whiche lif it ne my3t[e] nat embrace þe plente in dwellynge. *and* for þi yif we willen putte worþi name[s] to þinges *and* folwen plato. lat vs seyn þan soþely þat god is eterne. *and* þat þe worlde is perpetuel. þan syn þat euery iugement knoweþ *and* comprehendiþ by hys owen nature þinges þat ben subiect vnto hym. þere is soþely al-wey to god an eterne *and* presentarie estat. *and* þe

time, but rather by the simple and undivided properties of his nature. The infinite progression of temporel things imitates the ever-present condition of an immovable life: and since it cannot copy nor equal it from an immovable and simply present state, it passes into motion and into an infinite measure of past and future time. But since it cannot possess at once the whole extent of its duration, yet, as it never ceases wholly to be, it faintly emulates that whose perfection it can neither attain nor express, by attaching itself to 5041 the present fleeting moment, which, because it resembles the durable present time, imparts to those things that partake of it an appearance of existence. But as it cannot stop or abide it pursues its course through infinite time, and by gliding along it continues its duration, the plenitude of which it could not comprehend, by abiding in a permanent state. If we would follow Plato in giving things their right names, let us say that God is *eternal* and the world *perpetual*. His knowledge, surpassing the progression of time, is ever present, containing the infinite space

---

5032 *lyke*—lyk
5034 [*the*]—from C.
5039 *somde*[*l*]—somdel
5040 *fulfille*—fullfyllen
5041 *litel*—fr·m C., MS. lykly
5042 *whiche*—which
   lytele—from C., MS. lykly

5046 *ben* (1)—yben
   [*þat*]—from C.
5047 *swiche*—swych
5049 [*it*]—from C.
5051 *my3t*[*e*]—myhte
5052 *willen putte*—wollen putten

5052 *name*[*s*]—names
5053 *soþely*—sothly
5054 *worlde*—world
5055 *owen*—owne
5056 *soþely*—sothly
5057 *al-wey*—al-weys

DEFINITION OF PRESCIENCE. [BOOK 5. PROSE 6.

of past and future times, and embraces in his clear insight all things, as if they were now transacting. Prescience is, then, a foreknowledge, not of what is to come, but of the present and never-failing now (in which God [* fol. 39 b.] sees all things as if immovably present). Therefore foreknowledge is not so applicable a term as providence—for God looks down upon all things from the summit of the universe. Do you think that God imposes a necessity on things by beholding them? It is not so in human affairs. Does your view

5073 of an action lay any necessity upon it? B. No. P. By parity of reason it is clear that whilst you see only some things in a limited instant, God sees all things in his ever-present time. His Divine prescience therefore does not change the nature of things—but only beholds those things as present to him which shall in time be produced. Nor does he judge confusedly of them, but knows at one view what will necessarily and what will not necessarily happen. The eye of God, seeing all things, doth not alter the properties of things, for everything is present to him, though its temporal event is future.

science of hym þat ouer-passeþ alle temporel moe[ue]-ment dwelliþ in þe symplicite of hys presence *and* embraceþ *and* considereþ alle þe infinit spaces of tymes preteritȝ *and* futures *and* lokeþ in þis symple knowynge alle þinges of *preterit* ryȝt as þei weren ydoon presently ryȝt now ¶ yif þou wolt þan þenke *and* avise*n* þe prescience by whiche it knoweþ al[le] þinges *þou ne shalt nat demen it as prescience of þinges to comen. but þou shalt demen [it] more ryȝtfully þat it is science of presence or of instaunce þat neuer ne fayleþ. for whiche it nis nat ycleped prouidence but it sholde raþer be cleped purueaunce þat is establissed ful fer fro ryȝt lowe þinges. *and* byholdeþ from a-fer alle þinges ryȝt as it were fro þe heye heyȝte of þinges. whi axest þou þan or why disputest þou þan þat þilke þinges ben don by necessite whiche þat ben yseyen *and* yknowen by þe deuyne syȝt. syn þat for soþe men ne maken nat þilke þinges necessarie. whiche þat þe[i] seen be ydoon in hire syȝt. for addiþ þi byholdynge any necessite to þilke þinges þat þou byholdest present. ¶ Nay quod I. *p.* Certys þan yif men myȝte maken any digne comparisou*n* or collaciou*n* of þe presence diuine. *and* of þe presence of mankynde. ryȝt so as ȝe seen somme þinges in þis temporel presente. ryȝt so seeþ god alle þinges by hys eterne present. ¶ wherfore þis dyuyne prescience ne chaungeþ nat þe nature ne þe proprete of þinges but byholdeþ swyche þinges present to hym ward. as þei shollen bytiden to ȝow ward in tyme to come. ne it ne confoundeþ nat þe Iugementȝ of þinges but by of syȝt of hys þouȝt he knoweþ þe þinges to comen as wel necessarie as nat necessarie. ryȝt so as whan ȝe seen togidre a man walke on þe erþe *and* þe sonne arysen in [the] heuene. al be it so þat ȝe seen *and* byholden þat

---

5058 *alle*—al
  moe[ue]ment—moeuement
5063 *þenke*—thinken
  avisen—auyse
5064 *whiche*—which
  al[le]—alle

5066 *shalt*—shal
  (it)—from C.
5068 *whiche*—which
5074-76 *syȝt*—syhte
5075 *whiche*—which
  þe[i]—they

5085 *come*—comyn
5086 *of syȝt*—O syhte
5087 *he knoweþ*—MS. repeats
5090 *[the]*—from C.

oon *and* þat oþer to-gidre. ȝit naþeles ȝe demen *and* discerne þat þat oon is uoluntarie *and* þat oþer is necessarie. ¶ Ryȝt so þan [the] deuyne lokynge byholdynge alle þinges vndir hym ne troubleþ nat þe qualite of þinges þat ben certeynely pr*e*sent to hy*m* ward. but as to þe condici*ou*n of tyme for soþe þei ben futur*e*. for whiche it folwiþ þat þis nis non oppinioun. but raþer a stedfast knowyng ystrengeþed by soþenes. þat whan þat god knoweþ any þinge to be he ne vnwoot nat þat þilke þinge wanteþ necessite to be. þis is to seyn þat whan þat god knoweþ any þinge to bitide. he woot wel þat it ne haþ no necessite to bitide. *and* yif þou seist here þat þilke þinge þat god seeþ to bytide it ne may nat vnbytide. as who seiþ it mot bitide. ¶ and þilke þinge þat þat ne may nat vnbytide it mot bitide by necessite. and þat þou streine me to þis name of necessite. certys I wol wel confessen *and* byknowe a þinge of ful sadde trouþe. but vnneþ shal þere any wyȝt [mowe] seen it or comen þer-to. but yif þat he be byholder of þe deuyne þouȝte. ¶ for I wol answer*e* þe þus. þat þilke þinge þat is future whan it is referred to þe deuyne knowy*n*g þan is it necessarie. but certys whan it is vndirstonden in hys owen kynde me*n* sen it [is] vtterly fre *and* absolut from alle necessite. for certys þer ben two maneres of necessites. þat oon necessite is symple as þus. þat it byhoueþ by necessite þat alle men be mortal or dedely. an oþer necessite is condicionel as þus. yif þou wost þat a man walkiþ. it byhoueþ by necessite þat he walke. þilke þinge þan þat any wyȝt haþ yknowe to be. it ne may ben non oþer weyes þan he knoweþ it to be. ¶ but þis condicioun ne draweþ nat wiþ hir þilke necessite symple. For certys þis necessite condicionel.

When God knows that anything is to be, he knows at the same time that it is not under the necessity of being —but this is not conjecture, but certain knowledge founded upon truth. If you insist that *what God foresees shall and must happen*; *and that which cannot do otherwise than happen, must needs happen*, and so bind me to admit a necessity, I must confess that things are under such a restraint; but it is a truth that we scarce can comprehend, unless we be acquainted with the Divine counsels. For I will answer you thus. That the thing which is to happen in relation to the Divine knowledge is necessary; but, considered in its own nature, seems free and absolute. There are two kinds of necessity—one simple; as men must necessarily die—the other is conditional, as if you know a man walks he must necessarily walk —for that which is known cannot be otherwise than what it is apprehended to be. But this condition does not infer the absolute necessity, for the nature of the thing itself does not here constitute the necessity, but the necessity arises from the conjunction of the condition. No necessity compels a man to walk who does so

5092 *discerne*—discernen
5093 [*the*]—from C.
5097 *whiche*—which
5098 *stedfast*—stidefast
  soþenes—sothnesse
5102 *haþ*—MS. haþe
5104 *bitide*—bide

5108 *sadde*—sad
  vnneþ—vnnethe
  [*mowe*]—from C.
5109 *comen*—come
5110 þouȝte—thoght
  answere—answeren
5113 *sen*—MS. sene, C. sen

5113 [*is*]—from C.
5117 *dedely*—dedly
5119 *haþ*—MS. haþe
5121 *condicioun* — from C., MS. *necessite*

þe propre nature of it ne makeþ it nauȝt. but þe adieccioun of þe condicioun makiþ it. for no necessite ne constreyneþ a man to [gon / þat] gooþ by his propre wille. al be it so þat whan he gooþ þat it is necessarie þat he gooþ. ¶ Ryȝt on þis same manere þan. yif þat þe purucaunce of god seeþ any þing present. þan mot þilke *þinge be by necessite. al þouȝ þat it ne haue no necessite of hys owen nature. but certys þe futures þat bytyden by fredom of arbitre god seeþ hem alle to-gidre presentȝ. þise þinges þan [yif] þei ben referred to þe deuyne syȝt. þan ben þei maked necessarie to þe condicioun of þe deuyne knowynge. but certys yif þilke þinges ben considred by hem self þei ben absolut of necessite. and ne forleten nat ne cesen nat of þe liberte of hire owen nature. þan certys wiþ outen doute alle þe þingus shollen be doon whiche þat god woot by-forn þat þei ben to comen. but somme of hem comen and bitiden of [free] arbitre or of fre wille. þat al be it so þat þei bytiden. ȝit algates ne lese þei nat hire propre nature ne beynge. by þe whiche first or þat þei were doon þei hadden power nat to han bitidd. Boece. what is þis to seyn þan qŭod I. þat þinges ne ben nat necessarie by hire propre nature. so as þei comen in alle maneres in þe lykenesse of necessite by þe condicioun of þe deuyne science. Philosophie. þis is þe difference quod she. þat þo þinges þat I purposed[e] þe a litel here byforn. þat is to seyn þe sonne arysynge and þe man walkynge þat þerwhiles þat þilke þinges ben ydon. þei ne myȝten nat ben vndon. naþeles þat oon of hem or it was ydon it byhoued[e] by necessite þat it was ydon. but nat þat oþer. ryȝt so it is here þat þe þinges þat god haþ present.

5123 nauȝt—nat
5125 [gon þat]—from C.
    wille—wil
5128 mot—MS. mote, C. mot
5131 presentȝ—present
5132 [yif]—from C.
    syȝt—syhte
5137 wiþ outen—with-owte
5138 whiche—which

5139 somme—som
5140 [free]—from C.
5141 ne (2)—C. in
5142 whiche—which
    were doon—weeryn Idoon
5143 bitidd—MS. bitidde, C. bityd
5148 purposed[e] — pur posede

5150 ydon—MS. ydone, C. 1-doon
    myȝten—myhte
5151 vndon—MS. vndone, C. vndoon
5151-2 ydon—MS. ydone, C. 1-doon
5152 byhoued[e]—houyd
5153 haþ—MS. haþe

wiþ outen doute þei shulle ben. but somme of hem descendiþ of þe nature of þinges as þe sonne arysynge. *and* somme descendiþ of þe power of þe doers as þe man walkynge. ¶ þan seide I. no wronge þat yif þat þise þinges ben referred to þe deuyne knowynge þan ben þei necessarie. *and* yif þei ben considered by hem selfe þan ben þei absolut from þe bonde of necessite. ry3t so [as] alle þinges þat appiereþ or sheweþ to þe wittes yif þou referre it to resoun it is vniuersel. *and* yif þou referre it or look[e] it to it self. þan is it synguler. but now yif þou seist þus þat yif it be in my power to chaunge my pu*r*pose. þan shal I voide þe pu*r*ueaunce of god. whan þat pe*r*auenture I shal han chaunged þo þinges þat he knoweþ byforn. þan shal I answere þe þus ¶ Certys þou maist wel chaungen þi pu*r*pos but for as mochel as þe present sopenesse of þe deuyne pu*r*ueaunce byholdeþ þat þou mayst chaungen þi pu*r*pose. *and* whepir þou wolt chaunge it or no. *and* whider-ward þat þou tourne it. þou maist nat eschewen þe deuyne prescience ry3t as þou ne mayst nat fleen þe sy3t of þe present eye. al þou3 þat þou tourne þi self by þi fre wille in to dyue*r*se accioun. ¶ But þou mayst seyn a3eyne how shal it þan be. shal nat þe dyuyne science ben chaunged by my disposicioun whan þat I wol o þing now *and* now an oþer. *and* þilke prescience ne semeþ it nat to enterchaunge stoundes of knowynges. as who seiþ. ne shal it nat seme to vs þat þe deuyne prescience enterchaungeþ hys dyuers stoundes of knowynge. so þat it knowe somme tyme o þing *and* somme tyme þe contrarie. ¶ No for soþe. [*quod* I] for þe deuyne sy3t renneþ to-forne *and* seeþ alle futu*r*es *and* clepeþ hem a3ein

truth when I said that some things referred to the Divine knowledge are necessary, while considered in themselves they are not under the bond of necessity. In the same way everything that is an object of sense is *general* when considered in relation to reason—but particular when considered by itself. But you may say—If I am able to change my purpose I can deceive providence by changing that which she hath foreseen I would do.

P. You may perhaps alter your purpose—but as providence takes note of your intentions, you cannot deceive her; for you cannot escape the divine prescience though you have the power, through a free-will, to vary and diversify your actions. But you may say—Shall the divine knowledge be changed according to the mutability of my disposition, and the apprehensions of the Deity fluctuated with my changing purposes? No, indeed! The view of the Deity foreruns every future event, and brings it back into the presence of his own knowledge, which does not vary, as you imagine, to conform to your caprices, but remaining fixed, at once

---

5154 *wiþ outen*—with-owte
shulle—shollen
5156 *doers*—doeres
5157 *wronge*—wrong
5159 *selfe*—self
5160 *from*—fro
  bonde—bond
  [*as*]—from C.

5163 *look*[*e*]—loke
5166 *þo*—the
5169 *soþenesse*—sothnesse
5170 *chaungen*—chaunge
5173 *sy3t*—syhte
5175 *wille*—wyl
5177 *wol*—wole
5179 *enterchaunge*—MS. en-

terchaungyng, C. entrechaunge
5181 *hys*—hise
5182 *somme* (1)—slim
  somme (2)—som
5183 *sy3t*—syhte
5184 *to-forne*—to-forn

GOD'S KNOWLEDGE FIXED AND UNCHANGED. [BOOK 5. PROSE 6.

foresees and comprehends all your changes. This faculty of comprehending and seeing all things as present, God does not receive from the issue of futurities, but from the simplicity of his own nature. Here, then, is an answer to your former objection—that it is folly to think that our future actions and events are the causes of the prescience of God. For the Divine mind, em-
[* fol. 41 b.]
bracing and comprehending all things by a present knowledge, plans and directs all things and is not dependent upon futurity. Since no necessity is imposed

5200
upon things by the Divine prescience, there remains to men an inviolable freedom of will. And those laws are just which assign rewards and punishments to men possessing free-will. Moreover, God, who sits on high, foreknows all things, and the eternal presence of his knowledge concurs with the future quality of our actions, dispensing rewards to good and punishments to evil men. Nor are our hopes and prayers reposed in, and addressed to God in vain, which when they are sincere cannot be inefficacious nor unsuccessful. Resist and turn from vice—honour and

and retourniþ hem to þe presence of hys propre knowynge. ne he ne entrechaungeþ nat [so] as þou wenest þe stoundes of forknowyng [as] now þis now þat. but he ay dwellynge comiþ byforn *and* enbraceþ at o strook alle þi mutaciouns. and þis presence to comprehenden *and* to sen alle þinges. god ne haþ nat taken it of þe bitydynge of þinges forto come. but of hys propre symplicite. ¶ and her by is assoiled þilke þing þat þou puttest a litel her byforne. þat is to seyne þat it is vnworþi þinge to seyn þat oure futures ȝeuen cause of þe science of god ¶ For *certys* *þis strengþe of þe deuyne science whiche þat enbraceþ alle þinge by his presentarie knowynge establisseþ manere to alle þingus *and* it ne awiþ nat to lattere þinges. *and* syn þat þise þinges ben þus. þat is to seyn syn þat necessite nis nat in þinges by þe deuyne prescience. þan is þer fredom of arbitre. þat dwelleþ hool *and* vnwemmed to mortal men. ne þe lawes ne *purpose* nat wikkedly meedes *and* peynes to þe willynges of men þat ben vnbounde *and* quit of alle necessite. ¶ And god byholder *and* forwiter of alle þinges dwelliþ aboue *and* þe present eternite of hys syȝt renneþ alwey wiþ þe dyuerse qualite of oure dedes dispensyng *and* ordeynynge medes to good[e] men. *and* tourmentȝ to wicked men. ne in ydel ne in veyn ne ben þer nat put in god hope *and* prayeres. þat ne mowen nat ben vnspedful ne wiþ oute effect whan þei ben ryȝtful ¶ wiþstond þan *and* eschewe þou vices. worshippe *and* loue þou vertus. areise þi corage to ryȝtful hoopes. ȝelde þou humble *preiers* an heyȝe. grete necessite of prowesse *and* vertue is encharged *and* comaunded to ȝow yif ȝe nil nat dissimulen. ¶ Syn þat ȝe worchen *and* doon. þat is to seyn ȝoure dedes *and* ȝoure workes

5186 [*so*]—from C.
5187 [*as*]—from C.
5188 *comiþ*—comth
5190 *haþ*—MS. haþe
5193 *seyne*—seyn
5196 *whiche*—which
5198 *awiþ*—oweth

5199 *þat is to —— prescience*—omitted
5203 *vnbounde*—vnbownden *quit*—quite
5206 *syȝt*—sihte
5207 *good[e]*—goode
5211 *wiþstond* — MS. wiþ-

stonde, C. withstond
5213 *an heyȝe*—a heyȝh *grete*—Gret
5215 *worchen*—workyn
5216 *and* (2)—or

by-fore þe eyen of þe Iuge þat seeþ *and demeþ* alle love virtue, exalt your mind to God
þinges. [To whom be goye *and* worshipe bi Infynyt (the truest hope), offer up your
tymes / AMEN.] 5219 prayers with humility. If you
are sincere you
will feel that you are under an obligation to lead a good and virtuous life, inasmuch as all your
actions and works are done in the presence of an all-discerning Judge.

EXPLICIT LIBER QUINTUS. *ET VLTIMUS.*

5217 *by-fore*—by-forn	ends with the following	Finito libro sit laus *et*
5218 [*To whom——Amen*]—	rubric:	gloria *Christo*
from C.; MS. reads *et*	Explicit expliceat ludere	Corpore scribentis sit
cetera after 'þinges.' C.	scriptor eat	*gratia* cunctipotentis

APPENDIX.

[*Camb. Univ. MS.* Ii. 3. 21, *fol.* 52 *b.*]

Chawcer vp-on this fyfte metur of the second book

A Blysful lyf a paysyble *and* a swete
Ledden the poeples in the former age
They helde hem paied of the fructes þat þey ete
Whiche þat the feldes yaue hem by vsage   4
They ne weere nat forpampred wit*h* owtrage
Onknowyn was þ*e* quyerne *and* ek the melle
They eten mast hawes *and* swych pownage
And dronken wat*er* of the colde welle   8

¶ Yit nas the grownd nat wownded wit*h* þ*e* plowh
But corn vp-sprong vnsowe of mannes hond
þe which they gnodded *and* eete nat half .I.-nowh
No man yit knewe the forwes of his lond   12
No man the fyr owt of the flynt yit fonde
Vn-koruen and vn-grobbed lay the vyne
No man yit in the morter spices grond
To clarre ne to sawse of galentyne   16

¶ No Madyr welde or wod no litestere
Ne knewh / the fles was of is former hewe
No flessh ne wyste offence of egge or spere
No coyn ne knewh man which is fals or trewe   20
No ship yit karf the wawes grene *and* blewe
No Marchau*n*t yit ne fette owt-landissh ware
No batails trompes for the werres folk ne knewe
Ne towres heye *and* walles rownde or square   24

¶ What sholde it han avayled to werreye
Ther lay no profyt ther was no rychesse
But corsed was the tyme .I. dar' wel seye   [fol. 53.]
þat men fyrst dede hir swety bysynesse   28
To grobbe vp metal lurkynge in dirkenesse
And in þe Ryuerys fyrst gemmys sowhte
Allas than sprong' vp al the cursydnesse
Of coueytyse þat fyrst owr sorwe browhte   32

¶ Thyse tyrauntȝ put hem gladly nat in pres
No places wyldnesse ne no busshes for to wynne
Ther pouerte is as scith diogenes
Ther as vitayle ek is so skars and thinne   36
þat nat but mast or apples is ther Inne
But þer as bagges ben and fat vitaile
Ther wol they gon and spare for no synne
With al hir ost the Cyte forto a-sayle   40

¶ Yit was no paleis chaumbres ne non halles
In kaues and wodes softe and swete
Sleptin this blyssed folk' with-owte walles
On gras or leues in parfyt Ioye reste and quiete   44
No down of fetheres ne no bleched shete
Was kyd to hem but in surte they slepte
Hir hertes weere al on with-owte galles
Euerych of hem his feith to oother kepte   48

¶ Vnforged was the hawberke and the plate
þᵉ lambyssh poeple voyded of alle vyse
Hadden no fantesye to debate
But eche of hem wolde oother wel cheryce   52
No pride non enuye non Auaryce
No lord no taylage by no tyranye
Vmblesse and pes good feith the emperice
. . . .   56

39, 40 MS. transposes the lines   44 *On*—MS. Or
56 A line omitted, but no gap left for one.

¶ Yit was nat Iuppiter the lykerous
þat fyrst was fadyr of delicasie
Come in this world ne nembroth desyrous
To regne had nat maad his towres hye   60
Allas allas now may [men] wepe And crye
For in owre dayes nis but couetyse
Dowblenesse and tresoun and enuye
Poyson and manslawhtre and mordre in sondry wyse

      CAUSER / BALADES DE VILAGE SANZ PEINTURE

¶ This wrecched worlde-is transmutacioun
As wele / or wo / now poeere and now honour
With-owten ordyr or wis descresyoun
Gouerned is by fortunes errour   4
But natheles the lakke of hyr fauowr'
Ne may nat don me syngen thowh I. deye
Iay tout perdu moun temps et moun labour   [fol. 53 b.]
For fynaly fortune .I. the deffye   8

¶ Yit is me left the lyht of my resoun
To knowen frend fro foo in thi merowr'
So mochel hath yit thy whirlynge vp and down
I-tawht me for to knowe in an howr   12
But trewely no fors of thi reddowr'
To hym þat ouer hym self hath the maystrye
My suffysaunce shal be my socour'
For fynaly fortune I. thee deffye   16

¶ O socrates þou stidfast chaumpyoun
She neuer myht[e] be thi tormentowr
Thow neuer dreddest hyr oppressyoun
Ne in hyr chere fownde thow no sauour'   20
Thow knewe wel the descyte of hyr colour'
And þat hir' most[e] worshipe is to lye
I knew hir ek a fals dissimulour'
For fynaly fortune .I. the deffye   24

LE RESPOUNCE DE FORTUNE A PLEINTIF.

¶ No man ys wrechchyd but hym self yt wene
And he þat hath hym self hat suffisaunce
Whi seysthow thanne y am [to] the so kene
þat hast thy self owt of my gouernaunce   28
Sey thus graunt mercy of thyn haboundaunce
That thow hast lent or this why wolt þou stryue
What woost thow yit how y the wol auaunce
And ek thow hast thy beste frende a-lyue   32

¶ I haue the tawht deuisyoun by-twene
Frend of effect' and frende of cowntenaunce
The nedeth nat the galle of no hyene
þat cureth eyen derkyd for penaunce   36
Now se[st] thow cleer þat weere in ignoraunce
Yit halt thin ancre and yit thow mayst aryue
Ther bownte berth the keye of my substaunce
And ek þou hast thy beste frende alyue   40

¶ How manye haue .I. refused to sustigne
Syn .I. the fostred haue in thy plesaunce
Wolthow thanne make a statute on þy quyene
þat .I. shal ben ay at thy ordynaunce   44
Thow born art in my regne of varyaunce
Abowte the wheel with oother most thow dryue
My loore is bet than wikke is thi greuaunce
And ek þou hast thy beste frende a-lyue   48

LE RESPOUNCE DU PLEINTIF COUNTRE FORTUNE.

¶ Thy loore y dempne / it is aduersyte   [fol. 54.]
My frend maysthow nat reuen blynde goddesse
þat .I. thy frendes knowe .I. thanke to the
Tak hem agayn / lat hem go lye on presse   52
The negardye in kepynge hyr rychesse
Prenostik is thow wolt hir' towr' asayle

---

37 se[st]—partly erased and ist written on it in a later hand.
41 igne of sustigne is in a later hand.

Wikke appetyt comth ay before sykenesse
In general this rewle may nat fayle . 56

LE RESPOUNCE DE FORTUNE COUNTRE LE PLEINTIF

¶ Thow pynchest at my mutabylyte
For .I. the lente a drope of my rychesse
And now me lykyth to w*ith*-drawe me
Whi sholdysthow my realte ap*r*esse 60
The see may ebbe *and* flowen moore or lesse
The welkne hath myht to shyne reyne or hayle
Ryht so mot .I. kythen my brutelnesse
In general this rewle may nat fayle 64

LE PLEINTIF

¶ Lo excussyou*n* of the maieste
þ*a*t al purueyeth of his ryhtwysnesse
That same thinge fortune clepyn ye
Ye blynde beestys ful of lewednesse 68
The heuene hath p*ro*prete of sykyrnesse
This world hath eu*er* resteles trauayle
Thy laste day is ende of myn inter[e]sse
In general this rewele may nat fayle 72

LENUOY DE FORTUNE

¶ Prynses .I. prey yow of yowr*e* gentilesses
Lat nat this man on me thus crye *and* pleyne
And .I. shal quyte yow yowr*e* bysynesse
At my requeste as thre of yow or tweyne 76
þ*a*t but yow lest releue hym of hys peyne
Preyeth hys best frend of his noblesse
That to som beter*e* est*a*t he may attayne

GLOSSARIAL INDEX.

ABAIST = ABYEST, sufferest, endurest, 39/1014
ABAIST, abashed, 107/3047
ABASSEN, to be abashed, dismayed, 146/4213
ABESID (= ABAYSSHED), abashed, 7/92
ABIDE, to await, 7/93. 'ABIDE after' = look after, expect, 13/250; *p.p.* ABIDEN, waited, 86/2405
Abieþ, suffers, 109/3101
ABLYNGE, enabling, fitting (*aptans*), 26/624, 38/2440
Abood, abode, 63/1716
Aboven, above, 6/52
Abreggynge, curtailing; hence *gain* obtained by curtailment (*compendium*), 151/4355
Accoie, to soothe, quiet (*demulcere*), 38/967
Accordaunce, agreement, 143/4134
Accordaunt, agreeing, unanimous, 19/431
Accorde, to agree, 42/1080
Accoumpte, account, 47/1251
Accountyng, calculation, 8/110
Achat, purchase, 15/310
Acheve, to achieve, accomplish, 18/404
Achoken, to choke, 47/1235

Acomplise, Acomplisse, to accomplish, 92/2575, 118/3356
Acordable, agreeing, 62/1694
Acusor, informer, 72/1990
Addre (Nadre), adder, 170/4959
Adoune, down, downward, 7/92
Adounward, downwards, 7/87
Adrad, in fear, afraid, 43/1132
Adresse, to direct, control, 163/4721
Afer, afar, 164/4767
Agast, aghast, frightened, 76/2107
Agaste, to terrify, frighten, 141/4051
Agon, ago, 70/1907
Agreablete, goodwill, 42/1099
Agrisen, to be afraid, dread, 10/178, 31/777
Ajuge, to adjudge, 15/325
Aknowe, acknowledged, 17/367
Aldirmost, most of all, 124/3557
Algates, Algate, yet, nevertheless, 19/439, 68/1849, 81/2242, 162/4696, 4698
Allegge, to alleviate, 124/3529
Alouterly, utterly, entirely, 109/3090
Alþerfairest, fairest of all, 87/2422

Alþerfirst, first of all, 10/180
Alþermoste, most of all, 158/4563
Alþerworste, worst of all. 157/4562
Alyene, to alienate, 27/671
Amenuse, to lessen, diminish, 19/426, 40/1039
Amenusynge, diminution, 46/1192
Ameve, Amoeve, Amove, to move, 6/64, 23/551
Amoneste, to admonish, 171/4971
Amonestyng, admonition, exhortation, 149/4296
Amongus, amongst, 52/1380
Amonicioun, admonition, 13/253
Amynistre, to administer, 135/3891
Ancre, anchor, 41/1050
Angre, grief, misery, 41/1072
Anguisse, Angysse, anguish, 79/2177; to torment, 80/2198
Anguissous, anxious, sorrowful, 41/1062, 1606
Anoie, to be grieved, be sorry, 41/1058
Anoienge, 22/532
Anoies, hurtful, 47/1238
Anoious, annoying, hurtful, 7/102
An-oone, anon, 42/1086
Anoyously, dangerously, hurtfully, 80/2214
Apaise, to appease, 148/4278
Apasse, to pass away, go, 46/1195
Aperceive, to perceive, 16/344, 134/3845
Apertly, plainly, 17/386, 91/2543
Appaie, to please, satisfy, 47/1235
Appaire, to impair, 25/597
Apparaile, to clothe, adorn, 8/116
Apparaillement, clothing, ornament, 49/1300

Appertiene, to appertain, 73/1996
Applien, bend to, join, 161/4660
Apresse, to oppress, 184/60
Aprochen, to approach, 6/63, 66
Arace, Arase, Arrace, to tear, tear from, separate, 11/196, 27/671, 98/2774, 152/4278
Araise, Areise, Areyse, to raise, 51/1357, 118/3369, 178/5212
Arbitre, will, free will, 156/4500
Ardaunt, ardent, 106/3031
Aresten, to stop, arrest, 32/815
Aretten, to ascribe to, impute to, 40/1016
Arist, arises, 143/4138
Armurers, armours, arms, 51/1342
Armures, armour, 9/131
Arst, first, 95/2675
Arwe, arrow, 148/4262
Arysynge, rising, 22/512
Aryve, to bring to shore, 122/3479
Asayle, to assail, 181/40
Ascape, to escape, 8/129
Asondre, asunder, 64/1740
Aspre, sharp, rough, 32/806, 80/2216
Asprenesse, sharpness, 127/3627
Assaie, to essay, 42/1083
Assemble, to gather together, amass (money), 80/2203
Asseure, to assure, 16/330
Assoilen, to absolve, pay, unloose, dissolve, 149/4303, 154/4459
Astat, estate, state, 30/738
Astoned, astonished, 7/92, 63/1702; *stupidus*, 122/3471
Astonynge, Astonyenge, astonishment, 9/134, 132/3780
Ataste, to taste, 30/756
Ataynt, Ateint, attained, knowing, experienced, 31/772, 69/1905

Attayne, to reach, 12/227
Atte, at the, 95/2675
Attemperaunce, tempering, temperament, 138/3973, 144/4145
Attempre, to temper, moderate, 8/115, 111/3154; control, 163/4721; (*adj.*) modest, 29/728, 40/1033
Atteyne, to attain, 118/3358
Atwyne, in two, 98/2769
Avalen, to fall down, 143/4139
Avaunce, to advance, further, 41/1057
Avaunte, to boast, 5/26, 19/426
Auctorité, authority, 7/91
Aventerouse, fortuitous, 28/697, 40/1018
Aventure, event, 21/476
Autour, author, 58/1556
Auʒte, ought, 11/213
Avisen, to consider, 174/5063
Awaite, snare, 80/2214
Awaitour, one who lies in wait, 121/3463
Awiþ = aweþ, oweth (*debet*), 178/5198
Ay, ever, 184/55
Ay-dwellynge, ever-dwelling, 173/5044
Ayenis, against, 97/2749
Axe, to ask, 17/357, 24/579
Aʒeins, Aʒeynes, Aʒeynest, against, 10/183, 11/194, 12/221, 13/255
Aʒeinewarde, on the contrary, on the other hand, 42/1098

Bacine, basin, 133/3806
Batailen, to war on, do battle against, 18/412
Been, bees, 80/2200
Ber, did bear, 6/61
Bere, Bear, 143/4124

Beren on hond, to accuse falsely, 20/449
Bet, better, 63/1703
Bibled, covered over with blood, 48/1860
Bisien, to trouble, 8/112
Bitake. *See* Bytake.
Bitidd, happened, 176/5143
Bitwixen. *See* Bytwixen.
Blaundissinge, flattering, 30/749
Blaundyshing, flattery, blandishment, 34/866
Bleched, bleached, 181/45
Blemisse, to blemish, abuse (*lacero*), 20/472
Blyssed, blessed, 181/43
Blyþenesse, joyfulness, 37/957
Boch, botch, blain, sore, 72/1977
Bode, to foretell, 143/4130
Bole, bull, 148/4274
Boot, did bite, 53/1400
Bordure, border, hem, 6/50
Bosten, to boast, 79/2171
Botme, bottom, 12/234
Bounté, Bownté, goodness, kindness, 19/444, 46/1202, 183/39
Brenne (*pret*. Brende), to burn, 19/437, 106/3031
Brid, bird, 68/1867
Bristlede, bristly, 148/4281
Brode, broadly, plainly, 49/1298
Brutel, brittle, fragile, 45/1174
Brutelnesse, brittleness, frailty, 184/63
Burþe, birth, 78/2165
Busshel (corn), 15/312
Bydolven (*p.p.*), buried, 151/4348
Byen (for *abyen*), suffer, 125/3578
Byforen, BYFORN, BYFORNE, before, 20/454

Bygunne, didst begin, 37/941
Bygyle, to beguile, 25/615
Byhate, to hate, 75/2051
Byheste, promise, 149/4303
Byhete, to promise, 61/1651, 69/1903
Byhynde, Byhynden, behind, 108/3062, 110/3137
Byhyʒt, promised, 70/1925, 85/2374, 157/4558
Byknowen, Byknowe, to acknowledge, 146/4211, 175/5107; *p.p.* Byknowen, 90/2514
Byleve, believe, 28/695
Byname, an additional name, 84/2333
Byneþen, beneath, 49/1295
Bynomen (*p.p.*), taken from, 124/3527
Bynyme, to deprive of, take away, 43/1117, 70/1930
Byreft, bereft, 33/837
Byseche, to beseech, 86/2408
Bysmoked, besmoked, 5/49
Byspotte, to defile, 73/2009
Bystowe, to bestow, 24/585
Bysynesse, toil, 184/75
Bytake, to entrust, 32/808
Bytide (*pret.* BYTIDDE, *p.p.* BYTID), to befall, happen, 20/474, 151/4360, 155/4467
Bytwene, between, 6/54
Bytwixen, betwixt, 132/3785
Bytynge, biting, sharp, 63/1721
Bywepe, to weep for, 26/644
Byweyle, to bewail, 26/643

Caitif, Caytif, wretched, 21/489, 116/3289
Careyne, carcase, corpse, 116/3307
Cariages, taxes (*vectigalia*), 15/303
Celebrable, commendable, noted, 84/2320, 147/4257
Certein, certain, 170/4952
Cese, to cease, 36/904, 130/3716
Cesse, to cease, 133/3821
Chalenge, to claim, 52/1380
Chastie, Chastysen, to chastise, 125/3579, 145/4170
Chayere, chair, seat, 21/503
Cheminey, furnace (*caminus*), 12/236
Cheryce, to cherish, 181/52
Chesen, to choose, 76/2096
Cheyn, chain, 8/122
Chiere, CHERE, CHOERE, face, countenance, 8/123, 12/232, 108/3080
Chirkynge, groaning (*stridens*), 25/618
Clarré, a kind of wine, 50/1329
Cleer, serene, 45/1168
Clepe, to call, 4/17, 11/188, 17/369
Clifte, fissure, cleft, 130/3721
Cliven, CLIVE, to stick, cling, adhere to, 41/1050, 101/2858, 159/4600
Cloumben = CLOMBEN, climbed, ascended, 57/1533
Coempcioun, coemption, 15/309
Coeterne, coeternal, 172/5019
Colasioun, collation, 125/3569
Collacioun, comparison, 165/4805
Combred, troubled, 94/2642
Commoove, to move, 107/3043
Commoevyng, moving (*excitans*), 12/233
Communalité, commonwealth, 14/271, 142/4108
Comparisoune, to compare, 58/1567
Complyssen, to accomplish, 124/3534

GLOSSARIAL INDEX.

189

Compotent, having the mastery (*compos*), 172/5012
Compoune, to compose, form, 87/2419, 93/2598
Comprende, comprehend, 165/4807
Comunableté, commonwealth, 13/268
Comune, common, 9/140, 15/310
Confederacie, conspiracy, 53/1399
Confus, confused, 132/3788
Conjecte, to conjecture, 27/649, 114/3230
Conjoignen, to join, 92/2573
Conjuracioun, conspiracy, 18/394, 53/1399
Consequente, consequence, 84/2323
Constreyne, to constrain, contract, 5/38
Consuler (CONSEILER), consul, 51/1364, 1366
Consumpt (*consumptus*), consumed, 60/1632
Contek, contest, strife, 130/3745
Contene, Contienen, to contain, comprehend, 24/573, 116/3302
Contrarien, to be opposed to, adverse to, 154/4440
Contrarious, adverse, opposite, 21/488, 53/1420
Contrefeten, to counterfeit, 173/5031
Convenably, fitly, conveniently, 142/4089
Convict, convicted, 19/440
Cop, top, summit, 44/1159
Corage, mind, spirit, 118/3367, 119/3398
Corige, to correct, 125/3581
Corompe, Corrumpe, to become corrupt, 98/2766, 96/2697
Corone, Coroune, a crown, 119/3385, 91/2555

Corsed, cursed, 181/27
Corsednesse, cursedness, 90/2526
Corumpynge, corruption, 103/2927
Cosyne, cousin, 106/3020
Couche, to lay, set, 35/890
Coupable, guilty, 10/172
Couth, known, 25/592
Coveite, to covet, 51/1365
Covenable, fit, convenient, 97/2731
Covertour, Coverture, covering, 118/3361, 159/4622
Covetise, Coveytyse, covetousness, 20/451, 181/32
Covine, deceit, collusion, 21/493
Coyn, money, 180/20
Creat, created, 99/2796
Crike, creek, 82/2260
Croppe, top, 69/1877
Curacioun, cure (*curatio*), 26/632
Curage, 30/753. See Corage.
Cure, care, 64/1753

Dalf (*pret*. of *delven*), dug, delved, 51/1349
Damoisel, damsel, 30/762
Dampnacioun, condemnation, 16/352
Daunten, Dawnte, to subdue, daunt, 77/2115, 147/4258
Debonairly, mildly, 122/3490
Deboneire, gentle (*mitis*), 22/519; good, 88/2450
Deceivable, deceptive, 77/2124
Dede, did, 181/28
Dedid, made dead, 127/3623
Deef, deaf, 4/18
Deere, dear, 37/941
Deeþ, death, 4/15

Defaute, fault, defect, 18/402
Defende, to forbid, 34/859
Defleted, enfeebled, weakened 30/735
Defoule, to defile, 21/491, 68/1873
Degrees, steps, 6/54
Delices, delight, delights (*deliciæ*), 38/968, 41/1062, 66/1787
Delitable, delectable, 30/756
Delitably, delightfully, 108/3078
Delve, should dig, 151/4352
Delver, a digger, 151/4359
Delyé, thin, fine, 5/43. Fr. *délié*.
Dempne, to condemn, 183/49
Denoye, to deny, 88/2464
Departe, to separate, 29/719
Depelyche, deeply, 160/4647
Depeynte, to depict, 111/3146
Depper, deeper, 27/649
Derke, Derken, to darken, 7/90, 20/448
Derworþe, Derworþi, precious, 31/787, 41/1046
Desarmen, disarm, 13/241
Desceivaunce, deception, 81/2240
Desceive, Desseive, to deceive, 9/141, 38/967
Descryven, to describe, 99/2813
Desmaie, to dismay, 35/896
Desordene, inordinate, 36/912
Despoylynge, spoil, prey, 147/4259
Destempraunce, · severity, 97/2749
Destinal, fatal, 135/3884
Destourbe, disturb, 143/4123
Destrat, distracted, 80/2216
Destreine, to constrain, bind, 54/1441
Diffinisse, to define, 88/2459, 165/4808

Digne, worthy, just, 43/1124, 149/4297
Digneliche, worthily, 53/1427
Dirke, dark, 83/2306
Dirke, Dirken, to make dark, darken, 5/48, 49
Dirkenesse, darkness, 23/535
Disceyvable, deceptive, 4/23
Discordable, discordant, 143/4133
Discorde, to disagree, 94/2632, 102/2898
Discordyng, disagreeing, discordant, 68/1849
Discours, judgment, reason, 165/4804
Discressioun, discretion, 93/2594
Discussed, dispersed, scattered, 9/149
Disdaignen, to disdain (*indignari*), 146/4213
Disencrese, to decrease, 173/5035
Disordinaunce, disorder, 150/4324
Dispenden, to spend, expend, 45/1181
Dispone, to dispose, 135/3864
Disputisoun, disputation, 149/4314
Disseveraunce, separation, 96/2701
Dissimulen, to dissemble, 178/5215
Distempre, intemperate, 121/3466
Distingwed, distinguished, 47/1223
Dité, ditty, 134/3850
Divinour, diviner, 157/4541
Domesman, judge, 55/1467
Doom, judgment, 152/4395
Doumbe, dumb, 9/138
Doutous, Dowtos, doubtful, 5/37
Dowblenesse, duplicity, 182/63
Drede, dread, 21/497

GLOSSARIAL INDEX. 191

Dredeful, timid, 121/3468
Dredles, fearless, 106/3028
Dreint, Dreynt, drowned, drenched, 4/22, 7/99, 148/4271
Dresse, to direct, order, 137/3954, 142/4104
Drouppe, to drop, 20/455
Drow, drew, 15/300
Duely, duly, 22/530
Dulle, to become dull, 7/100
Dure, Duren, to last, 98/2755
Duske, to make dusk or dim, 5/48
Dyverses (*pl.*), divers, 8/120
Dyvynynge, divination, 157/4541

Echid, increased, 77/2134
Echynnys, sea-urchins, 82/2266
Egalité, equality, evenness (of mind), 42/1099
Egaly, equally, evenly, 43/1108, 157/4536
Egge, edge, 180/19
Egre, sharp, 25/610
Egren, to urge, excite, 141/4060
Eir, air, 45/1169
Ek, Eke, also, 40/1040, 181/36
Elde, old age, 5/48
Eldefadir, grandfather, 40/1042
Elder, older, 89/2493
Embelise, to embellish, 47/1223
Emperie, government, 51/1363
Emperisse, empress, 109/3098
Empoysenyng, poisoning, 11/206 (*venenum*).
Emprente, to imprint, 166/4839
Emprenten, obtain (translates the Latin, *impetrent*), 159/4596. Perhaps a mistake for *empetren*.
Emptid, exhausted, 5/34
Enbaissynge, a debasing, 109/3107
Enbrase, embrace, 142/4092

Enchaufen, to make hot, *chafe*, 73/2020
Encharge, to impose, 178/5214
Enchaunteresse, enchantress, 123/3504
Endamagen, to damage, 15/316
Endirken, to obscure, 120/3418
Enditen, to indite, 4/4
Enfourme, to inform, instruct, 11/212, 13/263
Enhaunse, Enhawnse, to raise, exalt (*enhance*), 33/825
Enlace, to bind, entangle, entertwine, perplex, 13/245, 80/2207, 149/4208
Enoynte, to anoint, 36/923
Enpeyren, to impair, 120/3418, 139/4015
Ensample, example, 9/151
Entalenten, to excite, 168/4876
Entecche, defile, pollute, 120/3431
Entendyng, intent, looking stedfastly on, 8/126
Entente, to intend, 150/4345
Ententes, endeavours, labours, 7/79
Ententif, attentive, intent, 12/223, 29/731
Ententifly, attentively, 103/2931
Enterchaunge, to interchange, 65/1785, 131/3753
Entercomunynge, commerce, communication, 57/1528
Entermedle, to intermix, 54/1436
Entré (*adytum*), 30/751
Entrechaunge, to interchange, 39/1003
Entrelaced, intermingled, entangled, 105/2981
Entremete, intermeddle, 104/2964
Enveneme, to poison, infect, 120/3437

Enviroune, to surround, 34/848, 88/2437
Environynge, circumference, 164/4769
Erþeliche, Erþelyche, earthly, 52/1378, 69/1888
Erye, to plough, ear, 71/1964
Eschapen, to escape, 41/1054
Eschaufe, to become hot, to burn, 22/524
Eschewen, to avoid, escape, 177/5172
Eschuynge, eschewing, 99/2802
Establisse, to establish, 15/311
Eterne, eternal; fro eterne = from eternity, 153/4422
Eternité, eternity, 171/4986
Evenliche, evenly, 25/599
Everyche, every, 11/190; each, 181/48
Evesterre, evening star, 22/510
Excussyoun, execution, 184/65
Exercen, to exercise, practise, 52/1389
Exercitacioun, exercise, 140/4034
Exilynge, banishment, 11/205
Exite, to excite, 168/4881
Eyen, eyes, 183/36
Eyer, air, 170/4962

Fader, father, 18/414
Familarité, familiarity, 30/740
Familers, familiars, 18/407
Fantesye, fancy, inclination, 181/51
Fasoun, fashion, 62/1693
Feffe, (?) 38/966
Fel, felle, fierce
Felawschipe, to accompany, 111/3141
Felefold, manifold, 30/738
Felliche, fiercely, 39/997

Felnesse, fierceness, 25/618
Felonous, wicked, depraved, 18/405
Felonye, crime, 124/3542
Fer, far, 23/554
Ferm, firm, 78/2148
Fermely, firmly, 157/4550
Ferne, fern, 64/1741
Ferne, distant, 60/1621
Ferþe, fourth, 56/1509
Festivaly, gaily, 59/1581
Festne, to fasten, fix, 10/166
Fette, fetched, 180/22
Fey, faith, truth, 112/3178
Ficchen, to fix, fasten, 45/1164, 88/2446
Fieblesse, feebleness, 81/2240, 112/3176
Fille, abundance, 48/1269
Flaumbe, flame, 98/2761
Fleme, to banish, 29/723
Fles, fleece, 180/18
Flete, Fleten, to float, flow, pass away, abound, 8/118, 28/690, 146/4223, 152/4376
Fletynge, flowing, 71/1961
Fley, flee, 149/4289
Fleyen, to flee, 125/3584
Flies, fleece, 50/1330
Flitte, to remove, 68/1853
Flittyng, changing, fickle, 78/2150
Flityng, flitting, 12/220
Flotere, to float, 99/2817
Floterynge, floating, 87/2420
Flouren, to flourish, 131/3763
Fodre, fodder, 148/4267
Foleyen, Folyen, to act foolishly, 67/1821, 1826
Folyly, foolishly, 12/220
Fooldest, foldest, 105/2984

GLOSSARIAL INDEX. 193

Forbrek, broke, interrupted, 108/3082
Fordoon, to undo, destroy, 62/1693
Fordryven, driven about, 12/215
Foreyne, foreign, 34/851
Forghe, furrow, 170/4959
Forheved, forehead, 16/346
Forknowyng, foreknowledge, 178/5187
Forleften, left (*pret.* of *forleve, linquo*), 9/150
Forlete, to cease, 96/2697; leave, forsake, 22/525
Forleten (*p.p.*), neglected, forsaken, 5/47
Forliven, degenerate from (*degenero*), 78/2163
Forlorn, lost, 34/858, 121/3452
Forme, an error for *ferme*, to make firm, 23/547
Forpampred, overpampered, 180/5
Fors, force; 'no fors,' no matter, 182/13
Forsweryng, perjury, 23/536
Forþenke, to be sorry, grieved, 41/1058
Forþere, to further, promote, 41/1057
Forþest, farthest, 136/3918
Forþi, therefore, 28/689
Fortroden, trodden upon, trampled, 109/3100
Fortunel, fortuitous, 152/4379
Fortunouse, Fortuouse, fortuitous, 26/639, 38/983, 132/3779
Forwes, furrows, 180/12
Forwiter, foreknower, 178/5204
Foryetyn, forgotten, 101/2872
Foundement, foundation, 98/2754
Fowel, bird, 107/3053
Fram, from, 70/1931
Freole, frail, 61/1658

Frete, to eat, devour, 147/4252
Frounce, flounce, 9/147
Fructe, fruit, 180/3
Frutefiyng, fructifying, fruitful, 6/72
Fulfilling, satisfying, 79/2178
Fycche, fix, 108/3073. See Ficchen.
Fyn, end, 69/1892

Gabbe, 'gabbe I?' am I deceived? 49/1308
Galentyne, a dish in ancient cookery made of sopped bread and spices (*Halliwell*), 180/16
Galles, galls, 181/47
Gapen, to desire, be greedy for, 15/324, 36/910
Gapinge, desire, 36/910
Gastnesse, terror, fear, 75/2079
Geaunt, giant, 104/2966
Gentilesse, nobility, 78/2154
Geometrien, geometrician, 91/2552
Gerdoned, rewarded, 120/3410
Gerdoun, reward, 13/265
Gerner, garner, 15/305
Gesse, Gessen, to deem, suppose, estimate, 17/378, 19/416, 65/1782
Gessinge, opinion, 21/475
Gest, guest, 38/979
Gideresse, a female guide, 108/3084
Gise, guise, mode, 71/1943
Giser, gizzard, 107/3054
Glotonus, greedy, 26/620
Gnodded, pounded, 180/11
Gobet, a bit (of gold), 51/1349
Godhed, divinity, 122/3492
Goost, spirit, ghost, 40/1036
Governaile, government (*gubernaculum*), 27/651

Governaunce, control, 32/813
Goye, joy, 179/5218
Grayþe, to devise, prepare, 19/438
Grobbe up, to grub up, 181/29
Grond, did grind, 180/15
Gynne, snare, trap, 82/2256
Gynner, beginner, 150/4330
Gyse, guise, mode, 134/3860

Habitacle, habitation, 57/1525
Habunde, to abound, 41/1073
Halden, to hold, 41/1053
Hale, to draw, drag, 61/1665
Halt, holds, 56/1504
Hardnesse, hardship, 132/3783
Hardyly, boldly, 34/857
Hastise, to hasten, 131/3746
Haunten, to frequent, 10/168; to practise, exercise, 52/1389
Heeres, hairs, 4/12
Heet, heat, 28/699
Hef, raised, heaved, 5/41
Hele, health, 93/2623
Henten, to seize, 15/326
Hepen, to heap up, increase, 153/4418
Herburghden, harboured, lodged, 53/1409
Herie, to praise, 109/3112
Hert, hart, 106/3027
Herted, hearted, 55/1466
Heve, to raise, heave, 171/4968
Heved, head, 4/13
Hevenelyche, heavenly, 8/105
Hevie, to make heavy, 171/4967
Hey, high, 22/523
Heyere, higher, 143/4117
Heyȝe, high, 171/4969
Hielde, pour, 35/899
Hiȝte, to adorn, 8/116

Hoke, hook, 16/347
Holily, wholly, entirely, 90/2503
Homelyche, homely, 105/3001
Hond, hand, 20/449
Honter, a hunter, 12/228
Hool, whole, 46/1191
Hoolnesse, wholeness, 164/4754
Hoope, to hope, 17/384
Hore, hoary, 4/13
Humblesse, humility, 80/2213
Hungry tyme, time of famine, 15/314
Hurtlen, to rush against, to oppose, 30/748, 167/4866
Hyene, hyæna, 185/35
Hyȝt, is called, 9/154, 25/619
Hyȝten, are called, 77/2126

Ibouȝt, bought, 157/4540
Ibowed, bent, turned, 137/3949
Icharged, loaded, 71/1962
Igete, gotten, 36/908
Ilorn, lost, 62/1677
Imperial, august (*imperiosus*), 7/91
Implie, to fold, enclose, 152/4379
Infortune, misfortune, 79/2197
Inmoeveable, immovable, 173/5030
Inmoeveableté, immobility, 173/5032
Inorschid, nourished, nurtured, 8/128
I-nowh, enough, 180/11
Inperfit, imperfect, 83/2291
Inplitable (*inexplicabilis*), 15/315
Inprente, to imprint, 166/4832
Inpressed, impressed, 167/4861
Inrest, innermost, 136/3913
Instaunce (*instantia*), presence, 174/5067

GLOSSARIAL INDEX.

Intil, into, 110/3139
Inwiþ, within, 32/801
Issest, issuest, 105/2983
Iwist, known, 156/4513

Jangland, chattering, 68/1867
Jape-worthi, ridiculous, 157/4540
Jolyté, pleasure, 79/2189
Jowes, jaws, 15/323
Joygnen, to join, 54/1455
Joynture, juncture, joining, 46/1207
Juge, a judge, 19/431; to judge, 53/1427
Jugement, judgment, 114/3253

Karf (*pret*. of Kerven), cut, 50/1337
Kembd, KEMBED, combed, 23/537
Kerve, to cut, 64/1740
Kevere, cover, obscure, 34/861
Keye, helm (*clavus*), 103/2926
Knowelechinge, knowledge, 168/4874
Knyȝt, soldier, 111/3142
Konnyng, knowledge, 16/351
Korue (*p.p.*), cut, rent, 6/58
Kuytten, to cut, 147/4246
Kyd, known, 181/46
Kyndeliche, Kyndely, naturally, 101/2850, 114/3228
Kythen, to make known, show, 184/63

Lache, slow, lazy, 122/3471
Lad (*p.p.*), led, 35/879
Laddre, ladder, 6/55
Lambyssh, lamb-like, 181/50
Languisse, to languish, 30/734, 130/3740
Lappe, flap, 9/146

Largesse, liberality, 45/1183
Lasse, less, 22/508
Leche, Leecher, physician, 13/250, 114/3254, 139/3990
Leef, dear, 37/941
Leesen, Leese, to lose, 22/509, 43/1133
Lene, to give, 139/3993
Lenger, longer, 52/1370
Lesynge, loss, 141/4066
Lesynge, leasing, lie, 156/4525
Leten, to leave, 10/176; to esteem, 61/1666
Leve, permission, leave, 128/3658
Leveful, allowable, lawful, 10/176
Ligge, to lie, 60/1632, 147/4251
Liifly, lively, lifelike, 5/33
Likerous, lecherous, 72/1989
Litargie, lethargy, 9/140
Litestere, a dyer, 180/17
Lokyng, sight, 10/167
Loos, praise
Looþ, loath, 40/1036
Lorel, a wretch, 21/495
Lorn, lost, 34/859
Lous, loose, free, 136/3926
Lykynge, pleasure, 31/771
Lymes, limbs, 71/1946
Lynage, lineage, 41/1070
Lythnesse, lightness, 98/2761
Lyȝte goodes, temporal goods, 4/21
Lyȝtly, easily, 12/220
Lyȝtne, to enlighten, 128/3655
Lyȝtnesse, light, brightness, 8/106

Maat, weary, dejected, 40/1037
Magistrat, magistracy, 72/1985
Maistresse, mistress, 10/169

Malice, *nefas*, wickedness, 20/466
Malyfice, *maleficium*, 20/468
Manace, menace, 12/232
Manase, to menace, 118/3365
Manassynge, threatening, 44/1158
Mareis, Mareys, marsh, 56/1513, 97/2735
Margarits, pearls, 94/2650
Marye, pith, marrow, 97/2744
Maugré, in spite of, 70/1928
Mede, meed, reward, 91/2555
Medle, to mix, *Medelyng*, mixing, mixture, 20/449, 122/3482, 126/3594
Meenelyche, moderate, 28/706
Meistresse, mistress, 17/363
Melle, mill, 180/6
Mene, the mean or middle path, 146/4228
Meremaydenes, mermaids, 7/83
Merken, to mark, 16/346
Mervaille, Merveile, marvel, 18/403, 132/3787
Merveilen, to marvel, 46/1205
Mervelyng, wondering, 10/161
Mest, most, 42/1081
Mesuren, to measure, 65/1782
Meyné, servants, domestics, 47/1243
Mirie, pleasant, sweet, 4/16
Mirinesse, pleasure, 66/1793
Misericorde, mercy, pity, 107/3057
Mistourne, to misturn, mislead, 69/1894
Mochel, great, 62/1674, 109/3110
Moeveable, mobile, fickle, 133/3817
Moeven, to move, 8/112, 150/4329
Moewyng, moving, motion, 130/3742

Mokere, to hoard up, 45/1182
Mokere, miser, 45/1182. A mistake for *mokerere*.
Molesté, trouble, grief, 85/2346
Monstre, prodigy, 18/403
More, greater, 129/3697
Morwe, morning, 22/513
Mosten (*pl.*), must, 166/4836
Mot, must, 40/1038
Mowen, be able, 25/608
Mowynge, ability, power, 124/3548
Myche, much, 21/475
Mychel, much, 46/1215
Myntynge, purposing, endeavouring, 7/101
Myrie, pleasant, 45/1165
Myrily, pleasantly, 59/1582
Myrþes, pleasures, 132/3782
Mys, badly, wrongly, 131/3772
Mysese, grievance, trouble, 15/299
Mysknowynge, ignorant, 61/1659
Mysweys, wrong paths, 149/4309

Naie, to refuse, 4/19
Nake, to make naked, 148/4288
Nameles, unrenowned, 131/3762
Namelyche, Namly, especially, 124/3550
Nare, were not, 10/176
Nart, art not, 23/556
Narwe, narrow, 57/1520
Nas, was not, 180/9
Naþeles, nevertheless, 6/57
Nat, not, 23/556
Necesseden, necessitated, 87/2419
Nedely, of necessity, 84/2334
Negardye, (*sb.*) misers, 183/53
Nere, were not, 26/646

Neþemaste, lowest, nethermost, 6/56
Neþereste, lowest, 6/50
Newe, to renew, 137/3938
Newliche, recently, 122/3489
Nice, foolish, 148/4287
Nil, will not, 107/3055
Nillynge, being unwilling, 97/2718
Nilt, wilt not, 112/3193
Nis, is not, 12/218
Niste, knew not, 102/2882
Noblesse, nobleness, 37/947
Nobley, nobility, nobleness, 37/945
Nolden, would not, 52/1369
Norice, nurse, 10/167
Norisse, to nourish, 79/2174
Norry, nursling, pupil, 10/173
Norssinge, nourishment, support, 47/1231; nutriment, 37/932
Not, know not (1st pers.), 27/649
Notful, useful, 7/85
Nounpower, impotence, 75/2074
Nouþir, neither, 160/4644
Noyse, to make a noise (about a thing), to brag, 79/2171
Nurry (see Norry), 86/2386
Nys, is not, 45/1175

O, one, 24/564
Obeisaunt, obedient, 13/266, 32/814
Object, presented, 168/4889
Occupye, to seize, 146/4227
Offence, hurt, damage, 180/19
Offensioun, offence, 20/473
Olifuntȝ, elephants, 80/2223
Onknowyn, unknown, 180/6
Onlyche, only, 171/4968

Onone, Onoon, at once, anon, 23/553, 74/2027
Ony, any, 21/488
Ooned, united, 135/3879
Oor, oar, 50/1338
Oosteresse, hostess, 122/3495
Or, ere, before, 9/143
Ordeinly, orderly, 140/4044
Ordenour, ordainer, 109/3110
Ordeyne, orderly, 109/3109
Ordinat, ordered, settled, 12/229
Ordinee, orderly, 102/2902
Ordure, filth, 29/716
Ostelmentȝ, furniture, goods, 48/1266
Oþerweyes, otherwise (aliter), 164/4772
Outerage, excess, 50/1326
Outerest, extremest, remotest, 55/1469, 89/2476
Outerly, utterly, 108/3081
Outraien, do harm (?), 78/2162
Over-comere, conqueror, 8/109
Overmaste, highest, uppermost, 6/57
Overmyche, overmuch, very much, 79/2191
Overoolde, very old, 11/209
Overþrowen, prostrate, 21/497
Overþrowyng, forward, headstrong, 7/99, 141/4058
Overtymelyche, untimely, 4/13
Owh, an exclamation (papæ), 112/3166
Owtrage, excess, 180/5

Paied, satisfied, 58/1549
Paleis, pale, 24/574
Palude, marsh, 148/4262
Paraventure, peradventure, 18/402
Parchemyn, parchment, 166/4835

Parsoners, sharers, partakers, 170/4942
Partles, without a share, 120/3409
Pas, paces, 19/442
Paysyble, peaceable, peaceful, 180/1
Peisible, quiet, placid, 23/550, 88/2450
Percen, to pierce, 81/2236
Perdurable, lasting, perpetual, 5/44, 21/503
Perdurableté, immortality, 58/1557
Perfitlyche, *Perfitly*, perfectly, 87/2426, 133/3833
Perfourny, to afford, furnish, 67/1823
Perisse, to perish, 96/2712
Perturbacioun, perturbation, 7/98
Perverte, to destroy, 11/201
Peyne, punishment, 121/3439
Piment, a kind of drink, 50/1329
Plenté, fulness, 173/5037
Plentevous, affluent, 67/1824
Plentivous, yielding abundantly, fertile, 64/1739
Plentivously, abundantly, 25/592
Plete, argue, plead, 33/833
Pletyngus, pleadings, debates (at law), 70/1933
Pleyne, to complain, 31/777
Pleynelyche, plainly, 28/681
Pleynt, complaint, 110/3122
Plonge, Ploungen, to plunge, 7/89, 65/1784
Ploungy, wet, rainy (*imbrifer*), 64/1745
Polute, polluted, 20/450
Pose, to put a case, cf. put a *poser*, 162/4686
Pousté, power, 131/3766

Pownage, pasturage, 180/7
Poyntel, style, 166/4838
Preiere, prayer, 107/3044
Preisen, to estimate, judge, 7/379
Preisynge, praising, 77/2131
Preke, to prick, 85/2346
Prenostik, prognostic, 183/54
Presentarie, present, 178/5196
Preterit, preterite, past, 171/4990
Pretorie, the imperial body-guard, 15/317
Prevé, secret, 121/3464
Preven, to prove, 90/2503
Prie, to pray, 25/600
Pris, value; 'worþi of *pris*,' precious, 24/583
Proche, to approach, 145/4182
Proeve, to approve, 154/4456
Punisse, to punish, 22/531
Puplisse, to publish, spread, propagate, 58/1549, 98/2753
Purper, purple, 25/617
Purpose, to propose, 176/5148
Purveaunce, providence, 134/3863
Purveiable, provident, foreseeing, 68/1854
Purveie, to ordain, order, 21/478
Purvyance, providence, 99/2795

Quereles, complaints, 70/1932
Quik, living, 134/3839
Quyene, queen, 183/43
Quyerne, a mill, 180/6

Rafte, bereft, 147/4259
Raþer, earlier, former, 30/735
Raviner, a plunderer, 12/228
Ravische, to snatch, 11/190
Ravyne, plunder, rapine, 15/302, 36/909

GLOSSARIAL INDEX.

Ravynour, plunderer, 121/3460
Ravysse, to carry off, 131/3774
Real, royal, 19/420
Recche, to care, reck, 33/827, 38 987
Recompensacioun, recompense, 130/3724
Recorde, to recount, recall, 92/2580, 101/2871
Reddowr, severity, rigour, 182/13
Redenesse, redness, flushing, 7/88
Redoutable, venerable, 131/3763
Redoute, to fear, 10/178, 57/1535
Redy = rody, red, ruddy, 39/995
Refet, refreshed, 143/4116
Reft (away), carried off, 22/521
Refut, refuge, 94/2644
Regne, kingdom, 67/1843
Regnen, to reign, rule, 29/726
Remewe, to remove, 19/441
Remorde, to vex, trouble, 140/4030
Remuable, able to remove from one place to another, 168/4898
Remuen, to remove, 52/1394
Renomed, renowned, 41/1070, 78/2143
Renovele, to renew, 98/2752
Replenisse, to replenish, 20/469
Reprere, to reprove, 167/4857
Repugnen, to be repugnant to, 154/4440
Requerable, desirable, 52/1377
Requere, to require, 99/2790
Rescowe, to recover, 133/3809
Rescowe, to rescue, 35/881
Resolve, to loosen, melt, 133/3814
Resoune, to resound, 107/3036
Rethoryen, rhetorical, 30/759
Rewlyche, pitiable, sorrowful, 35/878

Risorse = recourse (*recursus*), course, 8/108
Rody, ruddy, 143/4122
Roos, roes, 82/2258
Rosene, roseat, 8/117
Route, company, 47/1243
Royle, to run, roll, 29/717
Rynnyng, running, 50/1335
Ryʒtwisnesse, righteousness, equity, 16/331

Sachel, satchel, sack, 12/223
Sad, stable, 41/1064
Saddenesse, stability, 110/3123
Sarpuler, a sack made of coarse cloth (*Sarcinula*), 12/223
Sauuacioun, safety, salvation, 97/2723
Sauʒ, Say, saw, 8/106, 9/137
Saye, sawest, 37/958
Schad, shed, 4/13
Schrew, a wicked person, a wretch, 12/217
Schrewed, wicked, 18/398
Schrewednesse, wickedness, 18/401, 117/3324
Schronk, shrunk, 5/38
Schulden (*pl.*), should, 9/132
Schullen (*pl.*), shall, 25/605
Scom, foam, froth, 148/4281
Scripture, writing, 17/382
Sege, seat, 13/258
Seien (*pl.*), saw, 51/1344
Seien (*p.p.*), seen, 6/54
Selde, seldom, 133/3818
Seler, cellar, 35/890
Selily, happily, blissfully, 42/1076
Selve, very, 5/42
Semblable, like, 48/1279
Semblaunce, likeness, 142/4106
Semblaunt, appearance, countenance, 5/31

GLOSSARIAL INDEX.

Senglely, singly, 85/2369
Sensibilites, sensations, 166/4830
Servage, servitude, 153/4411
Sewe, to follow, 88/2441
Seye, sawest, 37/955
Seyntuaries, sanctuaries, 16/343
Shad, divided, spread, 136/3922
Sholdres, shoulders, 148/4281
Sich, such, 6/67
Sikerly, certainly, 94/2635
Singler, individual, single, 57/1529
Singlerly, singly, 135/3890
Sittyng, fitting, becoming, 10/176
Skilynge, reason, 137/3931
Slaken, to slake (hunger), 50/1326
Slede, sledge, 110/3131
Sleen, Slen, to slay, 53/1409, 55/1460
Slouȝ, slew, 55/1461
Smaragde, emerald, 94/2650
Smerte, to smart, pain, 39/1011
Smot, smote, 147/4254
Smoþe, smooth, 8/112
Sodeyn, sudden, 10/161
Somedel, somewhat, 25/606
Somer, summer, 22/517
Songen (*p.p.*), sung, 108/3078
Soory, sorry, grievous, 38/978
Soþe, true, 17/377, 118/3352
Soþefastly, truly, 89/2481
Soþely, truly, 169/4918
Soþenesse, truth, 26/641
Sothfast, true, 61/1652
Soun, sound, 68/1852
Soune, to sound, 37/929
Sounyng, sounding, roaring, 8/111
Sovereyne, supreme, 90/2508

Sovereynely, supremely, 91/2545
Sourmounte, to surpass, 80/2223
Spece, species, 165/4789
Speculacioun, looking, contemplation, 153/4408
Spedeful, Spedful, efficacious, conducive, 125/3570, 161/4671
Speden, to make clear, explain, 161/4667
Spere, sphere, 8/108
Sperkele, spark, 104/2971
Sprad, spread (*p.p.*), 9/156
Stableté, stability, 137/3950
Stablise, to establish, 134/3860
Stably, firmly, 135/3890
Stappe, step, 170/4963
Staunche, to satisfy, 71/1948, 1961
Stere, to move (*agitare*), 106/3015
Sterre, star, 36/903
Sterry, starry, 36/904
Sterten, to start, 104/2971
Stidefastnesse, stability, strength, 97/2748
Stidfast, steadfast, 182/17
Stien, to ascend, 88/2444
Stiere, *steer*, rudder (*gubernaculum*), 103/2926
Stiern, stern, 60/1628
Stoon, stone, 45/1165
Stormynge, making stormy, 29/712
Stont, stands, 9/154
Stoundes, times, 178/5187
Strauȝt, stretched, extended, 170/4957
Strengere, stronger, 12/221
Strenkeþ, strength, 12/240
Streyhte, stretched, 63/1702
Streyne, to restrain, 150/4325

Strond, strand, 51/1339
Strook, stroke, 153/4433
Strumpet, 6/66
Stye, to ascend, 143/4117
Stynte, to stop, 37/929
Styntynge, stopping, ceasing, 61/1638
Suasioun, persuasion (*suadela*), 30/759
Subgit, subject, 48/1273
Submytte, to compel, force (*summitto*), 19/434
Sudeyn, sudden, 30/752
Suffisaunce, sufficiency, 70/1922
Suffisaunt, sufficient, 70/1924
Suffisauntly, sufficiently, 133/3833
Summitte, Summytte, to submit, 49/1288, 136/3924
Superfice, surface, 81/2238
Supplien, to supplicate, 80/2210
Surté, security, 181/46
Sustigne, to sustain, 183/41
Sweighe, whirl, circular motion (*turbo*), 22/504
Swerd, sword, 19/438
Swety, sweaty, 181/28
Sweyes, whirlings, 32/816
Swich, such, 20/446
Swolwe, to swallow, 98/2777
Syker, secure, safe, 12/224, 16/333
Sykernesse, security, safety, 9/132
Symplesse, simplicity, 136/3914
Syn, since, 31/789
Syþen, since, 32/802

Talent, affection, desire, will, 6/71, 168/4887
Taylage, tollage, 181/524
Þar, need, 38/987

Þerwhiles, whilst, 176/5150
Þilke, the same, that, 99/2814
Þo, þoo (*pl.*), the, 11/200, 168/4886
Þondre, thunder, 45/1166
Þoruȝ, through, 11/202
Þreschefolde, threshold, 7/89
Þrest, thirst, 36/914, 71/1945
Þreste, þresten, thrust, 47/1237, 148/4283
Throf, throve, flourished, 74/2050
Þrust, thirst, 107/3053
Til, to, 69/1891
Tilier, a tiller, 151/4352
To-breke, break in pieces, 88/2447
Todrowen (*pl.*), drew asunder, 11/193
Toforne, before, 177/5184
Togidres, together, 53/1421
To hepe, together, 140/4029
Tokene, to token, 26/624
Tollen, to draw, 56/1496
Torenten (*pl.*), rent asunder, 11/194
To-teren, tear in pieces, 68/1865
Traas, Trais, trace, track, 170/4958, 4963
Transporten, throw on (*transferre*), 19/419
Travaille, labour, toil, 10/174
Travayle, to toil, labour, 64/1754
Travayle, labour, 148/4286
Tregedie, tragedy, 77/2126
Tregedien, tragedian, 77/2125
Trenden, to roll, turn, 100/2835
Troublable, troublesome, 118/3369
Trouble, turbid, stormy, 29/711
Troubly, troubled, cloudy (*nubilus*), 133/3819
Trowen, to trow, believe, 20/468, 152/4399

Twitre, to twitter, 68/1875
Twynkel, to wink, 38/971
Tylienge, tilling, 151/4347
Tyren, to tear, 107/3055

Umblesse, humility, 181/55
Unagreable, unpleasant, disagreeable, 4/25
Unassaieþ, untried, 42/1082
Unbitide, not to happen, 161/4678
Unbowed, unbent, 148/4284
Uncovenable, unmeet, importunate (*importunus*), 141/4058
Undefouled, undefiled, 40/1023
Undepartable, inseparable, 120/3422
Underput, put under, subject, 28/696
Understonde, to understand, 30/733, 43/1120
Undigne, unworthy, 54/1444
Undirneþ, underneath, 75/2074
Undiscomfited, not discomfited (*invictus*), 12/232
Undoutous, indubitable, 149/4315
Uneschewably, unavoidably, 157/4531
Ungentil, ignoble, 41/1070
Ungrobbed, ungrubbed, 180/14
Unhonestce, disreputableness, 24/587
Unhoped, unexpected, 139/4006
Université, whole, 165/4797
Unjoynen, Unjoygnen, to separate, 151/4373
Unknowyng, ignorant, 139/3997
Unknytten, to unloose (*dissolvere*), 154/4459
Unkonnyng, Unkunnynge, unknowing, ignorant, 7/76, 11/202
Unkorven, uncut, 180/14

Unkouþ, unknown, foreign, 34/870
Unlace, to disentangle, 105/2982
Unleveful, illicit, unlawful, 154/4456
Unmeke, fierce, cruel, 148/4267
Unmoeveable, immovable, 136/3901
Unmoeveableté, immobility, 136/3921
Unmyȝty, weak, impotent, 13/241
Unneþ, scarcely, 27/652
Unparygal, unequal, 63/1708
Unpitouse, cruel, 4/24
Unpleyten, to explain, 61/1647
Unplite, explain, unfold, 167/4843
Unpunissed, unpunished, 21/498
Unpurveyed, unforeseen, 30/743
Unraced, unbroken, whole, 110/3115
Unryȝtful, unjust, 10/185
Unryȝtfully, unrightfully, unjustly, 23/533
Unscience, unreal knowledge, no knowledge, 156/4515
Unsely, wretched, 39/1013
Unselynesse, wretchedness, 124/3544
Unskilfuly, unwisely, improperly, 18/407
Unsolempne, not famous, not celebrated, 11/210
Unsowe, unsown, 180/10
Unspedful, unsuccessful, 178/5210
Unstauncheable, unlimited, infinite, 58/1573
Unstaunched, uncurbed, unrestrained, 54/1439
Unsuffrable, intolerable, 79/2179
Unusage, unfrequency, 57/1528

GLOSSARIAL INDEX. 203

Untretable, inexorable, implacable, 61/1641
Unwar, unexpected, 35/886
Unwarly, unaware, unexpectedly, 4/10
Unwemmed, inviolate, 40/1023, 178/5201
Unwened, unexpected, 139/4006
Unwoot, knows not, 175/5099
Unworshipful, dishonoured, 75/2054
Uphepyng, heaping up, 37/951
Upsodoun, upside down, 48/1274, 156/4501
Upsprong, upsprung, 180/10
Used, accustomed, wonted, 22/512
Uterreste, extremest, outermost, 7/95

Vanisse, to vanish, 74/2027
Variaunt, varying, 22/518
Vengerisse, a she-avenger, 107/3048
Verray, Verrey, true, 19/429
Vilfully (Wilsfully), wilfully, 116/3295
Voide, having an empty purse (*vacuus*), 50/1316
Voyded (of), emptied of, free from, 181/50

Wakyng, watchful, 148/4263
Walwe, to toss, 51/1361
Walwyng, tossing, 29/712
Wan, did win, 147/4240
War, be aware, take care, 145/4200
Warne, to refuse, deny, 37/950
Wawe, a wave, 8/115
Wayk, weak, 28/706
Weep (*pret.*), wept, 35/883
Welde, wild, 180/17. It may

mean *boiled*, since another copy reads *wellyd*.
Weleful, Welful, prosperous, joyful, 4/15
Welefulnesse, Welfulnesse, prosperity, felicity, 11/188, 21/478
Welken, to wither, fade, 146/4224
Welkne, welkin, 184/62
Welle, well, source, 157/4548
Wende, weened, thought, 53/1397
Wenge, wing, 170/4961
Wenynge, opinion, 172/5022
Wepen (*p.p.*), wepi, 25/596
Wepli, tearful, 5/29
Werdes, fates, destinies, 4/10
Werreye, to make war, 181/25
Weten, to know, 156/4519
Wex, wax, 167/4840
Weyve, to waive, forsake, 29/722
Wham, whom, 89/2482
Whelwe, to toss, roll, 39/1001
Whiderward, whither, 177/5171
Whist, hushed, 51/1341
Wierdes, fates, destinies, 12/231
Wikke, wicked, bad, 64/1743
Willynge, desire, 178/5203
Wilne, to desire, 17/367
Wilnynge, desire, 98/2781
Wirche, to work, 12/235
Wirchyng, working, operation, 95/2677
Wist, known, 170/4937
Witen, to know, learn, 88/2458, 132/3776, 160/4624
Wiþdrow, withdrew, 64/1751
Wiþhalden, to withhold, 142/4105
Wiþoute forþe, outwardly, 165/4803
Wiþscid, denied, 90/2501

Wiþstant, withstand, 29/715
Wiþstonde (*p.p.*), withstood, 14/290
Witnesfully, attestedly, publicly, 131/3765
Witynge, knowledge, 156/4526
Wod, woad, 180/17
Wod, Wode, mad, raging, 12/225
Wode, wood, 39/995
Wodenesse, rage, madness, 45/1169, 107/3052
Wolen (*pl.*), will, 94/2645
Woltow, wilt thou, 97/2741
Wone, to dwell, 60/1627
Woode, Wode, furious, mad, 25/600
Woode, to rage, 123/3515
Woodnesse, rage, madness, 107/3052
Woot, knows, 43/1128
Wope, to weep, 36/905
Worchen, to work, 178/5215
Wost, knowest, 19/423
Woxe, to increase, wax, grow, 25/608
Woxen (*p.p.*), grown, 25/607
Wrekere, avenger, 128/3665
Wrekyng, vengeance, 147/4238
Wroþely, grieved, sad, 7/87
Wryþen, twist, turn, wrest, 154/4452
Wymple, to cover with a veil or wimple, 31/774
Wyt, sense, 164/4771
Wyʒt, wight, person, 19/425

Yave (*pl.*), gave, 180/4
Yben, been, 162/4698
Ybeyen, to obey, 105/2998
Ycauʒt, caught, captured, 118/3371
Ycleped, called, 150/4346

Ydel, '*in ydel*,' in vain, 5/43
Ydred, feared, 33/825
Yfelawshiped, associated, united, 53/1421
Yfeched, fixed, 136/3910
Yfinissed, finished, 125/3558
Yflit, flitted, removed, 8/108
Ygeten, gotten, 65/1776
Yhardid, hardened, 133/3814
Yheuied, made heavy, 171/4974
Ylad, led, 37/956, 172/5022
Ylete, permitted, 130/3730
Ylett, hindered, 161/4674
Ylorn, lost, 147/4250
Ymaginable, possessing imagination, 166/4812
Ymaked, made, 87/2426
Ymedeled, mixed, 140/4029
Ynouʒ, enough, 71/1947
Yplitid, pleated, folded, 9/147
YPORVEYID, YPURVEID, foreseen, 155/4467, 4468
Ysen, seen, 72/1982
Yshad, shed, scattered, 68/1874
Yshet, shut, 170/4955
Ysmyte, smitten, 80/2202
Ysped, made clear, determined, 161/4657; despatched, 149/4295
Yspendyd, examined (*expediero*), 161/4668
Ysprad, spread, 78/2140
Yspranid, sprinkled, mixed, 42/1102. *Read* yspraind.
Ystrengeþed, strengthened, 175/5098
Yþewed, behaved, 139/4008
Yþrongen, pressed, squeezed, 57/1521
Ytravailed, laboured, 155/4469
Ytretid, handled, performed, 131/3765

Yvel, evil, 105/2976
Ywened, believed, 145/4178
Ywist, known, 155/4475
Ywoven, woven, 6/51
Ywyst, known, 164/4759
Yȝeven, given, 141/4069

Ȝaf, gave, 8/130
Ȝeelde, Ȝelde, seldom, 39/1002, 52/1372
Ȝeld, yielded, 147/4253
Ȝelden, to yield, 149/4303
Ȝeve, to give, 149/4291
Ȝevyng, giving, 45/1188
Ȝif, if, 9/131
Ȝis, yes, 103/2919
Ȝisterday, yesterday, 171/4994
Ȝitte, yet, 156/4508
Ȝok, Ȝokke, yoke, 32/802, 60/1620
Ȝolde (*p.p.*), yielded, 25/599
Ȝonge, young, 35/889
Ȝouþe, youth, 10/168

Richard Clay & Sons, Limited
London & Bungay.

The Romance

of the

Cheuelere Assigne.

Early English Text Society.
Extra Series. No. VI.
1868.

DUBLIN: WILLIAM McGEE, 18, NASSAU STREET.
EDINBURGH: T. G. STEVENSON, 22, SOUTH FREDERICK STREET.
GLASGOW: OGLE & CO., 1, ROYAL EXCHANGE SQUARE.
BERLIN: ASHER & CO., UNTER DEN LINDEN, 20.
NEW YORK: C. SCRIBNER & CO.; LEYPOLDT & HOLT.
PHILADELPHIA: J. B. LIPPINCOTT & CO.
BOSTON, U.S.: DUTTON & CO.

The Romance

of the

Chevelere Assigne.

RE-EDITED FROM

THE UNIQUE MANUSCRIPT IN THE BRITISH MUSEUM,

WITH A PREFACE, NOTES, AND GLOSSARIAL INDEX,

BY

HENRY H. GIBBS, ESQ., M.A.,

OF EXETER COLLEGE, OXFORD.

LONDON:
PUBLISHED FOR THE EARLY ENGLISH TEXT SOCIETY,
BY N. TRÜBNER & CO., 60, PATERNOSTER ROW.

MDCCCLXVIII.

Extra Series,
VI.

JOHN CHILDS AND SON, PRINTERS.

PREFACE.

THIS short alliterative poem has already been edited by Mr Utterson, and presented by him in 1820 to the members of the Roxburghe Club ; but as the few copies then printed are very rare, and as the work is a curious specimen of unrimed alliterative poetry of a comparatively late date, it has been thought worth while that it should be edited again for the Extra Series of the Early English Text Society.

A mere reprint of the former edition would not have been desirable, both because there are several mistranscriptions, and because the glossary appended to that edition is excessively meagre, and in some cases erroneous: but so much advance has been made since the date of that publication in the knowledge of our ancient tongue, that however much this edition may leave to be desired, there will be no great difficulty in correcting the errors of the former one.

Wherever the new transcript differed from the Roxburghe edition, I have with especial care compared it with the manuscript, so as to satisfy myself of the correctness of the new reading.

The poem consists of 370 lines ; and is contained, with other pieces, in Caligula A. 2 of the Cotton MSS. in the British Museum. It professes to be taken from some other book (in the 7th line and elsewhere the author uses the expression, ' as þe book telleþe '), and appears to be an epitome of the first 1083 lines of the French poem, or rather 'lay' (in the sense in which Scott uses the word), which forms part of the volume marked 15 E. vj in the Royal Collection in the same library.

This French Manuscript contains many beautiful illuminations of excellent workmanship, two of which adorn the head of the first page (fo. 320) of the 'Chevalier au Signe.' The left-hand picture represents Queen Bietrix (as she is there called) sitting up in bed and looking very unhappy, while 'Matebrune' is carrying away a cot (nearly as big as the Queen's bed) with the seven children in it, clad four in green and three in purple, placed alternately. The right-hand picture represents the Knight 'Helyas,' armed, and in his ship alone ; the

Swan, 'ducally gorged, Or,' as a herald would say, sailing proudly before him. This picture is very like one of the compartments of the Ivory Casket, to which I shall presently refer.

Meanwhile, as this French chanson—so its author frequently calls it [1]—appears to be the original from whence our English author drew his poem, I will give an outline of the longer history told in its 6000 lines, comparing it from time to time with the very entertaining English Prose Romance, printed by Copland early in the 16th century, and edited in 1858 by Mr Thoms.

THE STORY OF THE KNIGHT OF THE SWAN.

Briefly told it is as follows:

Beatrix, Queen of King Oryens of Lilefort, after some years of childlessness, conceived seven children at one burden (as a punishment for disbelieving the possibility of twins being begotten by one man); and when she is brought to bed, in her husband's absence, his mother substitutes seven puppies for the seven children, whom she consigns to Marques, or Marcon, a serf of hers, with orders for their murder: when the King returns she shows him the whelps as the Queen's offspring, and demands her death; but the King only allows her to be imprisoned.

The children (who were miraculously born with silver chains about their necks) are of course not slain, but fed by a hind in the forest, and tended by a hermit in his cell.

They are unfortunately seen by the Forester Mauquarre, or Malquarrez, who tells the Queen; and by her desire he goes back to kill them and take away their chains. One, however, who is the hero of the tale, has gone out with the hermit to get food for the others; so that the forester finds only six of the children, and deprives them of their chains, upon which they are transformed into swans.

---

[1] The poem begins '*Escoutez seigneurs pour Dieu lespitable*
Que Ihus vous garisse de lamain au Dyable;'
and every now and then the minstrel addresses his hearers to call their attention to his song. Thus when Elyas first comes to Nimaye, the next sentence begins '*Seigneurs oez chanceon qui moult fait aloer.*' After the battle with the friends of the prevost, comes, '*Seigneurs or escoutez chanceon de grant baronaige;*' and again, '*Seigneurs or escoutez bonne chanceon;*' and '*Seigneurs oez chanceon de bonne enluminee;*' and '*Seigneurs oyez chanceon qui est vray.*'

PREFACE.

The old Queen questions Marcon, and revenges herself on him by putting out his eyes.

When the Queen has been 11 years in prison, Matebrune prevails on the King to condemn her to be burnt; and the day is fixed accordingly, and she is led to the stake.

Meanwhile an angel appears to the hermit and orders that the child should go to the city, be christened Helyas, and fight for his mother. He does so, meets the procession, accosts the King, obtains his consent to the battle, borrows from him horse and armour, slays Mauquarre, who is the champion on behalf of the accuser, and frees his mother.

Matebrune flees to a castle; Helyas prays to God, who restores Marques's sight. He tells his story to his newly-found father and mother, and all the court go to the water where the swans are swimming, and, their chains being restored to them, they resume their human form; all but one, who remains a swan.

Up to this time, as will be seen, the English poem faithfully accompanies the French one, excepting that as the poet means to make an end here, he summarily burns Matabryne, and says that the 6th brother continued *always* a swan for lack of his chain.

Moreover he makes no mention of the miracle of healing done on Marcus.

The French story proceeds with the abdication of King Oriant (on the plea that he has now lived a long time—*plus que c. ans*—) in favour of Helyas; with the siege of Matebrune's castle, the death of her champion Hendrys by the hand of Helyas; her capture, confession, and burning; whereafter

'*Lame emporterent dyables; ce fut la destinee.*'

The angel then appears to King Helyas and bids him leave his father and mother, and seek adventures under the guidance of his brother the swan, who waits for him with '*ung batel.*'

He abdicates, and leaves the kingdom to Orions, and divers governments to his other brothers.

From this differs the English Prose Romance of the Knight of the Swan, which makes no mention of King Oryens' great age, but makes

King Helyas surrender the kingdom again into his hands. Neither does he mention Helyas's departure at the bidding of the angel; but makes the swan-brother summon him by 'mervaylous cries,' to come into the boat which he has brought, and which he guides, without further adventure, to the city of Nimaye.

But in the French story he arrives soon at a city of Saracens, who assault him and his swan;—but he is rescued by 30 galleys under the guidance of Saint George (*qui fut bon chevalier*); and the four winds also helped, raising a storm and drowning the Saracens.

It then tells how Elyas went on alone in his boat, with the swan, till they came to a castle, called Sauvage, whose master was Agolant, brother of Matebrune; how their provisions being exhausted, they sought help at the castle; how Agolant received him well, but, after hearing his story, seizes, imprisons, and promises to burn him eight days thereafter.

But a page escapes and goes to Lilefort to King Orions, who goes with a great force to succour his brother. The men arrive when Helyas is already bound at the stake, and Agolant and all his men have to go out to repel them;—a friendly hand releases Helyas, who joins his brother's men, and slays Agolant.

Oryons goes back to Lilefort, and Helyas, summoning his brother the swan, pursues his way to Nimaye.

There, in a tournament, he slays an Earl [of Francbourck, says Copland], who, in a false plea before the Emperor Otho, is trying to deprive [Clarysse] Duchess Dabullon [of Bouillon] of her lands; and wins for himself the lands of Ardennes [of Dardaigne, in Copland] belonging to the Earl; and also gets to wife Beatrice, the fair daughter and heiress of the Duchess, by whom he has a daughter Idein or Ydain, who in time becomes the mother of Godfrey of Bouillon.

He leaves Nimaye and goes to his duchy of Bouillon, conquering in the way *Asselm le prevost* and many partisans of the deceased Earl, who had laid an ambush for him.

Many perilous adventures then befell him in Bouillon, which are recounted at considerable length; and afterwards the story tells how that, his wife having disobeyed his commandment which he laid upon her, not to inquire concerning his kith and kin, he departs from her, and rides away to Nimaye, to take leave of the Emperor, and bespeak his protection for his wife, daughter, and lands.

Thence, amidst great lamentation of the Emperor and all his barons, he departs in his boat with his brother the swan, and no more is known of him.

Oncq ne sceurent quelle part y fu tournes.

Then it passes on to tell of Godfrey Earl of Bouillon, his birth and deeds. How with the leave of the Emperor, Eustace Earl of '*Boulogne sur mer salee*' went a courting to Ydain '*a la fresce coulour*' (daughter of Helyas), then aged 13 years; how he married her; and how in the three years following she had three fair sons, Godfrey, Baldwin, and Eustace; and how that the eldest after many noble deeds went to Palestine, and took the Holy City. The poem ends with the assault and capture of Jerusalem and the crowning of Godfrey as its King.

The English Prose Romance takes up the story of Helyas where the French Poem leaves him, and tells how he arrived at Lilefort and is welcomed by his father and mother after his viij years' absence.

The Queen, it tells us, had a dream, in which she dreams that if they get the two cups which had been made of the 6th son's chain, and lay them on two altars, and set the swan on a bed betwixt the altars, and cause two masses to be said by devout priests who shall consecrate in the two chalices, the swan shall return to his own form: and 'Ryght so,' says Copland, 'as the priests consacred the body of our Lorde at the masse, the swanne retourned into his propre fourme and was a man,' and he was baptized, and named Emery.

'The whiche sith was a noble knight.'

'And thus,' he says, 'the noble king Oriant and the good queene Beatrice finabli recovered all their children by the grace of God, wherfore fro than forthon they lived holyly and devoutly in our Lorde.'

Now King Oriant had 'made a Religion' at the hermitage where his son Helyas had been brought up; and thither, after recounting his adventures, the good Knight of the Swan betook himself, with a simple staff in his hand, and made himself a 'Religious.'

And close to the convent he caused to be built a castle like to that of Bouillon, and he called it Bouillon, and the forest that was about it he called Dardayne, after the land that he had won from the Earl.

The English story here goes on to tell of the marriage of Eustace Earl of Boulogne and Ydain daughter of Helyas, and of the birth of her sons Godfrey, Baldwin, and Eustace ; and how that her mother, the Duchess of Bouillon, lamenting for the loss of her husband Helyas, sent messengers all over the world to find him ; and how that Ponce, one of these messengers, went to Jerusalem, and meeting there the Abbot Girarde of Saincteron, which is nigh to Bouillon, they determined as fellow-countrymen to return together. How they lose their way, and come to the castle of Bouillon *le restaure*, and are struck by the likeness to their own Bouillon; how they inquire of the Curate, and hear who it was who built the castle and named the forest.

And how that they make themselves known to Emery and Helyas, and also to the King and Queen, who had come to live at the castle, and how they returned to their country, bearing a token from Helyas to his wife.

Then it tells how the Duchess and the Countess Ydain, whose sons were by this time adolescent, set forth to see their husband and father Helyas, and how they found him lying sick unto death, and how shortly thereafter 'he desceased in our lorde Jesu Chryst.'

How the ladies returned to Bouillon, and how the three noble brethren prepared themselves by a knightly education for the day when it should please God to give the kingdom of Jerusalem into the hands of Godfrey of Bouillon, the eldest born. 'And thus,' says Copland, 'endeth the life and myraculous hystory of the most noble and illustryous Helyas knight of the swanne, with the birth of the excellent knyght Godfrey of Boulyon, one of the nyne worthiest, and the last of the three crysten.'

The English romance, printed by Copland, is in some parts much fuller even than the French poem, going more into detail as to the wooing of King Oryens, and the cause of the enmity of Matabryne ; but here and there the French 'chanson' has details which Copland's book does not give ; such as the troublous adventures of

Helyas in his journey between Lilefort and Nimaye, and the acts and prowess of Godfrey, and his conquest of his kingdom ; but as to the legendary hero of the story, the Knight of the Swan, the tale of his deeds until his retirement from the world is mainly the same, in the English prose and in the French verse.

THE CASKET.

This curious work, of which I have before made mention, is an ancient ivory one, of 14th-century workmanship, now belonging to Mr William Gibbs of Tyntesfield, co. Somerset, and formerly to his wife's family, the Crawley-Boeveys, Baronets, of Flaxley Abbey, co. Gloucester. It is 8 inches long, 5⅝ deep, and 5⅓ inches high; and in its thirty-six compartments it gives the history of the Knight of the Swan; going no further than our poem, except that it depicts the capture of Matabryne's castle and the leave-taking and departure of Helyas. It is this last compartment that so nearly resembles the illumination at the head of the French poem.

I now proceed to describe the carvings in the several compartments, which are all of them remarkable for their accurate detail of arms and costume, and some groups, especially in Nos. 23 and 24, very spirited in their execution.

The top of the casket.

1. The King, Queen, and Matabryne on the wall. Mother and Twins below.
2. The King and the Queen in bed.
3. The King discovers that the Queen is with child.
4. The Queen asleep in bed : Matabryne carries off the children.
5. Matabryne delivers the children to Marcus.
6. Matabryne drowns the bitch in a well.
7. Matabryne presents the whelps to the King, who wrings his hands.
8. Marcus exposes the children in the forest.
9. Malkedras (?) thrusts the Queen into prison.
10. The hermit finds the children.
11. A hind suckles them ; and Malkedras finds them.
12. Malkedras tells Matabryne.

The front of the casket.

13. Malkedras takes the chains from the children's necks.
14. They fly away as swans.
15. Matabryne praises and caresses Malkedras.
16. Matabryne taunts the King, and gets leave to burn the Queen.
17. A soldier is leading the Queen to execution: she has fallen on her knees and is praying. See l. 90, note.
18. The King is on his throne as if to see the burning. Matabryne and a man in armour behind him, counselling him.
19. The angel appears to the hermit and the child.
20. The hermit and the child set forth on their way.

The left side of the casket.

21. The King on his throne; the Queen presents the child as her champion, and Matabryne Malkedras as hers.
22. Combat between Helyas and Malkedras.
23. Helyas having slain Malkedras, bears away his head.
24. Flight of Matabryne.

The back of the casket.

25. Helyas presents the head of Malkedras to the King.
26. Reconciliation of King Oryens and Queen Beatrice.
27. The King and Queen embrace Helyas.
28. King Helyas with a kneeling figure before him. He seems to be giving something into his hand; and perhaps it is a commission to a captain 'to prepaire a lytle hoste,' as Copland has it.
29. His army march against Matabryne.
30. They prepare to assault
31. The castle and its defenders.
32. Capture of Matabryne.

The right side of the casket.

33. Helyas recounts his adventures to his father and mother.
34. The burning of Matabryne.

35. The King and the Queen gazing

36. At Helyas departing in his ship alone, led by his brother the Swan.

The letter from Mr Dallaway, and extract of a letter from Mr Way in the note below, give the opinion of those antiquaries on the date and artistic value of this casket.[1]

[1] 'Mr Dallaway's respectful compliments to Sir Thomas Crawley, with the cabinet he has so long detained. He should have returned it with more satisfaction had he been able to discover the whole of the history represented, which is too complicated for him to unravel.

'Upon the upper compartment is evidently shown the well-known Legend of Isenbard, Earl of Altorf, and Irmentruda his wife, with her supernatural progeny.

'The two sons, who were preserved, were called Guelfo and Ghibelino, and their descendants were leaders of the factions by which the Italian States were distracted in the 12th century.

'He is of opinion that the remainder of their legendary story is described around the sides of the cabinet, and is not without hopes that, when he can meet with a very scarce collection of German novels, entitled "Camerarii Horæ Subcesivæ," it will furnish him with the whole of the detail.

'The armour and weapons of some of the figures are decidedly those of the 14th century, when elaborate carving was in very general use, and many Greek artists were encouraged; which circumstance seems to establish the date of the specimen.

'The enclosed drawing Mr D. begs that Sir Thomas will accept, with many thanks, for the permission he has obtained to have it etched. He will take care that justice be done to it, and hopes that Sir T. will find room in his portfolio for some of the proof impressions.

'Jan. 5, 1793.

'Sir Thomas Crawley.'

'Wonham Manor,
'Reigate, Nov. 29, '60.

'Dear Sir Martin,

'Your kindness in permitting me to bring home your curious ivory casket has, as I anticipated, enabled me to ascertain the whole of the subjects represented upon it. After much fruitless research, and showing the casket to several learned friends, I have at length got the right clue, and all difficulty ceases. The subjects are all from one romance, known as the "Knight of the Swan," and not found in any of the abstracts of middle-age romances, by Ellis, Dunlop, or the Italian writer Ferrario. It has, however, been published, but the volumes containing it are of very great rarity.

'I hope to send you an account of the romance, detailing the subjects as they occur on the casket. . . . .

. . . . . . I should almost suggest only to repair the broken portions of the metal bands as they exist, not to renew those which have been

ORIGIN OF THE ROMANCE.

Little or nothing can be added, on this head, to what Mr Thoms has collected in his preface to the Knight of the Swan; and what I here write is chiefly drawn from that source.

Mr Utterson quotes Mr F. Cohen (Sir Francis Palgrave) for the opinion that the earliest form in which the story exists is in the Chronicle of Tongres, written by the Maitre de Guise, and incorporated in great part into the Mer des Hystoires. There is also, he says, an Icelandic Saga of Helis, the Knight of the Swan, in which he is called a son of Julius Cæsar; and a similar legend is introduced into the German romance of *Lohengrin*, of which an edition was printed at Heidelberg as late as 1813. The story is still popular in Flanders, where a Chap-book, entitled De Ridder Met de Zwaen, was of frequent occurrence early in this century.

The immediate parent of the English prose romances on the subject appears to be the French folio printed in 1504, and entitled LA GENEALOGIE AVECQUES LES GESTES ET NODLES FAITZ DARMES DU TRES PREUX ET RENOMME PRINCE GODEFFROY DE BOULION ET DE SES CHEUALEREUX FRERES BAUDOUIN ET EUSTACE, YSSUS & DESCENDUS DE LA TRES NOBLE & ILLUSTRE LIGNEE DU VERTUEUX CHEVALIER AU CYNE. AVECQUES AUSSI PLUSIEURS AUTRES CRONIQUES HYSTOIRES MIRACULEUSES; TANT DU BON ROY SAINCT LOYS COMME DE PLUSIEURS AULTRES PUISSANS & VERTUEUX CHEVALIERS.

It was the first thirty-eight chapters of this work that were published in an English form by Robert Copland (which is the version edited by Mr Thoms); and Ames speaks of a translation published by Wynkyn de Worde, in 1512; but it is not now known to exist.

lost. . . . . It is to be considered that these metal bands are not original. The ivory dates from about 1380; the metal work about 1550.
. . . .
'Believe me, very sincerely yours,
'ALBERT WAY.'
'Sir Martin Crawley-Boevey.'

Mr Way says in another letter that photographs had been taken of the casket. These I have never seen, but a set has been prepared expressly for this edition.

The tradition that the great Godfrey of Bouillon was descended from the Knight of the Swan, has always been a favourite one, and one of the most interesting stories in Otmar's Volksagen is founded on it. Nicolas de Klerc, in order to set right the common opinion in Flanders,

> Om dat van Brabant die Hertoghen
> Voormaels, dicke syn beloghen
> Alse dat sy quamen metten Swane
>
> [Forasmuch as the Dukes of Brabant
> have been heretofore much belied
> as that they came with a Swan],

professes to tell the truth about it in his Brabandshe Yeesten, written in 1318; and Marlaent refers to the same belief in his Spiegel Historiael.

On the other hand (through Godfrey, no doubt,) Robert Copland claims it as an honour for his patron, Edward Duke of Buckingham, that from the Knight of the 'Swan 'linially is dyscended my sayde Lorde.'

As to the portentous birth, which is the basis of the story, similar tales have been not unfrequently told. Amongst others there is one in which the house of Guelph is said to take its name from a like incident.

'Irmentrudes, wife of Isenbard Earl of Altorfe, accused a woman of adultery for bringing forth three children at a birth; adding withal that she was worthy to be sown in a sack, and thrown into the sea; and urged it very earnestly. It chanced in the year following, that she herself conceived, and in the absence of her husband, was delivered of twelve male children at one birth (though very little). But she, fearing the imputation and scandal she had formerly laid on the poor woman, and the law of like for like, caused her most trusty woman to make choice of one to be tendered to the father, and to drown all the residue in a neighbouring river. It fell out that the Earl Isenbard returning home, met this woman, demanding whither she went with her pail? who answered, "to drown a few baggage whelps in the river." The Earl would see them; and notwithstanding the woman's resistance, did so, and discovering the children, pressed her to tell the matter, which she also did; and he caused them all to be secretly nursed; and, grown great, were brought home unto him, which he placed in an open hall with the son whom his wife had brought up, and soon known to be brethren by their likelihood in every respect. The Countess confessed the whole matter (moved with the sting of conscience), and was forgiven. In remembrance whereof, the illustrious race of the Welfes (whelps) got that name, and ever since hath kept it.'

Westcote (whose words I transcribe, as his book is a privately printed one (1845) from his MS. c. 1600) quotes this story from one Camerarius (he says) of Nuremberg, as a companion to a story of the wife of a peasant of Chumleigh, co. Devon, who had seven children at a birth, and whose husband, for fear of having to maintain so many mouths, resolves to drown them, and declares to the Countess of Devon, who meets him while on his errand, that they are but whelps. She rescues them and provides for them.

In French history we have a story somewhat analogous, in the efforts of the monks to separate Robert Capet and his wife, by persuading him that she had given birth to a monster.

The after part of the story of our book is the old one told with many variations from the time of the Shepherd David until now, of extreme youth, with the aid of the grace of God, vanquishing in battle the evil-doer, though a man of war from his youth.

THE VERSIFICATION OF THE POEM.

Coming now to the versification of the poem: I have thought it useful to analyse it so as to ascertain how far the author has kept himself to the rules of alliterative verse, as collected by Mr Skeat in his Essay on the subject prefixed to the 3rd volume of the Percy Folio.

The author seems to have contented himself with preserving generally the proper swing of his metre, the accentuated syllables marking it, in most cases, fairly well: but it often halts, the soft or unaccentuated syllables being awkwardly and too prodigally used, and the rime-letters very frequently falling on those syllables.

In many couplets the alliteration is utterly irregular, and in 10 couplets[1] I can discover none at all.

[1] 21, 34, 106, 225, 232, 334-6, 343, 367.

In 22 others¹ he has satisfied himself with a feeble sprinkling of the same letter through the verse without any regard to the loud syllables; as

60. *at a* chamber dore *as* she forth sowȝte

sometimes also supplementing the weakness of one alliteration by adding a second in the same couplet; as

241. that *styked styffe* in her BRestes · þat wolde þe qwene BRenne

287. A *knyȝte kawȝte* nym by þe nonde · & ladde nym of þe route.

The couplets in which there are but two rime-letters are very many; no less than 143² out of the whole number of 370; and there are eight couplets³ with four rime-letters.

The other variations from the established rule are: (*a.*) The occurrence of the chief letter on the second instead of the first loud syllable of the second line, which is found 64 times,⁴ and of these 64, 29 (⁵) occur in couplets with but two rime-letters.

(*b.*) The occurrence of two rime-letters in the second line of the couplet, and but one in the first, in 37 couplets.⁶

(*c.*) The absence of the chief letter in the second limb of the couplet occurs 20 times.⁷

(*d.*) The rime-letters occur very often indeed upon unaccentuated or 'soft' syllables; so often, as to lead one to think that the author must have deemed his task fully done, if only there was any alliteration at all. The number is 72,⁸ besides three in the next class.

---

¹ 13-4, 32, 49, 52, 60, 81, 96, 113, 132, 145, 158, 165, 185, 199, 210-1, 218, 272, 281-2, 351.
² 5, 6, 8, 10-1, 16, 24, 30-1, 40-1, 45-6, 54, 58, 63, 65, 75-6, 80, 82, 88, 90, 95, 99, 101, 103-5, 108, 110, 114-5, 120-1, 127-9, 137, 139, 142, 146, 149-50, 154-5, 160-2, 166-7, 172, 174, 181, 184, 189, 191-2, 195-6, 200-1, 208, 222, 227-9, 231, 240-1, 244, 247, 250-3, 256, 258, 264-5, 268-9, 271, 273, 280, 285-6, 290, 292, 294, 296, 299, 300, 302-6, 309, 314-6, 320-1, 323, 325, 327-8, 338, 353-4, 368-70.
³ 2, 35, 42, 91, 152, 183, 239, 360.
⁴ 1, 4, 20, 25-6, 30, 42, 53, 69, 70, 112, 136, 156, 173, 179, 183, 202, 212, 217, 226, 236, 239, 248, 261, 295, 310, 313, 317, 319, 324, 329, 331, 334, 355, 359. (⁵) 22, 37-8, 48, 56, 64, 86, 123, 140, 144, 164, 177, 182, 187-8, 190, 194, 203, 205-6, 207, 214, 236, 238, 246, 254, 308, 312, 363.
⁶ 1, 12, 17, 23, 51, 78-9, 83-4, 107, 119, 135, 138, 141, 151, 159, 169, 170, 175, 198, 209, 223, 233-5, 237, 243, 255, 291, 293, 326, 340-2, 350, 356-7.
⁷ 19, 50, 59, 67, 125, 153, 157, 163, 215, 219, 257, 259, 277, 279, 289, 332, 346-7, 352, 364.
⁸ 2, 7, 23, 25-6, 28, 31, 35, 39, 40, 50-1, 66, 70, 73, 77, 79, 82, 102-3, 108-9,

(e.) Where the chief letter occurs in the initial catch of the second couplet.[1]

There are also *ten* couplets[2] with separate alliterations in each line, and

Seven,[3] in which there are no rime-letters in the first line.

And the couplets that appear to conform strictly to the canon of alliteration which provides that there shall be three rime-letters in each couplet, viz. two (sub-letters) in the accentuated syllables of the first line or limb of it, and one (the chief letter) on the first accentuated syllable of the second line, are 48 in number;[4] such as

<blockquote>
92. Now Leve we þis Lady · in Langour & pyne
147. They sToden alle sTylle · for sTere þey ne durste
</blockquote>

But of these 48, the alliteration is not always perfect, *w* having to do duty with words beginning with Oo (l. 29); *D* being once used as a rime-letter to *T* (l. 27), and the *G* in gladness being once considered mute, so as to rime the word with 'lay in langour' (l. 57).

The former editor draws attention to the existence of some rime-endings in this poem, but they seem to me to be accidental rather than intentional.

Mr Skeat enumerates them in his essay, and I set them down here, excepting those in lines 260-1, where he has been misled by the former editor's mistaking the long second *r* in *marre*, and reading it *marye;* and in 28, 29, where the editor has mistaken *leue* for *lene;*

12-13, *where* and *there*

31-32, *were* and *there*

158-159, *swyde* and *leyde*. This is not a rime at all.

166-167, *faste* and *caste*

198-199, } *swannes* and *cheynes*. A very doubtful rime.
350-351, }

---

[1] 116, 118, 120, 126-8, 141, 143, 152, 156, 159, 161, 168-9, 175-6, 178, 180, 186, 191, 195, 202, 204, 209, 217, 220-1, 234-5, 250, 256, 261-2, 267, 270, 274, 278, 280, 283-4, 287-8, 292, 294, 337, 341, 343, 347-8, 357.

[1] 55, 75, 96.

[2] 44, 72, 85, 111, 216, 249, 266, 275, 330, 365.

[3] 117, 198, 245, 318, 345, 350, 362.

[4] 3, 9, 15, 18, 27, 29, 33, 36, 39, 43, 47, 57, 61-2, 71, 74, 87, 89, 91-4, 97-8, 100, 124, 131, 133-4, 147-8, 171, 193, 197, 213, 260, 263, 276, 297-8, 301, 307, 311, 322, 339, 349, 360-1, 366.

237-238, *were* and *mysfare;*
and I may add 359-60, *mude* and *bledde.*

But among these there are but three rimes which are at all perfect; and it may be observed that in the 370 lines (from 200 to 570) of William of Palerne, which I have searched cursorily, there are as many:

As, 210, þat of horne ne of *hounde* · ne mizt he here *sowne·*
236-7, *telle* and *wille*
337-8, *speche* and *riche*
404, as euene as ani *wiȝt* · schuld attely bi *siȝt*
490-1, *wise* and *nyce*
563-4, *newe* and *shewe;*

so the rimes must, I think, be considered as an inadvertence on the part of the poet, and not as an intended embellishment.

CHARACTER OF THE MS.

The manuscript is neatly written in a handwriting of about 1460; and seemingly with few, if any, errors. At first sight the letter Thorn appears to be used indiscriminately for Th, but I find that it is *never* used at the beginning of a line, and *never* at the end of a word, whether it be written, for example, serveth, or servethe. The Th is used in proper names; and the few other cases where it is found are, with one exception (thykke), where the sound occurs before the vowel e. Thus Sythen, Murther, Ferther, Therefore, and Beetheth, are thus spelt whenever they are found; and Thefe is only once spelt þefe.

The ȝ is constantly used, representing *gh* in the middle of words and *y* at the beginning.

In most cases where we write *er* in our modern speech, and especially in word-endings, such as *after, water, together,* &c., the scribe uses a contraction representing *ur,* making the words *aftur, watur,* &c.

Where the double *l* is crossed (ƚƚ), a final *e* has been assumed.

DATE AND DIALECT OF THE POEM.

The date of our poem in its present form appears to be the latter end of the 14th century; and the dialect in which it is written is Midland, and probably East Midland, as will be seen by the following observations.

The present indicative plurals of regular verbs end everywhere in *-en*. There appears to be an exception to this in l. 72, 'hem that it *deservethe*;' but 'hem' may either be miswritten for 'her;' or else perhaps it is used indeterminately, as 'they' and 'them' are sometimes used now-a-days.

It is not West Midland; for the 3rd sing. indic. almost universally ends in *-eth;* the only exceptions being '*lykes*' in l. 134; '*wendes*' in ll. 155 and 178; '*launces*' in l. 323, and '*formerknes*' in l. 362, though this last (see the note on the line) is a doubtful instance. Robert of Brunne also uses this termination in *-es;* but always, apparently, for the sake of the rime.

The second person sing. indic. ends in *-est;* excepting the word '*fyndes*' in l. 305. 'Thou *were*' is used in lines 236-7.

In many instances the *e* final is omitted in the past tense of weak verbs; as, delyvered, 155 and 178; graunted, 189 and 246. See also ll. 18, 24, 28, 39, 62, 91, 107, 108, 255, 275, 281, and 339.

There are some terminations in *-eth*, used instead of *-ed* for the perfect participles of regular verbs. See ll. 78, 175, 200, 209, 310.

The plurals of nouns end almost universally in *-es;* the only exceptions being *lond-is*, l. 16, *lyon-ys*, l. 214, and *bell-ys*, l. 272 (which are perhaps only variations made by the copyist); *dom-us*, l. 91; and *chylderen*, ll. 20 and 82.

Fader is uninflected in the possessive case, l. 203. The other genitives are in *-es*.

Some nouns of time and measure are uninflected in the plural; as *ʒere*, l. 89, 243 (we say now 'a two-*year*-old colt'), and *myle*, l. 95 (we say now 'it is a *two-mile* course').

Of the personal pronouns—

I is always used, and not *Ic*.

All people alike, king and peasant, *Thou* and *Thee* one another, without the distinction of rank, such as is shown in William of Palerne, by the use of *Ye* and *You*. In one instance, l. 26, the King addresses the Queen as *Ye*. *Hym* is the objective singular, and *Hem* (in one instance *Ham*, probably for þam—a Northern form) the plural: *Them* is never used.

She is the 3rd person fem. nominative, and *Here* or *Her* objective, the latter being used 8 times in the poem, and the former 9.

Hit and *It* are used about equally, the latter rather more frequently. *They* is always used in the plural.

The possessive pronoun of the 3rd person feminine, is *Her* or *Here*. In the plural of all genders it is *Here*, and once *Her*.

The negative form of the verb To Be is once used in *Nere* = no were, l. 3.

The imperfect participles end always in -*ynge*.

This is contrary to early Midland usage, and seems to show that the dialect here employed must have been spoken in the Southern part of the East Midland district, -*inge* being a Southern form, though it is used in another East Midland book, 'Body and Soul,' l. 396 [brennynge], and by Robert of Brunne 'Handlyng Synne;' and by Chaucer. But as the peculiarities of each dialect were no doubt always understood by the neighbours on the borders of the several districts, and by degrees became naturalized beyond their ancient limits; so probably at the time when the Cheualere Assigne was written, the Southern and Midland dialects at least were beginning to blend and form a common language.

One peculiarity in this author's style is a strange mixing of past and present tenses; i. e. in the same sentence he constantly, as does also Chaucer sometimes, uses the historical present, and the perfect. Thus in l. 229,

'The chylde *stryketh* hym to, & *toke* hym by þe brydelle.'

See also lines 63, 115-16, 151, 155, 173, 178, 190, 221, 267, 332, 341, 355, 361-2, and 365.

Mr Morris writes, 'The Dialect in its *present form* is East Midland. But as we do not find [other] East Midland writers adopting alliterative measure in the 14th century, I am inclined to think that the original English text was written in the N. or N.W. of England, and that the present copy is a mere modified transcript. This theory accounts for the *es's* in the 3rd person [sing.], which are not required for the rime, and may be forms belonging to the earlier copy, and unaltered by the later scribe.'

I have to thank Mr Morris, Mr Skeat, and Mr Furnivall for their kind suggestions during the progress of my work, and I must make also my acknowledgments to Mr Brock for his faultless transcript.

Although, therefore, I suppose that, from their uncertain character, the dialect or grammatical peculiarities of this poem are not of any particular value in the history of the language, yet as it is at any rate a contribution to that history, and as I think that whatever is worth doing at all, is worth doing thoroughly, I have made the Glossary as copious and accurate as I could. Besides, there is some spirit and vigour in the Poem itself; and I hope the reading of the little book may be as entertaining to the members of the Early English Text Society, as the editing of it has been to me.

H. H. G.

.;. CHEUELERE .;. ASSIGNE .;.

[*Cotton MS. Caligula* A. ii., *fol.* 125 *b.*]

¶ Alle weldynge god · whenne it is his wylle,   God Almighty guards us,.
Wele he wereth his · werke wit*h* his owne honde :
For ofte harmes were hente · þat helpe we ne myȝte ;
Nere þe hyȝnes of hym · þat lengeth in heuene.   4
For this I saye by a lorde · was lente in an yle,   as we see by the story of King
That was kalled lyor · a londe by hym selfe.   Oryens,
The kynge hette oryens · as þe book tellet*he* ;
And his qwene bewtrys · þat bryȝt was & shene :   8   and Beatrice his queen, and his
¶ His moder hyȝte Matabryne · þat made moche sorwe ;   mother Matabryne.
For she sette her affye · in Sathanas of helle.
This was chefe of þe kynde · of cheualere assygne ;
And whenne þey sholde in-to a place · it seyth fulle
     wele where,   12
Sythen aft*ur* his lykynge · dwellede he þere,
Withe his owne qwene · þat he loue myȝte :
But alle in langou*r* he laye · for lofe of here one,
That he hadde no chylde · to cheue*n*ne his londis ; 16   He had no child to succeed him,
¶ But to be lordeles of his · whenne he þe lyf lafte :   which was a grief.
And þat honged in his herte · I heete þe for sothe.

Line 5. See note on l. 23.
6. lyor. In the French poem it is *Lilefort*, and in Copland also.
7—9. The King is called *Oriant* in the French version, and the Queen *Bietrix*, and the King's mother *Matebrune*.

11. 'This' must mean 'this King.'
12. I cannot make sense of this line. 'Sholde' = should go, and 'it' means the book.
18. honged in his herte = weighed upon his mind.

<small>The King and the Queen, talking on the wall, see beneath them a woman with her twins,</small>

As þey wente vp-on a walle · pleynge hem one,
Bothe þe kynge & þe qwene · hem selfen to-gedere: 20
The kynge loked a-downe · & by-helde vnder,
And sey3 a pore womman · at þe 3ate Sytte,
Withe two chylderen her by-fore · were borne at a byrthe;

<small>whereat he weeps.</small> And he turned hym þenne · & teres lette he falle. 24
¶ Sython sykede he on-hy3e · & to þe qwene sayde,
'Se 3e þe 3onder pore womman · how þat she is pyned
Withe twynlenges two · & þat dare I my hedde wedde.'

<small>The Queen says she disbelieves in twins. Each must have a father.</small>

The qwene nykked hym with nay · & seyde 'it is not
   to leue: 28
Oon manne for oon chylde · & two wymmen for tweyne;
Or ellis hit were vnsemelye þynge · as me wolde þenke,
But eche chylde hadde a fader · how manye so þer were.'

<small>The King rebukes her,</small>

The kynge rebukede here for her worþes ry3te þere; 32
¶ And whenne it drow3 towarde þe ny3te · þey wenten
   to bedde;

<small>and at night begets on her reasonably many children,</small>

He gette on here þat same ny3te · resonabullye manye.
The kynge was witty · whenne he wysste her with chylde,
And þankede lowely our lorde · of his loue & his
   sonde. 36

---

19. walle. The French has 'tour.'
23. Chaucer frequently omits the relative, as is done here.
26. 'is pyned' must mean 'has travailed,' or been in pain.
28. it is not to leue. The edition of 1820 has lene. In the French it is vous parlez de neant.
29. This means, 'One man can beget but one child, nor can one woman have more than one at a time by the same man. Two honestly-begotten children must needs have two mothers.' Twins were once thought to reflect on the mother's chastity.
The French poem has

Sa deux hommes ne sext lirree char-
  nellement.
31. how manye so = howso[ever] many.
32. ry3te there = On the spot.
33 & 37. drow3 and drow3e. 'The correct form is drow.'—R. Morris.
34. He gette, &c. It is printed gotte in the Roxb. ed., but the word is plainly gette in the MS. The French has

Engendra le seigneur en la dame
  vaillant
vij enfans celle nuit en ung engen-
  drement.

But whenne it drow3e to þe tyme · she shulde be de-
lyuered,
Ther moste no womman come her nere · but she þat
    was cursed,
His moder matabryne · þat cawsed moche sorowe;
For she thow3te to do þat byrthe · to a fowle ende. 40
¶ Whenne god wolde þey were borne · þenne brow3te
    she to honde
Sex semelye sonnes · & a dow3ter þe seueneth,   *to wit, six sons and a daughter,*

.;. MATABRYNE. .;.   [Fol. 128.]

Alle safe & alle sounde · & a seluer cheyne   *with silver chains about their necks.*
Eche on of hem hadde · a-bowte his swete swyre. 44
And she lefte hem out · & leyde hem in a cowche;
And þenne she sente aftur a man · þat markus was   *But Matabryne sends for her man Marcus,*
    called,
That hadde serued her-seluen · skylfully longe:
He was trewe of his feyth · & loth for to tryfulle; 48
¶ She knewe hym for swych · & triste hym þe better;
And seyde, 'þou moste kepe counselle · & helpe what
    þou may:
The fyrste grymme watur · þat þou to comeste, 51   *and bids him drown the children.*
Looke þou caste hem þer-In · & lete hym forthe slyppe:
Sythen seche to þe courte · as þou now3te hadde sene,
And þou shalt lyke fulle wele · yf þou may lyfe aftur.'

39. 'þat cawsed moche sorowe.' These words, and 'the cursede man in his feyth,' are, like the Homeric ποδας ωκυς and ποιμενα λαων, applied as a sort of verse-tag to fill up the line, and serve as constant epithets respectively to Matabryne and Malkedras.
40. do.. to a fowle ende. See l. 138. As in Shakespere, Much Ado about Nothing, V. 3: '*Done* to death with slanderous tongues.'
45. lefte = lifted.
46. Markus, called *Marques* and *Marcon* in the French poem.
49. knewe, should be *knew*; the *e* is superfluous; but it is so in the MS.
49. swych. Wrongly printed *swyth* in the Roxb. ed.
triste. Wrongly printed *tristed*, in the same, moste; the *e* is superfluous.
50. kepe counselle = be secret.
52. hym for *hem*.
53. seche = betake thyself. Comp. Ezekiel xiv. 10, 'him that seeketh unto him.'
54. lyke full wele = be well-liking = prosper. Comp. 'fat and well-liking,' Ps. xcii. 13; 'worse-liking,' Daniel i. 10. 'I believe the original construction was, "And it shal like þe ful wel" = and it shall please thee full well. See l. 134.'—R. Morris.

Marcus grieves, but dares not disobey.	Whenne he herde þat tale · hym rewede þe tyme; But he durste not werne · what þe qwene wolde. 56 ¶ The kynge lay in langour · sum gladdenes to here; But þe fyrste tale þat he herde · were tydynges febulle, Whenne his moder matabryne · browȝte hym tydynge. At a chamber dore · as she forthe sowȝte, 60
She takes seven whelps,	Seuenne whelpes she sawe · sowkynge þe damme, And she kawȝte out a knyfe · & kylled þe bycche; She caste her þenne in a pytte · & takethe þe welpes, And sythen come byfore þe kynge · & vp on-hyȝe she seyde, 64
and shows 'em to the King as the Queen's offspring, and bids him have her burnt.	¶ 'Sone paye þe with þy qwene · & se of her berthe.' Thenne syketh þe kynge · & gynnythe to morne, And wente wele it were sothe · alle þat she seyde. Thenne she seyde, 'lette brenne her a-none · for þat is þe beste.' 68
He refuses.	'Dame, she is my wedded wyfe · fulle trewe as I wene, As I haue holde her er þis · our lorde so me helpe!'
She vituperates.	'A, kowarde of kynde,' quod she · '& combred wrecche! Wolt þou werne wrake · to hem þat hit descruethe?'
He says, 'Stow her where thou wilt, so that I see it not.'	¶ 'Dame, þanne take here þy selfe · & sette her wher þe lykethe, 73 So þat I se hit noȝte · what may I seye elles?' Thenne she wente her forthe · þat god shalle confounde,
She falls foul of the Queen,	To þat febulle þer she laye · & felly she bygynnethe, 76 And seyde, 'a-ryse wrecched qwene · & reste þe her no lengur; Thow hast by-gylethe my sone · it shalle þe werke sorowe: Bothe howndes & men · haue hadde þe a wylle: Thow shalt to prisoun fyrste · & be brente aftur.' 80

60. sowȝte. See note on l. 53.
64. come. The correct form is com.
on-hyȝe = aloud.
68. lette brenne her = have her burnt.
72. descrueth. As to this termination in -eth, see Preface, p. xvi.
75. See note on l. 190.
78. by-gylethe. The final e is unnecessary; but there is a contraction representing it in the MS.

¶ Thenne shrykede þe ȝonge qwene · & vp on hyȝ and, in spite of her moans,
   cryethe,
'A, lady,' she seyde · 'where ar my lefe chylderen ?'
Whenne she myssede hem þer · grete mone she made.
By þat come tytlye · tyrauntes tweyne,   84
And by þe byddynge of matabryne · a-non þey her hente,
And in a dymme prysoun · þey slongen here deepe,   [Fol. 126 b.] has her thrown
And leyde a lokke on þe dore · & leuen here þere : 87 into prison, where she lies
Mote þey caste here a-downe · & more god sendethe. eleven years.

¶ And þus þe lady lyuede þere · elleuen ȝere,
And mony a fayre orysoun · vn-to þe fader made,
That saued Susanne fro sorowefulle domus · [her] to But God, who saved Susanna, hears her prayer
   saue als. also.
Now leue we þis lady· in langour & pyne,   92
And turne aȝeyne to our tale · towarde þese chylderen,
And to þe man markus · þat murther hem sholde ;
How he wente þorow a foreste · fowre longe myle, Marcus takes the children to drown
Thylle he come to a watur · þer he hem shulde in them.
   drowne ;   96

¶ And þer he keste vp þe clothe · to knowe hem bettur,
And þey ley & lowȝe on hym · louelye alle at ones : But they look on him in lovely
'He þat lendethe wit,' quod he · 'leyne me wyth sorowe, wise,
If I drowne ȝou to day · thowghe my deth be nyȝe.' 100 and he won't,
Thenne he leyde hem adowne · lappedde in þe mantelle, but leaves them all wrapped in a
And lappede hem, & hylyde hem · & hadde moche mantle, and commends them
   rewthe, to Christ.
That swyche a barmeteme as þat · shulde so be-tyde.
Thenne he takethe hem to criste · & aȝeyne turnethe. 104

---

81. See note on l. 64.
84. By þat = by that time, then.
tyrauntes. The French poem has Sers (serfs).
86. slongen. Roxb. ed. has flongen, which is an error of transcription.
90. This particular orison, with Susanna for its example, finds a place in the French poem, not at this point, but during the procession from the city to the place of burning, Matabryne's remark thereon being 'ça ne vault ung bouton.'
91. domus. This might be a miswriting for 'dom (= doom) us,' as the former edition reads it; but it is, no doubt, a plural in us, the word her having slipped out.
99. wit. Wrongly printed wth in the former edition.
103. swyche. See note on l. 49.

¶ But sone þe mantelle was vn-do · with mengynge of
her legges;
They cryedde vp on-hyӡe · with a dolefulle steuenne,
They chyuered for colde · as cheuerynge chyldren,

A hermit hears them sob,
They ӡoskened, & cryde out · & þat a man herde, 108
An holy hermyte was by · & towarde hem comethe :
Whenne he come by-tore hem · on knees þenne he felle,

and cries to Christ for succour;
And cryede ofte vpon cryste · for somme sokour hym
to sende,
If any lyfe were hem lente · in þis worlde lengur. 112

a hind comes and suckles them;
¶ Thenne an hynde kome fro þe woode · rennynge fulle
swyfte,
And felle be-fore hem adowñe · þey drowӡe to þe
pappes;
The heremyte prowde was þer-of · & putte hem to
sowke :

and the hermit takes them home and tends them.
Sethen taketh he hem vp · & þe hynde folowethe, 116
And she kepte hem þere · whylle our lorde wolde.
Thus he noryscheth hem vp · & criste hem helpe send-
ethe.
Of sadde leues of þe wode · wrowӡte he hem wedes.

Malkedras the Forester passes and sees them,
Malkedras þe fostere · þe fende mote hym haue, 120
¶ That cursedde man for his feythe · he come þer þey
wereñ,
And was ware in his syӡte · syker of þe chyldren;
He turnede aӡeyn to þe courte · & tolde of þe chaunce,

tells Matabryne,
And menede byfore matabryne · how mony þer were. 124
' And more merueyle þenne þat · Dame, a seluere cheyne
Eche on of hem hath · abowte here swyre.'
She seyde, ' holde þy wordes in chaste · þat none skape
ferther;
I wylle soone aske hym · þat hath me betrayed.' 128

---

119. sadde leues of þe wode. Fr. *feuilles de loriers.*
120. Malkedras is called in the French MS. *Malquarrez* and *Mauquarre.*

124. menede. Wrongly printed *meuede* in the Roxb. ed.
127. holde thy wordes in chaste = be silent.

¶ Thenne she sente aftur markus · þat murther hem *who questions Marcus,*
   sholde ;
And askede hym, in good feythe · what felle of þe
   chyldren :
Whenne she hym asked hadde · he seyde, 'here þe
   sothe ;
Dame, on a ryueres banke · lapped in my mantelle, 132 *and, hearing the truth, has his*
I lafte hem lyynge there · leue þou for sothe : *eyes put out ;*
I myȝte not drowne hem for dole · do what þe lykes.'
Thenne she made here alle preste · & (putt) out bothe
   hys yen.
Moche mone was therfore · but no man wyte moste. 136
¶ 'Wende þou aȝeyne malkedras · & gete me þe cheynes, *sends Malkedras to take the chains,*
And withe þe dynte of þy swerde · do hem to dethe ; *and slay the children.*
And I shalle do þe swych a turne · & þou þe tyte hyȝe,
That þe shalle lyke ryȝte wele · þe terme of þy lyue.' 140
Thenne þe hatefulle thefe · hyed hym fulle faste,
The cursede man in his feythe · come þer þey were.
By þenne was þe hermyte go in-to þe wode · & on of *He finds but six, one being away*
   þe children, *with the hermit.*
For to seke mete · for þe other sex,   144
¶ Whyles þe cursed man · asseylde þe other :
And he out withe his swerde · & smote of þe cheynes. *He smites off the chains ; and the*
They stoden alle stylle · for stere þey ne durste ; *children change into swans.*
And whenne þe cheynes felle hem fro · þey flowen vp
   swannes   148
To þe ryuere by-syde · withe a rewfulle steuenne.
And he takethe vp þe cheynes · & to þe cowrte
   turnethe,
And come by-fore þe qwene · & here hem bytakethe :
Thenne she toke hem in honde · & heelde ham fulle
   stylle ;   152
¶ She sente aftur a golde-smyȝte · to forge here a cowpe ;

   133. leue. Wrongly printed *lene* in of the MS. by the original scribe.
the edition of 1820.   138. do. See note on l. 40.
   135. The Roxb. ed. omits *putt*,   140. See note on l. 54.
which has been added in the margin

8 MATABRYNE HAS A CUP MADE OF THE SILVER.

The old Queen gives the chains to a goldsmith to make a cup of.

And whenne þe man was comen · þenne was þe qwene
 blythe,
And delyuered hym his weyȝtes · & he from cowrte
 wendes:
She badde þe wesselle were made · vpon alle wyse: 156
The goldesmyȝth goothe & beetheth hym a fyre · &
 brekethe a cheyne,

One chain multiplies so in the melting-pot, that half of one suffices.

And it wexeth in hys honde · & multyplycthe swyde :
He toke þat oþur fyue · & fro þe fyer hem leyde,
And made hollye þe cuppe · of haluendelle þe sixte. 160
¶ And whenne it drowȝe to þe nyȝte · he wendethe to
 bedde,

The goldsmith tells his wife, and asks her counsel.

And thus he seythe to his wyfe · in sawe as I telle.
'The olde qwene at þe courte · hathe me bytaken
Six cheynes in honde · & wolde haue a cowpe ;   164
And I breke me a cheyne · & halfe leyde in þe fyer,
And it wexedde in my honde · & wellede so faste,
That I toke þe oþur fyve · & fro þe fyer caste,
And haue made hollye þe cuppe · of haluendele þe
 sixte.'   168

She says, 'Keep the rest! The Queen has full weight. What would she have more?'
[Fol. 127 b.]

¶ 'I rede þe,' quod his wyfe · 'to holden hem stylle ;
Hit is þorowe þe werke of god · or þey be wronge
 wonnen ;
For whenne here mesure is made · what may she aske
 more ?'   171
And he dedde as she badde · & buskede hym at morwe ;

He gives the old Queen the cup and the half chain.

He come by-fore þe qwene · & bytaketh here þe cowpe,
And she toke it in honde · & kepte hit fulle clene.
'Nowe lefte ther ony ouur vn-werkethe · by þe better
 trowthe ?'
And he recheth her forth · haluendele a cheyne : 176

---

162. The conversation between the goldsmith and his wife is much longer and more dramatic in our poem than in the French.
170. þorowe. Wrongly printed *Thōre* in the Roxb. ed.

170. wronge wonnen=wrongly (i. e. wrongfully) acquired.
176. recheth. Misprinted *recketh*.
 forth. Misprinted *ferth* in the Roxb. ed.

¶ And she raw3te hit hym a3eyne · & seyde she ne *She gives him*
                                                 the half chain
row3te;   *and his pay.*
But delyuered hym his seruyse · & he out of cowrte
wendes.
'The curteynesse of criste,' q*uod* she · 'be wi*th* þese
    oþ*ur* cheynes!   179
They be delyuered out of þis worlde · were þe moder eke,
The*n*ne hadde I þis londe · hollye to myne wylle:
Now alle wyles shalle fayle · but I here dethe werke.'
At morn she come byfore þe kynge · & by ga*n*ne fulle *She scolds the*
                                                       King for leaving
    keene;   183 *his Queen so long*
                                                       unburnt,
'Moche of þis worlde so*n*ne · wondrethe on þe a*tt*one,
¶ That thy qwene is vnbrente · so meruelows longe,
That hath serued þe deth*e* · if þou here dome wyste:
Lette som*m*ene þy folke · vpon eche a syde,   *and bids him*
                                                       summon his folk.
That þey bene at þy sy3te · þe .xj. day assygned.' 188
And he here gra*u*nted þat · withe a grym*m*e herte;   *He grieves; but*
                                                       grants it.
And she wendeth here adowṅ · & lette hem a-none
    warne.
The ny3te byfore þe day · þat þe lady shulde bren*n*e, *The night before*
                                                       the burning
An Angell*e* come to þe hermyte · & askéde if he slepte: *comes an angel*
                                                         to the hermit.
¶ The angell*e* seyde, 'criste sendeth þe worde · of þese
    six chyldreṅ;   193
And for þe sauynge of hem · þanke þou haste seruethe:
They were þe kynges Oriens · wytte þou for sothe,

179. '*Puis dist entre ses dens assez*   and 'hy3e' in l. 141, after the French
bassetement   s'en *alla.* Comp. Shaksp. 2 Gent. of
Bien suis de ceulx delivre alez   Ver. IV. 4: 'I .. goes *me* to the fel-
sont voirement   low.' The phrase in the text seems
Se leur mere estoit arse ne me   to make it more probable that this *me*
chauldroit neant.   is the personal, and not the indeter-
And then,' she continues, 'by my en-   minate pronoun.
chantments I will cause that my son   194. þanke þou haste seruethe =
never marries again, and so I shall   thou hast deserved thanks. The final
have all the land at my command.'   *e* is too much. See note on l. 78.
  186. serued. In the Roxb. ed. this   195. They were the kynges Oriens =
is erroneously printed *dyserved*.   They were [the children] of the King
  if thou here dome wyste = if thou   Oriens. This expression is not unlike
knewest what her sentence ought to be.   that in Wm. of Palerne, l. 5437: þem-
  190. wendeth here. 'wend' is here   perours moder Willi*a*m.
used reflexively as 'went' is in l. 75,

Tells him that the six swan-children are sons of Oryens and Beatrice.	By his wyfe Betryce · she bere hem at ones, For a worde on þe walle · þat she wronge seyde; And ȝonder in þe ryuer · swymmen þey swannes; Sythen Malkedras þe forsworn þefe · byrafte hem her cheynes :	196
But that Christ formed the other child to fight for his mother.	And criste hath formeth þis chylde · to fyȝte for his moder.'	200
	¶ 'Oo-lyuynge god þat dwellest in heuene' · quod þe hermyte þanne,	
'How can this be?'	'How sholde he serue for suche a þynge · þat neuur none syȝe?'	
'Take him to Court and have him christened Enyas.'	'Go brynge hym to his fader courte · & loke þat he be cristened ; And kalle hym Enyas to name · for awȝte þat may be-falle, Ryȝte by þe mydday · to redresse his moder ; For goddes wylle moste be fulfylde · & þou most forthe wende.'	203
	The heremyte wakynge lay · & thowȝte on his wordes : Soone whenne þe day come · to þe chylde he seyde,	208
The hermit tells the child what he is to do, what a mother is, [Fol. 128.]	¶ 'Criste hath formeth þe sone · to fyȝte for þy moder.' He asskede hymm þanne · what was a moder. 'A womman þat bare þe to man · sonne, & of her reredde:' 'Ȝe, kanste þou, fader, enforme me · how þat I shalle fyȝte?' 'Vpon a hors,' seyde þe heremyte · 'as I haue herde seye.'	212

201. Oo. Wrongly printed *To* in the former edition. Oo-lyuynge = ever-living.

202. þynge. Wrongly printed ȝnge in the former edition.

204. Enyas; not *Ænyas*, as in the old edition. The French poem has *Elyas* or *Helyas*, which latter is the name given him in the English prose Romance.

A line seems to be omitted between 204 and 205, such as

'Let hym cair to þe court · þer þe kynge dwellethe.'

210. The conversation between the hermit and the child is more full in the English than in the French poem.

211. A very cramped line. 'A woman that bare thee to man, [my] son; and [thou wast] by her reared.'

'It means, "bare thee so that thou becamest a man." Such is the regular idiom ; [God] *wrouȝt me to man* = formed thee so that thou becamest a man, fashioned thee in man's shape; occurs in Piers Plowman, A. Pass. i. 1. 80.'—W. W. S.

'*Beau filz cest une femme quen ses flans te porta.*'

'What beste is þat?' quod þe chylde · 'lyonys wylde? *and what a horse, on which he is to*
Or elles wode? or watur' · quod þe chylde panne. *fight.*
'I sey3e neuur none,' quod þe hermyte · 'but by þe mater
　of bokes :　　　　　　　　　　　　　　　　216
¶ They seyn he hath a feyre hedde · & fowre lymes hye ;
And also he is a frely beeste · for-thy he man seruethe.'
'Go we forthe, fader,' quod þe childe 'vpon goddes halfe !' *The child is willing, and they*
The grypte eyþur a staffe in here honde · & on here wey *go forth on their way.*
　straw3te.　　　　　　　　　　　　　　　　220
Whenne þe heremyte hym lafte · an angelle hym suwethe, *The hermit leaves the child,*
Euur to rede þe chylde · vpon his ry3te sholder. *and an angel goes with him and counsels him.*
Thenne he seeth in a felde · folke gaderynge faste, *The child sees a*
And a hy3 fyre was þer bette · þat þe qwene sholde in *great crowd and*
　brenne,　　　　　　　　　　　　　　　　224 *a fire kindled in a field,*
¶ And noyse was in þe cyte · felly lowde, *and a great troop bringing the*
With trumpes & tabers · whenne þey here vp token ; *Queen from the city.*
The olde qwene at here bakke · betynge fulle faste ;
The kynge come rydynge a-fore · a forlonge & more ; 228 *The King rides in front.*
The chylde stryketh hym to · & toke hym by þe brydelle :
'What man arte þou?' quod þe chylde · '& who is þat *'Who art thou? and who are these?' quoth the*
　þe svethe?'　　　　　　　　　　　　　　*child.*

215. Or else [a] wood[-beast], or [a] water[-beast] ?
219. Comp. William of Palerne, l. 2803, 'Go we now on goddes halve.'
220. The grypte eyþur = They each seized.
221. suwethe. The Roxb. editor has mistaken this for seemeth.
221-2. rede. Here we find ride in the former edition ; but besides that it is not so written, the French original shows that it must be as in the text. This incident of the angel does not find its place here, in the French poem. There, it is when the child accosts the King that the author says,—
　Homme fol et sauvaige a merreilles
　　sembloit
　Lange a dieu le pere sur lespaule
　　avoit
　Que ce quil devoit dire trop bien lui
　　enseignoit.

224. brenne. The final e is illegible, being obliterated by a blot of ink.
bette. Comp. Sir Aldingar, l. 53 (Percy folio, vol. i. p. 168), 'And fayre fyer there shalbe bette.'
227. A tant est Matebrune qui
　　a-maine a grant cris
　Batant la bonne dame qui eust nom
　　Bietrix.
230. Here in the French poem follows,　　　　'Le roy ...
　Voulentiers en eust ris mais trop
　　dolent estoit.'
He then asks the child what his own name is ; and he answers that he has no name, except that with the hermit his name has been always Beau filz. Comp. Libius Disconius, ll. 25—30 and 62—66. Percy folio, vol. ii. p. 416 and 418.

12   HE OFFERS TO FIGHT FOR THE QUEEN.

'I am þe kynge of þis londe · & oryens am kalled,
The King answers, and tells the story.
And þe ʒondur is my qwene · betryce she hette,   232
¶ In þe ʒondere balowe fyre · is buskedde to brenne;
She was sklawnndered on-hyʒe · þat she hadde taken howndes;
And ʒyf she hadde so don · here harm were not to charge.'

'Thou dost ill to be led by Matabryne.
'Thenne . were þou noʒt ryʒ[t]lye sworne,' quod þe
chylde · 'vpon ryʒte Iuge,   236
Whenne þou tokest þe þy crowne · kynge whenne þou made were,
To done aftur matabryne · for þenne þou shalt mysfare,

She is fell and false, and shall go to the fiend.
For she is fowle felle & fals · & so she shalle be fownden,
And bylefte with þe fend · at here laste ende,   240
¶ That styked styffe in here brestes · þat wolde þe qwene brenne:

I am but 12 years old, but I will fight for the Queen.
I am but lytulle & ʒonge,' quod þe chylde · 'Iceue þou forsothe,
Not but twelfe ʒere olde · euen at þis tyme,
And I wolle putte my body · to better & to worse, 244
To fyʒte for þe qwene · with whome þat wronge seythe.'

The King is content.
Thenne graunted þe kynge · & Ioye he bygynnethe,
If any helpe were þer-Inne · þat here clensen myʒte.

The old Queen rebukes him.
By þat come þe olde qwene · & badde hym com þenne: 248

233. ʒondere. Misprinted ʒonders in the Roxb. ed.
235. hadde is erroneously printed shadde in the Roxb. ed.
here harm were not to charge = her death would not be a matter of concern to any one. ' Charge, in Chaucer, = a matter of difficulty, a matter of consideration.'—R. M.
236-7. The French corresponding to this passage is,
Arse! Dieu dist lenfant, fait as folle iugement

Nas pas a droit iuge comme roy loyaument.
vpon ryʒte Iuge = [hast not] rightly judged. These words are evidence that the French poem was the original of the English one; our poet having apparently taken the word *Iuge* into his text without translating it.
243. Not but = only. In modern Lancashire, *no but*, or *not but*.
245. with whom [soever it be] that wrong saith [of her].
248. þenne = thence.

¶ 'To speke wit/h suche on as he · þou mayste ryȝth
lothe thenke.'   249
'A, dame,' qu*od* þe kynge · 'thowȝte ȝe none synne? *He speaks up for his Queen, and*
Thow haste for-sette þe ȝonge qwene · þou knoweste   *[Fol. 128 b.] tells what the*
welle þe sothe :   *child says.*
This chylde þat I here speke withe · seyth þat he
wolle preue   252
That þou nother þy sawes · certeyne be neyther.'
And þenne she lepte to hym · & kawȝte hym by þe   *Matabryne rushes at the child and*
lokke ;   *tears his hair.*
That þer leued in here honde · heres an hondredde.
'A, by lyuynge god,' qu*od* þe childe · 'þat bydeste in
heuene,   256
¶ Thy hedde shalle lye on þy lappe · for þy false tu*r*nes. *'Thy head shall lie in thy lap!'*
I aske a felawe anone · a freshe knyȝte aftu*r*,   *quoth he. 'Give me a man to fight*
For to fyȝte wit/h me · to dryue owte þe ryȝte.'   *with!'*
'A, boy,' qu*od* she, 'wylt þou so · þou shalt sone
myskarye ;   260

254. hym, sc. the child. The passage
in the French poem is curious, the
writer exhibiting the rage of the con-
tending parties by a furious succession
of rimes in -*aige*, the Norman pronun-
ciation of -*age*.

Mere ce dist le roy vous nestes mie
    saige
Veez a ung enfant qui bien semble
    sauvaige
Qui dit que peche faictes et ennuy
    et hontaige
Que vous la dame a tort vous mettez
    sur putaige
Quant la vielle lentent a pou quelle
    nenrage
Aux chevculx prent lenfant plus de
    c. en arrache
Dieu aide dist lenfant ci a mal a
    comtaige
Ceste vielle hideuse a en son corps
    la raige
Plus fait a redoubter que mil lyon
    sauvaige.
La glorieuse dame en qui dieu print
    umbraige

Menvoye en cor vengence de ce
    villain hontaige ;
Ce ne me faisoit mie mon pere en
    lermitaige.
Tous ceulx qui lont oy huchent en
    leur langaige
Ha : roy de orient ne souffrez tel
    hontaige ;
Li enfant dit assez par les sains de
    cartaige.
Roy tien a lenfant droit bien pert
    de hault paraige,
Nulz homs ne puet mieulx dire tant
    soit de grant langaige,
Dieu te la envoye pour dire cest
    messaige.

256. bydeste. Sic in MS. 'It is
probably thrown in parenthetically,
and addressed to God. So in Havelok,
"Ihesu crist, þat made mone,
Þine dremes turne to ioye [sone]
Þat wite þw that sittes in trone."
It is very abrupt, certainly.'—W. W. S.
In Havelok also, there is a Thou in the
former part of the sentence, but here
there is none.

14   HE IS CHRISTENED ENYAS, AND IS DUBBED KNIGHT.

'Ha! boy! I'll get me a man that shall mar thee.'
I wylle gete me a man · þat shalle þe sone marre.'
She turneth her penne to malkedras · & byddyth hym take armes,

She sends Malkedras.
And badde hym bathe his spere · in þe boyes herte:
And he of suche one · gret skorne he þowȝte.   264

An Abbot christens the child Enyas.
¶ An holy abbot was þer-by · & he hym þeder bowethe,
For to cristen þe chylde · frely & feyre;
The abbot maketh hym a fonte · & was his godfader,
The erle of auñthepas · he was another,   268
The countes of salamere · was his godmoder;
They kallede hym Enyas to name · as þe book tellethe:
Mony was þe ryche ȝyfte · þat þey ȝafe hym aftur:

The bells ring of themselves all the fight through, betokening that Christ was well pleased.
Alle þe bellys of þe close · rongen at ones   272
¶ Withe-oute ony mannes helpe · whyle þe fyȝte lasted;
Wherefore þe wyste welle · þat criste was plesed with here dede.
Whenne he was cristened · frely & feyre,

The King dubs Enyas knight.
Aftur, þe kynge dubbede hym knyȝte · as his kynde wolde: 276
Thenne prestly he prayeth þe kynge · þat he hym lene wolde

The King lends him his good steed Feraunce, and armour, and a shield with a cross on it.
An hors with his harnes · & blethelye he hym grauntethe:
Thenne was feraunce fette forthe · þe kynges price stede,
And out of an hyȝe towre · armour þey halenne;   280
¶ And a whyte shelde with a crosse · vpon þe posse honged,
And hit was wryten þer-vpon · þat to enyas hit sholde:

261. marre. This is written in the MS. with a long r in the second place; and the former editor mistook it for a y, and wrote the word marye. The word 'miscarrye' in the line above might have undeceived him, for it also has the long r, followed by a real y.

262. þenne. Printed thence in the Roxb. ed.

265. An holy abbot. 'L'Abbe Gautier,' says the French book.

271. ȝyfte. This is misprinted ȝyste in the 1820 edition.

274. welle. Misprinted welt in the other edition.

279. Feraunce is Ferrant in the French poem.

281. posse. Perhaps miswritten for poste, as Utterson has printed it: it is, however, so written in the MS. Ayenbyte of Inwyt.

282. hit sholde [belong].

And whenne he was armed · to alle his ry3tes,   283
Thenne prayde he þe kynge · þat he hym lene wolde
Oon of his beste menne · þat he moste truste,
To speke with hym but · a speche whyle.
A kny3te kaw3te hym by þe honde · & ladde hym of
þe rowte :   287
'What beeste is þis,' quod þe childe · 'þat I shalle on
    houe ?'

¶ 'Hit is called an hors,' quod þe kny3te · 'a good & an
    abulle.'
'Why etethe he yren ?' quod þe chylde · 'wylle he ete
    no3the elles ?
And what is þat on his bakke · of byrthe, or on
    bounden ?'
'Nay, þat in his mowthe · men kallen a brydelle, 292
And that a sadelle on his bakke · þat þou shalt in
    sytte.'
'And what heuy kyrtelle is þis · withe holes so thykke ?
And þis holowe [on] on my hede · I may no3t wele
    here.'
'An helme men kallen þat on · & an hawberke þat
    other.'   296
¶ 'But what broode on is þis on my breste · hit bereth
    adown my nekke.'
'A bry3te shelde & a sheene · to shylde þe fro strokes.'
'And what longe on is þis · that I shalle vp lyfte?'
'Take þat launce vp in þyn honde · & loke þou hym
    hytte ;   300

Side notes:
Enyas takes counsel with a Knight whom the King lends him,
287 [of = from out of]
and learns what is a horse,
a saddle, a bridle, a hawberk, a helm, a shield, a lance, and a sword; and how to use them.
[Fol. 129.]
'See thou hit him.'

---

285. truste, pf. of trust; it is triste in l. 49.
286. a speche whyle. Comp. Shaksp. Two Gent. of Verona, IV. 3.
287. of = from out of.
288. houe. The Roxb. editor reads hone, and takes it to be the O.E. Hon = to hang, but it is doubtless Hove = abide, be.
290. The child puts this question to the King, in the French poem.

291. of byrthe = congenital, born with him, natural.
295. wele. This word is added in the margin in a later hand. It is omitted in the edition of 1820.
holowe = hollow one: the on has dropped out, because of the preposition following. See ll. 297, 299.
296. þat other. Misprinted þe other in the 1820 edition.

And whenne þat shafte is schyuered · take scharpelye another.'

'and if we come to ground?'
'Ȝe, what yf grace be · we to grownde wenden?'
'A-ryse vp lyȝtly on þe fete · & reste þe no lengur ; 303

'Get up again. Draw thy sword, smite him with the edge, anred him in pieces.'
And þenne plukke out þy swerde · & pele on hym faste,
¶ Alle-wey eggelynges down · on alle þat þou fyndes ;
His ryche helm nor his swerde · rekke þou of neyþur ;
Lete þe sharpe of þy swerde · schreden hym smalle.'

'But won't he smite again?'
'But wolle not he smyte aȝeyne · whenne he feleth smerte?'   308

'That will he! never mind! smite off his head!'
'Ȝys, I knowe hym fulle wele · bothe kenely & faste :
Euur folowe þou on þe flesh · tylle þou haste hym fallothe ;
And sythen smyte of his heede · I kan sey þe no furre.'

'Now þou haste tawȝte me,' quod þe childe · 'god I þe beteche :   312

¶ For now I kan of þe crafte · more þenne I kowthe.'

They run together, shiver their spears,
Thenne þey maden Raunges · & ronnen to-gedere,
That þe speres in here hondes · shyuereden to peces ;
And for [to] rennene aȝeyn · men rawȝten hem other, 316
Of balowe tymbere & bygge · þat wolde not breste ;
And eyther of hem · so smer[t]lye smote other,

smash their armour, and upset each other.
That alle fleye in þe felde · þat on hem was fastened,
And eyther of hem topseyle · tumbledde to þe erthe ; 320

The horses run round the lists.
¶ Thenne here horses ronnen forth · aftur þe raunges,
Euur feraunee by-forne · & þat other aftur ;

302. ȝe. Misprinted *Se* in the edition of 1820.
303. lyȝtly. Misprinted *lyȝt* in 1820.
305. eggelynges = edgewise. With the edge. The contrary of '*flatlings.*'
307. sharpe = sharp edge.
309. ȝys = yes. Its use here instead of ȝe, as in l. 302, is due to the negative in the question.
310. fallethe = felled.
316. rennene may be *rennenge, sb.;* but more probably the line should be as above, the *to* having been accident-ally omitted by the scribe.
320. topseyle. *Sic* in MS. Top = head,—as we say, 'from *top* to toe.' Should it be perhaps 'topteyle' ? Comp. Wm. of Palerne, l. 2776 :
'Set hire a sad strok so sore in þe necke
þat sche *top ouer tail* tombled ouer þe hacches.'
321. ronnen. Misprinted *rennen* in the Roxb. ed.
322. *Le destrier Elyas va, lautre poursuivant.*

Feraunce launces vp his fete · & lasschethe out his
yeñ :
The fyrste happe, other hele · was þat · þat þe chylde *Feraunce lashes out and blinds the other horse.*
hadde,   324
Whenne þat þe chylde þat hym bare · blente hadde his
fere :
Thenne thei styrte vp on hy · with staloworth shankes, *Enyas and Malkedras start up and draw their swerds.*
Pulledde out her swerdes · & smoten to-gedur.
'Kepe þy swerde fro my croyse' · quod cheuelrye *'Beware my cross!'*
assygne :   328
¶ 'I charde not þy croyse,' quod malkedras · 'þe valwe *'I don't care a cherry for your cross!'*
of a cherye ;
For I shalle choppe it fulle smalle · ere þenne þis werke
ende.'
An edder spronge out of his shelde · & in his body *An adder strikes him from out the cross; and a fire thereout blinds him.*
spynnethe ;
A fyre fruscheth out of his croys · & [f]rapte out his
yen :   332
Thenne he stryketh a stroke · Cheualere assygne, *Enyas cuts him down and takes [Fol. 129 b.] off his head.*
Euen his sholder in twoo · & down in-to þe herte ;
And he bowethe hym down · & ȝeldethe vp þe lyfe.
'I shalle þe ȝelde,' quod þe chylde · 'ryȝte as þe knyȝte
me tawȝte.'   336

323. yeñ. The transcriber for the Roxb. ed. mistook the curl over the n (ñ) for a d, as if it was rd, and wrote yerd, making nonsense of the line.
324. hele. The Roxb. ed. has *fele;* which is wrong.
325. chylde. This word seems to have crept in by mistake. The sense and alliteration would require 'blonk' = steed.
326. Thenne thei. The Roxb. ed. has *Thenne ether;* the transcriber having mistaken the last e in *then* for the beginning of the word *ether*.
staloworth. Miswritten for *stalworth*.
328. cheuelrye. *Sic* in MS.
330. þenne = the time when.

331. *Ung serpent a deux testes, oncques tel ne vit ho*mme
.... *saillit*.....
Tout droit a Mauquarre a sa veue se lance
Les deux testes lui crevent les deux yeulx sans doubtance.
332. rapte, in MS.; *frapte*, which is a common word enough, would suit the alliteration better.
333. Thenne. *Sic* in MS. The Roxb. ed. has *whenne*.
334. '*Schreding*,' or some such word, is wanted instead of, or after, *Even*.
336. I shall þe ȝelde = I shall render unto thee = I shall serve thee, I shall requite thee.

¶ He trussethe his harneys fro þe nekke · & þo hede
  wynnethe;
Sythen he toke hit by þe lokkes · & in þe helm leyde;
Thoo thanked he our lorde lowely · þat lente hym þat
  grace.

<small>Matabryne flees, but the child overtakes her and has her burnt to brown ashes.</small>

Thenne sawe þe qwene matabryne · her man so mur-
  dered;   340
Turned her brydelle · & towarde þe towne rydethe;
The chylde folowethe here aftur · fersly & faste,
Sythen browȝte here aȝeyne · wo for to drye,
And brente here in þe balowe fyer · alle to browne
  askes.   344

<small>The young Queen is unbound. Enyas tells his story to the King and Queen.</small>

¶ The ȝonge qwene at þe fyre · by þat was vnbouñdeñ;
The childe kome byfore þe kynge · & on-hyȝe he seyde,
And tolde hym how he was his sone · '& oþur sex
  childereñ,
By þe qwene betryce · she bare hem at ones,   348
For a worde on þe walle · þat she wronge seyde;
And ȝonder in a ryuere · swymmen þey swañnes;
Sythen þe forsworne thefe Malkadras · byrafte hem her
  cheynes.'   351
'By god,' quod þe goldsmythe ·'I knowe þat ryȝth wele;

<small>The goldsmith says he has five of the chains at home. They all go to the river and give the chains to the swans. Each choosing his own, turns to his human form. All but one. He, for want of his chain, remained always a swan.</small>

¶ Fyve cheynes I haue · & þey ben fysh hole.'
Nowe withe þe goldsmyȝthe · gon alle þese knyȝtes,
Toke þey þe cheynes · & to þe watur turneñ,   355
And shoken vp þe cheynes · þer sterten vp þe swannes;
Eche on chese to his · & turneñ to her kynde:
But on was alwaye a swanne · for losse of his cheyne.
Hit was doole for to se · þe sorowe þat he made;
He bote hym self with his bylle · þat alle his breste
  bledde,   360

---

345. by þat = by that time.
353. fysh hole = 'as sound as a roach,' as we say.
356. shoken. Sic in MS. The former edition has stroken.
357. turneñ. The former edition has turneden in this place; but not in l. 355.
chese to his = chose his own.
358. alwaye. Sic in MS. Edition of 1820 has alwayes.

¶ And all*e* his feyre federes · fomede vpon blode,
And all*e* formerknes þe wat*ur* · þer þe swanne swy*m*-
  methe :
There was ryche ne pore · þat my3te for rewthe,   'Twas sad to see
Lengere loke on hym · but to þe courte wenden. 364   his sorrow.
The*n*ne þey formed a fonte · & cristene þe children ;   They christen the
And callen Vryens þat on · and Oryens another,   children.
Assakarye þe thrydde · & gadyfere þe fowrthe ;
The fyfte hette rose · for she was a mayden ;   368
The sixte was fulwedde · cheuelere assygne.
And þus þe botenynge of god · brow3te hem to honde. ;.   So by God's help
.   they were
                restored.

.;. EXPLICIT .;.

362. formerknes. If this is *v.* land *-en.*
intr., and governed by the *sb.* water, 366. The names of the children in
it should have been by rights *former-* the French poem are *Orions, Orient,*
keneth ; but if it is *pl.* and *tr.* governed *Zacharias, Jehan,* and *Rosette.*
by *federes,* it has borrowed the North- 369. was fulwedde = had been bap-
ern *-es* termination instead of the Mid- tized already.

GLOSSARIAL INDEX.

ABBREVIATIONS.

Adj.	= Adjective.	*Obj.*	= Objective.
Adv.	= Adverb.	*O.E.*	= Old English, A. D. 500 —1200.
Allit.	= Early Engl. Alliterative Poems.	*Pf.*	= Perfect.
Art.	= Article.	*Pl.*	= Plural.
Comp.	= Comparative.	*P. pt.*	= Past Participle.
Conj.	= Conjunction.	*Pers.*	= Personal.
Cp.	= Compare.	*Poss.*	= Possessive.
Dem.	= Demonstrative.	*Prep.*	= Preposition.
Fem.	= Feminine.	*Pron.*	= Pronoun.
Fr.	= French.	*Refl.*	= Reflexive.
Gen.	= Genesis and Exodus.	*Rel.*	= Relative.
Germ.	= German.	*Sb.*	= Substantive.
Imp.	= Imperative.	*Sc.*	= Scottish.
Imp. pt.	= Imperfect Participle.	*Sing.*	= Singular.
Int.	= Interjection.	*Tr.*	= Transitive.
Intr.	= Intransitive.	*V.*	= Verb.

Wm. = William of Palerne.

A, *interj.* = Ah, 71, 82, 250, 255, 260.

A, *art.* 5, 6, &c. Perhaps as a numeral = one, 157, 165.

A, *prep.* = in, or on; O.E. & O. Sc. *An.* In l. 79 it means *at.*

Abbot, *sb.* 265.

Abowte, *prep.* 44, 126.

Abulle, *adj.* = fit, proper, able, 289.

Adowne, *adv.* = down, 21, 88, 101, 114; adown, 190, 297.

Affye, *sb.* = trust, 10.

Afore, *adv.* = in front, 228.

Aftur, *prep.* = along, 321; for, or in quest of, 46, 129, 153, 342; in accordance with, 13, 238; *adv.* = afterwards, 54, 80, 258, 271, 276; behind, 322.

Alle, *adj.* 43, 67, 98, &c.; *adv.* 15.

Alle-weldinge, *adj.* = Almighty, 1. O.E. *Eal-wealdende.*

Allewey. *See* Alwaye.

Allone, *adj.* = alone, 184.

Als, *conj.* = also, 91.

Also, *conj.* 218.

Alwaye, *adv.* 358; allowey, 305.

An, *art.* 5, 331, &c.

And, *conj.* 8, 18, &c. = an, if, 139.

Angelle, *sb.* 192, 193, 221.

Anon, *adv.* 85; anone, 68, 190, 258.

Another, *adj.* 268, 301, 366.

Ar, 3*d pl. pres. ind.* of *v.* Be, 82.

Armed, *p. pt.* of arm, *v. tr.* 283.

Armes, *sb. pl.* 262.

Armour, *sb.* 280.

Aryse, *v. intr.* 2*d sing. imper.* 77, 303.

As, *conj.* 7, 19, &c. = as though, 53.

Aske, *v. tr.* 128, 171; 3*d sing. pf.* askede, 130, 192; asskede, 210; *p. pt.* asked, 131.

Askes, *sb. pl.* = ashes, 344.

Asseylde, 3*d sing. pf. ind.* of asseyle, *v. tr.* 145.

Assygne = Fr. an cygne, 11, &c.

Assygyned, *p. pt.* of assign, *v. tr.* 188.

At, *prep.* 23, 60, 98.

Aw3te, *sb.* = aught, 204.

A3eyne, *adv.* = again, 93, 104, 137, 177, 343; a3eyn, 123.

Badde. *See* Bid.

Bakke, *sb.* = back, 291, 293.

Balowe, *adj.* O.E. *Bealu,* or *Bealo; Balo* or *Balu* = deadly, 233, 344, strong (?) 317.

Banke, *sb.* 132.

Barmeteme, *sb.* 103. This is the O.E. *Bearnteme,* and is miswritten for barnteme = brood, progeny, from barne = child, bairn; and teme, or teem (O.E. *teman*) = to produce, bring forth. *See* Gen. 954 and 3903. In Chalmers's Life of James 1. (prefixed to his 'Poetic Remains of the Scottish kings,' 1824), p. 15, he writes, "The Act of the former session was renewed in this; requiring the clergy to pray for the king, for the queen, and their *Bairntime,* which is now explained to mean, 'the children produced between them.'"

Bathe, *v. tr.* 263.

Bare, 3*d sing. pf. ind.* of bear, *v. tr.* 325, 348.

Be, *v. intr.* 17, 37, 80; 3*d pl. pres. subj.* bene (O.E. *beon*), 188; 3*d sing. subj.* 100, 302.

Bedde, *sb.* 33, 161.

Beetheth. *See* Bete.

Befalle, *v. intr.* 204.

Bene. *See* Be, *v. intr.*

Bere, *v. tr.* 3*d sing. ind.* bereth, 297; 3*d sing. pf.* 196. *See also* Bare, *p. pt.* borne, 23, 41.

Berthe. *See* Byrthe.

Beste, *sb.* = beast, 214; beeste, 218, 288.

Beste, *adj.* 68, 285.

Bete, *v. tr.* O.E. *betan* = to prepare, to kindle (said of fire); 3*d sing. pres. ind.* beetheth, 157; *p. pt.* bette, 224.

Bete, *v. tr.* = beat; *imp. pt.* betynge, 227.

Beteche, *v. tr. See* Bytake, 312.

Bette. *See* Bete.

Better, *adj.* 49, 175; bettur, *adv.* 97.

Betyde, *v. intr.* 103.

Betynge. *See* Bete.

Bid, *v. tr.* 3*d sing. pf.* badde, 156, 172, 248, 263; 3*d sing. pres.* byddyth, 262.

Bledde, 3*d sing. pf.* of bleed, *v. intr.* 360.

GLOSSARIAL INDEX.   23

Blente, *p. pt.* of blind, *v. tr.* O.E. *blendian,* 325.

Blethely, *adv.* = blithely, cheerfully, 278.

Blode, *sb.* = blood, 361.

Blythe, *adj.* 154.

Body, *sb.* 244.

Book, *sb.* 7, 270.

Borne. *See* Bere, *v. tr.*

Bote, 3*d sing. pf.* of bite, *v. tr.* 360.

Botenning, *sb.* = remedy, succour, 370; from boten, *v. tr.* formed from bote = remedy, from O.E. *gebetan* = to mend.

Bothe, *conj.* 20, 79 ; *adj.* 135.

Bounden, *p. pt.* of bind, *v. tr.* 291.

Boy, *sb.* 260 ; *poss.* boyes, 263.

Bowethe, 3*d sing. pres. ind.* of how, *v. tr.* 335; bowethe hym, 265 = turneth him, goeth.

Broke, *v. tr.* O.E. *brecan ;* 3*d sing. pres.* brekethe, 157 ; 1*st sing. pf. ind.* breke (now brake, or broke), 165.

Brenne, *v. tr.* = burn, 68, 241 ; *pf* brente, 344; *p. pt.* brente, 80; intransitively, 191, 224.

Breste, *sb.* 297, 360 ; *pl.* brestes, 241.

Breste, *v. inter.* = burst, 317.

Broode, *adj.* = broad, 297.

Browne, *adj.* 344.

Browʒte, 3*d sing. pf.* of bring, *v. tr.* 41, 49, 343, 370.

Brydelle, *sb.* 229, 292, 341.

Brynge, *v. tr.* 2*d sing. imp.* 203.

Bryʒt, *adj.* = bright, 8 ; bryʒte, 298.

Busk, *v. tr.* = prepare, make ready ; 3*d sing. pf. ind.* buskede, 172 ; *p. pt.* buskedde, 233.

But, *conj.* 15, 17, &c. = except, 38 ; only, 242.

By, *prep.* 196, 348 ; = of, concerning, 5 ; at, about, 84, 143, 205 ; through, 85, 216, *adv.* = near, 109.

Bycche, *sb.* = bitch, 62.

Bydeste = abidest, 256, 2*d sing. ind.* of byde, *v. intr.*

Byddynge, *sb.* = command, 85.

Byddyth. *See* Bid.

Byfore, *prep.* = before, 23, 64, 110, 124, &c., before, 114.

Byforne, *adv.* = before, 322 (Wm. *biforn.* Gen. *biforen*).

Bygyleth, *p. pt.* of beguile, *v. tr.* (for beguiled), 78.

Byginne, *v. tr.* 3*d sing. pres. ind.* bygynnethe, 76, 246 ; 3*d sing. pf.* byganne, 183.

Byhelde, 3*d sing. pf.* of byhold = behold; 21.

Bylefte, *p. pt.* of byleve, *or* beleave = abandon, 240.

Bylle, *sb.* = bill, 360.

Byrafte, 3*d sing. pf. ind.* of byreave *or* bereave. O.E. *bereafian ;* 199, 351.

Byrthe, *sb.* = birth, 23, 40, 291 ; berthe, 65.

Byside, *adv.* = beside, 149.

Bytake (*or* bitake) = betake, commit, deliver. O.E. *betæcan ;* 3*d sing. pres. ind.* bytakethe, 151; bytaketh, 173 ; *p. pt.* bytaken, 163; cp. Gen. 212.

Call, *v. tr.* 3*d pl. pres. indic.* callen, 366 ; kallen, 292, 296 ; 3*d pl. pf.* called, 46 ; kallede, 270 ; 2*d sing. imp.* kalle, 204 ; *p. pt.* called, 289 ; kalled, 6, 231.

Caste, *v. tr.* 52 ; 3*d pl. pres. ind.* caste, 88 ; 1*st sing. pf.* caste, 167 ; 3*d sing.* caste, 63.

Cawsed, 3*d sing. pf. ind.* of cause, *v. tr.* 39

Certeyne, *adj.* = certain, 253.

Charde, *v. intr.* = care, 329.

Charge, *sb.* concern, 235.

Chaste, *sb.* = chest, 127. See Note.

Chaunce, *sb.* 123.

Chefe, *sb.* = chief, 11.

Cherye, *sb.* = cherry, 329.

Chese, 3*d sing. pf.* of choose. Used with the *prep.* to, 357.

Cheualere, *sb.* 11, 333; cheuelere, 369.

Cheuelrye, *sb.* miswritten for cheuelere, 328.

Cheuene, *v. tr.* quasi chiefen = to rule over, 16.

Cheuerynge, *imp. pt.* of cheuer or chyuer, q. v.

Cheyne, *sb.* 43, 125, 137, 146, 148, 150, 157, 164, 165, 176, 179, 199, 351.

Choppe, *v. tr.* 330.

Chylde, *sb.* = child, 16, 29, &c. With chylde, 35; *pl.* chylderen, 23, 82, 93; chyldren, 107, 122, 130, &c.; children, 143; childeren, 347.

Chyuer, *v. intr.* = shiver, 3*d pl. pf.* chyuered, 107; *imp. pt.* cheuerynge, 107. Cp. Morte Arthur (Linc.) l. 3392.

Clene, *adj.* 174.

Clensen, *v. tr.* = to cleanse, 247.

Close, *sb.* = an enclosed field, or space of ground, 272.

Clothe, *sb.* = cloth, 97.

Colde, *sb.* 107.

Combred (*p. pt.* of combre (cumber) = to trouble) = miserable, 71.

Come, *v. intr.* 38; com, 248; 2*d sing. pres. indic.* comeste, 51; 3*d sing.* comethe, 109; *pf.* come, 64, 110, 142, 151, 173, 183, 208, 228, 248; Kome, 113, 346; *p. pt.* comen, 154.

Confounde, *v. tr.* 75.

Countes, *sb.* = countess, 269.

Counselle, *sb.* 50.

Courte, *sb.* 53, 123, 163, 203; cowrte, 150, 155, &c.

Cowche, *sb.* = bed, 45.

Cowpe, *sb.* = cup, 153, 164, 173, &c.

Crafte, *sb.* = business, 313.

Criste, 104; Cryste, 111.

Cristen, *v. tr.* = christen, 266; 3*d pl. pres. ind.* cristene, 365; *p. pt.* cristened, 203, 275.

Crosse, *sb.* 281.

Crowne, *sb.* 237.

Croyse, *sb.* = cross, 328-9; croys, 332.

Cry, *v. intr.* 3*d sing. pres. ind.* cryethe, 81; 3*d pl. pf.* cryedde, 106; cryde, 108; cryede, 111.

Cuppe, *sb.* 160, 168.

Cursed, *p. pt.* of curse, *v. tr.* 38, 145; used adjectively, cursede, 142; cursedde, 121.

Curteynesse, *sb.* = courteousness, 179.

Dame, *sb.* 69, 73, 125, 132, 250.

Damme, *sb.* = mother, 61.

Dare, *v. intr.* 1*st sing. pres. ind.* 27; 3*d sing. pf.* durste, 56; *pl.* 147.

Day, *sb.* 188, 191, 208.

Dedde. See Done.

Dede, *sb.* = deed, 274.

Deepe, *adv.* 86.

Delyuered, *p. pt.* of delyuer, *v. tr.* 37, 180; 3*d sing. pf.* 155, 178.

Deseruethe, 3*d sing. pres.* of deserve, *v. tr.* 72.

Deth, *sb.* 100; dethe, 138, 182, 186.

Do, *v. tr.* 139; done, 238; 3*d sing. pf.* 172; 2*d sing. imper.* do, 138 *p. pt.* don, 235.

Dole, *sb.* = sorrow, compassion, 134; doole, 359.
Dolefulle, *adj.* 106.
Dome, *sb.* = doom, 186; *pl.* domus, 91.
Dore, *sb.* 60, 87.
Down, *adv.* 305, 334, 335.
Dowȝter, *sb.* = daughter, 42.
Draw, *v. tr.* O.E. *dragan* (intransitively used, as in the phrase 'Draw near'); *3d sing.* and *pl.* drowȝ, 33; and drowȝe, 37, 114, 161.
Drowȝe = drew (Gen. l. 2360, dragen. O.E. *drog*). *See* Draw.
Drye, *v. tr.* (O.E. *dreogan.* Gen. *dregen*; Allit. *dryȝe*) = to dree, to suffer, 343.
Dryue, *v. tr.* dryue out = bring out, ascertain, 259.
Dubbede, *3d sing. pf. ind.* 276.
Durste. *See* Dare.
Dwellest, *2d sing. pres. ind.* of dwell, *v. intr.* 201; *3d sing. pf.* dwellede, 13.
Dymme, *adj.* = dim, dark, 86.
Dynte, *sb.* 138.

Eche, *adj.* = each, 31, 44, 126; each a, O.E. *ilka* = cach, every, 187.
Edder, *sb.* = adder, 331.
Eggelynges, *adv.* = edgelings, edgewise, with the edge (O.E. *Ecg.* = edge), 305.
Eke, *adv.* = also, 180.
Elles, *adv.* = else (Allit. *elleȝ*), 74, 215, 290; ellis, 30.
Elleven, *adj.* 89.
Ende, *sb.* 40, 240; *v. tr.* 330.
Enforme, *v. tr.* 212.
Er, *prep.* = ere, before, 70.
Erle, *sb.* 268.
Erthe, *sb.* 320.

Etethe, *3d sing. pres. ind.* of ete (eat), 290.
Euen, 243, 334.
Euur = ever, 222, 322.
Eyther = each, 220, 318, 320.

Fader, *sb.* = father, 90, 212, 219; *poss.* fader, 203.
Fallethe, *p. pt.* of fall = falled, 310. Perhaps miswritten for *felled;* which is the more likely, as the *p. pt.* of *fall* ought to be *fallen;* while *fell* would make *felled*. We say, however, sometimes, 'To *fall* timber.'
False, *adj.* 257; fals, 239.
Faste, *adv.* 141, 223, 227, 304, 309, 342.
Fastened, *p. pt.* of fasten, *v. tr.* 319.
Fayre, *adj.* 90; feyre, 217, 266, 275, 361.
Febull, *adj.* = sad, bad, 58; used *substantively*, 76.
Feder, *sb.* = feather; *pl.* federes, 361.
Felawe, *sb.* = fellow, 258.
Felde, *sb.* = field, 223, 319.
Felle, *adj.* = severe, stern, cruel, 239.
Felle, *pf.* of fall, *v. intr.* 110, 114; *3d pl.* 148; = befell, 130.
Felly, *adv.* = sternly, cruelly, fiercely, 76, 225. The word is used by Spenser.
Fende, *sb.* = fiend, devil, 120; fend, 240.
Fere, *sb.* = companion, 325.
Fersly, *adv.* = fiercely, 342.
Ferther, *adv.* (*comp.*) = further, 127.
Fete, *sb.* (*pl.* of foot) 303, 323.
Fette, *p. pt.* of fette, *v. tr.* = fetch, 279.

Feyth, *sb.* 48; feythe, 121, 130, 142.
Find, *v. ir. p. pt.* fownden, 239; *2d sing. indic.* fyndes, 305.
Flesh, *sb.* 310.
Fleye, *3d pl. pf.* of fly, *v. intr.* 319.
Flowen, *3d pl. pf.* of the same, 148 (Allit. *flowen;* Gen. *flogen*).
Folke, *sb.* 187, 223.
Folowe, *v. tr. 2d sing. imper.* 310; *3d sing. pres. ind.* foloweth, 116, 342.
Fomede, *3d pl. pf. ind.* of fome (foam), *v. intr.* 361.
Fonte, *sb.* 267, 365.
For, *conj.* 3, 5, &c.; *prep.* 15, 29, 49, &c.
Foreste, *sb.* 95.
Forge, *v. tr.* 153.
Forlonge, *sb.* = furlong, 228.
Formed, *3d pl. pf.* of form, *v. tr.* 365; *p. pt.* formeth = formed, 200, 209.
Formerken, *v. intr.* = darken; *3d sing. indic.* formerknes, 362. *See* Note.
Forsette, *v. tr.* = beset, entrap, betray, 251. O.E. *forsettan.* Cp. Allit. B. 78.
Forsothe, *adv.* 18, 195, 242.
Forsworn, *p. pt.* of forswear, *v. tr.* 199; forsworne, 351.
Forthe, *adv.* 52, 60, 75, &c. Forth, 176.
Forthy, *adv.* = wherefore, 218 (O.E.).
Fostere, *sb.* = forester, 120.
Fowle, *adj.* 40, 239.
Fownden. *See* Find.
Fowre, *numeral adj.* = four, 95.
Fowrth, *adj.* = fourth, 367.
Frapte, *pf.* of frap = strike, 332.
Frely, *adj.* = lordly, noble, 218,

266, 275. Cp. Allit. B. 162; Wm. 124.
Freshe, *adj.* 258.
Fro, *prep.* 113, 148, 159, 298, 328.
Frusch, *v. intr.* (properly *tr.* = strike. Fr. *froisser*) but here = rush; *3d sing. ind.* fruscheth, 332.
Fulfylde, *p. pt.* of fulfylle (fulfil), 206.
Fulle, *adv.* 12, 54, 69, 113, 141, &c.
Fulwen, *v. tr.* = baptize. O.E. *fulwian; p. pt.* fulwedde, 369.
Furre, *comp.* of fur = further, 311.
Fyfte, *adj.* = fifth, 368.
Fyndes. *See* Find, *v. tr.*
Fyre, *sb.* 224, 233, 332, 345; fyer, 159, 165, 167, 344.
Fyrste, *adj.* 51, 58; *adv.* 80.
Fysh, *sb.* = fish, 353.
Fyue, *numeral adj.* 159; fyve, 167.
Fyʒte, *v. intr.* = fight, 200, 209, 212, 245, 259; *sb.* 273.

Gader, *v. intr.* = gather; *imp. pt.* gaderynge, 223.
Gete, *v. tr.* = get, 261; *3d sing. pf. ind.* gette (properly ʒet or ʒat), 34; *2d sing. imper.* gete, 137.
Gladdenes, *sb.* 57.
Go, *v. intr. 3d sing. pres. ind.* goothe, 157; *3d pl.* gon, 354; *p. pt.* go, 143.
God, *sb.* 1, 40, &c.; *poss.* goddes, 206, 219.
Godfader, *sb.* 267.
Godmoder, *sb.* 269.
Goldsmyʒte, *sb.* 153, 157, 354; goldsmythe, 352.
Good, *adj.* 130, 289.
Grace, *sb.* 302, 339.

Graunt, *v. tr.* = grant; 2*d sing. pf. ind.* grauntethe, 278; 3*d sing.* graunted, 189, 246.

Grete, *adj.* = great, 83; gret, 264.

Grownde, *sb.* 302.

Grymme, *adj.* black, dark, 51; sad, 189. Cp. Allit. A. 1069.

Grypte, 3*d sing. pf.* of gryp, *v. tr.* 220.

Gynnyth, 3*d sing. pres. ind.* of gynne, *v.* (begin), 66.

Hadde. *See* Haue.

Halen, *v. tr.* = to haul; 3*d pl. indic.* halenne, 280.

Halfe, *sb.* 165; = side, behalf, 219.

Haluendele = half-deal = half, 176; halvendelle, 160.

Ham, *pers. pron. obj.* = them, 152.

Happe, *sb.* = hap (good), 324.

Harm, *sb.* 235; harme, 3.

Harnes, *sb.* = armour, 278; harneys, 337.

Hast. *See* Haue.

Hatefulle, *adj.* 141.

Hath. *See* Haue.

Haue, *v. tr.* 120; 1*st sing. pres. ind.* 70, 353; 2*d sing.* hast, 78; haste, 194, 251, 310; 3*d sing.* hath, 128; 3*d pl.* haue, 79; 3*d sing. pf.* hadde, 16, 44, 47; 1*st sing. pf. subj.* 181; 2*d sing.* 53; *p. pt.* hadde, 79.

Hawberke, *sb.* 296.

He, *pers. pron.* 2, 13, &c.

Hedde, *sb.* = head, 27, 217, 257; hede, 295; heede, 311.

Heelde. *See* Holden, *v. tr.*

Heete (or Hete), *v. tr.* = tell; 1*st sing. pres. indic.* 18.

Hele, *sb.* = pleasure, advantage, 324. O.E. *Hel* = health.

Helle, *sb.* 10.

Helme = helmet, *sb.* 296, 306, 338.

Helpe, *sb.* 118, 247, 273.

Helpe, *v. tr.* 50; 3*d sing. pres. subj.* 70.

Hem, *pron.* = 'em, them; 19, 20, 44, 45, 52, 83, 96, 97, 101, 102, 104, 109, 110, 112, 114—119, 126, 129, 133, 134, 138, 148, 151, 152, 159, 169, 190, 194, 196, 199, 316, 318—320, 348, 351.

Hemselfen = themselves, 20.

Hente, *v. tr.* = seize, take; 3*d pl. pf. ind.* hente, 85; *p. pt.* hente, 3.

Her, *poss. pron. fem.* 10, 32, 340, 341.

Her, *pers. pron. fem. obj.* 23, 35, 38, 47, 68, 70, 73, 85, 176, 262.

Her, *adv.* = here, in this place, 77.

Her = their. *See* Here.

Here, *poss. pron. fem.* = her, 171, 182, 240, 255.

Here, *pers. pron. fem. obj.* = her, 15, 32, 34, 86—88, 126, 131, 135, 151, 153, 189, 190, 226, 342—344.

Here, *poss. pron. pl.* = their, 126, 220, 235, 274, 315, 321; her, 105, 199, 327.

Here, *v. tr.* = hear, 57; 1*st sing. pf. ind.* herde, 213; 3*d sing.* 55, 58, 108; 2*d sing. imper.* 131.

Here, *sb.* = hair; *pl.* heres, 255.

Heremyte, *sb.* 115, 221; hermyte, 109, 192, 201.

Herseluen = herself, 47.

Herte, *sb.* (Germ. *herz*) = heart, 18, 189, 263, 334.

Hette, 3*d sing. pres. indic.* = is called, 232; 3*d sing. pf.* hette, 7; hyȝte, 9. (O.E. *hatan* = to be called.)

His, *poss. pron. masc.* 2, 8, 36, &c.; hys, 135.

Hit, *pers. pron. neut.* 30, 72, 74, &c.

Holden, v. tr. = to hold, 169;
 3d sing. pf. ind. heelde, 152; 2d
 sing. imper. holde, 127; p. pt.
 holde = accounted, 70.

Hole, sb. 294.

Hole, adj. = whole, 353.

Hollyc, adv. = wholly, 160, 168, 181.

Holy, adj. 109, 265.

Honde, sb. = hand, 2, 41, 152, 158, 164, 166, 174, 220, 255, 287, 300, 315, 370.

Hondredde = hundred, 255.

Honged, 3d sing. pf. of hongen, or hangen = hang, 18.

Hors, sb. = horse, 213, 289; pl. horses, 321.

Houe, v. intr. = to abide still, to hover, to wait, 288. Cp. Allit. B. 927; and Lancelot, 996.

How, adv. 26, 31, &c.

Hownde, sb. pl. howndes, 79, 234.

Hy, adj. = high, 326; hye, 217; hyȝ, 224; hyȝe, 280; on hyȝe = aloud.

Hylyde, 3d sing. pf. of hylen = hele = cover, 102.

Hym, pers. pron. masc. obj. = him, 4, 24, &c.

Hym for Hem = them, 52.

Hynde, sb. 113, 116.

Hytte, v. tr. 300.

Hyȝe, adj. See Hy.

Hyȝe, v. intr. = hie, go, 139; refl. 3d sing. pf. hyed hym, 141.

Hyȝnes, sb. = highness, 4.

Hyȝte = was called. See Hette.

I, pers. pron. 5, 18, &c.

If, conj. 192.

In, prep. 4, 5, &c.

Is, 3d sing. pres. ind. of Be, v. intr. 1, 26, &c.

It, pers. pron. neut. 1, 12, &c.

Joye, sb. 246.

Juge = judge, 236. See Note.

Kalled, &c. See Call.

Kan, v. tr. = can, i. e. know; 1st sing. pres. ind. kan, 311, 313; 2d sing. kanste, 212; 1st sing. pf. kowthe = knew, 313.

Kawȝte, 3d sing. pf. ind. of catch, 287; in l. 62 it = snatched. Cp. 'caught up.'

Keene, adj. 183; used adverbially.

Kenely, adv. 309.

Kepe, v. tr. = keep, 50; 3d sing. pf. ind. kepte, 117, 174; 2d sing. imper. kepe, 328.

Keste, 3d sing. pf. indic. of cast, 97.

Knee, sb. pl. knees, 110.

Knowe, v. tr. 97; 1st sing. pres. ind. 309, 352; 2d sing. knoweste, 251; 3d sing. pf. knewe, 49.

Knyfe, sb. 62.

Knyȝte, sb. = knight, 258, 276, 287, 289; pl. knyȝtes, 354.

Kome. See Come.

Kowarde, sb. 71.

Kowth. See Kan.

Kylled, 3d sing. pf. of kylle (kill); v. tr. 62.

Kynde, sb. (kind) = nature, condition, 71, 276; kin, family. 11. Cp. Gen. 650.

Kynge, sb. 7, 20, &c.; poss. kynges, 195.

Kyrtelle, sb. 294.

Ladde. See Lead, v. tr. Spenser uses this inflection, F. Q., I. i. 4: 'a milke white lamb she lad.'

Lady, sb. 82, 89, 92, 191.

Lafte. See Leve, v. tr.

Langour, sb. = languor, 15, 57, 92.

Lappe, sb. 257.

GLOSSARIAL INDEX. 29

Lappe, *v. tr.* = wrap ; 3*d sing.*
pf. lappede, 102 ; *p. pt.* lapped,
132 ; lappedde, 101.

Lassche, *v. tr.* = strike (lash out
= kick) ; 3*d sing pres. ind.* lassch-
eth, 323.

Laste, *adj.* 240.

Launce, *sb.* 300.

Launce, *v. tr.* = launce, dart,
throw ; 3*d sing. pres. ind.* launces,
323.

Laye. See Lye, *v. intr.*

Lead, *v. tr.* 3*d sing. pf. ind.*
ladde, 287.

Lefe, *adj.* = dear, 82.

Lefte, *pf.* of leve, q. v.

Lefte, 3*d sing. pf. ind.* of lift
(O.E. *lefan*), 45.

Lende, *v. intr.* a form of leng =
tarry, abide ; *p. pt.* lente, ' was
lente,' l. 5 = dwelt. Cp. Allit. B.
1084, ' waʒt lent.'

Lendeth, 3*d sing. pres. ind.* of
lend, *v. tr.* 99.

Lene, *v. tr.* = lend, grant, 277,
284 ; *p. pt.* lente, 112, 339.

Leng, *v. intr.* = tarry, dwell ; 3*d
sing. pres. ind.* lengeth, 4.

Lengur, *adv., comp.* of long, 77,
112, 303 ; lengere, 364.

Lente. See Lende, *v. intr.* ; and
Lene, *v. tr.*

Lepte, 3*d sing. pf. ind.* of lepe
(leap), *v. intr.* 254.

Let, *v. tr.* = allow, cause ; 3*d
sing. pf. ind.* lette, 24, 190 ; 2*d
sing. imper.* lette, 187 ; lete, 307 ;
2*d sing. subj.* lete, 52.

Leue, *v. tr.* = believe, allow, 28,
133 ; leeue, 242.

Leue, *v. tr.* = leave ; 1*st sing. pf.
ind.* lafte, 133 ; 3*d sing.* 17, 221 ;
1*st pl. imper.* leue, 92 ; 3*d pl. pres.
ind.* leuen, 87. Also *intransitively*
= remain ; 3*d sing. pf. ind.* lefte,
175 ; leued, 255.

Leues, *sb. pl.* of lefe (leaf), 119.

Ley. See Lye, *v. intr.*

Leyde, 1*st sing. pf. ind.* of lay ;
v. tr. 165 ; 3*d sing.* 87, 101, 159,
338.

Leyne, *v. tr.* = grant, requite,
reward, 99.

Lofe, *sb.* = love, 15.

Loke, *v. intr.* = look, 364 ; 3*d
sing. pf. ind.* loked, 21 ; 3*d sing.
imper.* looke, 52 ; loke, 203, 300.

Lokke, *sb.* of a door, 87 ; of hair,
254 ; *pl.* lokkes, 338.

Londe, *sb.* = land, 6, 181, 231 ;
pl. londis, 16.

Longe, *adj.* 95, 299 ; *adv.* 47,
185.

Lorde, *sb.* 5, 36, 70, &c.

Lordeles, *adj.* = having no lord,
or sovereign, 17.

Losse, *sb.* 358.

Lothe, *adj.* 249 ; loth, 48.

Loue, *sb.* 36.

Loue, *v. tr.* 14.

Louely, *adv.* 98.

Lowde, *adj.* 225.

Lowely, *adv.* = meekly, humbly,
36, 339.

Lowʒe, 3*d pl. pf. indic.* of laʒe,
v. intr. = laugh, 98.

Lye, *v. intr.* 257 ; 3*d sing. pf.
ind.* lay, 57, 207 ; laye, 76 ; 3*d pl.*
ley, 98 ; *imp. pt.* lyyinge, 133.

Lyf, *sb.* = life, 17 ; lyfe, 112,
335.

Lyfe, *v. intr.* = live, 54.

Lyfte, *v. tr.* 299.

Lyke, *v.* = like, 54 (*see* Note),
140 ; 3*d sing. pres. ind.* lykes, 134 ;
lyketh, 73.

Lykynge, *sb.* = liking, 13.

Lyme, *sb.* = limb ; *pl.* lymes, 217.

Lyonys, *pl.* of lyon ; *sb.* 214.

Lytulle, *adj.* 242.
Lyue, *v. intr.* = live ; 3*d sing. pf. ind.* lyuede, 89.
Lyue, *sb.* = life, 140.
Lyuinge, *adj.* = living, 256.
Ly3tly, *adv.* = lightly, 303.

Made. } *See* Make.
Maden. }
Make, *v. tr.* 3*d sing. pres. ind.* maketh, 267 ; 3*d sing. pf.* made, 9, 83, 90, 135, 359 ; 3*d pl.* maden, 314.
Man, *sb.* 46, 108, &c. ; manne, 29 ; *poss.* mannes, 273 ; *pl.* men, 79, 94 ; menne, 285.
Mantelle, *sb.* 101, 105, 132.
Many, *adj.* 31, 34, &c.
Marre, *sb.* = mar, *v. tr.* 261.
Mater, *sb.* = matter, 216.
May, 1*st sing. pres. ind.* of mowe = to be able = can, 74, 295 ; 2*d sing.* 50, 54 ; also mayste, 249.
Mayden, *sb.* 368.
Me, *indeterm. pron.* (Germ. *man* ; Fr. *on*) 30.
Me, *pers. pron. obj.* 70, 261.
Mene, *v. tr.* mention ; 3*d sing. pf. ind.* mencde, 124.
Mengynge, *sb.* = mingling, twisting, 125. From menge, *v. tr.* = mix.
Meruelows, *adj.* (used *adverbially*) 185.
Meruryle, *sb.* 125.
Mesure, *sb.* 171.
Mete, *sb.* = meat, 88, 144.
Moche, *adj.* = much, 9, 39, 102, 136 ; *substantively*, 184.
Moder, *sb.* = mother, 9, 39, 59, 180, 200, 205, 209, 210.
Mone, *sb.* = moan, 83, 136.
Mony, *adj.* 90, 124, 271.

More, *adj.* 88, 125, 171.
Morn, *sb.* = morning, 183.
Morne, *v. intr.* = mourn, 66.
Morwe, *sb.* = morrow, 172.
Most, *v.* = must, 2*d sing. ind.* of mot, 50, 206 ; 3*d sing.* 136, 206. *See* Mote.
Moste, *adv.* 285.
Mote, 3*d sing. pres. subj.* of mot, 120. The word has in this phrase an optative force. *See* Most.
Mowthe, *sb.* = mouth, 292.
Multiplyeth, 3*d sing. pres. ind.* of multiply ; *v. intr.* 158.
Murdered, *p. pt.* of murder, *v. tr.* 340.
Murther, *v. tr.* 94, 129.
My, *poss. pron.* 27, 78, 82, 100, &c
Mydday, *sb.* 205.
Myle, *sb.* 95.
Myne, *poss. pron.* 181.
Mysfare, *v. intr.* = go wrong, 238.
Myskarye, *v. intr.* = miscarry, 260.
Myssede, 3*d sing. pf. ind.* of mysse (miss), *v. tr.* 83.
My3te = might, 1*st sing. pf. ind.* of mowe, or mowen, *v.* 134 ; 3*d sing.* 14, 247, 363 ; 1*st pl.* 3.

Name, *sb.* 204, 270.
Nay, *interj.* 28.
Ne = not, 3, 147.
Nekke, *sb.* 297, 337.
Nere, *prep.* = near, 38.
Nere, *v.* = ne were, 4.
Neuur, *adv.* = never, 202, 216.
Neythur, *adv.* 253 ; *sb.* 306.
No, *adj.* 16, 38, 77.
None = ne one, 127, 216 : *adj.* 250.

Noryscheth, 3*d sing. pres. ind.* of norysch (nourish); *v. tr.* 118.
Not, *adv.* 28.
Nother, *conj.* = nor, 253.
Nowe, *adv.* 354.
Nowʒte, *sb.* = nought, 53.
Noyse, *sb.* 225.
Noʒt, *adv.* = not, 236, 295; noʒte, 74.
Noʒthe, *sb.* = nought, 290; nowʒte, 53.
Nykke, *v. tr.* = refuse, contradict; = ne (not), ikke (say); cognate with Latin *Negare*. With *ikke* compare Gothic *Aikan*; Sanskrit *Ah* = to say, to speak; Latin *Ajo* (agjo). Cp. also the Sanskrit *Aham* = I, with the O.E. *Ic.*
Nyʒe, *adj.* = nigh, 100.
Nyʒte, *sb.* = night, 33, 34, 161, 191.

Of, *prep.* 4, 10, &c. = from, out of, 287; = *adv.* off, 146, 311.
Ofte, *adv.* 3, 111.
Olde, *adj.* 163, 227, 243, &c.
On, *prep.* 34, 207.
On, *num.* = one, 44, 126, 143, 249, 295, 297, 299, 357, 358; oon, 29, 285.
One, *num.* 264.
One, *adj.* = alone, 15, 19.
Ones, *adv.* = at ones = at once, 98, 196, 272, 348.
On-hyʒe, *adv.* = aloud, 25, 64, 106, 234, 346; on hyʒ, 81; on-hy = up, 326.
Ony, *adj.* = any, 175, 273.
Oo-lyuynge, *adj.* = everliving, eternal, 201.
Oon. *See* On.
Orysoun, *sb.* = prayer, 90.
Other, *adj.* 144, 145, 296, &c.; othur, 159, 167, 347.

Other, *conj.* = or (Germ. *oder*), 324.
Our, *poss. pron.* 36, 70, 93, 117.
Out, *for* drew, *or* pulled out, 146.
Ouur, *adv.* = over, 175.
Owne, 2, 14, &c.

Pappe, *sb.* = breast, 114.
Paye, *v. tr.* = please, 65.
Peces, *pl.* of pece (piece), 315.
Pele, *v. intr.* smite, 'let drive,' 304. Cp. peal (of bells), *sb.*; also pelt, *v.* Mr Skeat writes, "Perhaps this is an instance of the word *Pelle*, which occurs in Havelok, and *nowhere else*, unless it is *here*. In Havelok it = drive forth, go; and seems to be the Lat. *pellere*.
The line in Havelok is,
' Shal ich neuere lenger dwelle,
To morwen shall ich forth *pelle*.'
    ll. 809-10.
[' I shall stay here no longer,
    I shall start off to-morrow!
It answers to our expression, 'go full drive.'"
Place, *sb.* 12.
Plesed, *p. pt.* of plese (please); *v. tr.* 274.
Plukke, *v. tr.* 2*d sing. imper.* 304.
Pore, *adj.* = poor, 22, 26, 363.
Posse, *sb.* Perhaps miswritten for Poste, 281.
Prayde, 3*d sing. pf. ind.* of pray; *v. tr.* 284; 2*d sing. pres.* prayeth, 277.
Preste, *adj.* = ready, 135.
Prestly, *adv.* = readily, quickly, 277.
Preve, *v. tr.* = prove, 252.
Price, *adj.* = worthy, noble, 279. Comp. Wm. l. 411.
Prisoun, *sb.* 80; prysoun, 86.

Prowde, *adj.* 115.

Pulledde, 3*d pl. pf.* of pulle; *v. tr.* 327.

Putte, *v. tr.*, 3*d sing. pf. ind.* putte, 115; putt, 135.

Pyne, *sb.* = suffering, 92. O.E. *pin; v. tr.* = to make to suffer, to torment, 26. O.E. *pinan.*

Pytte, *sb.* = pit, 63.

Quod *or* quoth, 3*d sing. pf. ind.* = said, 71, 99, 169, 214–216, 219, 230, 236, 242, 250, 256, 260, 288, 289, 290, 312, 328-29, 336, 352. O.E. *cwæð*, of *Cweðan* = to say.

Qwene, *sb.* = queen, 8, 14, &c.

Raunges, *sb. pl.* = lists, 314, 321. Cp. 'ringes' in Sir Eglamore, l. 1121, Percy folio, p. 382, vol. 2.

Raw3te (Raught). *See* Reche.

Reasonabullye, *adv.* = reasonably, 34.

Rebukede, 3*d sing. pf.* of rebuke, 32.

Reche, *v. tr.* = reach; 3*d sing. pres. ind.* recheth, 176; 3*d pl. pf.* raw3ten, 316.

Recke, *v. intr.* = reck, care; 3*d sing. pf. ind.* row3te, 177; 2*d sing. imper.* rekke, 306.

Rede, *v. tr.* = advise, 222; 1*st sing. pres. ind.* rede, 169.

Redresse, *v. tr.* 205.

Rekke. *See* Recke.

Rennen, *v. intr.* = run, 316 (?); *imp. pt.* rennynge, 113; 3*d pl. pf.* ronnen, 314, 321. *Rennene,* 316, may be *sb.* = rennenge *or* running, but is more likely the verb above.

Reredde, *p. pt.* of rere (rear); *v. tr.* 211.

Reste, *v. tr.* 77; 2*d sing. imper.* reste, 303.

Rewede, 3*d sing. pf. ind.* of rewe (rue); *v. tr.* = repent, be sorry for; used *impersonally*, 55; hym rewede = he was sorry.

Rewfulle, *adj.* 149.

Rewthe, *sb.* = ruth, sorrow, 102, 363.

Ring, *v. intr.*, 3*d pl. pf. ind.* rongen, 272.

Rongen. *See* Ring.

Rowte, *sb.* = crowd, 287.

Row3te. *See* Rekke, *v. intr.*

Ryche, *adj.* 271, 306, 363.

Rydethe, 3*d sing. pres. ind.* of ryde (ride); *v. intr.* 341; rydinge, *p. pt.* 228.

Ryuer, *sb.* 198; ryuere, 149, 350; *poss.* ryueres, 132.

Ry3te, *adj.* = right, 222, 236, 336, 352; *sb.* 259; *pl.* 'his ry3tes,' 283; *adv.* 32, 198, 205, 249.

Ry3[t]lye, *adv.* = rightly, 236.

Sadde, *adj.* 119. Perhaps = solid, massive (Cp. Wm. 1072); or else, and more probably = shed (O.E. *scaden,* from *scadan, v. tr.* Germ. *scheiden*). Cp. Gen. l. 58.

Sadelle, *sb.* 293.

Safe, *adj.* 43.

Same, *adj.* 34.

Saue, *v. tr.* 91; 3*d sing. pf. ind.* saued, 91.

Sauinge, *sb.* 194.

Sawe, *sb.* = that which is said, tale, 162, 253. *See also* Se, *v. tr.*

Sayde. *See* Seye.

Saye. *See* Se, *v. tr.*

Scharpelye, *adv.* 301.

Schreden, *v. tr.* = shred, 307.

Schyuered. *See* Shyuer.

Se, *v. tr.* = see, 359; 3*d sing. pres. ind.* seeth, 223; 1*st sing. pf.* saye, 5; sey3e, 216; 3*d sing.* sey3, 22; sy3e, 202; sawe, 61 340; 3*d sing. imper.* se, 26; used with *prep.*

GLOSSARIAL INDEX. 33

of, 65; 1*st sing. pres. subj.* 74; *p. pt.* sene, 53.

Seche, *v. tr.* = seek; 2*d sing. imper.* seche, 53; 3*d sing. pf. ind.* sowȝte, 60. Used intransitively in both places, in the sense of To betake oneself, go.

Seke, *v. tr.* = seek, 144.

Selfe, 73.

Selfen *or* Selven = self, and selves, 20, 47.

Seluer = silver, 43; seluere, 125.

Semelye, *adj.* = seemly, 42.

Sende, *v. tr.* 111; 3*d sing. pres. ind.* sendethe, 88, 118; sendeth, 193; 3*d sing. pf.* sente, 46, 129, 153.

Serue, *v. tr., intransitively* = be of use, 202; 3*d sing. pres. ind.* seruethe, 218; *p. pt.* serued, 47;= deserve, *p. pt.* serued, 186 · seruethe, 194.

Seruyse, *sb.* = pay for service, 178.

Sethen. *See* Sythen.

Sette, *v. tr.* = set, 73.

Seueneth, *adj.* = seventh, 42.

Seuenne, *numeral adj.* = seven, 61.

Sex, *numeral adj.* = six, 42, 144, 347. *See also* Six.

Sexte, *adj.* = sixth, 160; sixte, 168, 369.

Seyde. *See* Seye, *v. tr.*

Seye, *v. tr.* = say, 74; sey, 213; 3*d sing. ind. pres.* seyth, 252; seythe, 162, 245; 3*d pl.* seyn, 217; 3*d sing. pf.* sayde, 25; seyde, 28, 50, 64, 67-8, 77, 82, 127, 131, 177, 193, 197, 208, 213, 346, 349.

Seyȝ *and* Seyȝe. *See* Se, *v. tr.*

Shafte, *sb.* 301.

Shake, *v. tr.* 3*d pl. pf. ind.* shoken, 356.

Shalle, *v.* 1*st sing. pres. ind.* 75, 78, 139, 212, 239, 261, 288, 299, 330; 2*d sing.* shalt, 54, 80, 238,

260; 3*d sing. pf.* sholde, 94, 129, 202, 224, 232; shulde, 37, 96, 103, 191; 3*d pl.* sholde, 12.

Shanke, *sb., pl.* shankes, 326.

She, *pers. pron.* 10, 26, &c.

Shelde, *sb.* = shield, 281, 298, 331.

Shene, *adj.* = shining, beautiful, 8; sheene, 298.

Shoken. *See* Shake, *v. tr.*

Sholde = should. *See* Shalle.

Sholder, *sb.* 222, 334.

Shrykede, 3*d sing. pf. ind.* of shryke (shriek), 81.

Shulde = should. *See* Shalle.

Shylde, *v. tr.* = shield, 298.

Shyuer, *v. tr.* = smash, splinter; 3*d pl. pf. ind.* shyuereden, 315; *p. pt.* schyuered, 301.

Shyuereden. *See* Shyuer.

Six, *numeral adj.* 164, 193. *See* Sex.

Sixte, *adj.* = sixth, 369. *See also* Sexte.

Skape, *v. intr.* = escape, 127.

Sklawndered, *p. pt.* of sklawnder (slander); *v. tr.* = defame, accuse, 234.

Skorne, *sb.* 264.

Skylfully, *adv.* 47.

Slepte, 3*d sing. pf. ind.* of sleep; *v. intr.* 192.

Slongen, 3*d pl. pf. ind.* of sling; *v. tr.* = to throw, 86; perhaps involving the idea of letting down by ropes; as we *sling* horses in a transport-ship, or as we suspend an arm in a *sling*.

Slyppe, *v. intr.* = slip, 52.

Small, *adj.* 307, 330.

Smerte, *sb.* = smart, 308.

Smertlye, *adv.* = smartly, sharply, 318. It is miswritten *smerlye* in the MS.

Smyte, *v. tr.*, 3*d sing. pf. ind.* smote, 146, 313; 3*d pl.* smoten, 327; 2*d sing. imper.* smyte, 311.

So, *adv.* 31, 70, 74, 103.

Sokour, *sb.* = succour, 111.

Somme, *adj.* = some, 111.

Sommene, *v. tr.* = summon, 187.

Sonde, *sb.* that which is sent, gift, 36.

Sone, *sb.* = son, 65, 78, 209, 347; sonne, 184, 211.

Soone, *adv.* 128, 208; sone, 105, 260-61.

Sorowefulle, *adj.* 91.

Sorwe, *sb.* = sorrow, 9; sorowe, 39, 78, 99, 359.

Sothe, *sb.* = truth, 18, 67, 131, 133, &c.

Sounde, *adj.* 43.

Sowke, *v. tr.* = suck, 115; *imp. pt.* sowkynge, 61.

Sowȝte. *See* Seche, *v.*

Speche, *sb.* 286.

Speke, *v. intr.* 249; 3*d sing. pres. ind.* 252.

Spere, *sb.* = spear, 263, 315.

Spin, *v. intr.* = rush quickly; 3*d sing. pres. indic.* spynnethe, 331. It is still used colloquially.

Spring, *v. intr.*, 3*d sing. pf. ind.* spronge, 331.

Spronge. *See* Spring.

Spynnethe. *See* Spin.

Staffe, *sb.* 220.

Stalworth, *adj.* = stalwart, strong, 326.

Stand, *v. intr.*, 3*d pl. pf. ind.* stoden, 147.

Stere, *v. intr.* = stir, move, 147.

Sterte, *v. intr.* = start; 3*d pl. pres. indic.* sterten, 356; 3*d pl. pf.* styrte, 326.

Steuenne, *sb.* = voice, 106, 149.

Stoden. *See* Stand.

Strawȝte. *See* Stretch.

Stretch, *v. intr.*, 3*d pl. pf. ind.* strawȝte, 220.

Strike, *v. tr.*, 3*d sing. pres. ind.* stryketh, 333; also *intransitively* = go; as we say, 'to strike across a field,' 229.

Stroke, *sb.* 333; *pl.* strokes, 298.

Stryketh. *See* Strike.

Styffe, *adj.* 241.

Styked, 3*d sing. pf. ind.* of stick; *v. intr.* 241.

Stylle, *adj.* 147, 169.

Styrte. *See* Sterte.

Suche, *adj.* 202, 249, 264.

Sue, *v. tr.* = follow; 3*d sing. pres. ind.* suwethe, 221; sueth, 230.

Sum, *adj.* = some, 57.

Swanne, *sb.* 148, 198, 350, 356, 358, 362.

Swerde, *sb.* = sword, 138, 146, 304, 306-7, 327-8.

Swete, *adj.* 44.

Sworn, *p. pt.* of swear; *v. tr.* 236.

Swyche, *adj.* = such, 49, 103, 139.

Swyde *for* Swythe, *adv.* = quickly, 158.

Swyfte, *adv.* 113.

Swymmen, 3*d pl. pf. ind.* of swym (swim), 198, 350; 2*d sing. pres.* swymmethe, 362.

Swyre, *sb.* = neck (O.E. *sweora*), 44, 126.

Syde, *sb.* 187.

Syken, *v. intr.* = to sigh; 3*d sing. pres. ind.* syketh, 66; 3*d sing. pf.* sykede, 25.

Syker, *adj.*, used *adverbially* = surely, 122.

Synne, *sb.* = sin, 250.

GLOSSARIAL INDEX.

Sythen (Sithen) = since, then, 13, 25, 53, 64, 199; sethen, 116.
Sytte, v. intr. 22, 293.
Syȝe. See Se, v. tr.
Syȝte, sb. = sight, 122, 188.

Taber, sb. = tabor, 226.
Take, v. tr. = betake, commend, 104; also in its usual sense, 262; 2d sing. imper. 300; 3d sing. pres. ind. taketh, 116; takethe, 63, 150; 1st sing. pf. toke, 167; 2d sing. tokest, 237; 3d sing. toke, 159, 173, 229; 3d pl. 355; token, 226; p. pt. taken, 234.
Tale, sb. 55.
Tawȝte, p. pt. of teche (teach), 312, 336.
Telle, v. tr., 1st sing. pres. ind. 162; 3d sing. tellethe, 7, 270; 3d sing. pf. tolde, 123, 347.
Tere, sb. = tear; pl. teres, 24.
Terme, sb. 140.
þanke, sb. = 194.
Thanke, v. tr., 3d sing. pf. ind. thanked, 339; þankede, 36.
þanne, adv. = then, at that time, 73, 210.
þat, art. = the, 159, 296, 322, 366; rel. pron. 3, 4; dem. pron. 18, 27, &c.; by þat, 248, 345 = by that time; conj. 16, 26, &c.
The, art. 7, 11, 17, &c.
The, pers. pron. obj. = thee, 18, 65, 73, 77—79, 134, 139-40, 169, 184, 230, 237, 261, 311, 312, 336.
The, pers. pron. = they, 220, 274.
þeder, adv. = thither, 265.
Thefe, sb. 141, 199, 351.
Thei, pers. pron. See They.
Thenke, v. = think, 30, 249 (Cp. Wm. 4908); Germ. denken; 2d sing. pf. ind. thowȝte, 40, 207, 250, 264.
þenne, conj. = than, 125; adv. = when, 143; = at that time, 24,

41, 63, 67, &c.; ere thenne, 330 = before the time when; by thenne, 143 = by that time; = thence, 248.
þerby, adv. = near there, 265.
þere, adv. 13, 31, 87; = where, 76, 96, 121, 142, 362.
Therfore, adv. = on that account, 136.
þerin, adv. 52, 247.
þerof, adv. 115.
þerupon, adv. 282.
þese, dem. pron. pl. 93, 179, &c.
þey, pers. pron. pl. 12, 19, &c.; thei, 326. See also The.
This, dem. pron. 5, 92; er þis, 70 = before now.
Thoo, adv. = then, at that time, 339.
þorow, prep. = through, 95, 170.
þou, pers. pron. 50—54, &c.; thow, 80, 251.
þowghe, conj. = though, 100.
Thowȝte. See Thenke.
Thrydde, adj. = third, 367.
þus, adv. 89, 118.
þy, poss. pron. 65, 73.
Thykke, adj. = thick (closely covered), 294.
Thylle, conj. = till, 96.
Thynge, sb. 30, 202.
To, prep. 16, 17, &c.
Togedere, adv. = together, 20, 314; togedur, 327.
Toke } See Take.
Token }
Topseyle, adv. = headlong, 320. See Note.
Towarde, prep. 33, 93, 109, 341.
Towre, sb. 280.
Trewe, adj. = true, 48, 69.
Trist, v. tr. = trust; 3d sing. pf. ind. triste, 49; truste, 285.

Trowthe, *sb.* = truth, 175.

Trumpe, *sb.* = trumpet, 226.

Truss, *v. tr.* to remove (Cotgrave, trousser, to trusse, tuck, packe, bind, or gird in, pluck, or twitch up); 3*d sing. pres. ind.* trussethe, 327.

Truste, *v. tr.* 3*d sing. pf. ind.* 285.

Tryfulle, *v. intr.* = trifle, 48.

Tumbledde, 3*d pl. pf. ind.* of tumble; *v. intr.* 320.

Turne, *sb.* in a good sense (as we say, 'to do one a good turn'), 139; in a bad sense, trick, wile, 257.

Turne, *v. tr.*, 3*d sing. pres. ind.* turneth, 262; 3*d sing. pf.* turned, 24, 341; *intr.* 3*d pres. ind.* 104, 150; 3*d pl.* turnen, 355, 357; 3*d sing. pf.* turnede, 123; 1*st pl. imper.* turne, 93.

Twelfe, *numeral adj.* 243.

Tweyne, *numeral adj.* = two, twain, 29, 84.

Two, *numeral adj.* 23, 27, &c.; in two, 334.

Twynleng, *sb.* = a little twin, 27.

Tydynge, *sb.* 59; *pl.* tydynges, 58.

Tylle, *conj.* 310.

Tymber, *sb.* 317.

Tyme, *sb.* = time, 37, 55, 243.

Tyraunte, *sb.* = wicked, or evil man, 84. In Allit. the people of Sodom are called *tyrants*, B. 943.

Tyte, *adj.* = quick, 139. It is used here *adverbially*.

Tytlye, *adv.* = quickly, 84.

Unbounden, *p. pt.* of unbind; *v. tr.* 345.

Unbrente, *adj.* = unburnt, 185.

Under, *adv.* 21.

Undo = undone, *p. pt.* of undone, *v. tr.* = undo, 105.

Unsemelye, *adj.* 30.

Unto, *prep.* 90.

Unwerkethe, *adj.* = unworked, 175.

Up, *prep.* 64, 81, 97, &c.

Upon, *prep.* 19, 213, 222, 236, 281; = with, 361.

Valwe, *sb.* = value, 329.

Wakynge, *imp. pt.* of wake; *v. intr.* 207.

Walle, *sb.* 19, 349.

Ware, *adj.* 122.

Warne, *v. tr.* 190.

Was, 3*d sing. pf. ind.* of be, 5, 6, &c.

Water, *sb.* 355, 362 = a piece of water, 51, 96.

We, *pers. pron. pl.* 3, 92, 302.

Wedde, *v. tr.* = bet, pledge, 27; *p. pt.* wedded = married, 69.

Wede, *sb.* = dress, clothing, 119; *pl.* wedes.

Wele, *adv.* = well, 2, 54, 67, 140, 309, 352; welle, 251.

Well, *v. intr.* = to bubble, pour forth copiously (O.E. *wclan* = to boil); 3*d sing. pf. indic.* wellede, 166.

Welle, *adv.* 251.

Wende, *v. intr.* = go, 206; 3*d sing. pres. indic.* wendes, 155. 178; wendethe, 161; wendeth, 190 (*see* Note); 3*d pl. pres. indic.* wenden, 302, 364; 2*d sing. imper.* wende, 137.

Wene, *v. intr.* = ween, thinke (O.E. *wenan*); 1*st sing pres. ind.* wene, 69; 3*d sing. pf. indic.* wente, 67.

Wenten, 3*d pl. pf. ind.*, serving as past tense of go; *v. intr.* 33; wente, 19; 3*d sing.* (*reflexively* used) 75.

Were, 3*d pl. pf. ind.* of be, 41, 58, 142; 3*d sing. pf. subj.* 30, 67,

GLOSSARIAL INDEX. 37

156; 3*d pl.* 31; used for wast, 2*d sing. pf. ind.* 237 ; 3*d pl. pf. ind.* weren, 121.

Weren, *v. tr.* = defend (O.E. *werian;* Germ. *wehren*); 3*d sing. pres. ind.* wereth, 2.

Werke, *sb.* = work, 2, 170, 330 (Germ. *werke*).

Werke, *v. tr.* = work, 78, 182 (O. Germ. *werken*).

Werue, *v. tr.* = deny, refuse (O.E. *wyrnan*), 56, 72.

Wesselle, *sb.* = vessel ; or else silver plate. Fr. *vaisselle,* 156.

Wex, *v. intr.* = to wax, to grow ; 3*d sing. pres. indic.* wexeth, 158 ; *pf.* wexedde, 166.

Wey, *sb.* = way, 220.

Wey3te, *sb.* = weight, 155.

What, *rel. pron.* 56 ; *interrog.* 74.

Whelpe, *sb.* 61 ; welpe, 63.

Whenne, *adv.* = when, 1, 12, &c.

Where, *adv.* 12 ; *interrog.* 82.

Whyle, *adv.* 273 ; whyles, 145 ; whylle, 117 ; *sb.* 286.

Whyte, *adj.* 281.

With, *prep.* 2, 28, &c. ; withe, 14, 23, &c.; wyth, 99.

Witty, *adj.* = cheerful (?), 35.

Wo, *sb.* 343.

Wolle, *v.* ; 1*st sing. pres. ind.* 241; 3*d sing.* 252; 2*d sing.* wolt, 72 ; 3*d sing. pf. ind.* wolde, 30, 41, 56, 117, 164, 276. *See* Wylle.

Womman, *sb.* = woman, 22, 26, 38 ; *pl.* wymmen, 29.

Wondrethe, 3*d sing. pres. ind.* of wonder ; *v. intr.* 184.

Wonnen. *See* Wynne, *v. tr.*

Woode, *sb.* 113 ; wode, 119, 143, 215.

Worde, *sb.* 193, 207, 349 ; *pl.* worthes, 32.

Worlde, *sb.* 112, 180, 184.

Worse, *adj.* 244.

Worthes. *See* Word.

Wrake, *sb.* = punishment, 72. It is coupled with wrech = vengeance, in Gen. 552.

Wrecche, *sb.* = wretch, 71.

Wrecched, *adj.* = wretched, 77.

Wronge, *sb.* 245 ; *adj.* used adverbially = wrongly, 170, 197, 349.

Wrow3te = wrought, 3*d sing. pf. ind.* of work, 119.

Wryten, *p. pt.* of wryte ; *v. tr.* 282.

Wyfe, *sb.* = wife, 69, 162, 169, 196.

Wylde, *adj.* 214.

Wyle, *sb.* = wile, 182.

Wylle, *sb.* = will, 1, 79, 181, &c.

Wylle, *v.* ; 1*st sing. pres. ind.* 128, 261 ; 2*d sing.* 290; 2*d sing.* wylt, 260. *See* Wolle.

Wynne, *v. tr.* = win ; *p. pt.* wonnen, 170 ; 3*d sing. pres. ind.* wynnethe = getteth, taketh, 337 ; thus miners speak of winning or getting out ores, or coals.

Wyse, *sb.* = wise, manner, 156.

Wyste. *See* Wytte.

Wyte, *v. tr.* = blame, 136.

Wytte, *v. tr.* = know ; 2*d sing. imper.* 195 ; 2*d sing. pf. ind.* wysste, 35 ; 3*d pl. pf.* wyste, 274 ; 2*d sing. pf. subj.* 186.

Yen, *sb.* = eyen, eyne *or* eyes, 135, 323, 332.

Yf, *conj.* = if, 54.

Yle, *sb.* = isle, 5.

Yren, *sb.* = iron, 290.

Ʒafe, 3*d pl. pf. ind.* of give, 271.

Ʒate, *sb.* = gate, 22.

Ʒe = yea, 212, 302.

Ʒelde, *v. tr.* = yield, 335, 336. *See* Note.

Ȝere, *sb.* = year, 89, 243.

Ȝonder, *adj.* (preceded by an *article*) = yonder, 26; ȝondur, 232; ȝondere, 233; *adv.* 198, 350.

Ȝonge, *adj.* = young, 81, 242, 251, 345.

Ȝosken, *v. intr.* = to hiccough, to sob; 3*d pl. pf. ind.* ȝoskened, 108.

Ȝou, *pers. pron. obj.* = you, 100.

Ȝyf, *conj.* = if, 235.

Ȝyfte, *sb.* = gift, 271.

Ȝys = yes, 309.

www.ingramcontent.com/pod-product-compliance
Lightning Source LLC
Chambersburg PA
CBHW032057220426
43664CB00008B/1037